CW01072391

Mental Health Strategies for Zebras and Bicycles

Mabel Jox

ISBN: 978-1-77961-730-9
Imprint: Tween Twank Twinkies
Copyright © 2024 Mabel Jox.
All Rights Reserved.

Contents

Introduction

Understanding Mental Health

Definition of Mental Health

Mental health refers to a person's emotional, psychological, and social well-being. It encompasses how individuals think, feel, and behave, as well as how they handle stress, relate to others, and make choices. Mental health is not solely the absence of mental illness; rather, it is a state of overall well-being in which individuals can realize their own potential, cope with the normal stresses of life, work productively, and contribute to their communities.

At its core, mental health is about maintaining a healthy balance in all aspects of life - including physical, emotional, and social well-being. It is an essential component of overall health, just as important as physical health. In fact, mental and physical health are closely interconnected, and one can significantly impact the other. Ignoring mental health can have negative consequences on a person's overall well-being, leading to increased risk of physical health problems and decreased quality of life.

The World Health Organization (WHO) defines mental health as "a state of well-being in which every individual realizes his or her own potential, can cope with the normal stresses of life, can work productively and fruitfully, and is able to make a contribution to her or his community." This definition emphasizes the importance of individual potential, effective stress management, productivity, and social connectedness in achieving and maintaining good mental health.

It is crucial to understand that mental health is a continuum, ranging from optimal mental well-being to severe mental illness. Just like physical health, mental health exists on a spectrum, and individuals may experience different levels of mental well-being at different times in their lives. The goal is not to constantly strive for perfect mental health, but rather to develop strategies and skills that promote resilience and positive mental well-being, allowing individuals to effectively navigate and cope with the challenges of life.

Mental health involves many different aspects, including:

1. Emotional Well-being: This refers to the ability to recognize, understand, and manage one's emotions in a healthy and constructive manner. It involves being aware of and accepting a range of emotions, both positive and negative, and being able to express and regulate them appropriately.

2. Cognitive Functioning: Mental health encompasses cognitive processes such as thinking, perceiving, problem-solving, and decision-making. It involves having a clear and focused mind, being able to concentrate and learn, and applying critical thinking skills to various situations.

3. Social Interaction: Mental health is influenced by the quality of relationships and social connections. Maintaining healthy and supportive relationships with family, friends, and the community is essential for overall well-being. It also involves effective communication, empathy, and the ability to establish and maintain boundaries.

4. Resilience: Resilience refers to the ability to bounce back from adversity, stress, and life challenges. It involves adapting to changes, managing setbacks, and maintaining a positive outlook. Resilience is not the absence of difficulties, but rather the ability to effectively cope with them and move forward.

5. Purpose and Meaning: Mental health is closely linked to having a sense of purpose and meaning in life. It involves having goals, aspirations, and a sense of direction. Engaging in activities that align with personal values and beliefs contributes to a sense of fulfillment and well-being.

It is important to note that mental health is a multidimensional concept that can be influenced by various factors, including biological, psychological, social, and environmental factors. The interplay of these factors can impact an individual's mental well-being and may contribute to the development of mental health disorders.

In summary, mental health encompasses a person's emotional, psychological, and social well-being. It is a state of overall well-being in which individuals can realize their potential, cope with life's challenges, and contribute to their communities. Mental health is not the absence of mental illness but rather a continuum that requires active attention and care. By understanding and prioritizing mental health, individuals can improve their overall quality of life and well-being.

Historical Perspective on Mental Health

Mental health has been a topic of interest and concern throughout human history. Understanding the historical perspective on mental health allows us to trace the evolution of ideas, perceptions, and approaches towards mental well-being. It provides insights into the prevailing beliefs and practices that have shaped the field of mental health as we know it today. In this section, we will explore the key developments and milestones that have influenced the historical trajectory of mental health.

The ancient civilizations of Egypt, Greece, and Rome held diverse beliefs about mental health. In ancient Egypt, mental illness was often attributed to supernatural causes, and treatment involved rituals and magic. In contrast, ancient Greece embraced a more rational approach, with philosophers like Hippocrates proposing that mental disorders resulted from imbalances in bodily fluids, known as the theory of humorism. This theory classified mental disorders into categories such as melancholia and mania.

During the Middle Ages, religious and supernatural explanations of mental illness regained prominence in Europe. Mental health was often associated with demonic possession or witchcraft, leading to the widespread persecution of those deemed mentally ill. Treatments included exorcisms, torture, and confinement. This period was marked by a lack of scientific understanding and empathy towards individuals experiencing mental health challenges.

The Renaissance period witnessed a gradual shift towards a more humane and scientific understanding of mental health. Influenced by the emerging fields of medicine and psychology, scholars began to explore alternative explanations for mental illnesses. In the 18th century, the Enlightenment era emphasized reason, empirical observation, and human rights. Prominent figures like Philippe Pinel and William Tuke advocated for the humane treatment of those with mental illnesses. The introduction of moral therapy aimed to provide care, support, and social integration for individuals with mental health conditions.

The 19th and 20th centuries saw significant advancements in the understanding and treatment of mental health disorders. The development of psychiatric institutions, such as the Pennsylvania Hospital in the United States and the Bethlem Royal Hospital in London, provided a dedicated space for the care and treatment of those with mental illnesses. However, these institutions often faced issues such as overcrowding, abuse, and the segregation of patients from society.

The rise of psychoanalysis, pioneered by Sigmund Freud, brought a new level of introspection and understanding to the field of mental health. Freud's emphasis on the unconscious mind, childhood experiences, and the role of sexuality influenced the development of psychological therapies. With the advent of behavioral therapies, such as cognitive behavioral therapy (CBT), in the mid-20th century, there was a growing recognition of the role of thoughts and behaviors in mental health.

The latter part of the 20th century witnessed advancements in pharmacology and the introduction of psychotropic medications. The discovery of medications to manage symptoms of mental disorders, such as antipsychotics and antidepressants, revolutionized the field. However, the biomedical model, which focused on neurochemical imbalances as the primary cause of mental illness, overshadowed the role of psychosocial factors in mental health.

In recent decades, there has been a paradigm shift towards a more holistic and person-centered approach to mental health. The biopsychosocial model recognizes the interplay between biological, psychological, and social factors in mental health and emphasizes the importance of individual experiences and cultural context. This broader perspective has led to the integration of psychological therapies, medication, social support, and self-care strategies in the treatment and management of mental health disorders.

While the historical perspective on mental health provides valuable insights, it is essential to acknowledge the limitations and shortcomings of past approaches. Stigmatization, discrimination, and the marginalization of individuals with mental health challenges have been persistent issues throughout history. A comprehensive understanding of mental health requires a nuanced examination of the historical, social, and cultural factors that shape our understanding and treatment of mental health today.

Historical Perspective on Mental Health:

- Ancient civilizations and supernatural explanations of mental illness - The rational approach of ancient Greece and the theory of humorism - Religious beliefs and persecution during the Middle Ages - The humane and scientific understanding during the Renaissance period - The advent of moral therapy in the 18th century - Psychiatric institutions and advancements in the 19th and 20th centuries - The influence of psychoanalysis and the rise of behavioral therapies - The introduction of psychotropic medications - The paradigm shift towards a holistic and person-centered approach

Understanding the historical perspective on mental health allows us to appreciate the progress that has been made and the challenges that continue to persist. It reminds us of the importance of empathy, cultural sensitivity, and a comprehensive approach to promoting mental well-being. By examining the past, we can pave the way for a more inclusive and compassionate future in mental health.

Factors Influencing Mental Health

When it comes to mental health, there are numerous factors that can influence an individual's well-being. These factors can come from various domains of a person's life, including biological, psychological, social, and environmental elements. Let's take a closer look at some of the key factors that can impact mental health.

Biological Factors

Biological factors play a crucial role in mental health. They include genetic predisposition, brain chemistry, and hormonal imbalances. For example, certain mental health disorders, such as schizophrenia and bipolar disorder, have been found to have a strong genetic component. Research has identified specific gene variations that increase the risk of developing these disorders.

Brain chemistry also plays a significant role in mental health. Neurotransmitters, which are chemical messengers in the brain, regulate mood, emotions, and behavior. Imbalances in neurotransmitters like serotonin, dopamine, and norepinephrine can contribute to the development of mental health disorders, such as depression and anxiety.

Hormonal imbalances, particularly those related to the endocrine system, can also impact mental health. Fluctuations in hormone levels, such as those experienced during puberty, pregnancy, and menopause, can influence mood and emotional well-being.

Psychological Factors

Psychological factors refer to an individual's thoughts, emotions, and cognitive processes. These factors greatly influence mental health outcomes. Here are some of the key psychological factors that can impact mental well-being:

- **Perception and interpretation of events:** How a person perceives and interprets events can significantly impact their mental health. Negative thinking patterns, such as catastrophizing or overgeneralizing, can contribute to the development or exacerbation of mental health disorders.

- **Self-esteem and self-worth:** Low self-esteem and feelings of worthlessness can be detrimental to mental health. Negative self-perception can lead to depressive symptoms and increase vulnerability to anxiety disorders.

- **Coping strategies:** The ability to handle stress and difficult situations is crucial for mental well-being. Individuals who lack effective coping strategies may be more susceptible to the negative impact of stressors, which can contribute to the development of mental health disorders.

+ **Personality traits:** Certain personality traits, such as perfectionism or neuroticism, can increase the risk of developing mental health issues. For example, individuals with perfectionistic tendencies may be more prone to anxiety disorders or obsessive-compulsive disorder.

+ **Traumatic experiences:** Traumatic events, such as physical or sexual abuse, accidents, or witnessing violence, can have a profound impact on mental health. These experiences can lead to the development of post-traumatic stress disorder (PTSD) or other trauma-related disorders.

Social Factors

Social factors encompass the influence of relationships, social support, and cultural norms on mental health. Here are a few key social factors to consider:

+ **Family dynamics:** The quality of family relationships and the presence of supportive family members significantly impact mental health. Positive family dynamics and strong familial bonds can serve as protective factors against mental health disorders.

+ **Social support:** Having a strong support network of friends, peers, or community members can enhance mental well-being. Studies have shown that individuals with greater social support tend to have lower levels of depression and anxiety.

+ **Socioeconomic factors:** Socioeconomic status can influence mental health outcomes. Financial instability, limited access to resources, and socioeconomic disparities can contribute to increased stress levels and a higher risk of mental health disorders.

+ **Discrimination and stigma:** Discrimination and stigma related to mental health, race, gender, sexuality, or other characteristics can have a detrimental impact on mental well-being. Experiencing discrimination can lead to chronic stress, low self-esteem, and increased vulnerability to mental health disorders.

+ **Cultural factors:** Cultural norms, beliefs, and values shape our understanding and perception of mental health. Cultural factors can influence help-seeking behaviors, stigma, and the availability of culturally appropriate mental health services.

Environmental Factors

Environmental factors refer to the physical and social aspects of an individual's surroundings that can impact mental health. Key environmental factors include:

- **Exposure to trauma or violence:** Living in an environment characterized by high levels of violence or trauma can have a profound impact on mental health. Individuals exposed to war zones, crime-ridden neighborhoods, or natural disasters may experience heightened levels of stress and develop mental health disorders.

- **Access to healthcare and mental health services:** The availability and accessibility of mental health services play a critical role in individuals' mental well-being. Limited or inadequate access to mental health resources can hinder timely diagnosis, treatment, and support.

- **Physical environment:** Physical aspects of the environment, such as noise pollution, air pollution, or overcrowding, can contribute to stress levels and impact mental health outcomes.

- **Work and school environment:** The quality of the work or school environment can significantly affect mental health. High levels of stress, bullying, or a lack of support can increase the risk of mental health disorders.

Understanding the various factors that influence mental health is crucial for developing effective prevention strategies and interventions. By addressing these factors, healthcare professionals, policymakers, and individuals themselves can work towards improving mental well-being and reducing the burden of mental health disorders in our communities.

Stigma and Mental Health

Stigma has long been associated with mental health conditions, contributing to the burden and impact of these disorders on individuals and society as a whole. In this section, we will explore the concept of stigma and its effects on mental health. We will also discuss strategies for combating stigma and promoting understanding and acceptance.

Understanding Stigma

Stigma refers to the negative beliefs, attitudes, and behaviors associated with a particular characteristic or condition. In the context of mental health, stigma is a social construct that leads to the marginalization and discrimination of individuals with mental health disorders. It is based on stereotypes and misconceptions about mental illness.

Stigma can manifest in various ways, including:

- Public stigma: This occurs when society holds negative beliefs and attitudes towards individuals with mental health disorders. It can result in the social exclusion and isolation of individuals with mental illness.

- Self-stigma: This refers to internalized stigma, where individuals with mental health conditions adopt society's negative beliefs and attitudes and apply them to themselves. It can lead to feelings of shame, low self-esteem, and reluctance to seek help.

- Structural stigma: This refers to policies, laws, and practices in society that perpetuate discrimination and barriers to mental health care. It includes inadequate funding, lack of access to quality care, and stigma within healthcare systems.

Effects of Stigma on Mental Health

The impact of stigma on individuals with mental health disorders is significant and far-reaching. Stigma can:

- Delay or prevent help-seeking: Stigma creates barriers to seeking mental health care. Individuals may fear judgment and rejection, leading to delays in seeking help and receiving appropriate treatment.

- Worsen mental health outcomes: Stigma can contribute to feelings of shame and self-blame, worsening mental health symptoms and impairing recovery.

- Isolate individuals: Stigma isolates individuals with mental health disorders, leading to social withdrawal and limited support networks.

- Negatively impact relationships: Stigma can strain relationships, as individuals may face judgment and avoid disclosing their mental health condition to others.

+ Limit opportunities: Stigma can lead to employment discrimination, limited educational opportunities, and reduced social participation.

Strategies for Combating Stigma

Reducing stigma and promoting mental health acceptance require a multi-faceted approach. Here are some strategies that can help combat stigma:

+ Education and awareness: Promote accurate information about mental health conditions to dispel myths and misconceptions. Raise awareness of the prevalence of mental health disorders and their impact on individuals and society.

+ Challenging stereotypes: Encourage media outlets to portray mental health conditions accurately and sensitively. Highlight stories of recovery and resilience to challenge stereotypes.

+ Language matters: Use person-centered language that emphasizes the individual rather than their diagnosis. Avoid using derogatory terms or language that perpetuates stereotypes.

+ Encouraging help-seeking: Foster an environment where seeking mental health care is encouraged and supported. Provide resources and information about available services.

+ Support and inclusion: Foster supportive communities that embrace individuals with mental health disorders. Encourage inclusivity and respect in all settings, including workplaces, schools, and healthcare systems.

+ Advocacy and policy change: Advocate for policy changes that promote mental health awareness, reduce discrimination, and ensure access to quality mental health care.

Addressing Stigma in Practice

Addressing stigma requires the collective effort of individuals, communities, and society as a whole. Here are some practical steps that can be taken to address stigma:

+ Foster open dialogue: Create safe spaces for individuals to share their experiences and challenge stigma. Engage in open conversations about mental health to promote understanding and acceptance.

 ✦ Support mental health organizations: Contribute to or volunteer with organizations that work to reduce stigma and support individuals with mental health disorders.

 ✦ Advocate for change: Engage in advocacy efforts to challenge discriminatory policies and promote mental health awareness. Contact policymakers, participate in campaigns, and support legislation that addresses stigma.

 ✦ Role modeling: Be an advocate for mental health by educating others, challenging stigmatizing beliefs, and offering support to individuals facing mental health challenges.

 ✦ Seek support: If you are facing mental health challenges, reach out to supportive friends, family, or mental health professionals. Remember that you are not alone, and help is available.

By challenging stigma, we can create a society that supports and embraces individuals with mental health conditions. It is our collective responsibility to promote understanding, acceptance, and access to care for all. Together, we can make a difference.

Exercises

1. Reflect on your own beliefs and attitudes towards mental health. Are there any stigmatizing beliefs that you hold? How can you challenge and change these beliefs?

2. Conduct a media analysis of how mental health is portrayed in popular culture. Identify any stigmatizing portrayals and propose alternative narratives that promote understanding and acceptance.

3. Research local resources and organizations in your community that support individuals with mental health disorders. Explore opportunities to volunteer or contribute to these organizations.

4. Engage in a conversation with a friend, family member, or colleague about mental health. Share information and personal experiences to promote understanding and break down barriers.

5. Write a letter to a policymaker advocating for changes in mental health policies, such as increased funding for mental health services and improved access to care. Explain why these changes are necessary and how they can benefit individuals and society.

Remember, stigma can only be overcome through collective efforts. By taking action, we can create a more inclusive and supportive society for individuals with mental health disorders.

Importance of Mental Health Strategies

Mental health is a critical aspect of overall well-being and plays a vital role in an individual's ability to function and lead a fulfilling life. The importance of mental health strategies lies in their ability to promote, protect, and enhance mental well-being. These strategies aim to support individuals in maintaining optimal mental health, preventing the onset of mental health disorders, and managing the challenges they may face.

One of the primary reasons mental health strategies are important is the significant impact mental health has on daily functioning. When mental health is compromised, it can lead to difficulties in various areas of life, including personal relationships, work or school performance, and physical health. Mental health disorders, such as anxiety and depression, can hinder an individual's ability to concentrate, make decisions, and cope with stress. Therefore, implementing effective mental health strategies is crucial to improve overall functioning and quality of life.

Moreover, mental health strategies are vital in preventing the onset of mental health disorders. Just as physical health strategies aim to prevent illnesses, mental health strategies focus on reducing the risk and occurrence of mental health issues. This preventive approach involves promoting mental wellness, fostering resilience, and providing individuals with the tools and skills they need to cope with stress, manage emotions, and maintain a healthy mindset. By investing in prevention, resources can be directed towards early intervention and support, reducing the overall burden of mental health issues on individuals and society.

Another key aspect of the importance of mental health strategies is their role in managing the challenges and complexities of life. Mental health strategies equip individuals with coping mechanisms, resilience-building techniques, and support systems to navigate difficult situations effectively. These strategies help individuals develop a positive mindset, develop healthy coping mechanisms, and seek help when needed. By promoting resilience and providing individuals with the necessary tools to manage stressors, mental health strategies can minimize the negative impact of challenging circumstances on mental well-being.

Furthermore, mental health strategies play a crucial role in reducing stigma associated with mental health. Stigma often prevents individuals from seeking the help they need, leading to delayed diagnosis, inadequate treatment, and further deterioration of mental health. By implementing strategies that promote awareness, education, and acceptance of mental health issues, society can create an environment that encourages open conversations, reduces stigma, and fosters a culture of support and understanding.

In summary, the importance of mental health strategies cannot be overstated. They are essential for maintaining optimal mental well-being, preventing the onset of mental health disorders, managing life challenges effectively, and reducing stigma. By investing in mental health strategies, individuals, communities, and societies can create an environment that supports mental well-being and empowers individuals to lead healthier, happier lives. It is crucial to recognize that mental health is as important as physical health and to prioritize the development and implementation of effective mental health strategies in all aspects of life.

Overview of the Book

In this book, "Mental Health Strategies for Zebras and Bicycles," we explore various strategies and techniques to promote mental health and well-being. The book is designed to provide a comprehensive understanding of mental health, offer practical tools for maintaining mental wellness, and address the specific needs of different populations.

Understanding Mental Health

We begin by defining mental health and exploring its historical perspective. Mental health is not merely the absence of mental illness but encompasses a state of well-being where individuals can cope with daily stressors, maintain satisfying relationships, and function effectively. We delve into the factors that influence mental health, such as genetics, environment, and socio-cultural aspects. Additionally, we address the stigma associated with mental health and emphasize the importance of implementing effective strategies to combat it.

Mental Health Disorders

Building upon the foundation of understanding mental health, we delve into different mental health disorders, their prevalence, and the impact they have on individuals and society. We explore common mental health disorders such as anxiety, depression, and bipolar disorder, discussing diagnostic criteria and classification systems. We also debunk myths and misconceptions surrounding mental health disorders to promote accurate understanding and reduce stigma.

Zebras and Bicycles Metaphor

To enhance conceptual understanding, we introduce the metaphor of zebras and bicycles as a framework for mental health strategies. Zebras embody the uniqueness and diversity of individual experiences, highlighting the importance of personalized approaches to mental wellness. On the other hand, bicycles symbolize the need for balance and self-regulation in managing mental health. By combining the qualities of zebras and bicycles, individuals can cultivate empowerment, resilience, and adaptability.

The Mind-Body Connection

Recognizing the inseparable link between the mind and body, we explore the neurobiology of mental health. This section delves into brain structures, neurotransmitters, and the concept of neuroplasticity. We also highlight the role of psychoneuroimmunology and genetics in mental health. Additionally, we discuss the field of psychosomatic medicine, which elucidates the impact of stress on physical health and explores integrative approaches for holistic well-being.

Building a Foundation for Mental Health

To lay a strong foundation for mental health, we emphasize the importance of self-awareness and self-reflection. By recognizing and understanding our thoughts and emotions, we gain insight into our mental well-being. We explore various practices to cultivate self-awareness, such as mindfulness, journaling, and creative expression. Engaging in self-reflection techniques helps us develop compassion and self-compassion, fostering positive mental health outcomes.

Positive Psychology and Resilience

Drawing from the principles of positive psychology, we explore strategies to enhance resilience and well-being. By identifying and utilizing our strengths and virtues, we can navigate life's challenges more effectively. This section also highlights the importance of gratitude, optimism, and positive relationships in promoting mental health. We emphasize the integration of positive psychology principles into daily life to foster personal growth and resilience.

Emotional Intelligence and Self-Regulation

Emotional intelligence plays a vital role in mental health, enabling us to recognize, understand, and manage emotions effectively. We discuss the components of emotional intelligence, providing practical tools for emotional regulation. Additionally, we delve into empathy, social awareness, communication skills, and conflict resolution strategies. By honing these skills, individuals can foster healthy relationships and enhance their overall well-being.

Strategies for Mental Health Maintenance

This section focuses on strategies for maintaining mental health and well-being on a daily basis. We emphasize the importance of quality sleep and provide strategies for improving sleep hygiene. Physical activity and exercise are explored as effective tools for managing stress and enhancing mental well-being. Time management techniques, stress reduction strategies, and creating work-life balance are also discussed. Integrating these strategies into daily routines promotes overall mental health maintenance.

Mental Health Support Systems

Recognizing the interconnectedness between individuals and their social environments, we explore different mental health support systems. We discuss the role of mental health professionals and provide guidance on finding the right therapist. Peer support and group therapy are highlighted as valuable resources for individuals seeking social connections and understanding. Additionally, we address the importance of family and social support in promoting mental well-being and reducing stigma.

Mental Health Strategies for Specific Populations

Tailoring mental health strategies for specific populations is essential. We explore the unique challenges faced by children, adolescents, older adults, and the LGBTQ+ community. Strategies for promoting resilience, creating supportive environments, and addressing mental health disparities are discussed. We also provide insights into mental health in the workplace and education, emphasizing the importance of supportive environments and mental health literacy.

Crisis Intervention and Suicide Prevention

Recognizing the urgency of addressing mental health crises, we discuss the recognition, assessment, and de-escalation of crisis situations. We explore the role of mental health professionals in crisis intervention, collaborative crisis response, and post-crisis support. Suicide prevention and intervention strategies, including risk assessment, safety planning, and support for individuals in crisis, are also covered. Advocacy for mental health and suicide prevention is highlighted as a critical component of comprehensive mental health strategies.

Cultural Competence and Global Mental Health

Cultural influences significantly impact mental health, and cultural competence is essential for providing effective mental health services. We explore the intersection of culture and mental health and offer insights into culturally sensitive approaches to assessment and treatment. Moreover, we address global mental health initiatives, challenges, and the importance of cultural awareness in addressing mental health disparities. Indigenous mental health is also given special attention, with a focus on historical trauma, culturally sensitive healing approaches, and community-based services.

Overall, "Mental Health Strategies for Zebras and Bicycles" aims to empower individuals with the knowledge, skills, and strategies necessary for maintaining mental well-being. By addressing a wide array of topics and providing practical guidance, this book serves as a comprehensive resource for both individuals and professionals invested in mental health. Let's dive into this transformative journey together, embracing a holistic approach to mental health.

Mental Health Disorders

Common Mental Health Disorders

In this section, we will explore some of the most common mental health disorders that individuals may encounter. It is important to note that mental health disorders are complex and can vary in severity and presentation from person to person. Understanding these disorders can help raise awareness, reduce stigma, and promote early intervention and effective treatment.

Depression

Depression is a mood disorder characterized by persistent feelings of sadness, hopelessness, and a loss of interest or pleasure in activities. It affects how a person thinks, feels, and behaves, and can interfere with their daily functioning. Common symptoms of depression include:

+ Persistent sadness or a depressed mood

+ Loss of interest or pleasure in activities

- Changes in appetite or weight

- Sleep disturbances (insomnia or excessive sleeping)

- Fatigue or loss of energy

- Feelings of worthlessness or excessive guilt

- Difficulty concentrating or making decisions

- Recurrent thoughts of death or suicide

Depression can be caused by a combination of genetic, biological, environmental, and psychological factors. It is often treated through a combination of therapy, medication, and lifestyle changes. Cognitive-behavioral therapy (CBT) and interpersonal therapy (IPT) are effective forms of psychotherapy for depression.

Anxiety Disorders

Anxiety disorders are a group of mental health conditions characterized by excessive and persistent feelings of fear, worry, or anxiety. These disorders can significantly interfere with daily life and functioning. Some common types of anxiety disorders include:

- Generalized Anxiety Disorder (GAD): Excessive worrying about everyday problems and events, often accompanied by physical symptoms such as restlessness, muscle tension, and difficulty concentrating.

- Panic Disorder: Recurrent and unexpected panic attacks, which are sudden episodes of intense fear and physical discomfort. Panic attacks are often accompanied by a fear of having future attacks and a desire to avoid certain situations or places.

- Social Anxiety Disorder: Intense fear of social situations and a persistent worry about being embarrassed, humiliated, or judged by others. This fear can lead to avoidance of social interactions and significant distress.

- Specific Phobias: Excessive fear and avoidance of specific objects, situations, or activities. Common phobias include fear of heights, spiders, flying, and enclosed spaces.

Anxiety disorders can be caused by a combination of genetic, brain chemistry, and environmental factors. Treatment for anxiety disorders may include therapy (such as Cognitive-behavioral therapy or exposure therapy) and medication (such as selective serotonin reuptake inhibitors or benzodiazepines).

Bipolar Disorder

Bipolar disorder, also known as manic-depressive illness, is a mood disorder characterized by alternating periods of mania and depression. During manic episodes, individuals may experience an elevated mood, increased energy levels, impulsive behavior, and a decreased need for sleep. During depressive episodes, individuals experience symptoms similar to those of depression.

Common symptoms of bipolar disorder include:

+ Intense euphoria or irritability during manic episodes

+ Excessive talkativeness and racing thoughts

+ Increased goal-directed activity or agitation

+ Impulsive and risky behavior

+ Grandiose beliefs or inflated self-esteem

+ Decreased need for sleep

+ Fatigue and feelings of worthlessness during depressive episodes

The exact cause of bipolar disorder is still unknown, but it is believed to be influenced by genetic, biological, and environmental factors. Treatment typically involves a combination of medication (such as mood stabilizers) and psychotherapy (such as CBT or family-focused therapy).

Schizophrenia

Schizophrenia is a chronic and severe mental disorder that affects how a person thinks, feels, and behaves. It is characterized by symptoms such as hallucinations (seeing or hearing things that are not there), delusions (strongly held beliefs that are not based in reality), disorganized speech or behavior, and a loss of motivation and emotional expression.

Common symptoms of schizophrenia include:

- Hallucinations (most commonly auditory hallucinations)
- Delusions (such as paranoid delusions or delusions of grandeur)
- Disorganized speech (incoherent or illogical speech patterns)
- Disorganized behavior (such as unpredictable or inappropriate actions)
- Negative symptoms (e.g., lack of motivation, social withdrawal, diminished emotional expression)

The exact cause of schizophrenia is not fully understood, but research suggests a combination of genetic, brain chemistry, and environmental factors. Treatment typically involves a combination of antipsychotic medication and therapy, such as cognitive-behavioral therapy and psychosocial interventions.

Eating Disorders

Eating disorders are a group of mental health conditions characterized by disturbances in eating behaviors and attitudes towards food and body image. The most common types of eating disorders include:

- Anorexia Nervosa: Intense fear of gaining weight, leading to severe restriction of food intake and a distorted perception of body weight and shape. Individuals with anorexia may exhibit excessive exercise behaviors and have a preoccupation with food and weight.

- Bulimia Nervosa: Recurrent episodes of binge eating followed by compensatory behaviors such as self-induced vomiting, excessive exercise, or fasting. Individuals with bulimia often experience a sense of lack of control during binge episodes and have an intense concern about body weight and shape.

- Binge Eating Disorder: Recurrent episodes of binge eating without compensatory behaviors. Individuals with binge eating disorder may experience distress, shame, and guilt associated with their eating behavior, leading to feelings of loss of control and emotional distress.

The causes of eating disorders are complex and can involve a combination of genetic, environmental, psychological, and sociocultural factors. Treatment for eating disorders often includes a multidisciplinary approach involving medical, nutritional, and psychiatric interventions. Cognitive-behavioral therapy and interpersonal therapy are commonly used forms of psychotherapy.

Conclusion

This section provided an overview of some common mental health disorders, including depression, anxiety disorders, bipolar disorder, schizophrenia, and eating disorders. It is essential to recognize the signs and symptoms of these disorders to promote early intervention and effective treatment. Mental health disorders can significantly impact individuals' lives, but with appropriate support and resources, individuals can achieve recovery and lead fulfilling lives.

Diagnostic Criteria and Classification Systems

Diagnostic criteria and classification systems play a crucial role in the field of mental health. They provide a standardized framework for clinicians to assess, diagnose, and classify mental health disorders. In this section, we will explore the importance of diagnostic criteria and classification systems, examine some commonly used systems, such as the Diagnostic and Statistical Manual of Mental Disorders (DSM) and the International Classification of Diseases (ICD), and discuss their strengths and limitations.

Importance of Diagnostic Criteria

Diagnostic criteria are essential tools for clinicians in evaluating and diagnosing mental health disorders. They provide a common language and set of guidelines for clinicians to communicate and make accurate diagnoses. Diagnostic criteria help ensure consistency and reliability in the diagnosis process, allowing for improved treatment planning and research in the field of mental health. They also serve as a basis for insurance claims and reimbursement, as well as for determining eligibility for disability benefits.

Having clear and standardized diagnostic criteria is particularly important because mental health disorders often manifest with a wide range of symptoms and presentations. Diagnostic criteria help clinicians differentiate between various disorders that may share similar symptoms, ensuring appropriate treatment and support for individuals.

The Diagnostic and Statistical Manual of Mental Disorders (DSM)

The Diagnostic and Statistical Manual of Mental Disorders (DSM) is one of the most widely used classification systems in mental health. Published by the American Psychiatric Association (APA), the DSM provides a comprehensive set of diagnostic criteria for mental health disorders.

The DSM categorizes mental health disorders based on various criteria, such as the presence of specific symptoms, their duration and intensity, and the degree of impairment they cause. Each disorder in the DSM is accompanied by a detailed description, including information on prevalence, typical age of onset, possible causes, and associated features.

The DSM is currently in its fifth edition (DSM-5), which was published in 2013. It represents a significant update from its predecessors, incorporating new research findings and changes in the understanding of mental health disorders. The DSM-5 also introduced dimensional assessments, which aim to capture the severity or intensity of certain symptoms across disorders.

Despite its widespread use, the DSM has faced criticism and limitations. Some argue that the diagnostic criteria oversimplify complex conditions and may lead to overdiagnosis or misdiagnosis. Others highlight the influence of pharmaceutical companies and potential conflicts of interest in shaping diagnostic criteria.

The International Classification of Diseases (ICD)

The International Classification of Diseases (ICD) is a global classification system developed by the World Health Organization (WHO). Initially focused on physical health conditions, the ICD has expanded to include mental health disorders in its later editions. The current version, ICD-11, was released in 2019.

Like the DSM, the ICD provides diagnostic criteria for mental health disorders. It offers a broader perspective by incorporating social and environmental factors, as well as cultural considerations. The ICD also includes a broader range of conditions and disorders, making it a valuable resource for global mental health research and practice.

The ICD provides a multiaxial framework for diagnosis, considering not only the individual's symptoms but also their psychosocial and contextual factors. This holistic approach acknowledges the influence of various factors on mental health while emphasizing the importance of cultural sensitivity and diversity.

Strengths and Limitations

Both the DSM and the ICD have their strengths and limitations. The DSM is widely used in the United States and has contributed significantly to the field of mental health by enhancing diagnostic accuracy and consistency. Its categorical approach makes it easier to use in clinical practice and research studies.

On the other hand, the ICD offers a more comprehensive and culturally sensitive perspective. Its global reach and consideration of social determinants of health make it valuable for understanding mental health in diverse populations. The ICD's multiaxial framework allows for a more holistic assessment of the individual.

However, both classification systems have been criticized for their potential to pathologize normal human experiences and for their limited inclusion of culturally specific disorders. They also face challenges in keeping up with the evolving understanding of mental health disorders and the need for more personalized and dimensional diagnostic approaches.

Summary

Diagnostic criteria and classification systems are vital tools in mental health practice. The DSM and the ICD are two widely used systems that provide clinicians with guidelines for assessing and diagnosing mental health disorders. While both systems have their strengths and limitations, they serve as a foundation for standardizing and organizing mental health diagnoses. It is important for clinicians to be familiar with these classification systems to ensure accurate and effective assessment and treatment of individuals with mental health concerns.

Prevalence and Impact of Mental Health Disorders

Mental health disorders are pervasive in our society and have a significant impact on individuals, families, communities, and the overall healthcare system. Understanding the prevalence and impact of these disorders is crucial for developing effective strategies to promote mental well-being and provide appropriate support and care for those affected.

Prevalence of Mental Health Disorders

The prevalence of mental health disorders is staggering. According to the World Health Organization (WHO), approximately 1 in 4 people worldwide will experience a mental health disorder at some point in their lives. This means that an estimated 450 million people are currently living with a mental health condition.

In specific terms, some of the most common mental health disorders include depression, anxiety disorders, bipolar disorder, schizophrenia, and post-traumatic stress disorder (PTSD). These disorders can range in severity from mild to severe and can significantly impair a person's daily functioning and quality of life.

It is important to note that mental health disorders can affect anyone, regardless of age, gender, socioeconomic status, or cultural background. However, certain factors such as genetics, family history, traumatic experiences, chronic illness, substance abuse, and social isolation can increase the risk of developing a mental health disorder.

Impact of Mental Health Disorders

The impact of mental health disorders extends far beyond the individual experiencing the condition. It affects their relationships, work or academic performance, physical health, and overall well-being. The consequences can be devastating and long-lasting if left untreated or unsupported.

1.   Personal Relationship: Mental health disorders can strain personal relationships, leading to conflicts, misunderstandings, and feelings of isolation. Family members, friends, and romantic partners may struggle to understand the person's experiences and emotions, which can create additional stress and strain on the relationship.

2. Education and Employment: Mental health disorders often interfere with a person's ability to concentrate, learn, and perform well academically or professionally. This can lead to decreased productivity, frequent absences, job loss, and financial instability.

3. Physical Health: There is a strong correlation between mental and physical health. Individuals with mental health disorders may be at a higher risk of developing chronic physical conditions such as cardiovascular disease, diabetes, and obesity. Moreover, the burden of managing a mental health condition can make it more challenging to engage in healthy behaviors like regular exercise, proper nutrition, and adequate sleep.

4.   Community and Society: Mental health disorders have far-reaching implications on a community and society as a whole. The economic burden associated with mental health disorders includes healthcare costs, lost productivity, and the impact on the criminal justice system. Stigma and discrimination surrounding mental health can also lead to social exclusion, limiting opportunities for individuals with mental health conditions to fully participate in society.

5. Suicide: Perhaps the most devastating consequence of untreated mental health disorders is the risk of suicide. According to WHO, suicide is the second leading cause of death among individuals aged 15 to 29 globally. Mental health disorders, particularly depression and bipolar disorder, are significant risk factors for suicide.

Addressing Prevalence and Impact

Recognizing and addressing the prevalence and impact of mental health disorders is crucial for promoting overall well-being and reducing the burden on individuals and society. Some key strategies to address these challenges include:

1. Early intervention and prevention programs: By identifying mental health issues early on, appropriate interventions can be initiated, preventing the worsening of symptoms and the development of long-term consequences.

2. Promoting mental health literacy: Increasing awareness and knowledge about mental health disorders can help reduce stigma, encourage help-seeking behaviors, and promote empathy and understanding within communities.

3. Integration of mental healthcare into primary care settings: Integrating mental healthcare into primary care settings can ensure timely access to mental health services and facilitate a more holistic approach to healthcare.

4. Supporting research and innovation: Continued investment in mental health research can lead to the development of more effective interventions, treatment modalities, and prevention strategies.

5. Creating supportive environments: Building supportive environments that promote mental well-being and provide resources for those in need is essential. This can be achieved through policies that protect the rights of individuals with mental health conditions and promote inclusivity and equality.

In conclusion, mental health disorders are prevalent and have a profound impact on individuals and society. Recognizing the prevalence and understanding the consequences of these disorders is the first step towards developing effective strategies for prevention, intervention, and support. By addressing the root causes, reducing stigma, and providing appropriate care, we can work towards building a society that promotes mental well-being for all.

Co-occurring Disorders and Comorbidity

In the field of mental health, it is not uncommon for individuals to experience more than one mental health disorder simultaneously. This phenomenon, known as co-occurring disorders or comorbidity, occurs when a person meets the diagnostic criteria for two or more disorders. Co-occurring disorders can complicate diagnosis, treatment, and recovery, presenting unique challenges for individuals and mental health professionals.

Prevalence and Impact

Co-occurring disorders are highly prevalent, with research indicating that the majority of individuals with a mental health disorder experience comorbidity. For example, it is estimated that approximately 50% of individuals with depression also meet the criteria for an anxiety disorder. Similarly, substance use disorders often co-occur with other mental health disorders, such as mood, anxiety, and personality disorders.

The impact of co-occurring disorders can be significant, leading to increased symptom severity, functional impairment, and reduced quality of life. Individuals with comorbid disorders may experience more frequent and prolonged episodes of illness, increased rates of hospitalization, and higher suicide rates compared to those with a single disorder. Co-occurring disorders also pose challenges for treatment, as the presence of multiple disorders can complicate the effectiveness of interventions.

Common Co-occurring Disorders

There are certain combinations of mental health disorders that are more commonly observed to co-occur. Some of the most prevalent comorbidities include:

1. Depression and Anxiety Disorders: Depression often co-occurs with anxiety disorders, such as generalized anxiety disorder, panic disorder, and social anxiety disorder. These disorders share common risk factors and biological mechanisms.

2. Substance Use Disorders and Mental Health Disorders: Substance use disorders frequently co-occur with mental health disorders, particularly mood disorders (such as depression and bipolar disorder) and anxiety disorders. Co-occurring substance use and mental health disorders are commonly referred to as dual diagnosis or dual disorders.

3. Post-Traumatic Stress Disorder (PTSD) and Substance Use Disorders: Individuals with PTSD are at higher risk for developing substance use disorders, and individuals with substance use disorders are more likely to develop PTSD. This comorbidity often results from attempts to self-medicate symptoms of PTSD with substances.

4. Eating Disorders and Mood Disorders: Eating disorders, such as anorexia nervosa, bulimia nervosa, and binge eating disorder, often co-occur with mood disorders, particularly depression and anxiety. These disorders share common risk factors, such as low self-esteem and body dissatisfaction.

Causes and Mechanisms

The co-occurrence of mental health disorders is believed to be influenced by a combination of genetic, environmental, and psychosocial factors. Common underlying causes and mechanisms include:

1. Shared Vulnerability: Some individuals may have a genetic predisposition or susceptibility to developing multiple mental health disorders. Shared genetic factors can contribute to the co-occurrence of disorders.

2. Common Environmental Triggers: Certain environmental factors, such as childhood trauma, chronic stress, or substance abuse, can increase the risk of developing multiple mental health disorders. These shared environmental triggers can play a role in the onset and maintenance of comorbidities.

3. Bidirectional Relationships: Some mental health disorders can increase the risk of developing other disorders, and vice versa. For example, individuals with anxiety disorders may be more vulnerable to developing depression, and individuals with depression may be more likely to develop anxiety disorders.

4. Mediating and Moderating Factors: Various psychosocial and physiological factors can mediate or moderate the relationship between different mental health disorders. For example, the severity of one disorder may influence the severity or course of another disorder.

Treatment Considerations

The presence of co-occurring disorders necessitates tailored and integrated treatment approaches. It is essential to treat both disorders concurrently to achieve optimal outcomes. Treatment considerations for co-occurring disorders include:

1. Comprehensive Assessment: A thorough assessment is crucial to identify the different disorders and their specific symptoms, as well as any shared or unique treatment needs. This assessment should consider the person's social, biological, and psychological factors to develop an individualized treatment plan.

2. Integrated Treatment: Integrated treatment approaches that address both disorders simultaneously have been found to be more effective than treating them separately. Integrated treatment may involve a combination of medication, psychotherapy, support groups, and psychosocial interventions.

3. Holistic Approach: Given the complex nature of co-occurring disorders, a holistic approach that addresses the individual's physical, emotional, mental, and social well-being is essential. This approach may include lifestyle changes, stress management techniques, and self-care strategies.

4. Supportive Services: Co-occurring disorders often require ongoing support to prevent relapse and promote long-term recovery. Supportive services, such as case management, peer support, and community resources, can be instrumental in maintaining treatment gains and improving overall well-being.

5. Relapse Prevention: Individuals with co-occurring disorders may be more prone to relapse. Therefore, relapse prevention strategies should be integrated into the treatment plan, focusing on developing coping skills, recognizing triggers, and accessing support during challenging times.

6. Continuum of Care: The treatment of co-occurring disorders may require a continuum of care, including acute care, residential treatment, outpatient therapy, and aftercare services. This continuum ensures the continuity of care and provides ongoing support as individuals navigate recovery.

While treating co-occurring disorders can be challenging, it is important to remember that recovery is possible. With a comprehensive and individualized treatment approach, individuals can achieve improved mental health, enhanced quality of life, and increased resilience.

Case Study

A case study can help illustrate the challenges and complexities of co-occurring disorders. Let us consider the case of Sarah, a 30-year-old woman who presents with symptoms of major depressive disorder and generalized anxiety disorder.

Sarah has been experiencing persistent sadness, loss of interest, and difficulties concentrating, which are characteristic of depression. She also reports excessive worry, restlessness, and muscle tension, indicating symptoms of generalized anxiety disorder.

The presence of both disorders complicates Sarah's diagnosis and treatment. A comprehensive assessment would involve exploring the severity and duration of symptoms, any triggering events or traumas, and the impact of the disorders on her daily functioning and well-being.

Integrated treatment would be beneficial for Sarah, which may include a combination of antidepressant medication to target the depressive symptoms and anti-anxiety medication or cognitive-behavioral therapy techniques to address the anxiety symptoms. Therapy sessions would focus on identifying and challenging negative thought patterns, developing coping skills, and promoting self-care strategies.

Sarah's treatment plan would also incorporate supportive services, such as peer support groups or online communities, to provide ongoing encouragement and assistance. Regular follow-up appointments, monitoring of symptoms, and adjustments to treatment if needed would be essential to track progress and prevent relapse.

By addressing both the depressive and anxiety symptoms concurrently, Sarah has a better chance of achieving symptom remission, improved functioning, and enhanced overall well-being.

Conclusion

Co-occurring disorders, or comorbidity, present unique challenges in the mental health field. They are highly prevalent and can significantly impact individuals' lives and the effectiveness of treatment. Understanding the common co-occurring disorders, their causes, mechanisms, and treatment considerations is essential for mental health professionals and individuals seeking support.

Integrated and holistic treatment approaches that address both disorders simultaneously, along with supportive services and relapse prevention strategies, offer the best chances for recovery. By acknowledging the complexities of co-occurring disorders and providing comprehensive care, individuals can improve their mental health and achieve a better quality of life.

Myths and Misconceptions about Mental Health Disorders

Mental health disorders are often shrouded in myths and misconceptions that contribute to the stigma surrounding them. These misunderstandings can prevent individuals from seeking help and support, and can perpetuate harmful stereotypes. In this section, we will debunk some of the most common myths and misconceptions about mental health disorders, providing accurate and evidence-based information to promote understanding and empathy.

Myth 1: Mental health disorders are not real illnesses

There is a pervasive belief that mental health disorders are not legitimate medical conditions, but rather a result of personal weakness or character flaws. This is simply not true. Mental health disorders are recognized by leading medical and psychiatric associations, such as the American Psychiatric Association, as real illnesses that have a biological basis. Research has shown that mental health disorders are often caused by a combination of genetic, environmental, and neurochemical factors. They affect the structure and functioning of the brain, just like any other illness.

Myth 2: Mental health disorders are rare

Contrary to popular belief, mental health disorders are not uncommon. In fact, they are incredibly prevalent. According to the World Health Organization, approximately 1 in 4 people worldwide will experience a mental health disorder at some point in their lives. This means that millions of people are affected by these disorders, making it a global public health concern. It is important to recognize that mental health disorders can affect anyone, regardless of age, gender, socioeconomic status, or cultural background.

Myth 3: Mental health disorders only affect weak or unstable individuals

Another myth surrounding mental health disorders is that they only affect individuals who are weak, unstable, or incapable of coping with life's challenges. This misconception is not only stigmatizing but also incorrect. Mental health disorders can impact anyone, including individuals who are successful, resilient, and high-functioning. Factors such as genetics, traumatic life events, chronic stress, and biological vulnerabilities can contribute to the development of mental health disorders, regardless of a person's character or strength.

Myth 4: People with mental health disorders are violent or dangerous

One of the most harmful myths about mental health disorders is the belief that individuals who experience mental health issues are inherently violent or dangerous. In reality, research has consistently shown that people with mental health disorders are more likely to be victims of violence rather than perpetrators. The vast majority of individuals with mental health disorders pose no threat to others. It is crucial to challenge this misconception and promote empathy, understanding, and support for individuals with mental health disorders.

Myth 5: People with mental health disorders cannot recover or lead fulfilling lives

There is a common belief that people with mental health disorders cannot recover or achieve a high quality of life. This misconception is incredibly harmful and discourages individuals from seeking treatment and support. In reality, with appropriate interventions, access to treatment, and social support, individuals with mental health disorders can and do recover. Many people with mental health disorders lead fulfilling, productive lives and make significant contributions to their communities. It is important to emphasize hope, recovery, and the potential for growth and resilience.

Myth 6: Medication is the only effective treatment for mental health disorders

While medication can be a valuable tool in the treatment of mental health disorders, it is important to recognize that it is not the only effective intervention. Mental health disorders are multidimensional in nature, and treatment approaches need to address the complexity of individual experiences and needs. Evidence-based therapies, such as cognitive-behavioral therapy (CBT), dialectical behavior therapy (DBT), and psychodynamic therapy, have been shown to be effective in helping individuals manage symptoms, develop coping strategies, and improve their overall well-being. Additionally, holistic approaches that focus on lifestyle factors, such as exercise, nutrition, sleep, and stress management, are essential components of a comprehensive treatment plan.

Myth 7: Seeking help for mental health issues is a sign of weakness

Seeking help for mental health issues is not a sign of weakness; it is an act of courage and strength. It takes self-awareness and resilience to recognize when support is needed and to take steps towards getting that support. Just as individuals seek medical help for physical health conditions, seeking help for mental health disorders is an important and necessary part of overall well-being. Asking for help should be seen as a sign of strength, as it demonstrates a commitment to self-care and growth.

In conclusion, debunking myths and misconceptions about mental health disorders is essential for promoting understanding, empathy, and support. By challenging harmful beliefs and providing accurate information, we can break down the barriers that prevent individuals from seeking help and create a more inclusive and compassionate society. It is important to recognize that mental health is just as important as physical health, and everyone deserves access to appropriate care and support.

Zebras and Bicycles Metaphor

Understanding the Metaphor

The Zebras and Bicycles metaphor is a powerful tool that we can use to understand and navigate the challenges of mental health. In this section, we will delve deeper into the metaphor and explore its applications in mental health strategies.

The metaphor compares people with mental health struggles to both zebras and bicycles. Just as zebras are unique in their beautiful stripes, individuals with mental health issues have their own unique experiences and challenges. Similarly, bicycles require balance and coordination to function smoothly, emphasizing the importance of finding balance and equilibrium in our mental well-being.

The Zebras and Bicycles metaphor highlights the need to embrace our uniqueness and find harmony within ourselves. It encourages us to recognize and accept our individual differences, reminding us that mental health is not a one-size-fits-all concept.

This metaphor also emphasizes the importance of self-empowerment and resilience. Zebras, with their innate ability to adapt to their surroundings and survive in challenging environments, inspire us to harness our inner strength and overcome adversity. Bicycles, on the other hand, teach us the value of perseverance and continuous effort. Just like riding a bike, maintaining our mental health requires practice, patience, and a willingness to keep moving forward.

By understanding and embracing the Zebras and Bicycles metaphor, we can cultivate a more compassionate and inclusive approach to mental health. It reminds us that everyone's journey is unique and deserves respect and support. It teaches us to celebrate our individuality while also recognizing the interconnectedness of our experiences.

To apply this metaphor in mental health strategies, we can encourage individuals to explore and understand their own mental health in the context of their unique strengths and challenges. By acknowledging their "stripes" and accepting themselves as they are, individuals can develop a stronger sense of self-awareness and self-compassion.

Additionally, the metaphor prompts us to incorporate resilience-building practices into our mental health strategies. Just as zebras adapt and thrive in challenging environments, we can cultivate resilience through coping skills, positive relationships, and self-care practices. By incorporating mindfulness, yoga, art therapy, and other holistic approaches, individuals can nurture their mental well-being and find balance in their lives.

It is important to note that the Zebras and Bicycles metaphor should not be used to oversimplify or trivialize mental health issues. Instead, it should serve as a framework for understanding and promoting mental well-being, recognizing the diversity of experiences and the need for personalized approaches to mental health care.

In the next sections of this book, we will explore various strategies and techniques that can be employed to support mental health using the Zebras and Bicycles metaphor as a guiding principle. We will delve into the mind-body connection, lay the foundation for mental health, discuss maintenance strategies, and explore specific populations, workplaces, and crisis intervention.

Remember, understanding the Zebras and Bicycles metaphor is just the first step towards building a comprehensive and holistic approach to mental health. Let's embark on this journey together and empower ourselves to ride the bicycles of life with confidence and resilience.

Application to Mental Health Strategies

The Zebras and Bicycles metaphor is a powerful tool that can be applied to mental health strategies. Understanding how zebras and bicycles relate to our mental well-being can help us develop effective techniques for maintaining and improving our mental health. In this section, we will explore how the metaphor can be applied in practical ways to enhance our overall well-being.

One aspect of the Zebras and Bicycles metaphor is the idea of embracing our uniqueness. Just as zebras stand out with their distinctive stripes and bicycles come in various shapes, sizes, and colors, each person has their own individuality and strengths. This uniqueness should be celebrated and utilized in mental health strategies. By acknowledging and embracing our personal strengths, we can enhance our self-confidence, resilience, and overall mental well-being.

One practical application of this concept is to engage in activities that align with our strengths and interests. For example, if someone has a passion for art, incorporating art therapy into their mental health routine can be beneficial. Engaging in creative expression allows individuals to tap into their strengths and unique talents, fostering a sense of fulfillment and well-being.

Another important aspect of the metaphor is resilience. Zebras and bicycles both symbolize strength and the ability to overcome obstacles. Applying this concept to mental health, building resilience can be a powerful strategy for maintaining and improving well-being. Resilience refers to our ability to bounce back from adversity and cope with life's challenges.

To apply the concept of resilience, individuals can actively seek out opportunities to develop their coping skills. This can include participating in stress management programs, seeking support from others, and practicing positive self-talk. By developing resilience, individuals can better navigate through difficult times and maintain their mental well-being.

The Zebras and Bicycles metaphor also highlights the importance of balance and integration. Zebras are known for their ability to maintain a balanced and graceful gait, while bicycles require a harmonious integration of different components for smooth functioning. Similarly, mental health strategies should focus on achieving a balance in various aspects of life, such as work, relationships, self-care, and personal interests.

To apply this concept, individuals can prioritize self-care activities that promote balance and integration. This can include setting boundaries in work or personal relationships, scheduling regular breaks and leisure activities, and engaging in activities that promote both physical and mental well-being, such as exercise or mindfulness practices.

It's important to note that mental health strategies should be personalized and tailored to individual needs. Just as zebras and bicycles have their own unique qualities, each person has their own set of circumstances and challenges. Mental health strategies that work for one person may not work for another. Therefore, it is crucial for individuals to understand themselves and their specific needs when applying the Zebras and Bicycles metaphor to mental health.

In summary, the Zebras and Bicycles metaphor offers valuable insights that can be applied to mental health strategies. By embracing our uniqueness, developing resilience, and striving for balance and integration, individuals can enhance their mental well-being. It is essential to remember that mental health strategies should be personalized and tailored to individual needs. By understanding and applying the principles of the metaphor, individuals can develop effective strategies for maintaining and improving their mental health.

Empowerment and Resilience

Empowerment and resilience are key concepts in mental health strategies. They play a crucial role in promoting overall well-being, managing mental health disorders, and improving one's quality of life. In this section, we will explore the meaning of empowerment and resilience, their importance in mental health, and practical ways to cultivate these qualities within ourselves.

Understanding Empowerment

Empowerment is the process of gaining control, confidence, and autonomy over one's life. It involves recognizing one's strengths, abilities, and rights, and taking decisive actions to shape one's own destiny. Empowerment empowers individuals to make choices, set goals, and take responsibility for their own well-being.

In the context of mental health, empowerment encompasses the ability to advocate for oneself, collaborate with healthcare professionals, and actively participate in treatment decisions. It also involves challenging stigma, discrimination, and societal barriers that impede access to mental health care and support.

Cultivating Empowerment

Empowerment can be cultivated through various strategies and practices. Here are some practical ways to promote empowerment in your life:

1. Education and Information: Seek knowledge about mental health, mental health disorders, and available treatments. Understanding the intricacies of your condition will empower you to make informed decisions and actively participate in your treatment journey.

2. Assertiveness Skills: Develop assertiveness skills to effectively communicate your needs, rights, and boundaries. Learning how to advocate for yourself will enhance your ability to seek appropriate support and engage in meaningful conversations with healthcare providers.

3. Self-Advocacy: Take an active role in your treatment plan by providing input, asking questions, and expressing your concerns. Collaborate with your healthcare team to create a personalized and comprehensive approach to your mental health care.

4. Peer Support: Connect with others who have had similar experiences. Joining support groups or engaging in peer-led initiatives can provide a sense of belonging, validation, and shared empowerment.

5. Personal Growth and Development: Engage in activities and practices that promote personal growth and self-discovery. This can include exploring new hobbies, pursuing education or career goals, or engaging in self-reflection exercises.

6. Building Resilience: Building resilience, as discussed in the next section, is closely tied to empowerment. By developing resilience, you strengthen your ability to overcome challenges and setbacks, thereby enhancing your sense of empowerment.

Understanding Resilience

Resilience is the capacity to adapt, cope, and bounce back from adversity, trauma, or stress. It is not about avoiding or eliminating difficulties, but rather about developing the skills and mindset to navigate through them effectively.

In the context of mental health, resilience plays a crucial role in managing and recovering from mental health disorders. It involves developing protective factors that buffer against the impact of stressors and promote positive mental well-being. Resilience is not a fixed trait, but rather a set of skills and attitudes that can be cultivated and strengthened.

Cultivating Resilience

Cultivating resilience involves practicing specific strategies and adopting supportive attitudes. Here are some practical ways to build resilience in your life:

1. Positive Thinking: Foster a positive mindset by challenging negative thoughts and reframing them in a more optimistic light. Practice self-compassion and embrace a growth-oriented perspective that focuses on learning and improvement.

2. Social Support: Build and maintain strong social connections, as they provide a vital support network during difficult times. Seek out positive and trustworthy relationships that foster understanding, empathy, and encouragement.

3. Emotional Regulation: Develop emotional regulation skills to effectively manage and express emotions. This encompasses techniques such as deep breathing, journaling, or engaging in activities that promote relaxation and self-soothing.

4. Problem-Solving Skills: Enhance your problem-solving skills to tackle challenges effectively. Break down problems into manageable steps, brainstorm potential solutions, and take action towards finding constructive resolutions.

5. Self-Care: Prioritize self-care activities that nourish and rejuvenate your mind, body, and spirit. This can include engaging in regular exercise, getting enough sleep, practicing mindfulness or meditation, or pursuing activities that bring you joy.

6. Adaptive Coping Mechanisms: Identify and cultivate healthy coping mechanisms that help you navigate stress and adversity. This can include seeking support from loved ones, engaging in creative outlets, or practicing stress management techniques.

Remember that resilience is not a one-time achievement, but a lifelong journey. It is about embracing setbacks as opportunities for growth and learning. By cultivating resilience, you empower yourself to face life's challenges with strength, adaptability, and determination.

Conclusion

Empowerment and resilience are essential components of mental health strategies. By cultivating a sense of empowerment, you can take control over your own well-being and actively engage in your mental health care. Building resilience equips you with the skills and attitudes to overcome challenges and bounce back from adversity. Together, empowerment and resilience contribute to a more fulfilling and balanced life.

The Mind-Body Connection

Neurobiology of Mental Health

Brain Structures and Functions

To understand mental health and its strategies, it is crucial to explore the intricate network of brain structures and their functions. The brain is a complex organ that plays a vital role in regulating emotions, cognition, and behavior. In this section, we will delve into the key brain structures and their functions, shedding light on their contribution to mental health.

The Neuron: Building Block of the Nervous System

At the core of brain function lies the neuron, the fundamental unit of the nervous system. Neurons are specialized cells responsible for transmitting information throughout the brain and body. They are interconnected through networks, forming neural pathways that facilitate the transfer of electrical and chemical signals.

Neurons consist of several essential components. The cell body contains the nucleus, which houses the genetic material responsible for cell functioning. Dendrites are extensions that receive inputs from other neurons, while axons transmit electrical impulses to other neurons or target cells. At the end of the axon, terminal buttons release chemical messengers called neurotransmitters into the synapse, the tiny gap between neurons, enabling communication.

Understanding the structure and function of the neuron is crucial in comprehending how information is processed and relayed within the brain.

Central Nervous System: The Command Center

The central nervous system (CNS) is composed of two primary structures: the brain and the spinal cord. The brain serves as the command center, decoding and integrating information from various sources to generate appropriate responses.

The brain is divided into distinct regions, each responsible for specific functions. The cerebral cortex, the outermost layer of the brain, is associated with higher-order cognitive processes such as perception, thinking, and decision-making. It is further divided into four lobes: the frontal, parietal, temporal, and occipital lobes, which are responsible for different aspects of cognition and sensory processing.

Beneath the cerebral cortex, the limbic system plays a crucial role in regulating emotions, memory, and motivation. It includes structures such as the amygdala, hippocampus, and thalamus. These structures facilitate emotional responses, learning, and the formation of new memories.

At the base of the brain lies the brainstem, which connects the brain to the spinal cord. The brainstem controls essential bodily functions such as breathing, heart rate, and sleep-wake cycles.

Subcortical Structures: Orchestrating Behaviors and Emotions

Within the brain, there are several subcortical structures that perform critical functions in mental health. The basal ganglia are involved in voluntary movement control, procedural learning, and habit formation. Dysfunction in the basal ganglia can lead to movement disorders such as Parkinson's disease.

The thalamus acts as a relay station, receiving sensory information from various parts of the body and forwarding it to the respective regions of the cerebral cortex for processing. It also plays a role in regulating consciousness and alertness.

The hypothalamus, located just below the thalamus, is responsible for maintaining homeostasis by regulating body temperature, hunger, thirst, and the autonomic nervous system. It also plays a role in emotional regulation and the release of hormones.

The hippocampus, a seahorse-shaped structure within the limbic system, is critical for memory formation and spatial navigation. Damage to the hippocampus can lead to memory impairment, such as in Alzheimer's disease.

Hemispheric Specialization: Right and Left Brain Functions

The brain is divided into two hemispheres, left and right, connected by a bundle of nerve fibers called the corpus callosum. Each hemisphere exhibits functional specialization, meaning that certain tasks and cognitive functions are predominantly carried out by one hemisphere.

The left hemisphere is typically associated with language processing, analytical thinking, and logical reasoning. It plays a crucial role in reading, writing, and mathematical skills. The right hemisphere, on the other hand, excels in spatial awareness, creativity, and holistic thinking. It is involved in visual and spatial processing, recognizing faces, and interpreting emotions.

Understanding hemispheric specialization helps explain individual differences in cognitive and behavioral functions, as well as how brain injuries or disorders can affect specific functions more than others.

Neurotransmitters: Chemical Messengers of the Brain

Neurotransmitters are chemical messengers that transmit signals between neurons, allowing for communication within the brain. These molecules play a crucial role in regulating mood, emotions, cognition, and overall mental health.

There are various neurotransmitters in the brain, each with its unique functions. For example, serotonin is involved in mood regulation, sleep, and appetite. Dopamine is associated with reward and motivation, while gamma-aminobutyric acid (GABA) contributes to inhibitory signaling, reducing anxiety and promoting relaxation.

Imbalances in neurotransmitter levels can contribute to mental health disorders such as depression, anxiety, and schizophrenia. Medications targeting neurotransmitter systems can help restore balance and alleviate symptoms.

Neuroplasticity: The Brain's Ability to Adapt

The brain possesses an incredible capacity for change and adaptation, known as neuroplasticity. Neuroplasticity refers to the brain's ability to reorganize its structure, function, and connections in response to experiences, learning, and environmental changes.

Neurons can modify their connections, forming new pathways and networks. Through this process, the brain can compensate for damage by rerouting signals or recruit adjacent regions to perform specific functions.

Understanding neuroplasticity offers hope for individuals struggling with mental health disorders. By harnessing the brain's ability to adapt and rewire, interventions such as cognitive-behavioral therapy and mindfulness practices can shape neural pathways and improve mental well-being.

Summary

In this section, we explored the intricate network of brain structures and their functions. We began by understanding the neuron as the building block of the nervous system and its role in transmitting information. We then delved into the central nervous system, including the brain and spinal cord, as the command center for regulating various bodily functions. Subcortical structures within the brain, such as the basal ganglia and thalamus, were discussed in relation to behavior and emotion regulation. We also examined hemispheric specialization and the role of neurotransmitters in mental health. Lastly, we explored the brain's remarkable ability to adapt and rewire through neuroplasticity.

The knowledge of brain structures and functions lays the foundation for comprehending mental health strategies and interventions. By understanding the inner workings of the brain, we can develop effective approaches to promote mental well-being and provide support to individuals experiencing mental health challenges.

Now that we have a solid understanding of brain structures and functions, let us delve into the field of psychoneuroimmunology and its impact on mental health in the next section.

Neurotransmitters and Chemical Imbalances

Neurotransmitters are chemical messengers that facilitate communication between neurons in the brain and throughout the nervous system. These chemical substances play a crucial role in regulating various physiological and behavioral processes, including mood, cognition, emotions, and motor control. Imbalances in neurotransmitter levels can disrupt the normal functioning of the brain and contribute to the development of mental health disorders.

There are several key neurotransmitters involved in mental health, and their dysregulation is associated with specific conditions. Let's explore some of the major neurotransmitters and their role in mental health:

1. **Serotonin:** Serotonin is a neurotransmitter that regulates mood, sleep, appetite, and sexual function. It is commonly associated with feelings of well-being and happiness. Low levels of serotonin have been linked to depression, anxiety disorders, obsessive-compulsive disorder (OCD), and eating disorders.

2. **Dopamine:** Dopamine is involved in reward and motivation, as well as movement and coordination. It plays a crucial role in the brain's reward system, reinforcing behaviors that are pleasurable or rewarding. Imbalances in dopamine levels have been implicated in various mental health disorders, including schizophrenia, addiction, and attention-deficit/hyperactivity disorder (ADHD).

3. **Norepinephrine:** Norepinephrine, also known as noradrenaline, is important for attention, alertness, and the body's stress response. It helps regulate blood pressure, heart rate, and mood. Abnormal levels of norepinephrine have been associated with mood disorders, such as depression and bipolar disorder, as well as anxiety disorders.

4. **GABA:** Gamma-aminobutyric acid (GABA) is the primary inhibitory neurotransmitter in the central nervous system. It helps to reduce neuronal excitability and promote a state of relaxation. Low levels of GABA have been implicated in anxiety disorders, epilepsy, and insomnia.

5. **Glutamate:** Glutamate is the primary excitatory neurotransmitter in the brain, involved in learning, memory, and synaptic plasticity. Dysregulation of glutamate has been implicated in various mental health conditions, including schizophrenia, anxiety disorders, and mood disorders.

6. **Acetylcholine:** Acetylcholine is involved in memory, learning, and attention. It plays a crucial role in the functioning of the cholinergic system, which is disrupted in dementia and Alzheimer's disease.

Imbalances and Mental Health Disorders

Imbalances in neurotransmitter levels can have significant impacts on mental health, potentially contributing to the development of various disorders. It is important to note that these imbalances are often complex and can involve multiple neurotransmitters and their interactions.

For example, low levels of serotonin have been associated with depression, while excessive activity of dopamine has been linked to psychosis and schizophrenia. Imbalances in GABA have been implicated in anxiety disorders, and disturbances in glutamate signaling have been observed in mood disorders, such as major depressive disorder.

It is essential to remember that neurotransmitter imbalances are not the sole cause of mental health disorders. These imbalances often interact with genetic, environmental, and psychosocial factors to contribute to the development and progression of mental health conditions.

Treatment Approaches

Understanding the role of neurotransmitters in mental health has led to the development of various treatment approaches that aim to restore balance and alleviate symptoms. Medications known as psychotropic drugs can target specific neurotransmitter systems to regulate their levels or activity.

Selective serotonin reuptake inhibitors (SSRIs), for example, are commonly prescribed for depression and anxiety disorders. These medications enhance serotonin signaling by blocking its reuptake, thereby increasing its availability in the brain.

Antipsychotic medications used in the treatment of schizophrenia work by blocking dopamine receptors, reducing excessive dopamine activity. Medications targeting other neurotransmitter systems, such as norepinephrine and GABA, are also used in the treatment of various mental health disorders.

In addition to medication, other treatment approaches aim to modulate neurotransmitter levels through non-pharmacological means. Psychotherapy, including cognitive-behavioral therapy (CBT) and psychodynamic therapy, can help individuals develop coping strategies and improve their mental well-being.

Lifestyle changes, such as regular exercise, healthy diet, and stress reduction techniques, can also influence neurotransmitter levels and promote mental health. Engaging in activities that increase the release of endorphins, such as physical exercise and creative expression, can positively impact neurotransmitter levels associated with mood regulation.

It is important to note that addressing neurotransmitter imbalances may not be sufficient on its own for the treatment of mental health disorders. A holistic approach that considers the individual's unique needs and incorporates various therapeutic modalities is often necessary for optimal outcomes.

Conclusion

Neurotransmitters play a crucial role in mental health, regulating various physiological and behavioral processes. Imbalances in neurotransmitter levels can contribute to the development of mental health disorders. Understanding the role of neurotransmitters and their dysregulation provides valuable insights into the underlying mechanisms of these conditions, leading to more effective treatment approaches.

By targeting specific neurotransmitter systems through medication, therapy, and lifestyle interventions, individuals can improve their mental well-being and alleviate symptoms associated with mental health disorders. However, it is essential to consider the complex interplay of neurotransmitters with other factors when developing treatment plans, promoting personalized and holistic approaches to mental health care.

Neuroplasticity and Brain Development

Neuroplasticity refers to the brain's ability to change and adapt throughout a person's life. This phenomenon is crucial for brain development and learning. It allows the brain to form new connections between neurons and reorganize existing ones, enabling us to acquire new skills, recover from injuries, and adapt to changing environments.

Principles of Neuroplasticity

Neuroplasticity is based on several key principles:

+ **Use it or lose it**: The brain prunes unused connections while strengthening active ones. Just like muscles, the brain needs exercise to stay fit and functional.

+ **Specificity**: Neuroplastic changes are highly specific to the type of skill being learned. Different regions of the brain are responsible for different functions, and neuroplasticity occurs selectively in these regions based on the demands placed on them.

- **Repetition and practice:** Consistent practice and repetition of a skill facilitate neuroplastic changes. This is why frequent and focused practice leads to improved performance over time.

- **Intensity matters:** Intense and challenging mental and physical stimulation enhances neuroplasticity. Engaging in activities that push the limits of our abilities promotes greater rewiring of neural circuits.

- **Timing is important:** The brain is most receptive to neuroplastic changes during critical periods of development, such as early childhood. However, neuroplasticity continues throughout life and can be harnessed at any age.

- **Environmental influence:** The environment plays a crucial role in shaping neuroplasticity. Enriched environments that provide opportunities for learning, social interaction, and sensory stimulation have a positive impact on brain development.

Mechanisms of Neuroplasticity

Neuroplasticity involves various mechanisms at the molecular, cellular, and systems levels. Here are some key mechanisms:

- **Synaptic plasticity:** Synapses, the junctions between neurons, can undergo changes in strength through long-term potentiation (LTP) and long-term depression (LTD). LTP strengthens synaptic connections, while LTD weakens them. These changes in synaptic strength are believed to underlie learning and memory formation.

- **Neuronal growth and branching:** Neurons can grow new branches, called dendrites, and form new connections with other neurons. This process, known as dendritic arborization, occurs when neurons are repeatedly activated.

- **Axonal sprouting:** In response to injury or learning, undamaged neurons can sprout new axon terminals to form connections with nearby neurons. This rewiring promotes functional recovery and compensation.

- **Neurogenesis:** The adult brain can generate new neurons through a process called neurogenesis. Although more prevalent in certain brain regions, such as the hippocampus, neurogenesis can occur throughout the brain. It is influenced by various factors, including stress, exercise, and environmental enrichment.

+ **Myelination:** Myelin, a fatty substance that covers nerve fibers, facilitates faster and more efficient transmission of signals between neurons. Myelination continues into early adulthood, improving information processing speed and cognitive abilities.

Applications of Neuroplasticity

Understanding the principles and mechanisms of neuroplasticity has significant implications for various aspects of human life. Here are a few applications:

+ **Rehabilitation after brain injury:** Neuroplasticity forms the basis of rehabilitation programs for individuals with brain injuries. Through targeted therapy and repetitive exercises, damaged areas of the brain can rewire and regain lost functions.

+ **Treatment of neurological disorders:** Neuroplasticity-based interventions are used in the treatment of various neurological conditions, such as stroke, autism spectrum disorders, and Parkinson's disease. These interventions aim to promote functional recovery and alleviate symptoms.

+ **Boosting cognitive abilities:** By harnessing the principles of neuroplasticity, cognitive abilities such as memory, attention, and problem-solving can be enhanced. Mental exercises, brain-training programs, and certain learning strategies can stimulate neuroplastic changes to optimize cognitive functioning.

+ **Promoting healthy aging:** Engaging in mentally and physically stimulating activities throughout life can support healthy brain aging. Neuroplasticity research has shown that challenging the brain with new experiences and learning opportunities can help maintain cognitive vitality and reduce the risk of age-related cognitive decline.

Unleashing the Power of Neuroplasticity

To optimize neuroplasticity and promote brain health, here are some practical tips:

+ **Engage in lifelong learning:** Challenge yourself with new skills, hobbies, or subjects of interest. Continuous learning keeps your brain active and promotes neuroplasticity.

- **Physical exercise:** Regular aerobic exercise has been shown to enhance neuroplasticity and support brain health. Aim for at least 150 minutes of moderate-intensity exercise per week.

- **Mental stimulation:** Solve puzzles, play strategy games, or engage in activities that require mental effort and problem-solving. These activities stimulate neural connections and promote neuroplasticity.

- **Healthy lifestyle:** Maintain a balanced diet, get enough sleep, manage stress, and avoid harmful substances. A healthy lifestyle creates an optimal environment for neuroplasticity to thrive.

- **Social interaction:** Stay socially engaged and maintain strong relationships. Interacting with others stimulates brain activity and supports overall brain health.

By understanding and harnessing the power of neuroplasticity, we can optimize our brain health, enhance our cognitive abilities, and adapt to life's challenges at any age. So, let's embrace lifelong learning, challenge ourselves, and provide an environment that fosters neuroplasticity for ourselves and those around us.

Note: You can find additional exercises and resources on neuroplasticity and brain development in the appendix section of this book.

Psychoneuroimmunology and Mental Health

Psychoneuroimmunology (PNI) is an interdisciplinary field that studies the intricate relationship between the central nervous system, the immune system, and psychological factors. It explores how the mind, the brain, and the immune system interact and influence each other, ultimately impacting mental health.

Understanding the Mind-Body Connection

The mind-body connection refers to the bidirectional communication between the brain and the body, where psychological factors can influence physical well-being and vice versa. PNI focuses on deciphering the mechanisms and pathways involved in this connection.

The Immune System

The immune system is responsible for protecting the body against harmful pathogens and maintaining overall health. It consists of a complex network of organs, tissues, and cells that work together to identify and eliminate foreign invaders.

The immune system can be divided into two main components: the innate immune system and the adaptive immune system. The innate immune system provides the initial, rapid response to pathogens, while the adaptive immune system mounts a specific response tailored to each pathogen encountered.

Neuroendocrine System

The neuroendocrine system is a collective term for the hormones and neurotransmitters that regulate the communication between the nervous and endocrine systems. It encompasses various components, including the hypothalamus, pituitary gland, and adrenal glands, which play crucial roles in the stress response.

Stress and the Immune System

The stress response is a physiological reaction to a perceived threat or challenge. When activated, it triggers a cascade of hormonal and neurological changes in the body. Chronic stress can dysregulate the immune system and increase susceptibility to illness.

The stress response involves the release of stress hormones, such as cortisol and adrenaline, which can modulate immune function. While short-term stress can have a beneficial effect on immune response, prolonged or excessive stress can impair immune function, leading to a higher risk of infections and autoimmune disorders.

Psychological Factors and the Immune System

The field of PNI explores how psychological factors, such as stress, emotions, and social support, can modulate immune function. For example, studies have shown that chronic stress and negative emotions, such as depression and anxiety, can weaken immune responses and increase vulnerability to illness.

Conversely, positive emotions, social support, and engaging in stress-reducing activities have been found to enhance immune function and promote overall well-being. These findings highlight the importance of psychological interventions in improving mental health and boosting immune resilience.

Mind-Body Interventions

Mind-body interventions encompass a range of techniques aimed at promoting the connection between the mind and body to optimize health outcomes. These interventions, such as meditation, yoga, and relaxation techniques, have been shown to positively influence immune function and mental well-being.

Meditation practices, including mindfulness meditation, have been found to reduce stress, enhance emotional well-being, and modulate immune responses. Yoga combines physical postures, breathing exercises, and meditation, offering a holistic approach to improving both mental and physical health. Relaxation techniques, such as deep breathing and progressive muscle relaxation, help activate the body's relaxation response, reducing stress and its negative impact on the immune system.

The Gut-Brain Axis

The gut-brain axis refers to the bidirectional communication pathway between the gastrointestinal system and the central nervous system. Research has shown that the gut microbiota, the trillions of microorganisms residing in our digestive tract, play a crucial role in this communication.

The gut microbiota can influence brain function and mental health through various pathways, including immune modulation, production of neurotransmitters, and regulation of the stress response. Disruptions in the gut microbiota composition, known as dysbiosis, have been associated with psychiatric disorders such as depression, anxiety, and autism spectrum disorders.

Clinical Implications

Understanding the field of psychoneuroimmunology has important clinical implications for mental health. It highlights the need for a comprehensive approach that considers the interconnectedness of psychological, neurological, and immunological factors.

Interventions targeting the mind-body connection, such as mindfulness-based stress reduction programs or yoga therapy, can be effective adjunctive treatments for mental health disorders. Additionally, strategies aimed at promoting a healthy lifestyle, including regular exercise, good nutrition, and adequate sleep, can enhance overall immune resilience and mental well-being.

More research is needed to further elucidate the mechanisms linking psychoneuroimmunology to mental health. By embracing a holistic and interdisciplinary approach, we can continue to uncover innovative strategies for promoting mental health and well-being.

Exercises

1. Reflect on a situation in your life where stress had a significant impact on your physical health. Analyze the factors that contributed to this stress response and explore potential strategies that could have helped mitigate its negative effects.

2. Practice a mindfulness meditation session for 10 minutes each day for a week. Reflect on how this practice affects your mental state and overall well-being.

3. Research and identify different types of probiotics that are known to have positive effects on mental health. Experiment with incorporating these probiotics into your diet and observe any changes in your mood or overall mental well-being.

4. Design a comprehensive mental health and immune resilience program for a specific population, such as college students or healthcare workers. Consider integrating mind-body interventions, stress management techniques, and strategies to enhance social support.

5. Conduct a literature review on the role of nutrition in mental health and immune function. Summarize the key findings and provide recommendations for a balanced diet that supports both mental and physical well-being.

Remember to consult with healthcare professionals or mental health practitioners for personalized advice and guidance.

Genetics and Mental Health

Genetics plays a crucial role in mental health, influencing the development and expression of various mental health disorders. In this section, we will explore how genetics contributes to mental health and the implications for understanding and managing these conditions.

Genetic Factors and Mental Health

Genes are the basic units of heredity, carrying the instructions for building and maintaining our bodies. They determine our physical characteristics, such as eye color and height, but they also play a significant role in our mental health.

1. **Inherited Genetic Risk:** Certain mental health disorders have a clear genetic component, meaning that individuals with a family history of a particular disorder are more likely to develop it themselves. For example, studies have shown

that individuals with a first-degree relative (parent or sibling) who has schizophrenia are at a higher risk of developing the disorder.

2. **Gene-Environment Interaction:** While genetic factors contribute to the development of mental health disorders, they do not act alone. Gene-environment interactions play a crucial role in determining whether an individual will actually develop a disorder. Environmental factors, such as childhood trauma or chronic stress, can "trigger" the expression of certain genes associated with mental health conditions.

3. **Polygenic Nature of Mental Health:** Unlike some genetic disorders that are caused by a single gene mutation, mental health disorders are often polygenic, meaning that they result from the interaction of multiple genes. Each gene contributes a small effect to the overall risk, and the combination of these genetic variants can increase the likelihood of developing a disorder.

Genetic Research in Mental Health

Advancements in genetic research have provided valuable insights into the genetic basis of mental health disorders. Several approaches have been used to study the genetic factors involved, including:

1. **Family Studies:** By examining the occurrence of a disorder within families, researchers can assess the familial aggregation of mental health conditions. This helps to determine the heritability of the disorder and estimate the genetic risk.

2. **Twin Studies:** Twin studies involve comparing the prevalence of a disorder between monozygotic (identical) and dizygotic (fraternal) twins. By comparing the genetic similarity between twins, researchers can determine the contribution of genetic factors to the development of a disorder.

3. **Genome-wide Association Studies (GWAS):** GWAS involve scanning the entire genome of individuals to identify common genetic variants that are associated with a specific mental health disorder. These studies have helped identify potential candidate genes and pathways involved in the development of these conditions.

4. **Genetic Testing:** Genetic testing, such as DNA sequencing, can provide valuable information about an individual's genetic predisposition to certain mental health disorders. This information can help guide treatment decisions and interventions, as well as provide insights into potential risk factors.

Implications for Treatment and Prevention

Understanding the genetic factors involved in mental health disorders has significant implications for treatment and prevention strategies:

1. **Personalized Medicine**: Genetic information can help tailor treatment approaches to individuals based on their specific genetic profile. This can lead to more effective interventions and reduce the risk of adverse reactions to medications.

2. **Early Intervention**: Genetic testing can identify individuals at high risk for developing certain mental health disorders. Early intervention in these cases can help mitigate the impact of environmental triggers and promote better mental health outcomes.

3. **Preventive Strategies**: Knowledge of genetic risk factors can inform preventive strategies aimed at reducing the likelihood of developing a disorder. This may involve lifestyle modifications, psychoeducation, and targeted interventions focused on individuals with a high genetic predisposition.

4. **Targeted Therapies**: Genetic research can provide insight into the underlying biological mechanisms of mental health disorders, leading to the development of targeted therapies. This may include medications that specifically target gene-related pathways or gene-editing techniques that modify problematic genetic variants.

It is important to note that while genetics plays a significant role in mental health, it is not the sole determinant. Environmental factors, lifestyle choices, and individual resilience also contribute to an individual's mental well-being. A holistic approach that considers both genetic and environmental factors is crucial for understanding and managing mental health disorders effectively.

In conclusion, genetics plays a fundamental role in mental health. It influences the development and expression of mental health disorders through inherited genetic risk, gene-environment interactions, and the polygenic nature of these conditions. Genetic research provides valuable insights into the genetic basis of mental health disorders, informing treatment approaches, early intervention, preventive strategies, and the development of targeted therapies. However, a comprehensive approach that considers both genetic and environmental factors is essential for promoting mental well-being.

Psychosomatic Medicine

Overview of Psychosomatic Medicine

Psychosomatic medicine is an interdisciplinary field that focuses on the relationship between the mind and body in the context of health and disease. It recognizes that psychological factors can influence physical health and that physical conditions can impact mental well-being. Understanding this mind-body connection is essential for providing comprehensive and effective healthcare.

Historical Context

The origins of psychosomatic medicine can be traced back to the ancient Greeks, who believed that the mind and body were interconnected. However, it was not until the 19th century that the field began to take shape as a distinct discipline. Sigmund Freud, often regarded as the father of psychoanalysis, made significant contributions to understanding the influence of unconscious processes on physical symptoms.

In the early 20th century, several key figures expanded on Freud's work and laid the foundation for psychosomatic medicine as a holistic approach to healthcare. Pioneers such as Franz Alexander and George Engel emphasized the importance of considering psychological factors in the diagnosis and treatment of physical illnesses.

The Biopsychosocial Model

At the core of psychosomatic medicine is the biopsychosocial model, which recognizes that health and illness are influenced by a complex interaction of biological, psychological, and social factors. This model rejects the traditional biomedical approach, which views illness solely as a result of biological dysfunction. Instead, it takes into account the interplay between biological, psychological, and social determinants of health.

The biopsychosocial model emphasizes the importance of understanding the unique experiences and contexts of individuals. It recognizes that there are multiple pathways through which psychological and social factors can influence physical health outcomes. For example, chronic stress can lead to dysregulation of the hypothalamic-pituitary-adrenal axis, resulting in increased inflammation and a higher risk of developing certain diseases.

Psychosomatic Illnesses

Psychosomatic medicine focuses on the relationship between psychological factors and physical illnesses. It recognizes that psychological distress can contribute to the development, exacerbation, or maintenance of various medical conditions. Some common psychosomatic illnesses include:

- **Irritable bowel syndrome (IBS):** IBS is a chronic gastrointestinal disorder characterized by abdominal pain, bloating, and changes in bowel habits.

Psychological factors such as stress, anxiety, and depression can trigger or worsen symptoms.

+ **Hypertension:** Psychological factors, including chronic stress and negative emotions, can contribute to the development and progression of high blood pressure. Individuals with poorly managed stress are more likely to have elevated blood pressure levels.

+ **Asthma:** Emotional factors, such as anxiety or panic, can lead to the constriction of airways and exacerbate asthma symptoms. Stress can also weaken the immune system, making individuals more susceptible to respiratory infections and asthma attacks.

+ **Headaches:** Tension-type headaches and migraines can be influenced by stress, anxiety, and depression. Emotional factors play a role in triggering and exacerbating headaches in susceptible individuals.

Psychosomatic Interventions

Psychosomatic medicine employs various interventions to promote healing and well-being. These interventions target both the physical and psychological aspects of health, recognizing that addressing one without the other may lead to incomplete or ineffective treatment.

Therapeutic techniques commonly used in psychosomatic medicine include:

+ **Cognitive-behavioral therapy (CBT):** CBT is a psychological intervention that helps individuals identify and change negative thoughts and behaviors that contribute to physical symptoms. It has been particularly effective in managing conditions such as chronic pain and fibromyalgia.

+ **Relaxation techniques:** Practices such as deep breathing exercises, progressive muscle relaxation, and guided imagery can help individuals reduce stress, alleviate anxiety, and promote relaxation. These techniques have been found to be beneficial in managing a wide range of psychosomatic conditions.

+ **Mind-body interventions:** Approaches such as mindfulness-based stress reduction, yoga, and meditation are increasingly used in psychosomatic medicine to enhance self-awareness, reduce stress, and improve overall well-being. These interventions promote the integration of mind, body, and spirit in the healing process.

‣ **Supportive therapy:** Providing emotional support and validation to individuals with psychosomatic illnesses is crucial. Supportive therapy aims to create a safe and nonjudgmental environment where patients can explore and express their emotions, fears, and concerns.

Case Study: The Role of Stress in Psoriasis

Psoriasis is a chronic autoimmune skin condition characterized by red, scaly patches on the skin. While the exact cause of psoriasis is unknown, research has shown that psychological factors, particularly stress, play a significant role in the development and exacerbation of the disease.

Stress can trigger immune system dysregulation, leading to increased inflammation and the release of pro-inflammatory molecules that contribute to the development of psoriatic plaques. Additionally, stress can worsen existing symptoms and increase the risk of flare-ups.

In the case of a 35-year-old woman with psoriasis, a psychosomatic medicine approach would involve addressing both the physical symptoms and the underlying psychological factors. Treatment may include topical medications to manage the skin lesions, combined with stress management techniques such as relaxation exercises and mindfulness-based interventions. By targeting both the physical and psychological aspects of the disease, this holistic approach aims to improve overall well-being and quality of life.

Conclusion

Psychosomatic medicine recognizes the intricate connection between the mind and body in health and disease. By adopting a biopsychosocial perspective, it offers a comprehensive approach to healthcare that integrates biological, psychological, and social factors. Understanding the role of psychological factors in physical health and employing psychosomatic interventions can lead to improved outcomes and better overall well-being for individuals with psychosomatic conditions.

Impact of Stress on Physical Health

Stress is an unavoidable part of life, and it can have a significant impact on both our mental and physical well-being. When we experience stress, our body goes into a fight-or-flight response, releasing stress hormones such as cortisol and adrenaline. While this response is helpful in short bursts, chronic stress can have detrimental effects on our physical health.

One of the major ways that stress affects our physical health is through its impact on the immune system. When we are stressed, our immune system becomes suppressed, making us more susceptible to infections and illnesses. Research has shown that chronic stress can weaken the immune system, leaving individuals more vulnerable to colds, flu, and other respiratory infections.

Furthermore, stress can also contribute to the development and progression of chronic diseases, such as cardiovascular disease, diabetes, and autoimmune disorders. This is because stress increases inflammation in the body, which is a common underlying factor in many chronic conditions. The prolonged release of stress hormones can lead to persistent inflammation, which can damage tissues and organs over time.

Another way that stress affects physical health is through its impact on sleep. Chronic stress can disrupt our sleep patterns, leading to insomnia or poor-quality sleep. Lack of sleep has been linked to a wide range of health issues, including cardiovascular disease, obesity, diabetes, and mental health disorders. It is essential to prioritize good sleep hygiene and establish healthy sleep habits to mitigate the negative effects of stress on physical health.

Additionally, stress can also lead to unhealthy coping behaviors, such as overeating, excessive alcohol consumption, smoking, and substance abuse. These behaviors can have severe consequences for our physical health, increasing the risk of obesity, liver disease, cardiovascular problems, and addiction.

To mitigate the impact of stress on physical health, it is crucial to adopt effective stress management techniques. Regular exercise has proven to be an excellent stress reliever as it promotes the release of endorphins, which are natural mood-enhancing chemicals. Engaging in activities like yoga, tai chi, or aerobic exercises can help reduce stress levels and improve physical well-being.

Moreover, practicing relaxation techniques, such as deep breathing exercises, progressive muscle relaxation, and meditation, can activate the body's relaxation response. These techniques help decrease the production of stress hormones and promote a sense of calm and relaxation.

A healthy lifestyle that includes a balanced diet and adequate nutrition is also essential for managing stress and maintaining physical health. Research has demonstrated that certain nutrients, such as omega-3 fatty acids, B vitamins, and antioxidants, play a vital role in regulating the body's stress response. Including foods rich in these nutrients, such as fish, nuts, whole grains, fruits, and vegetables, can support overall well-being in the face of stress.

Lastly, social support and maintaining strong relationships can also buffer the impact of stress on physical health. Connecting with loved ones, seeking emotional support, and engaging in social activities can help reduce stress levels and promote resilience.

In conclusion, stress has a profound impact on physical health. Chronic stress can weaken the immune system, contribute to the development of chronic diseases, disrupt sleep patterns, and lead to unhealthy coping behaviors. By adopting effective stress management strategies, engaging in regular exercise, practicing relaxation techniques, maintaining a healthy lifestyle, and seeking social support, individuals can mitigate the negative effects of stress on physical health and promote overall well-being.

Additional Resources

1. Selye, H. (1974). Stress without distress. Psychology Today, 8(3), 47-50. 2. McEwen, B. S. (2006). Protective and damaging effects of stress mediators. New England Journal of Medicine, 338(3), 171-179. 3. Cohen, S., Janicki-Deverts, D., & Miller, G. E. (2007). Psychological stress and disease. JAMA, 298(14), 1685-1687. 4. National Institute of Mental Health. (2021). 5 things you should know about stress. Retrieved from https://www.nimh.nih.gov/health/publications/stress 5. American Psychological Association. (2021). Stress effects on the body. Retrieved from https://www.apa.org/topics/stress-body 6. Harvard Health Publishing. (2018). Understanding the stress response. Retrieved from https://www.health.harvard.edu/staying-healthy/understanding-the-stress-response.

Exercises

1. Think of a time when you experienced a particularly stressful situation. How did it impact your physical health? Share your experience and reflect on how you could have managed the stress differently. 2. Research and try out a relaxation technique that you haven't tried before, such as progressive muscle relaxation or guided imagery. Write about your experience and whether you found it helpful in reducing stress and improving your physical well-being. 3. Interview a healthcare professional or mental health expert about the impact of stress on physical health. Document their insights and recommendations for managing stress effectively. 4. Create a self-care plan that includes strategies for managing stress and promoting physical health. Share your plan with a friend or family member and discuss how you can support each other in following through with your self-care goals. 5. Conduct a small research project on the relationship between stress and a specific

chronic disease, such as cardiovascular disease or diabetes. Present your findings and propose ways in which individuals can reduce stress to mitigate the risk of developing or managing the disease.

Note: Remember to reflect on your experiences, feelings, and thoughts throughout the exercises. Self-reflection and introspection are essential components of personal growth and well-being.

Mind-Body Interventions

Mind-body interventions involve various techniques and practices that promote the connection between the mind and the body, aiming to enhance mental health and well-being. These interventions recognize the intricate relationship between psychological and physiological factors, emphasizing the influence of each on the other. By integrating the power of the mind and the body, individuals can cultivate a sense of balance, resilience, and relaxation.

Overview of Mind-Body Interventions

Mind-body interventions encompass a wide range of approaches that target the mind-body connection. Some of the common practices include meditation, yoga, biofeedback, guided imagery, and relaxation techniques. These interventions focus on harnessing the power of the mind to positively impact physical health and mental well-being. They can be practiced individually or in group settings, and they can complement traditional treatments or stand as independent practices.

Meditation

Meditation is a practice that involves training the mind to achieve a state of focused awareness and inner calm. It encompasses a variety of techniques, such as mindfulness meditation, loving-kindness meditation, and transcendental meditation. Through meditation, individuals learn to cultivate attention and awareness, develop a non-judgmental attitude towards their thoughts and emotions, and attain a sense of inner stillness and peace.

One of the most commonly practiced forms of meditation is mindfulness meditation. It involves focusing one's attention on the present moment, without judgment or attachment. Through mindfulness meditation, individuals develop the ability to observe their thoughts, emotions, and bodily sensations without getting swept away by them. This practice has been shown to reduce stress, improve emotional well-being, and enhance cognitive functions.

Yoga

Yoga is a mind-body practice that originated in ancient India and has gained popularity worldwide. It combines physical postures (asanas), breathing exercises (pranayama), and meditation to promote physical strength, flexibility, and mental clarity. Yoga focuses on the integration of mind, body, and breath, aiming to create a harmonious balance within oneself.

The physical postures of yoga help improve flexibility, strength, and body awareness. They can also release physical tension and promote relaxation. Combined with conscious breathing techniques, yoga can induce a state of relaxation and calm the mind. Regular practice of yoga has been shown to reduce anxiety, depression, and stress, while improving overall well-being and quality of life.

Biofeedback

Biofeedback is a technique that enables individuals to gain voluntary control over physiological processes through real-time feedback. It involves using electronic devices to measure and display information about bodily functions, such as heart rate, blood pressure, and skin temperature. By receiving immediate feedback, individuals can learn to identify and modify physiological responses that are typically outside conscious control.

For example, biofeedback can help individuals learn to regulate their breathing pattern, heart rate, or muscle tension. By actively participating in the process, individuals can gain a sense of control over their physical responses, leading to reduced stress and improved well-being. Biofeedback is often used in the treatment of conditions such as chronic pain, anxiety disorders, and hypertension.

Guided Imagery

Guided imagery is a technique that involves using visualization and imagination to evoke positive mental images. It utilizes the power of the mind to create sensory experiences that promote relaxation and healing. Through guided imagery, individuals are guided by a trained professional or through audio recordings to imagine themselves in peaceful and calming environments, engaging all their senses.

By engaging in vivid mental imagery, individuals activate the same neural pathways as they would in real-life experiences. This can induce a relaxation response, reduce stress, and promote a sense of well-being. Guided imagery is often used in the management of anxiety, pain, and sleep disorders.

Relaxation Techniques

Relaxation techniques encompass a variety of practices that aim to induce a state of relaxation and calmness. These techniques can include deep breathing exercises, progressive muscle relaxation, autogenic training, and mindfulness-based stress reduction. By activating the body's relaxation response, individuals can counteract the effects of stress and promote physical and mental well-being.

Deep breathing exercises involve taking slow, deep breaths, focusing on the inhalation and exhalation process. This practice helps slow down the heart rate, lower blood pressure, and reduce muscle tension. Progressive muscle relaxation involves sequentially tensing and releasing different muscle groups in the body to promote physical relaxation and relieve muscle tension. Autogenic training focuses on promoting a state of deep relaxation through self-suggestions of warmth and heaviness in the body. Mindfulness-based stress reduction combines mindfulness meditation, body awareness, and gentle movement to reduce stress and enhance well-being.

The Integration of Mind and Body

Mind-body interventions offer opportunities for individuals to take an active role in their mental health and well-being. By recognizing the connection between the mind and the body, individuals can engage in practices that influence both aspects, fostering a holistic approach to self-care. These interventions not only help manage symptoms of mental health disorders but also promote overall resilience, relaxation, and personal growth.

It is important to note that mind-body interventions should not be considered as standalone treatments but rather as complementary approaches that can enhance the effectiveness of traditional therapies. They can provide individuals with additional tools in their mental health toolkit, empowering them to actively participate in their healing process.

Unconventional yet Relevant

One unconventional but relevant mind-body intervention is laughter therapy. Laughter has been shown to have numerous psychological and physiological benefits. It releases endorphins, reduces stress hormones, and promotes a sense of well-being. Laughter therapy involves engaging in activities that induce laughter, such as watching a comedy show or participating in laughter yoga, where individuals engage in laughter exercises. Incorporating laughter into one's daily life can help alleviate stress, improve mood, and strengthen social connections.

Exercises

1. Mindfulness Meditation Practice: Find a quiet and comfortable space. Sit in a relaxed position and close your eyes. Take a few deep breaths, and then shift your attention to the sensation of your breath as it enters and leaves your body. Notice the rising and falling of your abdomen or the sensation of air passing through your nostrils. Whenever your mind wanders, gently bring your attention back to your breath. Practice this for 10 minutes each day and observe the impact on your mental and emotional state.

2. Yoga Postures for Relaxation: Try the Child's Pose (Balasana) and the Corpse Pose (Savasana) to promote relaxation. In Child's Pose, kneel on the floor, bring your big toes together, and sit on your heels. Slowly fold forward, resting your forehead on the mat and extending your arms forward or alongside your body. Breathe deeply and allow your body to relax. In Corpse Pose, lie flat on your back, arms by your sides, palms facing up. Close your eyes and focus on your breath, allowing your body to release tension. Practice these poses for a few minutes each day to experience the calming effects.

3. Biofeedback Practice: Using a biofeedback device (e.g., heart rate monitor or skin temperature sensor), measure your physiological response to a stressful situation, such as a challenging task or a difficult conversation. Observe how your heart rate, blood pressure, or other measurements change in response to stress. Then, practice relaxation techniques such as deep breathing or progressive muscle relaxation and monitor how your physiological responses change. Pay attention to the connection between your mind, body, and the effectiveness of the relaxation techniques.

4. Guided Imagery Exercise: Find a quiet space where you can relax comfortably. Close your eyes and imagine yourself in a peaceful natural setting, such as a beach, forest, or meadow. Engage all your senses to create a vivid mental image. Notice the sights, sounds, smells, and sensations in this environment. Stay in this imagery for several minutes, allowing yourself to feel a deep sense of relaxation and peace. Open your eyes when ready and reflect on the experience.

Resources

1. Kabat-Zinn, J. (2013). Full Catastrophe Living: Using the Wisdom of Your Body and Mind to Face Stress, Pain, and Illness. Bantam. 2. Benson, H., & Klipper, M. Z. (2000). The Relaxation Response. HarperTorch. 3. Farhi, D. (2011). The Breathing Book: Vitality and Good Health Through Essential Breath Work. Holt Paperbacks. 4. Siegel, R. D. (2010). The Mindfulness Solution: Everyday Practices

for Everyday Problems. Guilford Press. 5. Goleman, D., & Davidson, R. J. (2017). Altered Traits: Science Reveals How Meditation Changes Your Mind, Brain, and Body. Avery.

Remember, the mind and body are intricately connected, and by incorporating mind-body interventions into your life, you can nurture your mental and physical well-being. Experiment with different practices, find what resonates with you, and make them a part of your self-care routine.

Integrative Approaches to Health and Well-being

Integrative approaches to health and well-being encompass a wide range of practices and therapies that aim to promote holistic mental health. These approaches recognize the interconnectedness of the mind, body, and spirit, and seek to address mental health concerns by combining various methods from both conventional and complementary medicine. In this section, we will explore some of the key integrative approaches to health and well-being, including mindfulness, yoga, art therapy, complementary and alternative medicine, and nutrition.

Mindfulness

Mindfulness is a practice that involves intentionally focusing one's attention on the present moment, without judgment. It involves cultivating a state of awareness and acceptance of one's thoughts, emotions, and sensations. Mindfulness-based interventions have been shown to have a positive impact on mental health, including reducing stress, anxiety, and depression.

One powerful technique in mindfulness is meditation. This practice involves sitting quietly and paying attention to the breath, bodily sensations, or thoughts and emotions. By observing these experiences without attachment or judgment, individuals can develop a greater sense of self-awareness and a better ability to manage their mental and emotional states.

Another aspect of mindfulness is incorporating mindfulness into daily activities. This involves bringing mindful awareness to mundane tasks such as eating, walking, or washing dishes. By engaging fully in the present moment, individuals can cultivate a sense of calm and reduce stress.

Yoga

Yoga is a mind-body practice that originated in ancient India and has gained popularity worldwide as a form of exercise and relaxation. It combines physical postures, breathing techniques, and meditation to promote physical and mental well-being.

The physical aspect of yoga involves a series of postures, or asanas, that help build strength, flexibility, and balance. These postures can be adapted to suit a wide range of abilities and can be practiced by people of all ages.

In addition to the physical practice, yoga incorporates breath control techniques, known as pranayama, which help regulate the flow of energy in the body and calm the mind. By focusing on the breath, individuals can bring their attention away from distressing thoughts or emotions and find a sense of inner peace.

Yoga also includes meditation practices, such as mindfulness or loving-kindness meditation, which can help individuals cultivate a greater sense of self-compassion and connection with others.

Art Therapy and Expressive Arts

Art therapy is a form of psychotherapy that utilizes various art modalities, such as drawing, painting, and sculpture, to promote self-expression, insight, and healing. It can be particularly beneficial for individuals who find it difficult to verbalize their thoughts and emotions.

Through the process of creating art, individuals can explore and communicate their subconscious feelings and experiences. The art therapist provides a supportive and non-judgmental environment, allowing individuals to express themselves freely and use art as a medium for self-discovery and personal growth.

Art therapy has been shown to be effective in reducing symptoms of anxiety, depression, and trauma-related disorders. It can also enhance self-esteem, improve communication skills, and provide a sense of empowerment and control.

Expressive arts, a broader term that encompasses various creative modalities such as music, dance, and drama, can also be used as therapeutic tools to promote well-being and self-expression.

Complementary and Alternative Medicine

Complementary and alternative medicine (CAM) refers to a diverse set of medical and health care systems, practices, and products that are not considered a part of conventional medicine. These approaches are used alongside or in conjunction with conventional therapies to support and enhance overall health and well-being.

CAM practices can include herbal remedies, acupuncture, chiropractic care, naturopathy, and traditional healing systems such as Ayurveda and Traditional

Chinese Medicine (TCM). These approaches offer a holistic perspective on health, focusing on the balance of the mind, body, and spirit.

While some CAM practices have been extensively studied and have scientific evidence supporting their effectiveness, others may lack rigorous scientific research. It is important to consult with qualified practitioners and inform healthcare providers about any CAM therapies being used.

Nutrition and Mental Health

The food we consume plays a crucial role in our physical health, but it also impacts our mental well-being. A growing body of research suggests that a healthy diet can have positive effects on mental health, while a poor diet may contribute to the development or worsening of mental health disorders.

A diet rich in fruits, vegetables, whole grains, lean proteins, and healthy fats provides the necessary nutrients for optimal brain function. These nutrients, including Omega-3 fatty acids, B vitamins, and antioxidants, support neurotransmitter production, reduce inflammation, and promote overall brain health.

Conversely, a diet high in processed foods, sugar, unhealthy fats, and artificial additives may increase the risk of mental health issues such as depression and anxiety. Junk food and sugary drinks can lead to blood sugar spikes followed by crashes, affecting mood and energy levels.

In addition to a nutritious diet, it is essential to stay hydrated and practice mindful eating. Being aware of physical hunger cues and eating with intention and enjoyment can promote a healthier relationship with food and enhance overall well-being.

Integrative approaches to health and well-being recognize the importance of addressing mental health from a holistic perspective. By combining conventional and complementary practices, individuals can cultivate a greater sense of self-awareness, promote mental resilience, and improve overall mental well-being. It is important to consult with healthcare professionals or qualified practitioners to determine the most appropriate integrative approach for individual needs and preferences.

Remember, mental health is a journey, and finding the right combination of approaches and strategies is a highly personal process. The integrative approaches discussed in this section can serve as tools and resources to support and enhance mental health, but it is important to approach them with an open mind and willingness to explore what works best for each individual.

Holistic Approaches to Mental Health

Mindfulness and Meditation

In this section, we will explore the practice of mindfulness and meditation as powerful tools for promoting mental health and well-being. Mindfulness and meditation have gained significant popularity in recent years, as more and more people recognize their benefits in reducing stress, improving focus, and enhancing overall happiness. Let's dive in and explore the principles and practices of mindfulness and meditation.

Understanding Mindfulness

Mindfulness is a state of active, nonjudgmental attention to the present moment. It involves intentionally bringing one's awareness to the present experience, without getting caught up in thoughts or judgments about the past or future. By cultivating mindfulness, individuals can develop a greater sense of clarity, emotional resilience, and a deeper understanding of themselves and others.

Principles of Mindfulness

Mindfulness is grounded in several principles that guide its practice. These principles include:

1. **Non-judgment:** Practicing mindfulness involves observing thoughts, sensations, and emotions without labeling them as good or bad. Instead, individuals learn to accept whatever arises in their experience with an attitude of curiosity and openness.

2. **Present-moment awareness:** Mindfulness encourages individuals to anchor their attention in the present moment. Rather than dwelling on the past or worrying about the future, mindfulness cultivates an awareness of what is happening in the here and now. This practice helps individuals develop a sense of groundedness and calm.

3. **Acceptance:** Mindfulness emphasizes the importance of accepting things as they are, without trying to change or control them. This attitude of acceptance allows individuals to let go of resistance and find peace in the present moment.

4. **Non-striving:** Mindfulness involves letting go of the need to achieve or attain a particular outcome. Instead, individuals learn to simply be with

their experiences as they naturally unfold, without striving for a specific result.

Benefits of Mindfulness

The practice of mindfulness offers a wide range of benefits for mental health and well-being. Here are some key advantages:

- **Stress reduction**: Mindfulness has been shown to decrease stress levels and promote relaxation. By cultivating present-moment awareness and non-judgmental acceptance, individuals can develop more effective coping strategies for dealing with stress.

- **Improved focus and concentration**: Regular mindfulness practice can enhance attention and concentration. By training the mind to stay focused on the present moment, individuals can reduce distractions and improve productivity.

- **Emotional regulation**: Mindfulness helps individuals develop a greater ability to recognize and regulate their emotions. By observing emotions with non-judgmental awareness, individuals can respond to challenging situations in a more balanced and compassionate manner.

- **Enhanced self-awareness**: Mindfulness allows individuals to develop a deeper understanding of their thoughts, emotions, and patterns of behavior. This self-awareness can lead to greater self-compassion and personal growth.

- **Improved overall well-being**: Regular mindfulness practice has been linked to increased feelings of happiness and well-being. By cultivating a present-moment focus and accepting things as they are, individuals can experience a greater sense of contentment and fulfillment.

Types of Meditation

Meditation is a practice often associated with mindfulness, although there are various types of meditation techniques that can be used to cultivate mindfulness. Here are a few common types of meditation:

1. **Focused attention meditation**: This type of meditation involves directing one's attention to a specific object, such as the breath or a mantra. When the mind wanders, practitioners gently bring their attention back to the chosen object, training the mind to stay focused and present.

2. **Body scan meditation:** In body scan meditation, individuals systematically bring awareness to each part of their body, noticing any sensations or areas of tension. This practice helps cultivate a deeper connection between the mind and body, promoting relaxation and self-awareness.

3. **Loving-kindness meditation:** Loving-kindness meditation involves generating feelings of love, compassion, and goodwill towards oneself and others. Practitioners repeat specific phrases or visualizations to cultivate a sense of kindness and connection.

4. **Walking meditation:** Walking meditation is a form of meditation that involves maintaining present-moment awareness while walking slowly and deliberately. It encourages individuals to bring their attention to the sensations of walking, such as the feeling of the feet touching the ground.

Incorporating Mindfulness into Daily Life

Integrating mindfulness into daily life can greatly enhance its benefits. Here are some suggestions for incorporating mindfulness into your daily routine:

+ **Mindful eating:** Pay attention to the tastes, textures, and smells of your food. Eat slowly and savor each bite, fully engaging your senses.

+ **Mindful walking:** Take moments throughout the day to simply walk and be present. Notice the sensations in your body and the environment around you.

+ **Mindful breathing:** Take a few moments each day to focus on your breath. Observe each inhale and exhale, allowing yourself to fully relax.

+ **Mindful listening:** When engaged in conversations, practice active listening by fully attending to what the other person is saying without judgment or distraction.

+ **Mindful breaks:** Take short breaks during the day to bring your attention back to the present moment. You can do a quick body scan or simply take a few intentional breaths.

Resources for Mindfulness and Meditation

Here are some resources to explore further on mindfulness and meditation:

- Books: "The Miracle of Mindfulness" by Thich Nhat Hanh, "Wherever You Go, There You Are" by Jon Kabat-Zinn, and "The Power of Now" by Eckhart Tolle.

- Mobile apps: Headspace, Calm, and Insight Timer offer guided meditations and mindfulness exercises.

- Online courses: Websites such as Coursera and Udemy offer a variety of online courses on mindfulness and meditation, some of which are taught by renowned experts in the field.

- Local mindfulness centers: Many communities have mindfulness centers or meditation groups where you can learn and practice mindfulness with like-minded individuals.

Unconventional Approach: Mindful Technology Use

In today's digital age, technology is an integral part of our lives. However, excessive and mindless use of technology can contribute to stress and decreased well-being. An unconventional approach to mindfulness is to incorporate mindfulness into technology use itself.

For example, you can set aside dedicated time for technology use and practice being fully present and mindful during that time. Notice the sensations of the keyboard as you type, be aware of the sounds or vibrations of your phone notifications, and observe your emotional reactions as you engage with different online content. By bringing mindfulness to technology use, you can cultivate a more conscious and balanced relationship with digital devices.

Conclusion

Mindfulness and meditation offer powerful techniques for promoting mental health and well-being. By incorporating mindfulness into our daily lives and practicing different types of meditation, we can reduce stress, improve focus, regulate emotions, and enhance overall happiness. Whether it's taking a few deep breaths, practicing a body scan meditation, or simply being fully present as we engage with technology, mindfulness can bring about profound positive changes in our lives. Take the time to explore and experiment with mindfulness and meditation, and see how they can transform your mental health and your relationship with yourself and others.

Yoga and Tai Chi

Yoga and Tai Chi are ancient practices rooted in Eastern philosophy and have been gaining popularity in Western societies for their numerous mental and physical health benefits. These practices emphasize the mind-body connection and promote harmony, balance, and flexibility. In this section, we will explore the principles, benefits, and techniques of Yoga and Tai Chi as powerful mental health strategies.

Principles of Yoga

Yoga originated in ancient India and is a holistic approach to achieve physical, mental, and spiritual well-being. The word "yoga" means union, symbolizing the integration of body, mind, and spirit. It encompasses various practices, including physical postures (asanas), breath control (pranayama), and meditation (dhyana).

At its core, yoga is based on the following principles:

+ **Asanas:** Yoga poses or postures that promote strength, flexibility, and balance.

+ **Pranayama:** Breathing exercises that enhance mental clarity, energy, and relaxation.

+ **Meditation:** Focusing the mind to achieve a state of inner peace, concentration, and self-awareness.

+ **Yamas and Niyamas:** Ethical guidelines that encourage self-discipline, compassion, and integrity.

+ **Mantras and Chanting:** Repetition of sacred sounds or words to enhance focus and spiritual connection.

By practicing yoga, individuals are encouraged to cultivate a sense of presence, mindfulness, and self-compassion, which can positively impact mental health.

Tai Chi: The Art of Flowing Movement

Tai Chi, also known as Tai Chi Chuan, originated in ancient China and is often referred to as "moving meditation." It combines slow, continuous movements with deep breathing and mental focus. The practice is based on the principles of Taoism, aiming to harmonize the body, mind, and spirit.

The core principles of Tai Chi include:

+ **Slowness and Fluidity:** Tai Chi movements are slow, gentle, and continuous, allowing for a deep focus on body sensations and mental calmness.

+ **Alignment and Balance:** The practice emphasizes aligning the body in a relaxed and balanced posture, promoting stability and proper energy flow.

+ **Mindful Awareness:** Tai Chi cultivates a state of focused awareness, reducing mental chatter and enhancing present-moment experience.

+ **Taoist Philosophy:** The principles of yin and yang, harmony, and the Taoist concept of "non-doing" are fundamental to the practice of Tai Chi.

Tai Chi has been shown to improve physical strength, flexibility, and balance. Moreover, it has been found to decrease anxiety, depression, and stress while promoting relaxation and overall well-being.

Benefits of Yoga and Tai Chi for Mental Health

The regular practice of Yoga and Tai Chi offers numerous mental health benefits, including:

+ **Stress Reduction:** Both practices incorporate deep breathing and mindful movements, activating the relaxation response and reducing the physiological effects of stress.

+ **Improved Emotional Well-being:** Yoga and Tai Chi promote self-awareness, self-compassion, and emotional regulation. They can help manage symptoms of anxiety, depression, and mood disorders.

+ **Enhanced Cognitive Function:** Yoga and Tai Chi have been associated with improved attention, memory, and executive functioning. Regular practice may help prevent age-related cognitive decline.

+ **Better Sleep:** The relaxation techniques in Yoga and Tai Chi can improve sleep quality, reduce insomnia, and promote overall restfulness.

+ **Increased Resilience:** Both practices cultivate resilience by fostering a sense of inner strength, adaptability, and the ability to navigate challenges effectively.

It's important to note that while Yoga and Tai Chi are generally safe for most individuals, modifications may be necessary for those with specific physical limitations or health conditions. It is recommended to consult with a qualified instructor or healthcare professional before starting any new exercise program.

Practical Techniques and Tips

Here are some practical techniques and tips to incorporate Yoga and Tai Chi into your daily routine:

+ **Start with Beginner Classes:** If you're new to Yoga or Tai Chi, it's advisable to begin with beginner-level classes or seek guidance from a qualified instructor to learn proper techniques and postures.

+ **Practice Mindful Breathing:** Focus on your breath during the practice, inhaling deeply through the nose and exhaling slowly through the mouth. This can help induce relaxation and enhance the mind-body connection.

+ **Create a Serene Environment:** Designate a quiet and peaceful space for your practice, free from distractions. Consider adding calming elements such as candles, soft lighting, or soothing music.

+ **Set Realistic Goals:** Start with short sessions and gradually increase the duration and intensity of your practice. Be patient and kind to yourself, allowing for flexibility and adjustments in your routine.

+ **Practice Regularly:** Consistency is key. Engage in Yoga or Tai Chi practice at least a few times a week to experience the mental health benefits fully.

+ **Listen to Your Body:** Honor your body's limitations and avoid pushing yourself beyond your comfort zone. Modify poses or movements as needed to prevent injury and promote a sustainable practice.

Unconventional Application: Laughing Yoga

As an unconventional but relevant application of Yoga, Laughing Yoga combines laughter exercises with deep breathing and stretching. The principle behind Laughing Yoga is that voluntary laughter can lead to real and positive physiological and psychological changes in the body. Through the practice of deliberate laughter, participants often experience an uplifted mood, reduced stress levels, and enhanced social connections.

In a Laughing Yoga session, participants engage in various laughter exercises, often in a group setting, while maintaining eye contact and childlike playfulness. These exercises can range from laughing alone, to laughter in pairs or groups, all guided by a laughter leader.

The unconventional aspect of Laughing Yoga lies in its intentional use of laughter as a tool for promoting mental well-being. While it may initially feel forced or artificial, the contagious nature of laughter often leads to genuine, infectious laughter. The body cannot distinguish between voluntary and spontaneous laughter, and the physiological and psychological benefits are similar. Laughing Yoga can be a fun, unique, and effective practice for reducing stress and improving overall mental health.

Additional Resources

For those interested in exploring Yoga and Tai Chi further, here are some resources:

- ✦ Books:

  - – "Light on Yoga" by B.K.S. Iyengar

  - – "The Heart of Yoga: Developing a Personal Practice" by T.K.V. Desikachar

  - – "The Harvard Medical School Guide to Tai Chi" by Peter Wayne

  - – "Tai Chi for Beginners and the 24 Forms" by Paul Lam

- ✦ Websites and Apps:

  - – Yoga Journal: www.yogajournal.com

  - – DoYogaWithMe: www.doyogawithme.com

  - – Insight Timer: www.insighttimer.com (Meditation and Yoga App)

  - – Daily Yoga: www.dailyyoga.com (Yoga App)

  - – Tai Chi for Health Institute: www.taichiforhealthinstitute.org

- ✦ Local Classes or Instructors:

  - – Check with community centers, yoga studios, or fitness centers in your area for local Yoga and Tai Chi classes.

Remember, the goal of practicing Yoga and Tai Chi is to find what works best for you and to enjoy the journey of self-discovery and well-being. So take a deep breath, embrace the present moment, and embark on this transformative path towards better mental health with Yoga and Tai Chi.

Art Therapy and Expressive Arts

Art therapy is a form of therapy that utilizes the creative process of making art to improve mental and emotional well-being. It provides individuals with a way to express themselves and explore their thoughts and feelings through various art forms. In this section, we will explore the principles and benefits of art therapy, as well as different techniques and approaches that can be used.

Principles of Art Therapy

Art therapy is based on the principle that the creative process involved in making art can be healing and therapeutic. The focus is not on the end product but on the process of creating and the feelings and insights that arise during that process.

One of the key principles of art therapy is the non-verbal nature of art expression. Art allows individuals to communicate and express themselves without the limitations of language. This is particularly beneficial for individuals who may struggle to verbalize their thoughts and emotions.

Another principle of art therapy is that art can serve as a mirror, reflecting back to individuals their own experiences and emotions. By creating art, individuals can gain insight into their own thoughts, feelings, and experiences, and develop a greater understanding of themselves.

Benefits of Art Therapy

Art therapy offers numerous benefits for mental health and well-being. Some of the key benefits include:

- **Self-expression and communication**: Art therapy provides individuals with a safe and non-threatening way to express their thoughts, emotions, and experiences. It can help individuals communicate and share their inner world, even when words may be difficult to find.

- **Emotional release and stress reduction**: Engaging in the creative process can be cathartic and help individuals release pent-up emotions and reduce stress. It provides a healthy outlet for emotional expression and can promote relaxation and inner calm.

- **Self-discovery and personal growth**: Art therapy can foster self-awareness and self-exploration, allowing individuals to gain insights into their own thoughts, feelings, and experiences. It can also promote personal growth and facilitate positive changes in behavior and mindset.

+ **Enhanced problem-solving skills:** The process of creating art often requires problem-solving skills and encourages individuals to think creatively and outside the box. This can translate into improved problem-solving abilities in other areas of life.

+ **Increased self-esteem and self-confidence:** Accomplishing creative tasks and seeing the fruits of one's artistic efforts can boost self-esteem and confidence. Art therapy provides a sense of achievement and validation for individuals, regardless of their artistic abilities.

+ **Coping with trauma and emotional pain:** Art therapy can be particularly beneficial for individuals who have experienced trauma or emotional pain. It provides a safe space for exploring and processing difficult emotions, and can help individuals heal and regain a sense of control and empowerment.

Techniques and Approaches in Art Therapy

There are various techniques and approaches used in art therapy, depending on the individual's needs and goals. Some commonly used techniques include:

+ **Free art expression:** This approach allows individuals to create art freely without any specific guidelines or objectives. It promotes self-expression and encourages individuals to trust their intuition and let their creativity flow.

+ **Guided imagery and visualization:** Guided imagery involves using visual prompts or guided meditation to stimulate the imagination and create mental images. It can help individuals tap into their subconscious and address specific emotional or psychological concerns.

+ **Collage and mixed media:** Collage involves assembling various materials, such as magazine cutouts, photographs, and fabric, to create a visual composition. It encourages creativity and allows individuals to express themselves using different textures and elements.

+ **Painting and drawing:** Painting and drawing are versatile art forms that can be used in various art therapy techniques. They allow individuals to explore color, form, and symbolism to convey their thoughts and emotions.

+ **Sculpture and clay work:** Sculpting and working with clay offer a tactile and hands-on approach to art therapy. They can help individuals connect with their physical sensations and explore three-dimensional forms.

+ **Digital art and multimedia:** With the advancement of technology, digital art has also been incorporated into art therapy. It allows individuals to explore their creativity using digital tools and multimedia platforms.

Integrating Art Therapy into Mental Health Strategies

Art therapy can be integrated into various mental health strategies to enhance overall well-being. Here are some ways art therapy can be incorporated:

+ **Self-care routine:** Engaging in art therapy activities, such as painting or drawing, can be included as part of a regular self-care routine. It can provide a stress-relieving and rejuvenating experience.

+ **Group therapy:** Art therapy can be conducted in a group setting, allowing individuals to share their art and experiences with others. Group art therapy can foster a sense of community and support among participants.

+ **Mindfulness practice:** Art therapy can be combined with mindfulness techniques, such as mindful drawing or painting. This encourages individuals to engage fully in the present moment and immerse themselves in the sensory experience of creating art.

+ **Journaling and art:** Combining art therapy with journaling can provide a powerful tool for self-reflection and self-expression. Individuals can incorporate drawings, collages, or other art forms into their journal entries.

+ **Integrative therapy:** Art therapy can be used in conjunction with other therapeutic approaches, such as cognitive-behavioral therapy or psychodynamic therapy. The creative process can enhance the effectiveness of these therapies and provide additional insights and self-awareness.

+ **Community engagement:** Art therapy can also be utilized in community settings, such as schools, hospitals, or community centers. It can promote social connection and help individuals express themselves within a supportive environment.

Art therapy and expressive arts provide a unique and powerful approach to mental health and well-being. By tapping into the creative process, individuals can explore their emotions, enhance self-awareness, and develop coping strategies. Integrating art therapy into mental health strategies can offer a holistic and person-centered approach to supporting individuals on their path to mental wellness.

In the next section, we will explore complementary and alternative medicine approaches to mental health, including techniques such as acupuncture, herbal medicine, and aromatherapy.

Complementary and Alternative Medicine

Complementary and alternative medicine (CAM) refers to a diverse range of medical and healthcare systems, practices, and products that are not considered part of mainstream conventional medicine. CAM approaches are often used alongside or as alternatives to conventional medical treatments. CAM can encompass various modalities, including herbal medicine, acupuncture, chiropractic care, naturopathy, and mind-body practices such as meditation and yoga.

Principles of CAM

The principles underlying CAM approaches are rooted in a holistic view of health and well-being. CAM practitioners often emphasize the interconnectedness of mind, body, and spirit, and the importance of addressing the underlying causes of illness rather than simply alleviating symptoms. CAM also emphasizes the inherent healing abilities of the body and the importance of promoting self-care and self-healing.

Herbal Medicine

Herbal medicine, also known as botanical medicine, involves the use of plants and plant extracts to promote health and treat illness. It is one of the most widely practiced forms of CAM worldwide. Herbal remedies can be taken internally, such as in the form of teas, capsules, or tinctures, or applied topically as creams or ointments.

Different herbs have different medicinal properties and can be used to address a wide range of health concerns. For example, chamomile is often used to promote relaxation and relieve anxiety, while ginger is known for its anti-inflammatory properties and ability to relieve nausea. St. John's Wort is commonly used as a natural antidepressant.

It is important to note that while herbal remedies are considered natural, they can still have potent pharmacological effects. It is crucial to seek guidance from a qualified herbalist or healthcare professional to ensure the appropriate use and dosage of herbal remedies, as well as potential interactions with medications.

Acupuncture

Acupuncture is a key component of Traditional Chinese Medicine (TCM) and involves the insertion of thin needles into specific points on the body. According to TCM principles, these points are located along energy pathways known as meridians, and the stimulation of these points helps to balance the flow of energy, or Qi, within the body.

Acupuncture has been used for centuries to address a wide range of conditions, including pain management, stress reduction, and digestive disorders. It is now recognized as a viable treatment option by many healthcare systems worldwide.

Research has shown that acupuncture stimulates the release of endorphins, which are natural pain-relieving chemicals in the body. It can also have anti-inflammatory effects and promote relaxation. Acupuncture treatments are individualized, with the number of sessions and frequency varying depending on the specific condition and the individual's response to treatment.

Chiropractic Care

Chiropractic care focuses on the relationship between the spine and the nervous system and their impact on overall health. Chiropractors use a hands-on approach to diagnose, treat, and prevent musculoskeletal conditions, particularly those affecting the spine.

The goal of chiropractic adjustments is to restore proper alignment and mobility of the spine, allowing the nervous system to function optimally. This can help alleviate pain, improve physical function, and promote overall well-being. Chiropractors may also incorporate other complementary therapies, such as massage, exercises, and lifestyle recommendations, into their treatments.

Chiropractic care is commonly sought for conditions such as back pain, neck pain, headaches, and sports injuries. It is important to consult with a licensed chiropractor who has undergone appropriate training and certification to ensure safe and effective care.

Naturopathy

Naturopathy is a holistic approach to healthcare that emphasizes the body's innate ability to heal itself. Naturopathic doctors (NDs) combine conventional medical knowledge with a range of natural therapies and lifestyle interventions to address the root causes of illness and support overall wellness.

Naturopathic treatments may include dietary and nutritional counseling, herbal medicine, physical therapies, homeopathy, and lifestyle modifications. NDs consider the individual as a whole and take into account physical, mental, emotional, and environmental factors when developing treatment plans.

Naturopathic medicine aims to promote health, prevent illness, and support the body's natural healing processes. It can be used for various conditions, including chronic diseases, digestive disorders, hormonal imbalances, allergies, and stress management.

It is important to note that while naturopathic medicine can be beneficial, it is not a substitute for conventional medical care. It is advisable to consult with both a naturopathic doctor and a primary care physician to ensure comprehensive and coordinated healthcare.

Mind-Body Practices

Mind-body practices encompass various techniques and therapies that focus on the relationship between the mind and the body, and their impact on health. These practices aim to promote relaxation, reduce stress, and improve overall well-being.

Some common mind-body practices include:

+ **Meditation:** Meditation involves the practice of focused attention and mindfulness to cultivate a state of mental clarity and emotional calm. It has been shown to reduce stress, improve emotional stability, and enhance overall mental well-being.

+ **Yoga:** Yoga combines physical postures, breathing exercises, and meditation to promote physical strength, flexibility, and relaxation. It has been found to have numerous benefits for mental health, including reducing anxiety, improving mood, and enhancing self-awareness.

+ **Tai Chi:** Tai Chi is an ancient Chinese martial art that involves slow, gentle movements and deep breathing. It promotes balance, flexibility, and relaxation. Studies have shown that practicing Tai Chi can reduce stress, improve mental clarity, and enhance overall physical and mental well-being.

+ **Art Therapy:** Art therapy involves the use of artistic expression, such as painting, drawing, or sculpting, to explore emotions, reduce stress, and enhance self-awareness. It can be particularly beneficial for individuals experiencing trauma, grief, or mental health disorders.

+ **Complementary and Alternative Medicine:** Various other mind-body practices, such as biofeedback, hypnotherapy, and music therapy, can also be used to promote relaxation, reduce pain, and improve overall well-being.

While mind-body practices are generally safe, it is important to learn from qualified instructors and practitioners to ensure proper technique and avoid potential injury. These practices can be integrated into daily routines as self-care strategies or as part of a comprehensive treatment plan in collaboration with healthcare professionals.

Integrating CAM with Conventional Medicine

Integrative medicine involves combining the use of CAM approaches with conventional medical treatments to provide a comprehensive and individualized approach to healthcare. Integrative medicine recognizes the value of both conventional and complementary therapies and aims to bridge the gap between them.

Integrative healthcare professionals work collaboratively to develop treatment plans that address the unique needs and preferences of each patient. This approach can help optimize health outcomes, reduce side effects of conventional treatments, and enhance overall well-being.

It is important to communicate openly and honestly with healthcare providers about the use of CAM therapies to ensure safe and effective integration with conventional treatments. Healthcare professionals can provide guidance, monitor interactions, and support the use of evidence-based CAM approaches.

Caveats and Considerations

While many CAM therapies can be beneficial, it is important to exercise caution and be aware of potential risks and limitations. Some key considerations include:

+ **Safety:** Although many CAM therapies are generally safe, there can be risks associated with certain practices or products. It is crucial to seek guidance from qualified practitioners and ensure the use of high-quality and reputable sources.

+ **Evidence Base:** While some CAM therapies have a growing body of scientific evidence supporting their effectiveness, not all approaches have been extensively researched. It is important to stay informed and evaluate the available evidence before incorporating any new therapy.

+ **Comprehensive Approach:** CAM therapies should be viewed as part of a comprehensive approach to health and well-being. They should not be used as a substitute for necessary medical treatments or as a sole solution to complex health conditions.

+ **Collaboration:** To ensure safe and effective care, it is essential to maintain open communication and collaboration with healthcare providers. This includes sharing information about CAM therapies being used and discussing any potential interactions with medications or conventional treatments.

By considering these caveats and working with qualified practitioners, individuals can make informed decisions about the integration of CAM therapies into their overall healthcare strategies.

Conclusion

Complementary and alternative medicine offers a broad range of approaches that can be used to complement or provide alternatives to conventional medical treatments. From herbal medicine and acupuncture to chiropractic care and mind-body practices, CAM encompasses a diverse array of therapies that emphasize holistic health and wellness.

While CAM therapies can offer numerous benefits, it is important to approach them with caution and in collaboration with healthcare professionals. By combining the principles of CAM with evidence-based practice, individuals can develop a comprehensive approach to healthcare that addresses their unique needs and promotes optimal well-being.

Nutrition and Mental Health

Good nutrition plays a crucial role in our overall well-being, including our mental health. The food we eat provides the necessary nutrients for our brain to function optimally and influences our mood, cognition, and emotional well-being. In this section, we will explore the link between nutrition and mental health, discuss key nutrients that support mental well-being, and provide practical strategies for incorporating a healthy diet into daily life.

The Gut-Brain Axis

Before delving into the specifics of nutrition and mental health, it is important to understand the gut-brain axis. The gut and the brain are connected through a bidirectional communication system, which means that the health of our gut directly impacts our mental health. The gut microbiota, a diverse community of microorganisms residing in the digestive tract, plays a crucial role in this communication. These microorganisms produce neurotransmitters, such as serotonin and dopamine, which are vital for regulating mood and cognition.

Key Nutrients for Mental Health

1. Omega-3 Fatty Acids: Omega-3 fatty acids, found in fatty fish (e.g., salmon, mackerel) and walnuts, are essential for brain health. They support the structure and function of brain cells and help reduce inflammation in the brain, which is associated with mental health disorders such as depression and anxiety.

2. B Vitamins: B vitamins, particularly B6, B12, and folate, are important for the production of neurotransmitters and the formation of red blood cells. Deficiencies in these vitamins have been linked to an increased risk of depression and cognitive decline. Sources of B vitamins include whole grains, legumes, leafy green vegetables, and fortified cereals.

3. Antioxidants: Antioxidants, such as vitamins C and E, help protect the brain from oxidative stress, which can contribute to mental decline and neurodegenerative disorders. Foods rich in antioxidants include berries, citrus fruits, nuts, and seeds.

4. Magnesium: Magnesium plays a role in regulating neurotransmitters and promoting relaxation. Low magnesium levels have been associated with an increased risk of depression and anxiety. Good sources of magnesium include dark leafy greens, legumes, nuts, and whole grains.

5. Zinc: Zinc is involved in neurotransmitter synthesis and has been linked to mood regulation. Foods high in zinc include oysters, red meat, poultry, legumes, and nuts.

6. Probiotics: Probiotics, found in fermented foods like yogurt and sauerkraut, help maintain a healthy gut microbiota. They have been shown to reduce symptoms of depression and anxiety, improve stress resilience, and enhance overall mental well-being.

The Mediterranean Diet

One dietary approach that has gained attention for its positive impact on mental health is the Mediterranean diet. This diet emphasizes whole foods, such as fruits, vegetables, whole grains, legumes, nuts, seeds, and olive oil, while limiting processed foods, red meat, and added sugars.

Research suggests that following a Mediterranean diet is associated with a reduced risk of depression and other mental health disorders. The high intake of omega-3 fatty acids, antioxidants, and other nutrients in this diet may contribute to its beneficial effects on mental well-being.

Practical Tips for a Healthy Diet

1. Eat a variety of whole foods: Include a rainbow of fruits and vegetables, whole grains, lean proteins, and healthy fats in your diet. This ensures that you receive a wide range of nutrients necessary for optimal brain function.

2. Limit processed foods and added sugars: Highly processed foods, such as fast food, sugary snacks, and sodas, may negatively impact mental health. Opt for whole, unprocessed foods whenever possible.

3. Stay hydrated: Dehydration can affect cognitive function and mood. Aim to drink plenty of water throughout the day.

4. Practice mindful eating: Pay attention to your hunger and fullness cues. Slow down and savor your meals, enjoying the flavors and textures of the food.

5. Plan and prepare meals: Take time to plan and prepare healthy meals and snacks in advance. This can help you make better choices and prevent reliance on unhealthy convenience foods.

6. Seek professional guidance: If you have specific dietary concerns or mental health conditions, consider consulting a registered dietitian or mental health professional for personalized guidance and support.

Caveats and Considerations

While nutrition can greatly influence mental health, it is important to note that diet alone is not a cure for mental health disorders. It is a complementary approach that can support overall well-being. If you are experiencing mental health symptoms, it is crucial to seek professional help and follow evidence-based treatments.

Additionally, individual nutritional needs may vary, and it is always best to consult with a healthcare professional or registered dietitian to determine the best dietary approach for your specific needs.

Conclusion

Nutrition plays a significant role in promoting mental health and well-being. By incorporating nutrient-rich foods into our diet, such as omega-3 fatty acids, B vitamins, antioxidants, and probiotics, we can support brain function, reduce inflammation, and improve overall mental well-being. Embracing a healthy and balanced diet, such as the Mediterranean diet, along with other mental health strategies, can contribute to a more resilient and positive mental outlook. Remember, nourishing your body is an essential part of taking care of your mind.

Building a Foundation for Mental Health

Self-Awareness and Self-Reflection

Recognizing Thoughts and Emotions

In order to improve our mental health, it is important to develop self-awareness and gain insight into our thoughts and emotions. This section will explore the process of recognizing thoughts and emotions, and the significance of this skill in promoting overall well-being.

The Role of Thoughts and Emotions

Our thoughts and emotions play a crucial role in shaping our mental health. Thoughts form the basis of our beliefs, perceptions, and interpretations of the world around us. They can be rational or irrational, positive or negative, and influence our mood and behavior. Emotions, on the other hand, are our internal responses to different situations and experiences. They can range from joy and happiness to sadness, anger, fear, and anxiety.

The interaction between our thoughts and emotions is complex. Our thoughts can influence our emotions, and our emotions can influence our thoughts. For example, if we have negative thoughts about ourselves, it can lead to feelings of low self-esteem and sadness. Likewise, experiencing a traumatic event can trigger fearful thoughts and anxiety.

Recognizing Thoughts

Recognizing our thoughts involves becoming aware of the continuous stream of thinking that occurs in our minds. Often, we may not pay attention to our thoughts and may not even be aware of the impact they have on our mental well-being. Developing the ability to recognize our thoughts allows us to identify patterns of thinking, challenge negative or irrational thoughts, and develop more positive and constructive thinking patterns.

Here are some strategies to help recognize and identify our thoughts:

1. **Mindfulness:** Practicing mindfulness involves paying attention to the present moment without judgment. It allows us to observe our thoughts as they arise without getting caught up in them. By observing our thoughts without judgment, we can gain insight into the patterns and content of our thinking.

2. **Journaling:** Keeping a journal can be a powerful tool for recognizing and documenting our thoughts. By writing down our thoughts and reflecting on them, we can gain a deeper understanding of our thinking patterns and emotions associated with them.

3. **Self-reflection:** Taking time for self-reflection enables us to introspect and examine our thoughts and emotions. This can be done through activities such as meditation, introspective writing, or engaging in meaningful conversations with trusted individuals.

4. **Thought labeling:** When we notice a thought arising in our minds, we can label it without judgment. For example, if a negative thought comes up, we can simply acknowledge it as a negative thought rather than getting carried away by its content.

5. **Cognitive restructuring:** Cognitive restructuring involves challenging and replacing negative or irrational thoughts with more positive and realistic ones. By identifying unhelpful thinking patterns, we can reframe our thoughts and develop healthier perspectives.

Recognizing Emotions

Recognizing and acknowledging our emotions is an essential aspect of self-awareness. Emotions provide valuable information about our inner experiences and can guide our actions and decision-making. Being able to recognize our emotions allows us to better understand ourselves and others, manage our emotional reactions, and take appropriate steps towards improving our mental well-being.

Here are some strategies to help recognize and identify our emotions:

1. **Body awareness:** Our emotions are not just experienced in our minds but also manifested in our bodies. Paying attention to bodily sensations can help us identify and label our emotions. For example, a racing heart and sweaty palms may indicate anxiety, while a warm and open chest may indicate happiness or joy.

2. **Emotion labeling:** Like thought labeling, emotion labeling involves simply acknowledging and naming the emotions we are experiencing without judgment. This can be done internally or by expressing our emotions through verbal or written communication.

3. **Mindfulness of emotions:** Practicing mindfulness can also help us become more aware of our emotions. By observing our emotions without judgment or attachment, we can develop a greater understanding of how emotions arise and subside within us.

4. **Emotion tracking:** Keeping a record of our emotions throughout the day can provide valuable insights into our emotional patterns and triggers. This can be done using a journal or a mobile app dedicated to tracking emotions.

5. **Seeking feedback:** Sometimes, others may be able to recognize and identify our emotions more accurately than we can ourselves. Trusted friends, family members, or mental health professionals can provide valuable feedback and insights into our emotional experiences.

The Benefits of Recognizing Thoughts and Emotions

Developing the skill of recognizing thoughts and emotions can have numerous benefits for our mental health and overall well-being. Here are some of the benefits:

- **Increased self-awareness:** Recognizing our thoughts and emotions allows us to gain a deeper understanding of ourselves, our values, and our belief systems. This self-awareness provides a foundation for personal growth and development.

- **Improved emotional regulation:** Being able to accurately identify and label our emotions helps us regulate our emotional responses and cope with challenging situations more effectively. It allows us to respond to emotions in a more balanced and constructive manner.

+ **Enhanced problem-solving skills:** Recognizing our thoughts enables us to identify distorted thinking patterns and replace them with more accurate and rational thoughts, leading to improved problem-solving skills and decision-making.

+ **Strengthened relationships:** By recognizing our own emotions, we can also become more attuned to the emotions of others. This empathy and understanding can strengthen our relationships and improve communication.

+ **Reduced stress and anxiety:** Recognizing and understanding our thoughts and emotions can help us identify stressors and triggers, leading to reduced stress and anxiety. It allows us to develop appropriate coping strategies and resilience.

Exercise: Thought and Emotion Awareness

Take a few moments to engage in an exercise to practice thought and emotion awareness.

1. Find a quiet and comfortable space where you can relax without distractions.

2. Close your eyes, take a few deep breaths, and bring your attention to the present moment.

3. Begin by focusing on your thoughts. Notice any thoughts that arise in your mind, without judgment. Observe the content of your thoughts, their frequency, and any patterns that emerge.

4. Shift your focus to your emotions. Pay attention to any emotions you are experiencing in the present moment. Notice the sensations in your body associated with these emotions.

5. Take a few moments to reflect on the connection between your thoughts and emotions. Are there any thoughts that seem to trigger specific emotions? How do these thoughts and emotions interact with each other?

6. After observing your thoughts and emotions, gently return your focus to the present moment and open your eyes.

By regularly practicing this exercise, you can enhance your ability to recognize and understand your thoughts and emotions, leading to improved self-awareness and mental well-being.

Conclusion

Recognizing thoughts and emotions is a crucial skill for promoting mental health and overall well-being. By becoming aware of our thoughts and emotions, we can develop a deeper understanding of ourselves, regulate our emotions more effectively, and cultivate healthier thinking patterns. Through mindfulness, journaling, self-reflection, and cognitive restructuring, we can enhance our ability to recognize and harness the power of our thoughts and emotions. So, take the time to develop this skill and embark on a journey of self-discovery and growth.

Mindfulness Practices for Self-Awareness

In this section, we will explore the concept of mindfulness and its application as a practice for cultivating self-awareness. Mindfulness is an ancient practice rooted in Eastern traditions, and it has gained significant recognition and popularity in the field of mental health in recent years. It involves paying attention to the present moment, with a non-judgmental and accepting attitude. By practicing mindfulness, individuals can develop a deeper understanding of their thoughts, emotions, and bodily sensations, which leads to a heightened sense of self-awareness.

The Essence of Mindfulness

Mindfulness is often described as the art of being fully present in the moment. It entails actively paying attention to one's experiences, both internally (thoughts, emotions) and externally (sensory stimuli), without getting caught up in judgment, attachment, or resistance. The core of mindfulness is curiosity, or what is commonly referred to as the "beginner's mind." This attitude allows individuals to observe their inner and outer experiences with a sense of openness and without preconceived notions.

Moreover, mindfulness involves cultivating an attitude of acceptance or non-reactivity towards one's experiences. Rather than trying to change or avoid certain thoughts or emotions, individuals are encouraged to acknowledge and accept them as they arise, without judgment or criticism. This non-reactive stance allows for a more objective and compassionate observation of inner experiences, fostering self-awareness and reducing emotional reactivity.

Mindfulness Meditation

One of the most well-known and widely practiced forms of mindfulness is mindfulness meditation. Mindfulness meditation involves intentionally directing one's attention to a particular focus, such as the breath, bodily sensations, sounds, or thoughts. The individual aims to maintain a relaxed, non-judgmental awareness of the chosen focus, continuously bringing their attention back whenever it wanders.

To begin a mindfulness meditation practice, find a quiet and comfortable space where you can sit or lie down without distraction. Close your eyes and bring your attention to your breath. Notice the sensation of your breath as it enters and leaves your body. Whenever your mind starts to wander, gently bring your attention back to the breath, without judgment or frustration.

As you continue the practice, you may become aware of various thoughts, emotions, or bodily sensations arising in your awareness. Instead of engaging with them or trying to push them away, acknowledge their presence and let them pass, returning your attention to the breath. Through this process, you develop the ability to observe your thoughts and emotions with detachment, nurturing self-awareness and reducing the tendency to react automatically.

Mindful Daily Activities

Mindfulness is not limited to formal meditation practice; it can also be integrated into daily activities, turning routine tasks into opportunities for self-awareness and presence. Engaging in mindfulness during daily activities helps to anchor our attention in the present moment and cultivate a sense of connection with our lived experiences.

For example, while eating, bring your full attention to the sensory experience of the food – the aroma, texture, taste, and sound. Notice the physical sensations of chewing and swallowing. By savoring each bite and paying attention to the sensations and flavors, you can enhance the pleasure and experience of the meal.

Another mindfulness practice is mindful walking. As you walk, direct your attention to the physical sensations of each step, the feeling of your feet touching the ground, and the movement of your body. Take notice of the sights, sounds, and smells around you, without getting caught up in thoughts or worries. Engaging in mindful walking can help to clear the mind, reduce stress, and increase overall self-awareness.

Benefits of Mindfulness for Self-Awareness

Cultivating self-awareness through mindfulness practices has numerous benefits for mental health and well-being. Here are some key advantages:

+ Increased self-understanding: Mindfulness enhances our ability to observe our thoughts, emotions, and bodily sensations without judgment. This deeper self-awareness allows us to recognize patterns, triggers, and underlying beliefs that influence our behavior and emotional states.

+ Emotional regulation: By practicing mindfulness, individuals develop the capacity to observe their emotions in the present moment, without being overwhelmed by them. This awareness enables them to recognize and regulate their emotional responses more effectively.

+ Improved attention and focus: Mindfulness practice trains the mind to sustain attention on a chosen object or task. This skill is transferable to other areas of life, improving concentration and reducing mind-wandering.

+ Reduced stress and anxiety: Mindfulness has been shown to reduce stress and anxiety levels. By bringing awareness to the present moment, individuals can interrupt the cycle of worrying about the future or ruminating on the past, bringing a sense of calm and relaxation.

+ Enhanced self-compassion and resilience: Mindfulness fosters a compassionate and non-judgmental attitude towards oneself. This self-compassion supports resilience in the face of difficulties and cultivates a kinder relationship with oneself.

Exercise: Mindful Breathing

A simple yet powerful exercise to cultivate mindfulness and self-awareness is mindful breathing. Find a comfortable position, either sitting or lying down, and close your eyes. Take a few deep breaths to relax your body and settle into the present moment. Then, bring your attention to your breath, noticing the sensation of each inhalation and exhalation. Follow the breath as it flows in and out, without trying to control or manipulate it. Whenever your mind wanders, gently bring your focus back to the breath. Practice this exercise for a few minutes each day, gradually extending the duration as you become more comfortable.

Resources

There are many resources available for individuals interested in exploring mindfulness further. Here are a few recommendations:

- "Wherever You Go, There You Are" by Jon Kabat-Zinn: This book provides an excellent introduction to mindfulness and offers practical guidance for integrating mindfulness into daily life.

- Mindfulness-Based Stress Reduction (MBSR) programs: MBSR is an evidence-based mindfulness program developed by Jon Kabat-Zinn. Many local centers and clinics offer MBSR courses, providing guided instruction and support in developing mindfulness skills.

- Mobile apps: There are various mindfulness apps available, such as Headspace, Calm, and Insight Timer, which offer guided meditation practices, mindfulness reminders, and other helpful resources.

Remember, mindfulness is a skill that improves with practice and consistency. As you continue to explore mindfulness practices, you will gradually deepen your self-awareness and experience the transformative effects it can have on your mental well-being.

In conclusion, mindfulness practices provide a powerful avenue for developing self-awareness. By cultivating a non-judgmental and curious attitude towards our experiences, we can gain a deeper understanding of our thoughts, emotions, and bodily sensations. Through formal meditation and integrating mindfulness into daily activities, we can enhance our self-awareness, regulate our emotions, improve our focus, and reduce stress. Mindfulness empowers us to live more fully in the present moment and cultivate a compassionate relationship with ourselves.

Journaling and Creative Expression

Journaling and creative expression are powerful tools in promoting self-awareness and enhancing mental well-being. They provide a means for individuals to explore and express their thoughts, emotions, and experiences in a safe and reflective manner. In this section, we will delve into the benefits of journaling and creative expression, the different techniques and approaches that can be used, and how to incorporate them into daily life.

Benefits of Journaling

Journaling is a practice of writing down one's thoughts, feelings, and experiences in a structured manner. It serves as a form of self-reflection and can provide numerous benefits for mental health.

1. **Emotional Release**: Journaling allows individuals to express and release their emotions in a healthy and non-judgmental way. It provides a safe space to vent frustrations, process difficult emotions, and gain clarity.

2. **Self-Discovery**: By regularly journaling, individuals can gain a deeper understanding of themselves. It helps in uncovering patterns, beliefs, and values, leading to self-awareness and personal growth.

3. **Stress Reduction**: Writing down one's thoughts and concerns can help reduce stress and anxiety. It allows individuals to externalize their worries, making them feel more manageable.

4. **Problem-Solving**: Journaling can be an effective tool for problem-solving. It helps individuals organize their thoughts, generate alternative perspectives, and come up with creative solutions.

5. **Memory Enhancement**: Writing about past experiences and events can improve memory retention and recall. It allows individuals to reflect on their experiences and learn from them.

Journaling Techniques

There are various techniques and approaches that can be used in journaling. Here are a few examples:

1. **Free Writing**: Set aside a designated time, grab your pen and paper, and let your thoughts flow. Write without censoring or worrying about grammar or punctuation. The key is to keep writing without stopping for a set period.

2. **Prompted Journaling**: Use a specific prompt or question to guide your journaling. It could be something like "What are you grateful for today?" or "What is one challenge you are currently facing?" Prompts can help focus your thoughts and ensure a meaningful reflection.

3. **Stream of Consciousness**: Write whatever comes to your mind without any filters or judgments. Allow your thoughts to flow naturally, capturing the stream of consciousness. This technique encourages self-expression and may uncover hidden insights.

4. **Gratitude Journaling**: Write down things that you are grateful for each day. This practice cultivates a positive mindset and shifts the focus towards the positive aspects of life.

5. **Visual Journaling**: Incorporate images, drawings, and collages into your journaling practice. Use colors, symbols, and visual elements to express your thoughts and emotions. This technique engages the creative side of the brain and can be particularly helpful for individuals who find it challenging to express themselves through words alone.

Incorporating Creative Expression

Creative expression goes beyond writing and encompasses a wide range of artistic activities. It encourages individuals to explore different modes of self-expression, including visual arts, music, dance, and more. Here are some ways to incorporate creative expression into your mental health strategies:

1. **Art Therapy**: Engage in art therapy to explore and process emotions, beliefs, and experiences. Art therapists use various art modalities to help individuals gain insight, reduce stress, and promote self-discovery. Painting, drawing, clay work, and collage-making are some common techniques used in art therapy.

2. **Music and Dance**: Use music and dance as forms of self-expression and emotional release. Listen to uplifting or calming music that resonates with your emotions. Engage in dance or movement practices to connect with your body and express yourself physically.

3. **Creative Writing**: Expand your journaling practice by exploring different forms of creative writing. Write poetry, short stories, or personal essays to express your thoughts and emotions in a creative and imaginative way.

4. **Photography**: Grab your camera or smartphone and go on a photo walk. Capture images that speak to you and represent your emotions or experiences. Photography can be a therapeutic and visually compelling way to express yourself.

5. **Crafts and DIY Projects**: Engage in crafting or DIY projects as a means of creative expression. Knitting, sewing, woodworking, and other hands-on activities can provide a sense of accomplishment and offer a meditative space for the mind.

Journaling and Creative Expression Exercises

To give you a hands-on experience, here are two exercises that combine journaling and creative expression:

1. **Collage of Emotions**: Gather magazines, newspapers, and art supplies. Start by journaling about a recent emotional experience. Then, flip through the magazines and cut out images and words that represent your emotions. Collage these images onto a blank page, creating a visual representation of your feelings.

2. **Music and Mood Journal**: Create a journal combining written entries and a curated playlist. Each day, journal about your mood, emotions, and experiences. Then, select a song that reflects your mood and add it to your playlist. Over time, you'll have a collection of entries and songs that document your mental and emotional journey.

Caveats and Precautions

While journaling and creative expression can be beneficial for mental health, it is essential to consider a few caveats:

1. **Safety first:** If you are experiencing severe distress or mental health issues, it's important to seek professional help. Journaling is not a substitute for therapy or medical treatment.

2. **Respect boundaries:** Be mindful of your comfort level and only share what you feel comfortable sharing. Not everything you write or create needs to be shared with others.

3. **Take breaks:** Journaling and creative expression should be enjoyable and not add pressure. If you feel overwhelmed or stuck, take a break and come back to it later.

Resources

Here are some resources to explore further:

- *The Artist's Way* by Julia Cameron

- *Writing Down the Bones* by Natalie Goldberg

- *The Creative Habit* by Twyla Tharp

- International Journal of Art Therapy: `https://www.tandfonline.com/loi/uart20`

- American Journal of Dance Therapy: `https://www.springer.com/journal/10465`

Conclusion

Journaling and creative expression offer powerful means of self-reflection, emotional release, and personal growth. They can be used as effective tools in promoting mental well-being. By incorporating journaling techniques and engaging in various forms of creative expression, individuals can deepen their self-awareness, reduce stress, and foster personal transformation. So grab your pen, paintbrush, or music player, and embark on a journey of self-discovery and creativity. Take the time to explore the world within and express yourself in ways that bring joy and healing.

Self-Reflection Techniques

Self-reflection is a powerful tool for personal growth and self-awareness. It involves stepping back from our thoughts, feelings, and actions to gain a deeper understanding of ourselves and our experiences. In this section, we will explore various techniques that can be used to facilitate self-reflection and promote mental well-being.

Journaling

Journaling is a popular and effective self-reflection technique that involves writing down our thoughts, emotions, and experiences. It provides a safe space for self-expression and allows us to explore our inner thoughts and feelings. Journaling can be done in different formats, such as free writing, guided prompts, or bullet points. The key is to write without judgment or criticism, allowing the thoughts to flow freely.

To start journaling, find a quiet and comfortable space where you can focus without distractions. Begin by setting a specific time for journaling, whether it's in the morning, before bed, or during breaks throughout the day. Write about whatever comes to mind, without worrying about grammar or spelling. The goal is to capture your thoughts and feelings in the moment.

To deepen the self-reflection process, you can ask yourself thought-provoking questions, such as:

+ What are my current thoughts, feelings, and emotions?

+ What experiences or events have impacted me recently?

+ What are my hopes, dreams, and goals?

+ What challenges or obstacles am I facing?

+ What can I learn from my past experiences?

Journaling can help us gain clarity, release pent-up emotions, and identify patterns or triggers that affect our mental well-being. It serves as a valuable tool for self-discovery and self-expression.

Visualization

Visualization is a powerful technique that uses mental imagery to enhance self-reflection and promote positive change. It involves creating vivid mental pictures of our desires, goals, or ideal outcomes. Visualization engages our senses and taps into the power of our imagination.

To practice visualization, find a quiet and comfortable space where you can relax. Close your eyes and take a few deep breaths to calm your mind. Then, create a mental image of what you want to reflect upon or achieve. Visualize the details, colors, and sensations associated with your desired outcome. Immerse yourself in the image and engage all your senses.

For example, if you are reflecting on a challenging situation at work, visualize yourself confidently navigating the situation and achieving a positive outcome. See yourself communicating effectively, resolving conflicts, and feeling a sense of accomplishment. Imagine the emotions, sounds, and smells associated with your desired experience.

Visualization can help us gain clarity, boost motivation, and enhance our problem-solving abilities. By creating a mental image of our desired outcomes, we can tap into our subconscious mind and unlock our full potential.

Mindful Reflection

Mindful reflection involves practicing mindfulness while reflecting on our thoughts, feelings, and experiences. It combines the principles of mindfulness meditation with the process of self-reflection. Mindfulness is the practice of paying attention to the present moment with an attitude of curiosity and non-judgment.

To practice mindful reflection, find a quiet and comfortable space where you won't be disturbed. Begin by bringing your awareness to your breath, noticing the inhale and exhale without judgment. Allow your thoughts and emotions to arise and pass, observing them with curiosity and acceptance.

Next, bring your attention to the topic or experience you want to reflect upon. Notice the thoughts, feelings, and bodily sensations that arise as you reflect. Instead of getting caught up in the stories or judgments associated with the experience, simply observe them without attachment.

If your mind wanders, gently bring your attention back to the present moment and the reflection process. Be kind to yourself and practice self-compassion as you navigate the thoughts and emotions that arise.

Mindful reflection allows us to cultivate a deeper understanding of ourselves and our experiences. By bringing a non-judgmental and curious attitude to our reflections, we can gain insights, develop self-compassion, and make more intentional choices in our lives.

Creative Expression

Creative expression is a powerful tool for self-reflection and self-discovery. It involves using various art forms, such as painting, drawing, writing, or music, to express our thoughts, emotions, and experiences. Engaging in creative activities allows us to tap into our subconscious mind and express ourselves in a non-verbal way.

To explore creative expression as a self-reflection technique, choose an art form that resonates with you. It could be drawing, painting, writing poetry, playing a musical instrument, or any other artistic medium that you enjoy. Set aside dedicated time for creative expression, free from distractions.

Allow yourself to freely express your thoughts and emotions through the chosen art form. Let go of any expectations or judgments and focus on the process rather than the outcome. Use colors, words, or sounds to convey your feelings and experiences. Let your creativity flow without limitations.

Engaging in creative expression can provide a new perspective on our thoughts and emotions. It allows us to access deeper layers of our subconscious mind and tap into our intuition. Through creative expression, we can gain insights, release emotions, and discover new aspects of ourselves.

Reflection Prompts

To enhance your self-reflection practice, here are some reflection prompts to consider:

- What are my core values, and how do they align with my actions?

- What are my strengths, and how can I utilize them in achieving my goals?

- What limiting beliefs or negative thought patterns hold me back, and how can I challenge them?

- How can I cultivate more self-compassion and kindness towards myself?

- What are my sources of inspiration and how can I incorporate them into my daily life?

- How do my relationships impact my mental well-being, and how can I nurture healthy connections?

Reflection prompts can serve as a guide to delve deeper into our thoughts, emotions, and experiences. They provide a starting point for self-exploration and can uncover valuable insights and self-awareness.

Putting It Into Practice

To incorporate self-reflection techniques into your daily life, consider the following suggestions:

+ Set aside dedicated time each day or week for self-reflection.

+ Create a quiet and comfortable space where you can engage in self-reflection without distractions.

+ Experiment with different self-reflection techniques, such as journaling, visualization, mindful reflection, or creative expression.

+ Utilize reflection prompts to guide your self-reflection practice.

+ Be patient and compassionate with yourself as you navigate the self-reflection process.

+ Consider seeking support from a therapist or counselor to deepen your self-reflection practice.

Remember, self-reflection is a continuous journey of self-discovery and personal growth. By incorporating these techniques into your life, you can cultivate self-awareness, gain insights, and promote your mental well-being.

Conclusion

Self-reflection is a valuable practice that promotes self-awareness, personal growth, and mental well-being. Techniques such as journaling, visualization, mindful reflection, and creative expression can help us gain deeper insights into our thoughts, emotions, and experiences. By setting aside dedicated time for self-reflection and incorporating these techniques into our daily lives, we can enhance our understanding of ourselves, cultivate self-compassion, and make intentional choices for our mental health and overall well-being.

Cultivating Compassion and Self-Compassion

In the journey towards mental health and well-being, cultivating compassion and self-compassion plays a crucial role. Compassion involves both understanding and empathy for others' suffering, while self-compassion centers on extending the same kindness and understanding to oneself. This section will explore the importance of these qualities, the benefits they bring, and practical strategies to develop and strengthen compassion and self-compassion.

Understanding Compassion and Self-Compassion

Compassion is the ability to recognize and respond to the suffering of others with kindness, empathy, and genuine concern. It goes beyond mere sympathy by encouraging action and helping alleviate the pain experienced by others. Self-compassion, on the other hand, involves treating oneself with the same empathy, understanding, and kindness that one would extend to a loved one facing a difficult situation.

Both compassion and self-compassion have immense benefits for mental health. They promote positive emotions, foster social connections, and enhance overall psychological well-being. Research has shown that individuals who cultivate compassion and self-compassion are more resilient, experience increased life satisfaction, and have better self-esteem.

The Importance of Compassion and Self-Compassion

Compassion is essential for creating a more caring and supportive society. By developing a compassionate mindset, we can enhance our relationships with others, foster empathy, and promote a sense of belonging. Compassion allows us to celebrate diversity, reduce discrimination, and promote social justice. Moreover, it encourages an open-minded and non-judgmental attitude towards oneself and others.

Self-compassion, often neglected in our demanding and fast-paced world, is crucial for mental health. It involves being understanding and forgiving towards oneself, especially during times of failure, disappointment, or self-criticism. Self-compassion helps to counteract negative self-judgment and self-deprecation, enabling individuals to embrace their imperfections with self-kindness and self-acceptance. This practice can lead to reduced stress, improved resilience, and enhanced emotional well-being.

Strategies for Cultivating Compassion and Self-Compassion

1. Mindful Self-Compassion Meditation: Engage in mindfulness meditation practices that specifically cultivate self-compassion. This involves redirecting our attention towards self-kindness and acceptance, acknowledging our struggles without judgment, and comforting ourselves like a supportive friend.

2. Loving-Kindness Meditation: Practice loving-kindness meditation to cultivate compassion for oneself and others. This involves sending well-wishes and unconditional love to oneself, loved ones, acquaintances, and even difficult individuals.

3. Cognitive Restructuring: Challenge self-critical thoughts and negative self-talk by reframing them with self-compassionate and realistic perspectives. Replace harsh self-judgment with kind and understanding statements, acknowledging that everyone makes mistakes and faces challenges.

4. Savoring Positive Experiences: Take time to savor and appreciate positive experiences and accomplishments. Practice self-compassion by acknowledging and celebrating personal growth, even in small victories.

5. Cultivating Empathy and Active Listening: Engage in active listening and seek to understand others' perspectives and experiences. Practice empathy by acknowledging and validating others' emotions, offering support, and providing a safe space for them to express themselves.

6. Engaging in Acts of Kindness: Actively seek opportunities to perform acts of kindness towards oneself and others. Random acts of kindness, whether big or small, can foster compassion and improve well-being for both the giver and the recipient.

7. Building Supportive Relationships: Surround yourself with supportive and compassionate individuals. Seek out communities and social groups that prioritize compassion and cultivate meaningful connections with others.

Remember, cultivating compassion and self-compassion is an ongoing practice that requires persistence and patience. Start with small steps, and over time, you will witness positive changes in your mindset and overall well-being.

Exercise: Compassion Journal

To strengthen your compassion and self-compassion, you can start a compassion journal. Set aside a few minutes each day to reflect on acts of compassion you witnessed, participated in, or received. Write down your thoughts, emotions, and any insights gained from these experiences. Additionally, reflect on how you offered yourself compassion and kindness during challenging moments. This exercise can help you become more aware of compassionate actions and reinforce positive behaviors in yourself and others.

By cultivating compassion and self-compassion, you not only enhance your own well-being but also contribute to promoting a more compassionate and empathetic society. Practice these strategies regularly, and you will embark on a transformative journey towards mental health and resilience.

Resources for Further Exploration

1. Germer, C. K., & Neff, K. D. (Eds.). (2019). *The Oxford Handbook of Compassion Science*. Oxford University Press.

2. Gilbert, P. (2010). *Compassion Focused Therapy: Distinctive Features*. Routledge.

3. Neff, K. D. (2011). *Self-Compassion: Stop Beating Yourself Up and Leave Insecurity Behind*. HarperCollins.

4. Salzberg, S. (1997). *Lovingkindness: The Revolutionary Art of Happiness*. Shambhala Publications.

5. The Center for Compassion and Altruism Research and Education (CCARE) at Stanford University: `https://ccare.stanford.edu/`

Remember, building compassion and self-compassion is a personal journey, and it is essential to seek professional help if you are experiencing significant challenges or mental health concerns.

Positive Psychology and Resilience

Understanding Positive Psychology

Positive psychology is a branch of psychology that focuses on studying and understanding the factors that contribute to human well-being, happiness, and flourishing. It is a relatively new field, emerging in the late 20th century as a response to the traditional focus of psychology on mental disorders and pathology.

In positive psychology, the emphasis is shifted from studying what is wrong with individuals to exploring what is right with them. It seeks to identify the strengths, virtues, and positive aspects of human behavior and experiences. The field aims to provide individuals with the knowledge and tools to enhance their overall well-being and lead fulfilling lives.

1. The Three Pillars of Positive Psychology

Positive psychology is built upon three key pillars: positive emotions, positive traits, and positive institutions.

1.1 Positive Emotions

Positive emotions refer to feelings such as joy, gratitude, hope, love, and contentment. These emotions not only contribute to our subjective well-being but also lead to a range of positive outcomes in various domains of life. Research has shown that experiencing positive emotions can improve physical health, enhance relationships, increase creativity, boost resilience, and improve overall life satisfaction.

1.2 Positive Traits

Positive traits are the personal characteristics and qualities that contribute to the development of well-being and positive functioning. Examples of positive traits include optimism, gratitude, resilience, perseverance, curiosity, and self-control. These traits can be learned, cultivated, and developed, which can have a significant impact on individuals' overall well-being and success in life.

1.3 Positive Institutions

Positive institutions are the social structures, organizations, and systems that promote the well-being and flourishing of individuals and communities. Examples of positive institutions include schools that foster positive education, workplaces that prioritize employee well-being and engagement, and communities that promote social connections and support. These institutions play a crucial role in creating environments that nurture the development of positive emotions and traits.

2. Core Concepts in Positive Psychology

2.1 Authentic Happiness

Authentic happiness is a central concept in positive psychology, referring to the experience of genuine and lasting well-being. It goes beyond temporary feelings of pleasure or happiness and encompasses a deeper sense of satisfaction and fulfillment in life. Authentic happiness is achieved when individuals align their actions, values, and goals with their authentic selves, leading to a sense of purpose and meaning.

2.2 Subjective Well-being

Subjective well-being refers to an individual's subjective evaluation of their own happiness, life satisfaction, and overall well-being. It includes both hedonic well-being (the presence of positive emotions and absence of negative emotions) and eudaimonic well-being (the sense of purpose, fulfillment, and personal growth). Subjective well-being is influenced by various factors, including genetics, life circumstances, and intentional activities.

2.3 Character Strengths

Character strengths are the positive qualities and virtues that individuals possess, which contribute to their overall well-being and success. These strengths, such as courage, kindness, honesty, and perseverance, are considered the building blocks of positive behavior and can be cultivated and developed through intentional practice. Understanding and leveraging one's character strengths can enhance resilience, improve relationships, and promote personal growth.

3. Applications of Positive Psychology

Positive psychology has wide-ranging applications in various domains of life, including education, healthcare, organizations, and therapy. Here are a few examples:

3.1 Positive Education

Positive education incorporates the principles and practices of positive psychology into the education system. It aims to foster the well-being and holistic development of students by promoting positive emotions, character strengths, and a sense of purpose. Positive education programs focus not only on academic achievement but also on the development of life skills, social-emotional competencies, and positive relationships.

3.2 Positive Therapy

Positive therapy, also known as positive psychotherapy, is an approach that integrates positive psychology principles into therapeutic interventions. It emphasizes the exploration and cultivation of positive emotions, strengths, and positive relationships to promote well-being and alleviate symptoms of mental disorders. Positive therapy aims to help individuals identify their strengths and build resilience, leading to improved psychological functioning and overall well-being.

3.3 Positive Organizational Psychology

Positive organizational psychology applies the principles of positive psychology to the workplace context. It focuses on creating positive work environments, fostering employee well-being and engagement, and promoting a culture of growth and development. Positive organizational interventions, such as gratitude practices, strengths-based approaches, and employee recognition programs, have been shown to improve job satisfaction, productivity, and organizational performance.

In conclusion, positive psychology provides a framework for understanding and promoting human well-being and flourishing. By shifting the focus from pathology to strengths and positive experiences, positive psychology offers practical strategies and interventions that can enhance individual and collective well-being across different life domains. Understanding the principles and concepts of positive psychology can help individuals lead more fulfilling lives and contribute to the creation of positive and supportive environments.

Identifying Strengths and Virtues

Identifying our strengths and virtues is an important aspect of promoting mental health and well-being. This process involves recognizing our unique qualities, positive attributes, and personal characteristics that contribute to our overall happiness and success. By understanding and harnessing these strengths, we can develop strategies to navigate life's challenges and cultivate resilience.

Understanding Strengths and Virtues

Strengths can be defined as positive qualities that enable individuals to thrive and excel in various aspects of their lives. They are the capabilities, talents, and traits that bring out the best in us. Virtues, on the other hand, are deeply ingrained moral qualities that shape our character and guide our actions.

In the field of positive psychology, researchers Martin Seligman and Christopher Peterson developed the Values in Action (VIA) classification of strengths and virtues. This framework consists of 24 character strengths that are grouped into six broad categories: wisdom, courage, humanity, justice, temperance, and transcendence. Examples of these strengths include creativity, bravery, kindness, fairness, self-control, and spirituality.

Assessing Strengths

To identify our strengths and virtues, we can use various assessment tools and techniques. One of the most widely used assessments is the VIA Survey, which is available online and provides a comprehensive report of an individual's strengths profile. This survey consists of 120 questions that measure the presence and intensity of each of the 24 character strengths.

In addition to formal assessments, we can also engage in self-reflection and introspection to gain insight into our strengths. Asking ourselves questions such as "What am I good at?" and "What activities bring me joy and fulfillment?" can help us uncover our unique strengths and virtues.

It is important to note that strengths may vary among individuals. Each person possesses a combination of different strengths, and there is no single set of strengths that is better or more desirable than others. Embracing our individual strengths allows us to celebrate our uniqueness and cultivate authenticity.

Developing Strengths

Once we have identified our strengths and virtues, we can utilize them in various ways to enhance our mental health and overall well-being. Here are some strategies for developing and leveraging our strengths:

1. Purposeful Practice: Engage in activities and tasks that align with our strengths. By practicing and honing our skills in areas where we excel, we can experience a sense of mastery and fulfillment.

2. Strengths-Based Goal Setting: Set goals that utilize our strengths. By leveraging our strengths in pursuit of our goals, we can increase our motivation, engagement, and chances of success.

3. Capitalizing on Strengths in Relationships: Recognize and appreciate the strengths of others. By acknowledging and valuing the strengths of those around us, we can build stronger and more positive relationships.

4. Strengths in Problem-Solving: Utilize our strengths to navigate challenges and solve problems. By tapping into our unique abilities, we can approach difficulties with confidence and creativity.

5. Strengths-Based Self-Talk: Use positive affirmations and self-talk centered around our strengths. By reminding ourselves of our capabilities and past successes, we can cultivate a positive mindset and resilience.

Case Study: Applying Strengths in a Work Setting

Let's consider an example of how identifying strengths and virtues can be beneficial in a work setting. Sarah, an employee in a marketing firm, has recently undergone a strengths assessment and discovered that one of her top strengths is creativity. Armed with this knowledge, she approaches her supervisor and offers to take the lead on a new advertising campaign for a client.

Sarah's supervisor recognizes her strength in creativity and believes she is the perfect fit for the project. As a result, Sarah is given the opportunity to showcase her talents, which leads to a highly successful and innovative campaign. Not only does Sarah excel in her role, but her confidence and job satisfaction also increase as she feels aligned with her strengths.

Resources for Identifying Strengths and Virtues

1. VIA Institute on Character: The official website of the VIA Survey and other valuable resources on character strengths. (`www.viacharacter.org`)

2. Positive Psychology Program: Offers a comprehensive list of free assessments and resources for identifying strengths and virtues. (`www.positivepsychologyprogram.com`)

3. StrengthsFinder 2.0 by Tom Rath: A book that helps individuals identify and maximize their strengths.

Enhancing Resilience and Coping Skills

Resilience and coping skills play a crucial role in maintaining and promoting mental health. Life can be challenging and unpredictable, and developing these skills can help individuals navigate through difficult times, bounce back from adversity, and maintain a sense of well-being. In this section, we will explore the concept of resilience, different approaches to enhancing resilience, and various coping strategies that can be helpful in managing stress and overcoming obstacles.

Understanding Resilience

Resilience can be defined as the ability to adapt and thrive in the face of adversity, trauma, or significant stress. It involves the capacity to maintain mental and emotional well-being, recover from setbacks, and continue functioning in a positive and meaningful way.

Research has shown that resilience is not an innate trait, but rather a set of skills and behaviors that can be cultivated and strengthened over time. It is influenced by a combination of genetic, environmental, and personal factors. Building resilience can help individuals better cope with life's challenges and improve their overall mental health.

Approaches to Enhancing Resilience

There are several approaches that can be effective in enhancing resilience. These approaches focus on developing skills, attitudes, and behaviors that promote adaptability and emotional well-being. Here are some key strategies:

Developing a Positive Mindset A positive mindset is essential for building resilience. It involves cultivating a hopeful and optimistic outlook, even in the face of adversity. Individuals with a positive mindset tend to have greater emotional well-being and are better equipped to cope with stress and setbacks. Practicing gratitude, reframing negative thoughts, and focusing on strengths and accomplishments are all effective ways to develop a positive mindset.

Building Social Connections Social support is a critical factor in resilience. Having a network of supportive relationships can provide emotional comfort, practical assistance, and a sense of belonging. Building and maintaining positive relationships with family, friends, and community members can strengthen resilience. Engaging in activities that foster social connections, such as joining clubs or volunteering, can also be beneficial.

Developing Problem-Solving Skills Developing strong problem-solving skills is essential for enhancing resilience. This involves the ability to identify and assess challenges, generate effective solutions, and implement them successfully. Problem-solving skills can be honed through practice and learning from past experiences. Seeking support and guidance from trusted individuals can also be helpful in developing effective problem-solving strategies.

Practicing Self-Care   Taking care of oneself is crucial for maintaining resilience. This involves engaging in activities that promote physical, mental, and emotional well-being. Regular exercise, adequate sleep, and a balanced diet are all important aspects of self-care. Engaging in hobbies, practicing relaxation techniques such as deep breathing or meditation, and engaging in activities that bring joy and fulfillment can also contribute to self-care and enhance resilience.

Cultivating Flexibility and Adaptability   Flexibility and adaptability are key qualities of resilient individuals. Being open to change, embracing uncertainty, and adjusting to new circumstances are essential skills in navigating life's challenges. Cultivating flexibility can involve trying new experiences, exposing oneself to different perspectives, and actively seeking opportunities for growth and learning.

Coping Strategies

Coping strategies are specific techniques and behaviors that individuals use to manage stress, regulate emotions, and navigate difficult situations. Developing effective coping strategies can significantly contribute to resilience. Here are some commonly used coping strategies:

Problem-Focused Coping   Problem-focused coping strategies involve taking direct action to address the source of stress or challenge. This can include problem-solving, seeking information or support, and making changes to the situation. Problem-focused coping is especially useful in situations where the individual has some control or influence over the stressor.

Emotion-Focused Coping   Emotion-focused coping strategies focus on regulating emotions and managing the emotional distress associated with stressful situations. This can involve techniques such as relaxation exercises, deep breathing, meditation, or engaging in activities that promote emotional well-being. Emotion-focused coping is particularly helpful when the individual has little control over the stressor itself.

Seeking Support   Seeking support from others is a crucial coping strategy. This can involve reaching out to friends, family, or a support group to share feelings, seek advice, or simply receive emotional support. Connecting with others who have experienced similar challenges can be particularly beneficial, as it provides a sense of validation and understanding.

Engaging in Self-Care Activities   Engaging in self-care activities is an important coping strategy for maintaining mental well-being. This can include activities such as exercising, practicing relaxation techniques, engaging in creative outlets, or spending time in nature. Self-care activities provide a reprieve from stress and promote a sense of balance and self-nurturing.

Cognitive Restructuring   Cognitive restructuring is a coping strategy that involves reframing and challenging negative thoughts and beliefs. It involves identifying and replacing irrational or unhelpful thoughts with more realistic and positive ones. Cognitive restructuring can help individuals develop a more adaptive and resilient mindset.

In conclusion, enhancing resilience and developing effective coping skills are crucial for maintaining and promoting mental health. By cultivating a positive mindset, building social connections, developing problem-solving skills, practicing self-care, and engaging in effective coping strategies, individuals can strengthen their resilience and navigate life's challenges with greater ease. Remember, resilience is not about avoiding difficulties but rather about developing the skills to face them head-on and emerge stronger.

Gratitude and Optimism Practices

Gratitude and optimism practices are essential tools in promoting mental health and well-being. They involve cultivating a positive mindset, focusing on gratitude, and embracing optimism. In this section, we will explore the benefits of gratitude and optimism, as well as various strategies to develop and incorporate these practices into daily life.

The Power of Gratitude

Gratitude is the practice of acknowledging and appreciating the good things in one's life. Research has shown that cultivating gratitude can have a profound impact on mental health, leading to increased happiness, life satisfaction, and overall well-being. It has been found to reduce stress, anxiety, and depression, while also improving sleep quality and enhancing relationships.

One effective gratitude practice is keeping a gratitude journal. Each day, take a few minutes to write down three things you are grateful for. These can be simple things like a warm cup of coffee, a kind gesture from a friend, or a beautiful sunset. By focusing on the positive aspects of life, you train your mind to notice and appreciate the good, even in the face of challenges.

Another gratitude practice is expressing gratitude to others. Take the time to thank people who have made a positive impact on your life. This could be through a heartfelt conversation, a handwritten note, or a small act of kindness. Not only will this strengthen your relationships, but it will also enhance your own sense of well-being.

Embracing Optimism

Optimism involves adopting a positive outlook on life and anticipating favorable outcomes. It is a mindset that helps individuals approach challenges with resilience and hope. Research has shown that optimistic individuals are more likely to experience better mental health, recover more quickly from setbacks, and have a higher quality of life.

One way to embrace optimism is by practicing positive self-talk. Pay attention to your internal dialogue and replace negative thoughts with positive and empowering ones. For example, instead of saying "I can't do this," reframe it as "I am capable and will give it my best shot." This shift in mindset can have a significant impact on your overall outlook and well-being.

Another strategy is to focus on solutions rather than dwelling on problems. When faced with a challenge, approach it with a mindset of finding creative solutions. This helps to shift your attention from the problem itself to the steps you can take to overcome it. By adopting this proactive approach, you can cultivate a sense of optimism and empowerment.

Applying Gratitude and Optimism Practices

Integrating gratitude and optimism practices into your daily life can be achieved through several strategies. Here are some effective techniques to help you apply these practices:

1. **Setting a Gratitude Reminder:** Choose a specific time each day, such as in the morning or before bed, to reflect on what you are grateful for. Use this reminder as a prompt to focus on the positive aspects of your life.

2. **Finding Joy in Small Moments:** Take notice of the small, everyday pleasures that bring you joy. It could be the smell of blooming flowers, the taste of your favorite snack, or the laughter of loved ones. Appreciating these moments can enhance your overall sense of gratitude and optimism.

3. **Practicing Mindfulness:** Engage in mindfulness exercises, such as deep breathing or meditation, to cultivate a present-moment awareness. This helps to shift your focus away from worries and encourages a positive perspective.

4. **Surrounding Yourself with Positive Influences:** Surround yourself with supportive and positive individuals who uplift and inspire you. Their optimism and gratitude will greatly influence your own mindset and well-being.

5. **Engaging in Random Acts of Kindness:** Perform small acts of kindness for others, such as holding the door open, offering a compliment, or volunteering your time. These acts not only benefit others but also boost your own sense of gratitude and well-being.

It is important to note that gratitude and optimism practices do not deny or dismiss the challenges of life. Instead, they provide a perspective that allows individuals to navigate difficulties with resilience and hope. By incorporating gratitude and optimism into your daily routine, you can enhance your mental health and cultivate a more positive and fulfilling life.

Exercise: Gratitude Journal

One practical exercise to develop gratitude is keeping a gratitude journal. Start by dedicating a few minutes each day to reflect on three things you are grateful for. Write them down in your journal and take a moment to appreciate the positive impact these things have had on your life. Remember to be specific and detailed in your entries to fully immerse yourself in the experience.

To further deepen your gratitude practice, try to identify why you are grateful for each item on your list. This exercise will help you uncover the underlying reasons and reinforce your sense of appreciation. Over time, you will find that gratitude becomes a natural habit, and you will notice even more things to be grateful for.

Remember, your gratitude journal is personal, and there is no right or wrong way to approach it. The key is consistency and sincerity. Make it a daily ritual, and watch as your perspective shifts towards a more positive and grateful outlook on life.

Resources for Further Exploration

If you are interested in delving deeper into gratitude and optimism practices, the following resources may be helpful:

- Books:

  - "The Gratitude Diaries: How a Year Looking on the Bright Side Can Transform Your Life" by Janice Kaplan.
  - "Learned Optimism: How to Change Your Mind and Your Life" by Martin E.P. Seligman.

- Apps:

  - Gratitude Journal App: A digital platform that allows you to create and maintain a gratitude journal on your phone or tablet.
  - Headspace: A meditation app that offers guided meditations on topics like gratitude and optimism.

- Websites:

  - Greater Good Science Center: Provides research-backed articles and practices on gratitude and positive psychology.
  - PositivePsychology.com: Offers resources, exercises, and articles on various positive psychology topics, including gratitude and optimism.

Remember, developing gratitude and embracing optimism is a journey that requires practice and commitment. Be patient with yourself and allow these practices to unfold naturally in your life. By nurturing gratitude and optimism, you can cultivate a more positive and fulfilling mental health journey.

Building Positive Relationships

Building positive relationships is essential for maintaining good mental health. Our social connections and interactions play a significant role in our overall well-being and can greatly impact our mental state. In this section, we will explore the importance of positive relationships, the key components for building and maintaining them, and strategies for improving our social connections.

The Importance of Positive Relationships

Positive relationships provide numerous benefits for our mental health. When we have strong connections with others, we experience a sense of belonging, support, and validation, which can contribute to increased happiness and life satisfaction. Positive relationships also provide opportunities for personal growth, self-discovery, and emotional resilience.

Research shows that individuals with strong and supportive social connections tend to have lower levels of stress, anxiety, and depression. They also have higher levels of self-esteem, self-confidence, and overall well-being. Positive relationships can serve as buffers against the impacts of stress and adversity, providing emotional and practical support during challenging times.

Furthermore, positive relationships foster a sense of purpose and meaning in our lives. When we feel connected to others, we are more likely to engage in activities that align with our values and contribute to the greater good. This sense of purpose and contribution enhances our overall mental wellness.

Key Components of Positive Relationships

Building positive relationships requires attention, effort, and genuine care. Here are some key components that contribute to the development and maintenance of positive relationships:

1. **Communication:** Effective communication is the foundation of any healthy relationship. It involves active listening, empathy, and clear expression of thoughts and feelings. Listening attentively to others and expressing ourselves honestly and respectfully fosters trust, understanding, and connection.

2. **Trust and Mutual Respect:** Trust and mutual respect are essential for creating and maintaining positive relationships. When we trust and respect others, we feel safe, valued, and supported. Trust is built over time through consistent actions, reliability, and open communication.

3. **Empathy and Understanding:** Being empathetic and understanding towards others allows us to connect on a deeper level. It involves putting ourselves in someone else's shoes, seeking to understand their perspective, and validating their experiences and emotions. Genuine empathy strengthens emotional bonds and promotes a sense of belonging.

4. **Shared Interests and Values:** Shared interests and values provide a foundation for meaningful connections. Engaging in activities together that align with our passions and values promotes a sense of belonging and shared purpose. It also provides opportunities for collaboration and mutual growth.

5. **Support and Encouragement:** Offering support and encouragement to others is crucial for building positive relationships. Being there for someone in both good times and bad, celebrating their successes, and providing a shoulder to lean on during difficult times fosters trust, intimacy, and a sense of belonging.

Strategies for Building Positive Relationships

Developing and maintaining positive relationships requires effort and intentionality. Here are some practical strategies to enhance your social connections:

1. **Develop Active Listening Skills:** Practice active listening by giving your full attention to the person speaking, maintaining eye contact, and responding with empathy. Avoid interrupting or dismissing their thoughts and feelings. Active listening shows that you value and respect the other person's perspective.

2. **Nurture Existing Relationships:** Prioritize and invest in your existing relationships. Reach out to friends, family, or colleagues regularly to check in, engage in shared activities, or simply spend quality time together. Show interest in their lives and actively support their goals and aspirations.

3. **Expand Your Social Network:** Seek opportunities to meet new people and expand your social network. Join clubs, organizations, or community groups that align with your interests. Attend social events, workshops, or seminars where you can connect with like-minded individuals.

4. **Practice Openness and Vulnerability:** Foster deeper connections by being open and vulnerable with others. Share your thoughts, feelings, and experiences honestly, allowing others to see your authentic self. This encourages others to reciprocate and creates a space for genuine and meaningful connections to flourish.

5. **Resolve Conflict Creatively:** Conflict is a normal part of any relationship. When conflicts arise, strive to resolve them creatively and constructively. Practice active problem-solving skills, engage in open and honest

EMOTIONAL INTELLIGENCE AND SELF-REGULATION   113

communication, and seek compromise. Remember that maintaining the relationship's well-being is more important than "winning" the argument.

6. **Express Gratitude and Appreciation:** Take time to express gratitude and appreciation to those around you. Acknowledge their support, kindness, or positive influence on your life. Small gestures like a heartfelt thank you note or a sincere compliment can strengthen bonds and foster a positive atmosphere in your relationships.

A Real-World Example: The Power of Building Positive Relationships

Consider the story of Sarah, a college student struggling with anxiety and feelings of isolation. Sarah decided to join a student-run mental health support group at her university. In this group, she found a safe space to share her experiences, receive validation, and connect with others who understood her challenges. Over time, she developed close friendships with group members, regularly meeting outside of group sessions for study groups, movie nights, and social outings. These positive relationships provided Sarah with a sense of belonging, support, and empowerment on her mental health journey.

Conclusion

Positive relationships are vital for our mental health and overall well-being. They provide us with emotional support, a sense of belonging, and opportunities for personal growth. By practicing effective communication, trust, empathy, and support, we can build and maintain positive relationships. Investing in our social connections enriches our lives and contributes to our mental wellness. So, let's prioritize building positive relationships and nurture the connections that bring joy and support to our lives.

Emotional Intelligence and Self-Regulation

Components of Emotional Intelligence

Emotional intelligence refers to the ability to recognize, understand, and manage our own emotions, as well as the emotions of others. It plays a crucial role in our personal and professional lives, influencing our relationships, decision-making, and overall well-being. In this section, we will explore the components of emotional intelligence and how they contribute to our mental health strategies.

Self-awareness

Self-awareness is the foundation of emotional intelligence. It involves being conscious of our own emotions, strengths, weaknesses, values, and motivations. When we have a high level of self-awareness, we are able to accurately recognize and understand our own emotional reactions and patterns of behavior.

One way to cultivate self-awareness is through self-reflection. Taking the time to examine our thoughts and emotions allows us to gain insights into our inner world. Journaling, mindfulness practices, and creative expression can be helpful tools in this process. By regularly engaging in self-reflection, we can develop a deeper understanding of ourselves and our emotional landscape.

Self-regulation

Self-regulation refers to the ability to manage and control our emotions and impulses. It involves being able to respond to situations in a calm and composed manner, rather than reacting impulsively. Self-regulation allows us to adapt to changing circumstances and make thoughtful decisions.

One technique for improving self-regulation is emotional regulation. This involves recognizing and labeling our emotions, understanding the triggers that may lead to emotional reactions, and developing strategies to manage and express our emotions in a healthy way. Techniques such as deep breathing, grounding exercises, and progressive muscle relaxation can help us regulate our emotions and maintain emotional balance.

Empathy

Empathy is the ability to understand and share the feelings of others. It involves being able to recognize and consider the perspectives, needs, and concerns of others. Empathy allows us to connect with others on a deeper level and build meaningful relationships.

To enhance empathy, it is important to practice active listening. This involves giving our full attention to others, suspending judgment, and seeking to understand their emotions and experiences. Asking open-ended questions and reflecting back on what others are saying can help us demonstrate empathy and create a safe and supportive environment for open communication.

Social awareness

Social awareness pertains to being aware of the emotions and needs of others in social situations. It involves recognizing social cues, understanding social norms, and displaying appropriate behavior. Social awareness allows us to navigate social interactions effectively and build positive connections with others.

To develop social awareness, it is helpful to pay attention to non-verbal cues such as facial expressions, body language, and tone of voice. Actively observing and engaging in social settings can provide valuable insights into social dynamics and help us understand the emotions and needs of others. By practicing empathy and actively seeking to understand others, we can enhance our social awareness.

Effective communication

Effective communication is essential for expressing our thoughts, emotions, needs, and concerns clearly and assertively. It involves both verbal and non-verbal communication skills, such as listening, speaking, and body language. Effective communication facilitates understanding, resolves conflicts, and builds stronger relationships.

To improve communication skills, it is important to practice active listening and consider the impact of our words and actions on others. Clarifying our thoughts and emotions before communicating them can help us express ourselves more effectively. Additionally, being open to feedback and practicing empathy in our interactions can contribute to more meaningful and productive communication.

Putting it into practice

To enhance our emotional intelligence, it is important to cultivate these components in our everyday lives. Here are a few exercises and strategies that can help:

1. Self-reflection journal: Set aside regular time for journaling, where you can reflect on your emotions, thoughts, and experiences. Use this as an opportunity to gain self-awareness and identify patterns or areas for growth.

2. Emotional regulation techniques: Practice deep breathing, progressive muscle relaxation, or other relaxation techniques to help you regulate your emotions and respond more calmly to stressful situations.

3. Practicing empathy: Engage in active listening and try to understand the perspective of others. Put yourself in their shoes and reflect on their emotions and experiences. Practice empathy in your daily interactions and seek to create a supportive environment for open communication.

4. Social observation: Pay attention to social cues and dynamics in your environment.   Observe non-verbal cues, such as body language and facial expressions, and practice social awareness by considering the emotions and needs of others.

5. Effective communication exercises: Practice active listening, assertive communication, and seeking clarification in your interactions. Pay attention to both verbal and non-verbal aspects of communication and aim to express yourself clearly and assertively.

Remember, developing emotional intelligence is an ongoing process.   By incorporating these strategies and exercises into your daily life, you can enhance your emotional intelligence and improve your mental well-being.

Conclusion

Emotional intelligence is a vital aspect of our mental health strategies.   By cultivating self-awareness, self-regulation, empathy, social awareness, and effective communication, we can enhance our ability to navigate emotions, build positive relationships, and make thoughtful decisions.   Incorporating exercises and strategies into our daily lives allows us to strengthen our emotional intelligence and improve our overall well-being. By embracing and developing these components of emotional intelligence, we can cultivate resilience and better cope with the challenges and stresses of life.

Recognizing and Managing Emotions

In this section, we will explore the importance of recognizing and managing emotions for maintaining good mental health. Emotions play a crucial role in our daily lives, influencing our thoughts, behavior, and overall well-being. By developing emotional intelligence and learning effective strategies to regulate our emotions, we can enhance our mental resilience and improve our relationships with others.

Understanding Emotions

Emotions are complex physiological and psychological responses to specific stimuli or situations. They arise from the interplay between our thoughts, feelings, and bodily sensations. Emotions can range from basic, instinctual responses such as fear and anger to more complex emotions like joy, sadness, and love.

Recognizing emotions requires self-awareness and the ability to identify and label our feelings accurately. It involves paying attention to the physical sensations and behavioral cues associated with different emotions. For example, feeling a knot in your stomach and increased heart rate may indicate anxiety, while a warm, contented feeling may indicate happiness.

The Importance of Emotional Recognition

Recognizing our emotions is crucial for several reasons. Firstly, it allows us to gain insight into our inner experiences and understand the underlying causes of our emotional state. By acknowledging and accepting our emotions, we can better address and cope with them effectively.

Emotional recognition also helps us understand the emotions of others. By being attuned to non-verbal cues, facial expressions, and body language, we can empathize with others and respond appropriately. This fosters better communication, deeper connections, and more meaningful relationships.

Strategies for Recognizing Emotions

Developing the skill of recognizing emotions requires practice and self-reflection. Here are some strategies to help you improve your emotional awareness:

1. **Mindfulness:** Practice being fully present in the moment and pay attention to your thoughts, feelings, and bodily sensations without judgment.

2. **Journaling:** Keep a journal to record your thoughts, emotions, and experiences. This can help you identify patterns and triggers that influence your emotional state.

3. **Body scan:** Perform a body scan meditation where you systematically bring your attention to each part of your body, noticing any physical sensations or tension that may indicate an emotional response.

4. **Seek feedback:** Ask trusted friends, family members, or mental health professionals for feedback on how they perceive your emotions. Their insights can provide valuable perspectives.

5. **Reflect on past experiences:** Take time to reflect on past situations that elicited strong emotions. What were the triggers? How did you respond? Understanding these patterns can help you become more aware in the present moment.

Managing Emotions

Recognizing emotions is only the first step. It is equally important to learn how to manage and regulate them effectively. Emotion regulation involves understanding and modifying our emotional responses to better adapt to different situations and maintain mental well-being.

Here are some strategies to help you manage your emotions:

1. **Deep breathing:** Practice deep breathing exercises to calm your body and mind during moments of stress or emotional intensity. Breathe in deeply through your nose, hold for a few seconds, and exhale slowly through your mouth.

2. **Cognitive reappraisal:** Challenge and reframe negative thoughts that may be contributing to negative emotions. Look for alternative perspectives and focus on more positive interpretations.

3. **Self-care:** Engage in activities that promote self-care and relaxation, such as taking a bath, going for a walk in nature, listening to music, or practicing hobbies. These activities can help reduce stress and promote emotional well-being.

4. **Social support:** Reach out to trusted friends, family members, or support groups to share your feelings and seek validation and understanding. Sometimes, simply talking about your emotions can help alleviate their intensity.

5. **Problem-solving:** If your emotions are primarily driven by a specific problem or issue, focus on developing effective problem-solving strategies. Break the problem down into smaller steps and work towards a solution.

Remember, managing emotions is a learned skill that takes time and practice. Be patient with yourself and seek professional help if you are struggling to regulate your emotions effectively.

Case Study: Managing Anger

Anger is one of the most common and powerful emotions. Let's consider a case study to understand how recognizing and managing anger can contribute to mental well-being.

Imagine Sarah, a young professional, frequently gets angry at her colleagues for not meeting deadlines. This anger is negatively impacting her work relationships and job satisfaction. To manage her anger, Sarah first needs to recognize the physical and emotional signs of anger. She notices that her face becomes flushed, her heart rate increases, and she feels a strong urge to yell or argue.

Once Sarah becomes aware of her anger, she can implement strategies to manage it. For example, she can:

- Take a few deep breaths and count to ten to calm herself down before responding.

- Remind herself that getting angry will not solve the problem and may damage her professional relationships.

- Engage in problem-solving by discussing the issue calmly with her colleagues or exploring alternative ways to meet deadlines effectively.

- Seek support from a mentor or supervisor to gain insights and guidance on managing work-related stress and anger.

By recognizing and managing her anger, Sarah can improve her emotional well-being, enhance her professional relationships, and create a more positive work environment.

Conclusion

Recognizing and managing emotions are essential skills for maintaining good mental health. By becoming more aware of our emotions and developing effective strategies to regulate them, we can improve our overall well-being, enhance our relationships, and navigate life's challenges more effectively. Practice self-reflection, seek support when needed, and be patient with yourself as you learn to recognize and manage your emotions. Remember, emotional intelligence is a lifelong journey.

Emotional Regulation Techniques

Emotions are an integral part of our lives, influencing our thoughts, behaviors, and overall well-being. Sometimes, however, emotions can become overwhelming and difficult to manage. This is where emotional regulation techniques come into play. Emotional regulation refers to the process of effectively managing and modulating our emotions in order to promote emotional well-being and maintain healthy relationships. In this section, we will explore various techniques that can help individuals regulate their emotions and navigate through challenging situations.

Identifying and Labeling Emotions

The first step in emotional regulation is to accurately identify and label our emotions. Many people struggle with recognizing and understanding their emotions, which can impede their ability to regulate them effectively. It is important to develop emotional awareness by paying attention to bodily sensations, behaviors, thoughts, and facial expressions that accompany different emotions.

One effective technique for identifying and labeling emotions is called "emotional check-ins". This involves regularly taking the time to tune in to our emotions and ask ourselves how we are feeling. Journaling can also be a helpful tool for tracking and documenting emotions. By developing this habit, individuals can become more in tune with their emotional experiences and better equipped to regulate them.

Cognitive Reappraisal

Cognitive reappraisal is a powerful technique that involves reframing and reinterpreting the meaning of a situation in order to change our emotional response. Our emotions are often influenced by our thoughts and interpretations of events. By challenging and reshaping these thoughts, we can alter our emotional reactions.

One way to practice cognitive reappraisal is through the use of positive self-talk and reframing. Encouraging oneself with optimistic and realistic statements can help shift the perspective and reduce negative emotions. For example, instead of catastrophizing a situation, such as an upcoming exam, one could reframe it as an opportunity for growth and learning. This can alleviate anxiety and promote a more positive emotional state.

Mindfulness and Acceptance

Mindfulness is a practice that involves paying attention to the present moment without judgment. It allows individuals to observe their thoughts, emotions, and sensations without becoming overwhelmed by them. Mindfulness-based techniques can be particularly helpful in emotional regulation as they promote non-reactivity and acceptance.

One mindfulness technique that can be used for emotional regulation is the R.A.I.N. method. R.A.I.N. stands for Recognize, Allow, Investigate, and Nourish. It involves recognizing and acknowledging emotions, allowing them to be present without trying to suppress or control them, investigating the underlying causes of the emotions, and nurturing oneself with self-compassion and self-care.

Additionally, practicing acceptance can be a valuable tool in emotional regulation. Acceptance involves acknowledging and acknowledging that emotions are a natural part of the human experience, and that it is normal to experience a range of emotions. By accepting our emotions without judgment, we can reduce resistance and create space for emotional regulation.

Emotion Regulation Strategies

In addition to the techniques mentioned above, there are several practical strategies that can be implemented to regulate emotions effectively.

1. Deep Breathing: Deep breathing exercises can help activate the body's relaxation response and calm the mind. By taking slow, deep breaths and focusing on the sensations of the breath, individuals can reduce anxiety and promote emotional regulation.

2. Physical Activity: Engaging in physical activities such as yoga, running, or dancing can release endorphins and promote a positive mood. Regular exercise has been shown to alleviate symptoms of depression and anxiety, and improve overall emotional well-being.

3. Social Support: Connecting with others and seeking support from friends, family, or support groups can provide a sense of validation, understanding, and comfort. Talking about our emotions and sharing our experiences can contribute to emotional regulation.

4. Creative Expression: Engaging in creative activities such as painting, writing, or playing music can serve as a form of emotional release. These activities allow individuals to express and process their emotions in a healthy and constructive way.

5. Time Management and Organization: A structured and organized environment can reduce stress and create a sense of control. Effective time management techniques, such as prioritizing tasks and setting realistic goals, can reduce feelings of overwhelm and contribute to emotional regulation.

It is important to remember that emotional regulation is a skill that takes time and practice to develop. Different techniques may work better for different individuals, so it is essential to find what strategies resonate with you personally. Experimenting with different approaches and seeking support from mental health professionals can be beneficial in mastering emotional regulation.

In conclusion, emotional regulation techniques are essential for promoting emotional well-being and maintaining healthy relationships. By identifying and labeling emotions, practicing cognitive reappraisal, incorporating mindfulness and acceptance, and implementing practical strategies, individuals can effectively regulate their emotions and navigate through life's challenges. Learning and mastering these techniques can contribute to a more balanced and fulfilling emotional life.

Empathy and Social Awareness

Empathy and social awareness play crucial roles in promoting mental health and fostering positive relationships. Empathy is the ability to understand and share the feelings of another person, while social awareness is the ability to recognize and understand the emotions, needs, and perspectives of others in a social context. In this section, we will explore the importance of empathy and social awareness in mental health strategies and provide practical tips for cultivating these skills.

The Importance of Empathy

Empathy is a fundamental aspect of human interaction and is essential for building and maintaining healthy relationships. When we empathize with others, we demonstrate that we value their emotions and experiences. This helps create a sense of trust, connection, and support, which are essential for overall mental health and well-being.

Empathy allows us to put ourselves in someone else's shoes, allowing us to better understand their perspectives, emotions, and needs. This can lead to improved communication, conflict resolution, and problem-solving skills. It also helps us develop stronger connections with others and fosters a sense of community and belonging.

Furthermore, empathy plays a crucial role in reducing stigma and promoting understanding of mental health issues. By empathizing with individuals experiencing mental health challenges, we can cultivate a more compassionate and inclusive society.

Developing Empathy

Empathy is a skill that can be developed and improved with practice. Here are some strategies to enhance your empathetic abilities:

1. **Active Listening:** Give your full attention when someone is speaking to you. Maintain eye contact, nod, and provide verbal and non-verbal cues to show that you are engaged and interested in what the person is saying. Avoid interrupting or imposing your own judgments or assumptions.

2. **Put Yourself in Their Shoes:** Try to imagine how the other person is feeling and what they might be going through. Consider their perspective, life experiences, and cultural background. This can help you better understand their emotions and reactions.

3. **Practice Perspective-Taking:** Take the time to view situations from different angles. Consider how others might interpret or respond to the same situation based on their unique experiences and beliefs. This can help broaden your understanding and empathy towards diverse perspectives.

4. **Validate Emotions:** When someone shares their feelings with you, acknowledge and validate their emotions. Let them know that their feelings are valid and understandable. Avoid dismissing or minimizing their experiences.

5. **Practice Empathetic Language:** Use language that shows you care and understand. Express empathy by saying things like, "I can imagine that must have been really difficult for you" or "I understand how you feel." This shows that you are actively trying to empathize and connect with the person.

6. **Be Mindful of Non-Verbal Cues:** Pay attention to the non-verbal cues such as facial expressions, body language, and tone of voice. These cues often provide valuable insights into a person's emotions and can help you better understand their experiences.

Social Awareness

Social awareness is closely connected to empathy and involves being attuned to the emotions, needs, and dynamics of a social context. It involves understanding social norms, cultural sensitivities, and power dynamics. Developing social awareness can contribute significantly to positive mental health outcomes and is a core component of effective communication and relationship-building.

Here are some strategies to enhance your social awareness:

1. **Cultivate Cultural Competence:** Educate yourself about different cultures, traditions, and customs. Learn about social norms, values, and communication styles of diverse communities. This will help you navigate social interactions with sensitivity and respect.

2. **Practice Active Observation:** Pay attention to the dynamics and interactions within social groups. Observe how individuals communicate,

express emotions, and respond to each other. This can help you better understand and adapt to social contexts.

3. **Develop Empathetic Curiosity**: Approach social interactions with curiosity and genuine interest. Ask open-ended questions and actively listen to understand other people's experiences, perspectives, and needs. This can help build stronger connections and foster a sense of understanding.

4. **Seek Feedback and Learn from Others**: Be open to feedback and constructive criticism from others. Engaging in honest and respectful conversations can provide valuable insights into your blind spots and help you develop a deeper understanding of social dynamics.

5. **Practice Cultural Humility**: Recognize that your own cultural perspective may be limited and that there is always more to learn. Embrace a mindset of continuous learning and growth, and be open to challenging your own assumptions and biases.

The Power of Empathy and Social Awareness

Empathy and social awareness have the power to create meaningful change in individuals, relationships, and communities. By developing these skills, we can:

- Foster more supportive and inclusive social environments.

- Strengthen relationships and enhance communication.

- Reduce conflicts and promote peaceful resolutions.

- Improve understanding and support for individuals with mental health challenges.

- Promote a sense of belonging and connection.

It is important to note that empathy and social awareness should be practiced in a balanced way. It is crucial to establish healthy boundaries and prioritize self-care to prevent emotional exhaustion or burnout. Remember to also be empathetic towards yourself and seek support when needed.

Putting Empathy and Social Awareness into Action

To put empathy and social awareness into action, consider the following practical exercises:

1. **Journaling Reflection:** Take a few minutes each day to reflect on interactions you had with others. Identify moments where you exercised empathy or social awareness, and those where you could have done better. Write down your thoughts, feelings, and insights.

2. **Volunteer or Engage in Community Service:** Find opportunities to contribute to your community or support organizations that promote empathy and social awareness. This could involve volunteering at a local shelter, participating in community projects, or joining advocacy groups.

3. **Practice Empathy in Everyday Interactions:** Challenge yourself to consciously practice empathy in your daily interactions. This could involve actively listening to a friend, offering support to someone in need, or engaging in a compassionate conversation with a colleague.

Remember, developing empathy and social awareness is an ongoing process that requires continuous practice and self-reflection. By integrating these skills into your life, you can contribute to a more compassionate and understanding society, while also enhancing your own well-being.

Communication Skills and Conflict Resolution

Effective communication skills are essential for maintaining healthy relationships and resolving conflicts. Communication is the foundation of all human interactions, and developing strong communication skills can greatly enhance mental health and overall well-being. In this section, we will explore various aspects of communication skills and conflict resolution techniques that can be applied in different contexts.

Understanding Effective Communication

Effective communication involves both verbal and non-verbal aspects. Verbal communication refers to the use of words, while non-verbal communication includes body language, facial expressions, tone of voice, and gestures. Both forms of communication play a crucial role in conveying messages accurately.

To enhance verbal communication, it is important to speak clearly, use appropriate tone and volume, and choose words carefully to convey thoughts and emotions accurately. Active listening is also a vital component of effective communication. It involves fully focusing on and comprehending what the other person is saying, without interrupting or formulating responses prematurely.

Non-verbal communication can often communicate messages more powerfully than words. Paying attention to body language cues, such as eye contact, postures, and facial expressions, can help interpret the underlying emotions and intent behind someone's words. For instance, crossed arms and a tense posture might indicate defensiveness or disagreement.

Conflict Resolution Strategies

Conflicts are an inevitable part of life, especially in interpersonal relationships. However, mastering conflict resolution skills can contribute to better mental health and long-lasting relationships. Here are some strategies for effectively resolving conflicts:

1. Active Listening: Actively listening to the other person's perspective without interrupting or judging allows for deeper understanding. Restating what the other person said can validate their feelings and show empathy.

2. Expressing Emotions: Honest expression of emotions is important in conflict resolution. Use "I" statements to communicate how you feel without blaming the other person. For example, instead of saying, "You always ignore me," say, "I feel ignored when I don't receive a response."

3. Finding Common Ground: Seek areas of agreement or shared interests to create a foundation for resolving conflicts. Identifying common goals can help shift the focus from adversarial positions to mutually beneficial solutions.

4. Problem-Solving and Negotiation: Collaborate with the other person to find win-win solutions. Brainstorm possible solutions and evaluate them based on feasibility and potential impact. Compromise when necessary to ensure a fair outcome.

5. Managing Emotions: Emotions can escalate conflicts, making them harder to resolve. Practice emotional self-regulation techniques, such as deep breathing or taking a break, to calm yourself and approach the conflict in a more constructive manner.

6. Addressing Underlying Issues: Superficial conflicts often stem from deeper underlying issues. Take the time to explore these root causes and discuss them openly. Addressing the core issues can lead to more effective resolution and prevent recurring conflicts.

7. Seeking Mediation: In some cases, involving a neutral third party can help facilitate conflict resolution. A trained mediator can provide an unbiased perspective

and guide the discussion towards a mutually satisfactory resolution.

It is important to remember that conflict resolution is a process and may not always result in a perfect resolution. However, employing these strategies can foster open communication, strengthen relationships, and promote overall mental well-being.

Conflict Resolution in the Digital Age

In today's digital age, conflicts often arise in online spaces, such as social media platforms and online communities. Resolving conflicts in these contexts requires additional considerations:

1. Mindful Online Communication: When engaging in online discussions, practice mindfulness and awareness of your own emotions and reactions. Be mindful of the tone and content of your messages to avoid miscommunication.

2. Respectful Disagreements: Online platforms can foster heated debates and arguments. Maintain respectful dialogue, even when faced with opposing views. Treat others with kindness and empathy, and avoid personal attacks or derogatory language.

3. Unplugging and Setting Boundaries: Online conflicts can be overwhelming and emotionally taxing. It's important to set boundaries and take breaks when needed. Disconnecting from social media or online platforms temporarily can help reduce stress and maintain mental well-being.

4. Reporting and Blocking: In cases of online harassment or abusive behavior, it is crucial to report the issue to the platform administrators or authorities. Blocking individuals who consistently engage in harmful behavior can be an effective way to protect oneself.

5. Seeking Support: Online conflicts can have a significant impact on mental health. Reach out to trusted friends, family members, or online support groups to share your experiences and seek guidance. Connecting with others who have experienced similar conflicts can provide validation and support.

It is important to approach online conflicts with the same principles of effective communication and conflict resolution as in face-to-face interactions. Building a positive online presence and promoting respectful communication can contribute to a healthier online environment.

Putting It into Practice

To enhance your communication skills and conflict resolution abilities, here are some exercises and resources you can explore:

1. Reflect on a recent conflict you experienced. Analyze your communication style and identify areas for improvement. How could active listening, expressing emotions, or finding common ground have led to a better resolution?

2. Engage in active listening with a partner or friend. Take turns sharing a personal experience while the other person demonstrates active listening by reflecting back their understanding of the story.

3. Practice expressing emotions using "I" statements. Write down a conflict scenario and rephrase it using "I" statements to convey your emotions without blaming the other person.

4. Role-play conflict resolution scenarios with a friend or family member. Take turns playing different roles and practice applying the strategies discussed in this section.

Resources:

- "Nonviolent Communication: A Language of Life" by Marshall B. Rosenberg. - "Crucial Conversations: Tools for Talking When Stakes Are High" by Kerry Patterson, Joseph Grenny, Ron McMillan, and Al Switzler. - Online courses and workshops on conflict resolution and effective communication offered by reputable organizations or universities.

Remember, mastering communication skills and conflict resolution takes practice and patience. By investing time and effort into developing these skills, you can foster healthier relationships, resolve conflicts effectively, and promote your own mental well-being.

Strategies for Mental Health Maintenance

Sleep and Restorative Practices

Importance of Sleep for Mental Health

Sleep is an essential function of our daily lives, playing a crucial role in maintaining our overall health and well-being. It is a complex biological process that allows our body and mind to rest, restore, and rejuvenate. In the context of mental health, sleep has a profound impact on our cognitive processes, emotional regulation, and overall psychological functioning. In this section, we will explore the importance of sleep for mental health and discuss strategies for improving sleep quality.

The Sleep-Wake Cycle

Before delving into the specifics of sleep and mental health, let's first understand the basic mechanisms of the sleep-wake cycle. Our sleep-wake cycle, also known as the circadian rhythm, is regulated by an internal biological clock located in the suprachiasmatic nucleus (SCN) of the brain. This clock is influenced by external cues such as daylight and darkness.

The sleep-wake cycle consists of two main phases: wakefulness and sleep. During wakefulness, we are alert and engaged in daily activities. As the day progresses, our body's sleep drive increases, leading to a gradual transition into sleep. Sleep is divided into multiple stages, including rapid eye movement (REM) sleep and non-REM sleep, each with its own unique characteristics.

129

Cognitive Functioning and Memory Consolidation

One of the primary functions of sleep is to support optimal cognitive functioning. Sleep plays a crucial role in memory consolidation and learning processes. During sleep, our brain processes and consolidates information acquired during wakefulness, allowing us to retain and recall this information more effectively.

Research has shown that sleep enhances our ability to learn new information, consolidate memories, and improve problem-solving skills. Lack of adequate sleep can impair cognitive processes, such as attention, concentration, and decision-making. It can also negatively impact our memory formation and retrieval abilities, leading to difficulties in academic or work-related tasks.

Emotional Regulation and Mood Stability

Sleep also plays a pivotal role in emotional regulation and mood stability. Sufficient sleep allows us to regulate our emotions effectively, while sleep deprivation can lead to emotional dysregulation and mood disturbances.

During sleep, our brain processes and regulates emotions, helping us to maintain emotional well-being. It is during REM sleep that we often experience vivid dreams, which serve as a mechanism for processing and integrating emotions. Insufficient sleep can disrupt this process, leading to heightened emotional reactivity, irritability, and poor stress management.

Furthermore, inadequate sleep is closely linked to the development and exacerbation of mental health disorders, such as depression and anxiety. Sleep disturbances are common symptoms of these disorders, and addressing sleep problems can significantly improve overall mental health outcomes.

Psychological Resilience and Coping Mechanisms

Adequate sleep is crucial for building psychological resilience and effective coping mechanisms. When we are well-rested, we are better equipped to navigate and cope with life's challenges. Sleep deprivation, on the other hand, can weaken our ability to cope with stress, making us more vulnerable to mental health issues.

Research has consistently shown that individuals who consistently get enough sleep are more resilient to stress, have better emotional regulation skills, and experience improved mental well-being. By prioritizing sleep and ensuring its quality, we can build a strong foundation for psychological resilience and better manage the adversities we face.

Strategies for Improving Sleep Quality

Now that we understand the significance of sleep for mental health, let's explore some strategies for improving sleep quality:

- Establish a consistent sleep schedule: Going to bed and waking up at the same time every day, even on weekends, helps regulate your body's internal clock.

- Create a sleep-friendly environment: Make sure your bedroom is quiet, dark, and at a comfortable temperature. Invest in a comfortable mattress and pillow that support your sleep posture.

- Practice good sleep hygiene: Avoid stimulating activities, such as using electronic devices or consuming caffeine close to bedtime. Establish a relaxing bedtime routine to signal your body that it's time to sleep.

- Manage stress: Engage in stress management techniques, such as mindfulness meditation or deep breathing exercises, to calm your mind before bed.

- Regular physical activity: Engaging in regular exercise during the day can promote better sleep. However, avoid intense workouts close to bedtime, as it may interfere with sleep.

- Limit exposure to blue light: Blue light emitted by electronic devices can disrupt your sleep-wake cycle. Limit your exposure to these devices before bedtime or use blue light-blocking filters.

- Avoid napping late in the day: If you need to nap, keep it short and avoid napping too close to your bedtime, as it may interfere with your ability to fall asleep at night.

- Seek professional help if needed: If you have persistent sleep problems or suspect an underlying sleep disorder, consult a healthcare professional for a comprehensive evaluation and appropriate treatment options.

Incorporating these strategies into your daily routine can significantly improve your sleep quality and, in turn, positively impact your mental health and overall well-being.

Real-World Example

To illustrate the importance of sleep for mental health, let's consider the case of Sarah, a working professional experiencing chronic sleep deprivation. Sarah consistently sacrificed sleep to meet work demands, resulting in persistent fatigue, poor concentration, and increased irritability. As a consequence, her overall mood and job performance suffered, leading to heightened stress levels and strained interpersonal relationships.

Recognizing the detrimental effects of sleep deprivation on her mental health, Sarah decided to prioritize sleep by implementing the strategies mentioned earlier. She established a consistent sleep schedule, created a sleep-friendly environment, and practiced relaxation techniques before bed. Over time, Sarah experienced significant improvements in her sleep quality, cognitive functioning, and emotional well-being. She became more resilient to stress and noticed enhanced productivity and job satisfaction.

Sarah's story exemplifies the powerful impact of prioritizing sleep on mental health outcomes. By recognizing the importance of sleep and taking proactive steps to improve sleep patterns, individuals can significantly enhance their overall mental well-being and quality of life.

Conclusion

In conclusion, sleep is an essential component of mental health. It influences various aspects of our cognitive, emotional, and psychological functioning. Prioritizing and improving sleep quality can have a profound positive impact on our mental well-being, cognitive abilities, emotional regulation, and overall resilience. By implementing strategies to optimize sleep, individuals can effectively support their mental health and enhance their overall quality of life. Remember, a good night's sleep is not a luxury, but a vital investment in our mental and emotional well-being.

Sleep Disorders and Strategies for Improvement

Sleep is a fundamental aspect of our overall well-being and plays a vital role in maintaining good mental health. However, millions of people worldwide suffer from sleep disorders that can significantly impact their quality of life. In this section, we will explore different types of sleep disorders and discuss strategies to improve sleep.

Types of Sleep Disorders

Sleep disorders can be broadly categorized into three main types: insomnia, sleep apnea, and circadian rhythm disorders.

Insomnia is characterized by difficulty falling asleep, staying asleep, or experiencing non-restorative sleep. It can be caused by various factors such as stress, anxiety, depression, medical conditions, medications, or poor sleep hygiene.

Sleep apnea is a disorder characterized by pauses in breathing or shallow breaths during sleep. The two main types of sleep apnea are obstructive sleep apnea (OSA) and central sleep apnea (CSA). OSA occurs when the airway becomes blocked or collapsed, leading to snoring, gasping, and interrupted sleep. CSA occurs when the brain fails to send proper signals to the muscles that control breathing during sleep.

Circadian rhythm disorders are conditions that disrupt the body's internal clock, leading to difficulties in falling asleep or waking up at the desired times. Examples of circadian rhythm disorders include jet lag, shift work sleep disorder, delayed sleep-wake phase disorder, and advanced sleep-wake phase disorder.

Strategies for Improvement

Improving sleep quality and managing sleep disorders require a multifaceted approach. Here are some strategies that can help individuals with sleep disorders:

1. Implement good sleep hygiene practices: Establishing a regular sleep schedule, creating a comfortable sleep environment, and avoiding stimulating activities before bedtime can improve sleep quality. It is important to maintain a consistent sleep routine, even on weekends.

2. Manage stress and anxiety: Stress and anxiety can significantly impact sleep. Engaging in relaxation techniques such as deep breathing exercises, meditation, and yoga can promote a state of calmness and aid in falling asleep.

3. Cognitive Behavioral Therapy for Insomnia (CBT-I): CBT-I is a highly effective therapeutic approach for treating insomnia. It focuses on identifying and changing negative thoughts and behaviors that contribute to sleep disturbances. CBT-I techniques may include sleep restriction therapy, stimulus control therapy, and relaxation training.

4. Sleep environment optimization: Creating a sleep-friendly environment can contribute to better sleep. This includes keeping the bedroom cool, dark, and quiet, investing in a comfortable mattress and pillows, and minimizing disturbances from electronic devices.

5. Medical interventions: In certain cases, medical interventions may be necessary to manage sleep disorders. Continuous Positive Airway Pressure (CPAP) therapy is the primary treatment for obstructive sleep apnea. Medications may be prescribed for conditions like insomnia or circadian rhythm disorders, but they should be used under the guidance of a healthcare professional.

Case Study: The Impact of Sleep Disorders on Mental Health

Let's consider the case of Sarah, a 35-year-old woman who has been experiencing chronic insomnia. She struggles to fall asleep and wakes up frequently during the night, leading to daytime fatigue and irritability. Her insomnia has started affecting her mental health, and she often feels anxious and depressed.

To address Sarah's sleep disorder and its impact on her mental health, a comprehensive approach is needed. Sarah can benefit from implementing the following strategies:

1. Sleep hygiene practices: Sarah can establish a consistent sleep schedule, create a comfortable sleep environment, and avoid stimulating activities before bedtime. She can also incorporate relaxation techniques into her bedtime routine.

2. Stress management: Sarah can practice stress management techniques such as deep breathing exercises or meditation to help calm her mind before sleep.

3. Cognitive Behavioral Therapy for Insomnia (CBT-I):   Sarah can undergo CBT-I to address her negative thoughts and behaviors surrounding sleep. This therapy can help her establish healthier sleep patterns and reduce anxiety related to sleep.

4. Medical evaluation: Sarah should consult with a healthcare professional to rule out any underlying medical conditions contributing to her insomnia. A sleep study may be recommended to assess the severity of her sleep disorder.

By implementing these strategies, Sarah can improve her sleep quality, reduce the impact of insomnia on her mental health, and regain a sense of well-being.

Conclusion

Sleep disorders can significantly impact one's mental health and overall quality of life. Understanding the different types of sleep disorders and implementing effective strategies for improvement is crucial in promoting better sleep and well-being. By addressing sleep disorders and prioritizing healthy sleep habits, individuals can enhance their mental resilience and overall mental health. Remember, good sleep is the foundation of a healthy mind.

Relaxation Techniques and Stress Reduction

In today's fast-paced and stressful world, finding ways to relax and reduce stress is essential for maintaining good mental health. In this section, we will explore various relaxation techniques that have proven effective in managing stress and promoting overall well-being. These techniques can be easily incorporated into your daily routine, providing you with the necessary tools to navigate stressful situations and find inner peace.

Progressive Muscle Relaxation

Progressive muscle relaxation (PMR) is a technique developed by Edmund Jacobson in the early 20th century, which involves systematically tensing and then releasing different muscle groups in the body. This technique helps to release tension and promote a sense of deep relaxation.

To practice PMR, find a comfortable and quiet space where you can sit or lie down. Close your eyes and take a few deep breaths to center yourself. Starting from your toes, gradually tense the muscles in your feet by curling your toes for a few seconds, then release the tension and feel the relaxation spreading through your feet. Move on to the next muscle group, such as your calves, thighs, and buttocks, repeating the process of tensing and releasing.

Continue this process, gradually working your way up through your body, including your abdomen, chest, arms, and neck. Pay attention to any areas of tension or discomfort and consciously release the tension as you exhale. Finally, finish by tensing and releasing the muscles in your face and scalp.

Practicing PMR regularly can help you become more aware of the physical sensations related to stress and tension in your body. By deliberately relaxing these muscles, you can release built-up stress and promote a sense of calmness and relaxation.

Deep Breathing Exercises

Deep breathing exercises are a simple yet powerful technique for reducing stress and promoting relaxation. When we're stressed, our breathing tends to become shallow and rapid. This can further contribute to feelings of anxiety and tension. Deep breathing exercises help to slow down the breathing, activate the body's relaxation response, and promote a sense of calm.

To practice deep breathing, find a comfortable position either sitting or lying down. Place one hand on your abdomen and the other on your chest. Take a slow, deep breath in through your nose, allowing your abdomen to rise as you fill your lungs with air. As you exhale through your mouth, imagine all the tension, stress, and negative energy leaving your body.

Repeat this process several times, focusing on the sensation of your breath entering and leaving your body. As you become more comfortable with deep breathing, you can gradually extend the duration of your inhalations and exhalations.

Deep breathing exercises can be done anywhere and at any time, making them a convenient tool for managing stress in various situations. Incorporate this practice into your daily routine or whenever you feel overwhelmed or anxious.

Guided Imagery

Guided imagery is a relaxation technique that involves using your imagination to create a visual and sensory experience that promotes relaxation and reduces stress. It taps into the power of the mind-body connection, allowing you to create a calming mental retreat.

To practice guided imagery, find a quiet and comfortable space where you won't be disturbed. Close your eyes and take a few deep, slow breaths to relax your body and mind. Choose a peaceful and calming scenario or location in your mind, such as a serene beach, a tranquil forest, or a cozy mountain cabin.

Begin to engage your senses by visualizing the details of this place. Imagine the colors, shapes, and textures around you. Notice any sounds, whether it's the gentle lapping of waves, the rustling of leaves, or the crackling of a fireplace. Allow yourself to feel the temperature, the softness of the sand or the warmth of the fire.

As you continue to explore this mental sanctuary, let go of any worries or stressors that may be weighing on your mind. Embrace the peace and tranquility of this imaginary place, focusing on the positive sensations and emotions it evokes.

You can find guided imagery scripts or recordings online or use your own creative visualization skills to guide yourself through this practice. Regular practice of guided imagery can help you cultivate a sense of inner calmness and provide a mental escape during times of stress.

Mindfulness Meditation

Mindfulness meditation is a practice rooted in ancient Buddhist traditions that has gained tremendous popularity in recent years. It involves intentionally bringing your attention to the present moment without judgment, allowing you to cultivate a sense of awareness and acceptance.

To practice mindfulness meditation, find a comfortable position, either sitting or lying down. Close your eyes and take a few deep breaths to center yourself. Bring your attention to the sensations of your breath, focusing on the physical sensations of each inhale and exhale. Notice the rise and fall of your abdomen or the coolness of the air entering your nostrils.

As you engage with your breath, thoughts, emotions, and bodily sensations will naturally arise. Instead of getting caught up in these thoughts, simply acknowledge them without judgment and gently redirect your attention back to your breath.

You can start with short periods of mindfulness meditation, such as five or ten minutes, and gradually increase the duration as you become more comfortable. With regular practice, mindfulness meditation can help you develop a greater capacity to observe your thoughts and emotions without getting entangled in them. This can be particularly helpful in managing stress and cultivating a sense of inner calmness.

Aromatherapy

Aromatherapy is a holistic healing practice that utilizes essential oils to promote physical and psychological well-being. Essential oils are highly concentrated plant extracts that have distinct therapeutic properties. They can be used in various ways, including inhalation, topical application, or diffusion.

Certain essential oils have been found to have calming and relaxing effects, making them ideal for stress reduction. Lavender, bergamot, chamomile, and ylang-ylang are common essential oils known for their relaxation properties. These oils can be added to a diffuser, diluted in a carrier oil for massage, or added to bath water for a soothing soak.

To create a calming atmosphere, you can also use essential oils in combination with other relaxation techniques. For example, you can diffuse lavender oil while practicing deep breathing exercises or incorporate a lavender-scented candle into your guided imagery practice.

When using essential oils, it's important to follow proper dilution guidelines and choose high-quality oils from reputable sources. Some oils may cause skin irritation or interact with medications, so it's always wise to consult a qualified aromatherapist or healthcare professional before using them.

Unconventional Relaxation Techniques

In addition to the well-known relaxation techniques mentioned above, there are also some unconventional methods that can be effective in reducing stress and promoting relaxation. These techniques may not be widely known or practiced but have shown promise in relieving stress for some individuals.

One such technique is laughter yoga, a practice that combines intentional laughter exercises with yogic breathing techniques. Laughter has been scientifically proven to reduce stress hormone levels and improve mood. Laughter yoga involves simulated laughter, which often leads to genuine laughter and a release of tension. This practice can be done alone or in a group setting and is a fun way to reduce stress and promote overall well-being.

Another unconventional technique is sound therapy, which uses the vibrations and frequencies of specific sounds or instruments to induce a state of relaxation. Sound baths, for example, involve lying down and being immersed in the sounds of instruments such as singing bowls, gongs, or tuning forks. The resonant sounds create a sense of harmony and can help you achieve deep relaxation.

While these unconventional techniques may not be suitable for everyone, they can offer alternative ways to reduce stress and promote relaxation. Explore different options and find what resonates with you personally.

Conclusion

Incorporating relaxation techniques into your daily routine can have a profound impact on your mental health and well-being. Progressive muscle relaxation, deep breathing exercises, guided imagery, mindfulness meditation, and aromatherapy are some of the effective techniques you can try. Experiment with different methods and find what works best for you. Remember that consistency and practice are key to reaping the full benefits of these techniques. By making relaxation a priority, you can reduce stress, improve your overall mental health, and create a greater sense of balance and peace in your life.

Mindfulness-Based Sleep Practices

In this section, we will explore the concept of mindfulness-based sleep practices and how they can contribute to improved sleep and overall mental well-being. Sleep is a vital part of our daily lives, and getting sufficient restful sleep is crucial for maintaining good mental health. However, many individuals struggle with sleep-related issues such as insomnia, restless sleep, or difficulty falling asleep. Mindfulness-based sleep practices offer a unique and effective approach to addressing these challenges and promoting better sleep hygiene.

Understanding Mindfulness

Before delving into mindfulness-based sleep practices, it is important to have a clear understanding of what mindfulness entails. Mindfulness is a practice derived from Buddhist meditation, which involves paying deliberate attention to the present moment with a non-judgmental and accepting attitude. It is about being fully present and aware of our thoughts, emotions, bodily sensations, and the surrounding environment.

In the context of sleep, mindfulness can be applied to cultivate a state of relaxation and readiness for sleep. By practicing mindfulness, we can train our minds to let go of racing thoughts, worries, and distractions that often keep us awake. It allows us to be more attuned to our body's signals and helps create a sense of calm and tranquility conducive to sleep.

Techniques for Mindfulness-Based Sleep Practices

There are several techniques and practices that can be incorporated into a mindfulness-based sleep routine. These practices aim to relax the mind and body, reduce stress, and create an optimal environment for restful sleep. Let's explore some of them:

1. Body Scan Meditation One technique widely used in mindfulness-based sleep practices is the body scan meditation. This practice involves systematically focusing your attention on different parts of the body and observing any sensations or tension present. By bringing awareness to each part of the body, you can consciously relax and release any physical tension that may be interfering with sleep.

To practice body scan meditation, find a comfortable position in bed, close your eyes, and start by bringing your attention to your toes. Notice any sensations, warmth, or tension in this area. Gradually move your attention up through each part of your body, from your feet to your head, bringing awareness to each body part and allowing any tension to melt away.

2. Mindful Breathing   Another effective technique for promoting relaxation and sleep is mindful breathing. This practice involves paying attention to the natural rhythm of your breath, anchoring your focus to the sensation of each inhalation and exhalation. By focusing on your breath, you can redirect your attention away from racing thoughts and create a sense of calm.

To practice mindful breathing, find a comfortable position in bed and bring your attention to your breath. Observe the sensation of the breath entering and leaving your body, without trying to control or manipulate it. If your mind wanders, gently bring your attention back to your breath, without judgment.

3. Guided Visualization   Guided visualization is another mindfulness-based practice that can help induce a state of relaxation before sleep. It involves using the power of imagination to create calming mental images that promote a sense of peace and tranquility.

To practice guided visualization, lie down comfortably in bed and close your eyes. Start by imagining yourself in a peaceful and serene setting, such as a beach or a forest. Engage your senses by visualizing vivid details, such as the sound of waves crashing or the smell of fresh pine trees. Allow yourself to fully immerse in this mental imagery, letting go of any tension or stress.

Benefits of Mindfulness-Based Sleep Practices

Mindfulness-based sleep practices offer numerous benefits for improving sleep quality and overall mental well-being. Here are some of the key advantages:

1. Stress Reduction   Mindfulness has been shown to effectively reduce stress and anxiety, which are common factors contributing to sleep disturbances. By practicing mindfulness before bed, you can alleviate stress and promote a sense of calm, making it easier to fall asleep and stay asleep throughout the night.

2. Enhanced Relaxation and Sleep Onset   The relaxation techniques involved in mindfulness-based sleep practices help create an optimal mental and physical state for sleep initiation. By calming the mind and easing physical tension, you can improve sleep onset, reducing the time it takes to fall asleep.

3. Improved Sleep Quality   Engaging in mindfulness-based sleep practices can enhance the overall quality of sleep. By reducing intrusive thoughts, worries, and distractions, you can experience deeper and more restorative sleep. This leads to waking up feeling refreshed and energized.

4.   Increased Self-Awareness   Mindfulness cultivates self-awareness, which includes recognizing sleep patterns, identifying potential sleep disruptors, and being attuned to the body's sleep needs. By developing this self-awareness, you can make more informed choices regarding sleep habits and create a sleep-friendly environment.

5.   Better Emotional Regulation   Mindfulness-based sleep practices can also contribute to better emotional regulation during waking hours. Improved sleep quality leads to increased emotional resilience, reduced irritability, and better management of daily stressors.

Applying Mindfulness-Based Sleep Practices

To effectively apply mindfulness-based sleep practices, it is important to incorporate them into a consistent sleep routine. Here are some tips to help you get started:

1. Establish a Bedtime Ritual   Create a calming bedtime ritual that includes mindfulness-based sleep practices. This can involve engaging in a body scan meditation, practicing mindful breathing, or engaging in guided visualization. The key is to make these practices a regular part of your nightly routine.

2.   Create a Sleep-Friendly Environment   Ensure your sleep environment is conducive to relaxation and sleep. Keep your bedroom cool, dark, and quiet, and remove any distractions that may interfere with sleep. Consider using scents, such as lavender, known for their soothing and sleep-inducing properties.

3.   Consistency is Key   Consistency is crucial when it comes to mindfulness-based sleep practices. Try to practice these techniques every night, even if it feels challenging at first. With time and regular practice, you will begin to reap the benefits of improved sleep and mental well-being.

4. Seek Support if Needed   If you continue to experience sleep difficulties despite incorporating mindfulness-based sleep practices, consider seeking support from a mental health professional or sleep specialist. They can provide guidance tailored to your specific needs and help address any underlying sleep disorders or conditions.

In conclusion, mindfulness-based sleep practices offer valuable tools to promote better sleep and overall mental well-being. By incorporating techniques such as body scan meditation, mindful breathing, and guided visualization into your bedtime routine, you can reduce stress, enhance relaxation, and improve sleep quality. Remember, patience and consistency are key when incorporating these practices into your daily life. So, why not give mindfulness-based sleep practices a try and experience the positive impact on your sleep and mental health?

Creating a Sleep-Friendly Environment

Having a sleep-friendly environment is crucial for promoting restful and quality sleep. When our sleep environment is optimized, it can help improve the quantity and quality of our sleep, leading to overall better mental health and well-being. In this section, we will explore various strategies and tips for creating a sleep-friendly environment.

Optimizing the Bedroom

The bedroom plays a significant role in our sleep quality. It should be a sanctuary dedicated to sleep and relaxation. Here are some tips to create a sleep-friendly bedroom:

1. Darkness: Ensure that your bedroom is as dark as possible during sleep. Use blackout curtains or blinds to block out external sources of light, such as streetlights or sunlight. Light exposure at night can disrupt the natural sleep-wake cycle.

2. Noise Reduction: Minimize noise disturbances or mask them with soothing sounds. Use earplugs, a white noise machine, or a fan to block or mask noise that may disrupt your sleep. If you live in a noisy area or share the space with others, consider using a soundproofing solution.

3. Comfortable Mattress and Pillows: Invest in a comfortable mattress and pillows that suit your sleeping preferences. The right mattress and pillows can alleviate aches and pains, promote proper spinal alignment, and improve sleep quality.

4. Temperature Regulation: Keep your bedroom at a cool and comfortable temperature. The optimal temperature for sleep is typically between 60 to 67 degrees Fahrenheit (15 to 19 degrees Celsius). Use fans, air conditioners, or heaters to adjust the temperature according to your preference.

5. Decluttering: Keep your bedroom clean and free of clutter. A cluttered space can create a sense of chaos and make it difficult to relax. Organize your belongings and create a peaceful atmosphere that promotes relaxation and calmness.

6. Non-Stimulating Colors: Choose calming and soothing colors for your bedroom decor. Colors like soft blues, greens, and neutral tones can create a tranquil ambiance conducive to sleep. Avoid bright and stimulating colors, as they can have an energizing effect and hinder sleep.

7. Scent and Aromatherapy: Experiment with soothing scents or aromatherapy to create a relaxing atmosphere in your bedroom. Lavender, chamomile, and jasmine are known for their calming properties. Consider using essential oils, scented candles, or pillow sprays to enhance relaxation.

Establishing a Bedtime Routine

A consistent bedtime routine can signal to your body that it is time to wind down and prepare for sleep. It helps transition from wakefulness to sleep by promoting relaxation and reducing stress. Here are some essential elements to include in your bedtime routine:

1. Screen-Free Time: Power down electronic devices like smartphones, tablets, and laptops at least 30 minutes before bedtime. The blue light emitted by these devices can suppress the production of melatonin, a hormone that regulates sleep.

2. Relaxation Techniques: Engage in relaxation techniques that help calm the mind and body before sleep. This may include deep breathing exercises, progressive muscle relaxation, guided imagery, or gentle stretching.

3. Light Reading: Read a book or magazine that interests you but avoid stimulating or suspenseful material. Reading can promote relaxation and distract the mind from anxious or racing thoughts.

4. Herbal Tea: Enjoy a cup of herbal tea, such as chamomile or valerian root tea, which have natural calming properties. Avoid caffeinated beverages, as they can interfere with sleep.

5. Dim Lighting: Create a dim and cozy ambiance in your bedroom during your bedtime routine. Use soft lighting, such as bedside lamps or dimmers, to prepare your body for sleep.

6. Journaling: Take a few minutes to jot down your thoughts, worries, or reflections in a journal. This can help unload any mental burdens and promote a sense of peace before bedtime.

7. Regular Sleep Schedule: Establish a consistent sleep schedule by going to bed and waking up at the same time each day, even on weekends. Consistency helps regulate your body's internal clock and improves sleep quality.

Optimizing External Factors

In addition to the bedroom and bedtime routine, several external factors can influence your sleep quality. Consider the following strategies to optimize these factors:

1. Light Exposure: Exposure to natural light during the day can help regulate your circadian rhythm, promoting better sleep. Spend time outside, open curtains, or position your workspace near windows to maximize natural light exposure.

2. Limiting Stimulants: Reduce consumption of stimulants, such as caffeine and nicotine, especially close to bedtime. These substances can interfere with your ability to fall asleep and stay asleep.

3. Minimizing Fluid Intake: Limit your fluid intake close to bedtime to minimize disruptions from bathroom visits. However, ensure that you remain adequately hydrated throughout the day to support overall health.

4. Regular Exercise: Engage in regular physical activity, but avoid intense exercise close to bedtime. Exercise promotes better sleep, but the timing is crucial, as exercising too close to sleep can increase alertness and make it harder to fall asleep.

5. Limiting Napping: If you have trouble falling asleep or staying asleep at night, limit daytime napping. If you nap, keep it short (around 20-30 minutes) and avoid napping late in the day.

6. Reducing Stress: Practice stress management techniques, such as meditation, deep breathing, or engaging in hobbies you enjoy. High levels of stress can disrupt sleep, so it's important to find healthy ways to manage and reduce stress.

7. Creating a Tech-Free Zone: Keep electronic devices out of the bedroom or designate the bedroom as a tech-free zone. The presence of devices can be distracting and disrupt sleep. Use an alarm clock instead of relying on your phone for wake-up calls.

Creating a sleep-friendly environment involves optimizing various aspects of your bedroom, establishing a bedtime routine, and considering external factors that impact sleep. By implementing these strategies, you can create an atmosphere conducive to restful and rejuvenating sleep, which is essential for overall mental well-being. Remember, finding the right sleep environment may require some experimentation and personalization to suit your individual needs and preferences.

Physical Activity and Mental Health

Benefits of Exercise for Mental Well-being

Exercise has long been recognized as a key component of maintaining physical health, but its benefits extend far beyond that. Research has shown that engaging in regular physical activity can have a profound impact on mental well-being. In this section, we will explore the various ways in which exercise can improve mental health and provide strategies for incorporating exercise into your daily routine.

The Connection between Exercise and Mental Health

Before diving into the specific benefits of exercise for mental well-being, it's important to understand the underlying mechanisms that contribute to this connection. Exercise has been found to:

- **Neurochemical Effects:** Exercise stimulates the release of endorphins, which are chemicals in the brain that act as natural painkillers and mood elevators. Additionally, exercise increases the production of neurotransmitters like serotonin and dopamine, which play crucial roles in regulating mood and emotions.

* **Stress Reduction:** Physical activity has been shown to reduce levels of cortisol, the primary stress hormone in the body. Regular exercise can help alleviate symptoms of stress and anxiety, leading to a calmer and clearer mind.

* **Cognitive Enhancement:** Exercise promotes the growth and development of new neurons in the brain, particularly in areas associated with memory and learning. It also improves blood flow to the brain, increasing oxygen and nutrient delivery, which enhances cognitive function.

* **Social Interaction:** Many forms of exercise provide opportunities for social interaction, such as group fitness classes or team sports. Social connections are essential for mental well-being, as they provide support, companionship, and a sense of belonging.

Now that we understand the underlying mechanisms, let's explore the specific benefits of exercise for mental well-being.

Improvement in Mood and Emotional Well-being

One of the most well-known benefits of exercise for mental health is its ability to improve mood and emotional well-being. Engaging in physical activity stimulates the release of endorphins, which are known as "feel-good" chemicals. These endorphins interact with the receptors in your brain, reducing pain perception and creating a sense of happiness and euphoria. This boost in mood can be particularly helpful in alleviating symptoms of depression and anxiety.

Regular exercise has also been shown to reduce symptoms of stress and improve overall emotional well-being. When you engage in physical activity, you are providing an outlet for built-up tension and stress. This can lead to a greater sense of calm and relaxation, as well as improved sleep quality. Exercise can also serve as a distraction from negative thoughts and worries, allowing you to focus on the present moment and let go of stressors.

In addition to the neurochemical effects, the act of exercising itself can provide a sense of accomplishment and self-confidence. Setting and achieving fitness goals, no matter how small, can boost self-esteem and foster a positive body image. This can have a significant impact on mental well-being, as it promotes self-acceptance and a more positive outlook on life.

Reduction in Symptoms of Depression and Anxiety

Exercise has been widely studied as a potential treatment for depression and anxiety, and the results have been promising. Numerous studies have shown that regular physical activity can reduce symptoms of both conditions and improve overall mental health.

In the case of depression, exercise not only improves mood but also increases energy levels and reduces feelings of fatigue. It serves as a natural antidepressant by increasing the production of neurotransmitters like serotonin and dopamine, which are often imbalanced in individuals with depression.

For anxiety, exercise acts as a form of exposure therapy. When you engage in physical activity, your body experiences some of the same physiological responses as it does during moments of anxiety, such as increased heart rate and sweating. By repeatedly exposing yourself to these sensations in a controlled and non-threatening environment, you can build resilience and reduce anxiety symptoms over time.

It's important to note that exercise should not replace traditional therapies for depression and anxiety, but rather be used as a complementary strategy. If you are experiencing symptoms of depression or anxiety, it's important to seek professional help and consider incorporating exercise into your overall treatment plan.

Enhanced Cognitive Function and Memory

Exercise not only benefits our mood and emotional well-being, but it also has the power to enhance cognitive function and improve memory. Research has consistently shown that regular physical activity is associated with better cognitive performance across all age groups.

Physical activity increases blood flow to the brain, delivering oxygen and nutrients that are essential for optimal brain function. It also promotes the growth of new neurons in the hippocampus, a region of the brain that plays a key role in memory and learning. This neurogenesis, combined with increased neurotransmitter production, leads to improved cognitive function, enhanced focus, and better information retention.

Additionally, exercise helps to regulate stress hormones, such as cortisol, which can impair cognitive function when present in excessive amounts. By reducing stress levels, exercise allows for clearer thinking and improved mental clarity.

Tips for Incorporating Exercise into Your Routine

Now that we understand the benefits of exercise for mental well-being, let's discuss some practical tips for incorporating physical activity into your daily routine:

1. **Start Slow:** If you're new to exercise or haven't been active for a while, start with small steps. Begin by incorporating short walks into your day and gradually increase the duration and intensity of your workouts.

2. **Find Activities You Enjoy:** Choose activities that you find enjoyable and that align with your interests. Whether it's dancing, swimming, or hiking, engaging in activities you love will make it easier to stick to an exercise routine.

3. **Set Realistic Goals:** Set realistic and achievable goals that align with your current fitness level. This will help you stay motivated and track your progress over time.

4. **Make it Social:** Consider joining a fitness class, sports team, or exercise group to make your workouts more social. Not only will this provide you with motivation and support, but it will also enhance your overall well-being.

5. **Mix it Up:** Vary your exercise routine to prevent boredom and engage different muscle groups. Try different forms of exercise, such as cardiovascular workouts, strength training, and flexibility exercises.

6. **Fit it into Your Schedule:** Find pockets of time throughout your day where you can incorporate physical activity. Whether it's taking the stairs instead of the elevator or doing a quick workout during your lunch break, every little bit counts.

Remember, the goal is to make exercise a consistent and enjoyable part of your life. By finding activities you love and integrating them into your routine, you can reap the many mental health benefits of physical activity.

In conclusion, exercise is not only beneficial for physical health but also plays a crucial role in promoting mental well-being. From improving mood and reducing symptoms of depression and anxiety to enhancing cognitive function and memory, physical activity has a profound impact on mental health. By incorporating exercise into your daily routine and finding activities you enjoy, you can reap the numerous benefits and improve your overall quality of life.

Types of Physical Activity for Optimal Mental Health

Physical activity has been widely recognized as a key component of maintaining good physical health. However, research has also shown that engaging in regular physical activity can have significant benefits for mental health and overall well-being. In this section, we will explore different types of physical activities that have been found to be particularly effective in promoting optimal mental health.

Aerobic Exercise

Aerobic exercise, also known as cardiovascular exercise, refers to activities that increase your heart rate and improve the efficiency of your cardiovascular system. This type of exercise is known to have numerous mental health benefits. When you engage in aerobic exercise, your body releases endorphins, which are natural chemicals that act as mood enhancers and reduce feelings of stress and anxiety.

Some common forms of aerobic exercise include jogging, swimming, cycling, and dancing. These activities can be easily incorporated into your daily routine and can be done individually or in groups. Engaging in aerobic exercise for at least 30 minutes a day, five days a week, has been shown to have significant positive effects on mental health.

Strength Training

Strength training, also referred to as resistance or weight training, involves using resistance to build muscular strength and endurance. While the primary focus of strength training is often physical fitness and body composition, research has shown that it also has notable benefits for mental health.

Strength training promotes the release of endorphins, similar to aerobic exercise, which can help to alleviate symptoms of depression and anxiety. Additionally, strength training can improve self-esteem and body image, leading to a greater sense of well-being and confidence.

Various forms of strength training can be practiced, including using free weights, weight machines, or even your own body weight. Aim to incorporate strength training exercises into your routine at least two to three times a week, focusing on different muscle groups each session.

Mind-Body Exercises

Mind-body exercises combine physical movement with mental focus to promote relaxation, mindfulness, and overall mental well-being. These activities are particularly effective in reducing stress and improving mental clarity.

Yoga is one of the most well-known mind-body exercises. It involves a series of poses, breathing techniques, and meditation to promote physical and mental balance. Regular practice of yoga has been shown to reduce anxiety, improve mood, and increase resilience to stress.

Tai Chi is another mind-body exercise that originated in ancient China. It involves slow and controlled movements, alongside deep breathing and mental concentration. Tai Chi has been found to have positive effects on mental health, including reducing symptoms of depression and improving cognitive function.

Outdoor Activities

Engaging in physical activity outdoors provides additional mental health benefits compared to indoor activities. Spending time in nature has been shown to promote relaxation, boost mood, and reduce symptoms of stress and anxiety. The fresh air, natural scenery, and exposure to sunlight can greatly contribute to your overall well-being.

Outdoor activities can vary widely and can include walking or jogging in a local park, hiking in the mountains, cycling along scenic trails, or participating in outdoor sports such as soccer or basketball. Aim to spend time outdoors regularly to reap the mental health benefits that nature has to offer.

Team Sports and Group Activities

Participating in team sports or group activities can have significant positive effects on mental health. Engaging in physical activity with others fosters social connections and a sense of belonging, which are important for overall well-being.

Team sports such as soccer, basketball, or volleyball not only provide physical exercise but also promote teamwork, cooperation, and communication skills. The camaraderie and support from teammates can enhance mood, reduce stress, and improve self-esteem.

Group activities such as dance classes, group fitness workouts, or martial arts training can also provide similar mental health benefits. The social interaction and shared experiences in these activities can boost mood and create a sense of community.

Conclusion

Engaging in regular physical activity is essential for optimal mental health. The types of physical activities discussed in this section, including aerobic exercise, strength training, mind-body exercises, outdoor activities, and team sports/group activities, offer unique benefits for mental well-being. Incorporate a variety of these activities into your routine to enjoy the physical and mental health benefits they provide. Remember, physical activity should be enjoyable, so choose activities that you genuinely enjoy and that fit your individual preferences and abilities. Stay active, and take care of your mental health while doing so.

Exercise as a Coping Mechanism

Exercise has long been recognized as a powerful tool for promoting physical health and well-being. But its benefits extend beyond the physical realm, as it also plays a significant role in maintaining and improving mental health. In this section, we will explore how exercise can be used as a coping mechanism for managing stress, anxiety, and other mental health challenges.

Understanding the Connection between Exercise and Mental Health

Exercise affects the brain in a variety of ways, leading to positive changes in mood, cognition, and overall mental well-being. When we engage in physical activity, our bodies release chemicals called endorphins, which are known to promote feelings of happiness and reduce pain perception. Additionally, exercise increases the production of neurotransmitters such as serotonin, dopamine, and norepinephrine, all of which play a vital role in regulating mood and emotions.

Regular exercise has been shown to alleviate symptoms of anxiety and depression. It can help reduce feelings of stress, improve sleep quality, and boost self-esteem. Exercise also provides a healthy outlet for releasing pent-up energy and emotions, allowing individuals to manage their mental health challenges in a positive and constructive way.

Types of Exercise for Optimal Mental Health

While any form of physical activity can have mental health benefits, certain types of exercise have been found to be particularly effective in promoting optimal mental well-being. Here are some examples:

- **Aerobic exercise:** Activities such as brisk walking, running, cycling, swimming, and dancing increase heart rate and oxygen flow to the brain. Aerobic exercise has been linked to improved mood, reduced symptoms of depression, and enhanced cognitive function.

- **Strength training:** Engaging in resistance and weightlifting exercises not only improves physical strength and body composition but also enhances mental resilience. Strength training has been found to reduce symptoms of anxiety and depression and boost self-esteem.

+ **Mind-body exercises:** Practices like yoga, tai chi, and qigong combine physical movement with relaxation and mindfulness techniques. These exercises promote a sense of calm, improve body awareness, and reduce stress levels.

+ **Team sports and group activities:** Participating in team sports or group exercise classes provides opportunities for social interaction and support, which can have positive effects on mental health. Being part of a supportive group can boost motivation, provide a sense of belonging, and enhance overall well-being.

It's important to find an exercise routine that suits your preferences and fits into your lifestyle. Experimenting with different activities can help you discover what works best for you and brings you the most enjoyment.

Integrating Exercise into Daily Life

Incorporating exercise into your daily routine doesn't have to be complicated or time-consuming. Here are some strategies to help you make exercise a regular part of your life:

+ **Start small:** If you're new to exercise or have been inactive for a while, begin with small, achievable goals. Gradually increase the duration and intensity of your workouts as you build strength and stamina.

+ **Make it enjoyable:** Choose activities that you genuinely enjoy and look forward to. If you find exercise fun, you will be more likely to stick with it in the long run. Consider trying new activities or joining exercise classes that align with your interests.

+ **Build movement into your day:** Look for opportunities to incorporate physical activity into your daily routine. Take the stairs instead of the elevator, walk or cycle to work or school, or schedule active breaks during sedentary tasks.

+ **Set realistic goals:** Set realistic and achievable goals for yourself, both in terms of fitness milestones and time commitment. This will help you stay motivated and prevent feelings of overwhelm or burnout.

+ **Find an exercise buddy:** Exercising with a friend or family member can make the experience more enjoyable and provide additional motivation and accountability.

Remember, the key is to establish a sustainable exercise routine that you can maintain in the long term. Consistency is more important than intensity, so focus on creating a habit of regular physical activity rather than pushing yourself to the limit.

Exercise and Mental Health - A Real-World Example

To illustrate the positive impact of exercise on mental health, let's consider the case of Sarah, a 30-year-old office worker experiencing chronic stress and anxiety. Sarah decides to incorporate regular exercise into her daily routine to help manage her symptoms.

She starts by scheduling three 30-minute walks during her lunch breaks each week. During these walks, she takes deep breaths, focuses on her surroundings, and appreciates the natural beauty around her. Gradually, Sarah increases the duration and intensity of her walks, transforming them into brisk walking sessions.

After a few weeks, Sarah notices that her walks not only have a positive effect on her physical health, but also help her manage stress and anxiety more effectively. She feels calmer, more energized, and better able to concentrate at work. Sarah becomes more motivated to continue her exercise routine, eventually adding strength training and yoga classes to her schedule.

Sarah's story exemplifies how exercise can serve as a coping mechanism for managing stress and improving mental health. By incorporating exercise into her daily routine and adapting it to her preferences, Sarah takes an active role in her mental well-being and experiences positive changes in her overall quality of life.

Key Takeaways

+ Exercise has a profound impact on mental health by improving mood, reducing stress, and boosting self-esteem.

+ Aerobic exercise, strength training, mind-body exercises, and group activities all contribute to optimal mental well-being.

+ Finding enjoyable activities and integrating exercise into your daily routine can make it easier to stick with an exercise routine.

+ Start small, set realistic goals, and seek support from exercise buddies to maintain motivation and accountability.

- Exercise as a coping mechanism can lead to significant improvements in mental health, allowing individuals to better manage stress and other mental health challenges.

Exercise is a powerful tool that individuals can harness to support their mental health. By incorporating regular physical activity into their lives, individuals can experience the many benefits that exercise offers in terms of mood enhancement, stress reduction, and overall well-being. So put on your sneakers, step outside, and discover the positive impact exercise can have on your mental health.

Integrating Physical Activity into Daily Routine

Physical activity plays a crucial role in promoting optimal mental health and overall well-being. Engaging in regular exercise has been linked to a myriad of benefits, including improved mood, reduced stress levels, increased cognitive function, and enhanced self-esteem. However, finding the time and motivation to incorporate physical activity into our busy daily routines can be a challenge. In this section, we will explore strategies and practical tips for integrating physical activity into our daily lives.

Understanding the Importance of Physical Activity

Before delving into the specific strategies, it is essential to understand the significance of physical activity for mental health. Exercise has been shown to increase the production of endorphins, which are neurotransmitters responsible for elevating mood and reducing feelings of pain and stress. Additionally, regular physical activity stimulates the release of serotonin and dopamine, neurotransmitters associated with feelings of happiness and pleasure.

Moreover, exercise improves blood circulation, which ensures optimal oxygen and nutrient delivery to the brain. This increased blood flow enhances cognitive function, memory, and concentration. Research has also shown that physical activity promotes the growth of new neurons and strengthens neural connections, leading to improved brain health and resilience.

Identifying Opportunities for Physical Activity

Many of us mistakenly believe that physical activity can only be achieved through structured exercise programs or gym workouts. However, integrating physical activity into our daily routines does not necessarily require a significant time commitment or the need for specialized equipment. Here are some simple yet effective ways to incorporate physical activity into your daily life:

1. Active commuting: Consider walking, biking, or using public transportation for your daily commute instead of relying solely on cars or elevators. This can provide an opportunity to engage in physical activity while also reducing carbon footprint.

2. Taking active breaks: Break up prolonged periods of sitting or desk work by incorporating short bursts of physical activity. You can perform stretching exercises, go for a short walk, or do a few sets of squats or lunges. These quick activity breaks not only energize you but also prevent the negative health effects of prolonged sitting.

3. Active household chores: Engage in household chores that require physical exertion, such as gardening or cleaning. These activities not only contribute to maintaining a tidy living space but also provide an opportunity for physical activity.

4. Lunchtime walks: Instead of spending your lunch break at your desk, use that time to go for a brisk walk. Walking outdoors in nature can have additional mental health benefits, such as reducing stress and promoting relaxation.

5. Stair climbing: Make a conscious effort to use the stairs instead of elevators whenever possible. Climbing stairs is an excellent cardiovascular exercise that also strengthens leg muscles.

6. Active socializing: Rather than meeting friends or colleagues in a sedentary environment, opt for activities that involve movement. This could include going for a hike, playing a sport, or even taking a dance class together.

Creating an Exercise Routine

While incorporating incidental physical activity into your daily routine is beneficial, it is also essential to establish a regular exercise routine. Having a structured exercise plan ensures that you engage in physical activity at a level that promotes cardiovascular fitness and strength. Here are some tips for creating an exercise routine:

1. Set realistic goals: Start by setting achievable goals that consider your current fitness level and schedule. Gradually increase the intensity and duration of your exercise sessions over time.

2. Find activities you enjoy: Experiment with different types of exercise, such as jogging, swimming, cycling, or dancing, to find activities that you genuinely enjoy. Enjoyment increases the likelihood of sticking to an exercise routine.

3. Mix it up: Avoid monotony by incorporating a variety of exercises into your routine. This not only keeps things interesting but also helps to work different muscle groups and prevent overuse injuries.

4. Schedule regular exercise sessions: Dedicate specific time slots for exercise in your daily or weekly schedule, treating them as non-negotiable appointments. Consistency is key for reaping the long-term benefits of exercise.

5. Monitor your progress: Keep track of your exercise sessions, noting the duration, intensity, and type of activity. This can help you set new goals and motivate you by visualizing your progress.

6. Seek support and accountability: Consider exercising with a friend or joining group exercise classes. Having a workout buddy or a fitness community can provide support, motivation, and accountability.

7. Listen to your body: Pay attention to how your body feels during and after exercise. Take rest days when needed and modify your routine if you experience any pain or discomfort.

Utilizing Technology and Apps

In the digital age, there are numerous technology-driven tools and apps available to support physical activity and make it more engaging. Here are some examples:

1. Fitness tracking devices: Wearable fitness trackers, such as smartwatches or fitness bands, can monitor your physical activity levels, heart rate, and sleep patterns. These devices provide real-time feedback and motivate you to achieve your fitness goals.

2. Exercise apps: There are plenty of smartphone apps available that offer guided workouts, exercise routines, and progress tracking. These apps can help you structure your workouts and maintain consistency.

3. Virtual classes: Online platforms and fitness apps provide access to a wide range of virtual exercise classes, including yoga, HIIT, and dance. These classes can be done from the comfort of your home, providing flexibility and convenience.

4. Gamification: Some fitness apps incorporate gamification elements, turning physical activity into a fun and interactive experience. These apps may use challenges, rewards, and virtual characters to motivate and engage users.

Prioritizing Self-Care and Rest

It is important to strike a balance between regular physical activity and rest and recovery. Giving your body the time it needs to rest and recuperate is crucial for preventing burnout and injuries. Here are some self-care practices to incorporate into your routine:

1. Rest days: Schedule regular rest days to allow your body to recover from exercise. Engage in activities that promote relaxation and rejuvenation, such as taking a bath, practicing mindfulness, or engaging in a hobby.

2. Quality sleep: Ensure that you are getting adequate sleep to support your physical activity levels. Prioritize establishing a consistent sleep routine and create a sleep-friendly environment.

3. Proper nutrition: Fueling your body with a balanced diet is essential for optimal physical performance and recovery. Consume a variety of nutrient-dense foods, including protein, complex carbohydrates, healthy fats, and fruits and vegetables.

4. Hydration: Stay well-hydrated before, during, and after exercise to support your body's functions and prevent dehydration. Listen to your body's thirst signals and drink water regularly throughout the day.

An Unconventional Approach: Deskercise

For individuals with sedentary jobs that require long hours of sitting, it can be challenging to incorporate physical activity into their workday. However, there is an unconventional approach called "deskercise" that can help combat the negative effects of prolonged sitting. Deskercise involves performing simple exercises or stretches at your desk to break up sedentary behavior. Here are some examples:

1. Seated leg raises: While sitting, extend one leg straight and hold for a few seconds. Lower it back down, and repeat with the other leg. This exercise helps strengthen the leg muscles and improve blood circulation.

2. Shoulder rolls: Sit up straight and roll your shoulders backward, then forward, in a circular motion. This helps relieve tension in the neck and shoulder muscles.

3. Chair squats: Stand up from your chair and lower yourself back down as if you were going to sit, but stop just before your bottom touches the seat. Repeat this movement several times to engage your leg muscles.

4. Wrist stretches: Extend one arm in front of you with your palm facing up. With the other hand, gently pull back your fingers and hold for a few seconds. This exercise stretches the muscles in your forearm and can help prevent wrist pain.

5. Neck stretches: Slowly tilt your head to one side, bringing your ear toward your shoulder. Hold this stretch for a few seconds, then repeat on the opposite side. This exercise helps relieve tension in the neck and upper back.

Deskercise can be tailored to individual preferences and work constraints. Incorporating these short exercises throughout the workday improves circulation, reduces muscle stiffness, and boosts overall energy levels.

Conclusion

Integrating physical activity into our daily routines is crucial for maintaining optimal mental health. By identifying opportunities for physical activity, creating a structured exercise routine, utilizing technology and apps, prioritizing self-care and rest, and trying unconventional approaches like deskercise, we can make physical activity an integral part of our lives. Remember, even small and consistent efforts towards incorporating physical activity can have a significant positive impact on our well-being. So, let's get moving and reap the many rewards of an active lifestyle.

Mind-Body Forms of Exercise

In this section, we will explore the concept of mind-body forms of exercise and their significance in promoting mental health. These forms of exercise focus on the connection between the mind and body, emphasizing the integration of physical movement with mental awareness and mindfulness.

Understanding the Mind-Body Connection

The mind-body connection refers to the intricate relationship between our thoughts, emotions, and physical well-being. It recognizes that our mental and emotional states can significantly impact our physical health and vice versa. Mind-body forms of exercise aim to leverage this connection by incorporating mindful movement and intentional awareness into physical activities.

Mind-Body Exercise Techniques

There are various mind-body exercise techniques that individuals can incorporate into their routine to enhance mental health and well-being. Let's explore some common and effective techniques:

1. Yoga   Yoga is a popular mind-body exercise that combines physical postures, breathing techniques, and meditation. It promotes flexibility, strength, and balance, while also fostering mental clarity, stress reduction, and relaxation. Practicing yoga can help calm the mind, improve concentration, and cultivate a sense of inner peace.

2. Tai Chi   Tai Chi is an ancient Chinese martial art that involves slow, flowing movements combined with deep breathing and focused attention. This gentle and low-impact exercise promotes balance, flexibility, and coordination. Tai Chi also encourages relaxation, stress reduction, and increased energy levels. It can be particularly beneficial for individuals seeking a mind-body exercise that is accessible to people of all ages and fitness levels.

3. Pilates   Pilates is a body conditioning method that focuses on core strength, flexibility, and body awareness. It incorporates controlled movements and emphasizes proper alignment, breathing, and balance. Through Pilates, individuals can improve their physical strength, posture, and stamina, while also enhancing concentration, body-mind connection, and overall relaxation.

4.   Qigong   Qigong is an ancient Chinese practice that combines gentle movements, breath control, and guided meditation. It aims to balance and enhance the flow of energy in the body, promoting overall well-being. Qigong exercises are often characterized by slow, repetitive motions, designed to cultivate a calm mind, reduce stress, and restore inner harmony.

Benefits of Mind-Body Forms of Exercise

Mind-body forms of exercise offer numerous benefits for mental health and well-being. Here are some key advantages:

1. **Stress Reduction**   Engaging in mind-body exercises can help alleviate stress and promote relaxation. By focusing on the present moment and connecting with the body's movements, individuals can experience a sense of calm and reduced mental tension. The combination of physical movement and mindfulness allows for the release of endorphins, which are natural stress-fighting chemicals in the body.

2. **Improved Mental Clarity and Focus**   Mind-body exercises require mental focus and concentration, which can enhance cognitive function and mental clarity. Regular practice can sharpen attention, improve memory, and increase overall mental acuity. By engaging both the mind and body, these exercises can help individuals cultivate mindfulness, enabling them to stay present and focused.

3. **Emotional Well-being**   Mind-body exercises have a positive impact on emotional well-being by promoting self-awareness and emotional regulation. The mindful approach to movement allows individuals to connect with their emotions and develop a greater understanding of their mental states. This increased self-awareness can lead to improved emotional intelligence, better coping mechanisms, and a greater sense of overall emotional well-being.

4. **Physical Fitness and Flexibility**   While mind-body exercises prioritize mental well-being, they also offer physical fitness benefits. These exercises help improve strength, flexibility, balance, and posture. Regular practice can help individuals increase body awareness, prevent injuries, and enhance overall physical fitness. The combination of physical and mental benefits makes mind-body exercises a holistic approach to well-being.

Incorporating Mind-Body Forms of Exercise into Your Routine

To incorporate mind-body forms of exercise into your routine, consider the following tips:

1. **Start Slowly**   If you are new to mind-body exercises, start with beginner-friendly classes or tutorials. Begin by practicing for shorter durations and gradually increase the intensity and duration as you become more comfortable.

2. Find a Qualified Instructor   Seek out certified instructors who specialize in the specific form of exercise you are interested in. A qualified instructor can guide you through proper techniques, offer modifications, and ensure your safety during the practice.

3. Practice Regularly   Consistency is key when it comes to mind-body exercises. Aim to incorporate these exercises into your routine at least a few times a week to experience the maximum benefits. Establishing a regular practice will help you develop mindfulness skills and see long-term improvements in mental and physical well-being.

4. Listen to Your Body   Pay attention to your body's limitations and avoid pushing yourself beyond your capabilities. Mind-body exercises are meant to be gentle and non-competitive. Honor your body's needs and practice self-care by modifying movements or taking breaks when necessary.

5. Combine with Other Strategies   Remember that mind-body exercises are just one component of a comprehensive mental health strategy. Combine these exercises with other self-care practices such as healthy eating, quality sleep, and consistent stress management techniques for optimal results.

Conclusion

In conclusion, mind-body forms of exercise offer a powerful approach to promoting mental health and overall well-being. Incorporating these exercises into your routine can reduce stress, improve mental clarity, enhance emotional well-being, and foster physical fitness and flexibility. By embracing the mind-body connection, you can achieve a holistic balance that nurtures both your body and mind. So, why not embark on your journey towards optimal mental health by exploring one of these mind-body exercises today?

Remember, the key is to start slow, seek guidance from qualified instructors, practice regularly, and listen to your body. Embrace the mind-body connection and reap the incredible benefits these exercises have to offer. Trust the process, be patient with yourself, and enjoy the journey to a healthier mind and body.

Time Management and Productivity

Strategies for Effective Time Management

Effective time management is crucial for maintaining good mental health and overall well-being. It involves prioritizing tasks, setting goals, and utilizing tools and techniques to optimize productivity. In this section, we will explore various strategies for managing time effectively and achieving a healthy work-life balance.

Prioritizing Tasks

One of the fundamental principles of time management is prioritizing tasks based on their importance and urgency. By focusing on the most critical and time-sensitive tasks first, you can ensure that you are making progress on the most essential aspects of your work or personal life.

To prioritize effectively, you can use different approaches, such as the Eisenhower Matrix. This matrix categorizes tasks into four quadrants:

- **Urgent and Important:** Tasks that require immediate attention and are critical to your goals. These tasks should be your top priority.

- **Important but not Urgent:** Tasks that contribute to your long-term goals but don't require immediate attention. Dedicate specific time slots to work on these tasks to ensure they are not neglected.

- **Urgent but not Important:** Tasks that demand immediate attention but don't align with your long-term goals. Delegate or postpone these tasks whenever possible to focus on more critical activities.

- **Not Urgent and not Important:** Tasks that have little to no impact on your goals or overall well-being. Minimize or eliminate these tasks to free up time for more important activities.

By using the Eisenhower Matrix or a similar method, you can enhance your ability to prioritize effectively and allocate time to the most valuable tasks.

Setting SMART Goals

Setting goals is essential for staying motivated and maintaining a sense of direction. However, it's crucial to set goals that are specific, measurable, attainable, relevant, and time-bound (SMART).

Specific goals provide clarity and focus. Instead of setting a vague goal like "increase productivity," a specific goal would be "complete three major project tasks by the end of the week."

Measurable goals allow you to track progress and celebrate achievements. For example, you could set a goal to "increase sales by 10% within three months."

Attainable goals are challenging yet realistic. It's important to set goals that push you outside your comfort zone but are still within your capabilities.

Relevant goals align with your overall vision and aspirations. They reflect what is truly important to you and contribute to your long-term success and well-being.

Time-bound goals have a specific deadline or timeline. This helps create a sense of urgency and prevents procrastination. For example, you could set a goal to "complete a chapter of the book by the end of the month."

By following the SMART goal framework, you can effectively structure your time and efforts towards meaningful outcomes.

Applying Time Blocking Techniques

Time blocking is a popular time management technique that involves scheduling specific blocks of time for different tasks or activities. It helps create structure and eliminates the tendency to multitask or get distracted.

To apply time blocking effectively, start by identifying your most productive hours. These are the times when you are most focused and motivated. Schedule your most critical and challenging tasks during these peak hours.

Break your day into manageable chunks and allocate specific time blocks for different activities. For example, you could allocate a block from 8 am to 10 am for deep work, another block from 10 am to 11 am for meetings, and so on.

When time blocking, it's essential to be realistic about the time required for each task. Allow buffer time between blocks for breaks and unexpected interruptions.

Remember to include time blocks for personal activities and self-care, such as exercise, relaxation, and spending time with loved ones. This helps maintain a healthy work-life balance and prevents burnout.

Utilizing Technology Tools

In today's digital age, numerous time management tools and apps can help streamline and optimize your workflow. These tools can assist with task tracking, project management, and time tracking, among others.

Task management tools like Todoist, Asana, or Trello can help organize and prioritize tasks. They allow you to create to-do lists, set deadlines, and track progress.

Digital calendars, such as Google Calendar or Microsoft Outlook, can help you manage your schedule effectively. You can block out time for specific tasks, set reminders, and synchronize your calendar across different devices.

Time-tracking apps like Toggl or RescueTime can provide insights into how you spend your time. They help identify time-wasting activities and highlight areas for improvement.

Additionally, productivity apps like Forest or StayFocusd can help limit distractions caused by social media or other online platforms.

While technology tools can be beneficial, it's important to use them strategically and not become overwhelmed by the sheer number of options. Choose tools that align with your needs and preferences, and experiment to find the ones that work best for you.

Effective Delegation and Outsourcing

Effective delegation is a valuable skill in time management. Learning to delegate tasks to capable individuals or outsourcing certain activities can free up your time for more critical responsibilities.

When delegating, consider the strengths and expertise of your team members or colleagues. Assign tasks that align with their skills and provide clear instructions and expectations.

Outsourcing is another option for tasks that can be handled by external professionals or services. For example, you might consider outsourcing administrative work or hiring a virtual assistant to manage your emails.

Remember that effective delegation requires trust and effective communication. Regularly check in with the individuals or services you have delegated to, provide necessary support, and ensure that the tasks are on track.

The Pomodoro Technique

The Pomodoro Technique is a time management method developed by Francesco Cirillo. It involves breaking work into intervals called "Pomodoros," traditionally 25 minutes in duration, separated by short breaks.

To apply the Pomodoro Technique, follow these steps:

1. Choose a task to work on.

2. Set a timer for 25 minutes and focus solely on the task during this time.

3. When the timer goes off, take a short break of around five minutes.

4. Repeat the process, completing four Pomodoros, and then take a longer break of 15-30 minutes.

The Pomodoro Technique helps improve focus and prevent burnout by breaking work into manageable chunks and providing regular breaks for rest and rejuvenation.

Avoiding Procrastination

Procrastination can seriously hinder effective time management and productivity. Recognizing the factors that contribute to procrastination and implementing strategies to overcome it can significantly improve your ability to manage time effectively.

One effective strategy to combat procrastination is the "5-Second Rule" introduced by Mel Robbins. When faced with a task, count down from five and then take immediate action. This simple technique helps you overcome the initial resistance and momentum loss associated with procrastination.

Another strategy is to break large or overwhelming tasks into smaller, more manageable subtasks. This approach makes the task appear less daunting and allows you to make progress gradually.

Identifying and eliminating distractions is crucial for minimizing procrastination. Turn off notifications on your phone, close unnecessary tabs on your computer, and create a distraction-free environment that enables focused work.

Lastly, integrating accountability measures can help combat procrastination. Share your goals and deadlines with a trusted friend, colleague, or mentor who can hold you accountable. Alternatively, use apps or productivity systems that track your progress and provide reminders.

Unconventional yet Effective Techniques

While traditional time management techniques are valuable, it can be beneficial to experiment with unconventional approaches to optimize productivity and manage time effectively. Here are a few unconventional techniques that have yielded positive results for many individuals:

+ **The Two-Minute Rule:** If a task takes less than two minutes to complete, do it immediately instead of adding it to your to-do list. This prevents small, quick tasks from piling up and creating mental clutter.

+ **The 80/20 Rule (Pareto Principle):** The 80/20 rule states that 80% of the results come from 20% of the efforts. Identify the tasks or activities that yield the most significant results and prioritize them accordingly.

+ **Time Capsule Technique:** Set a specific time limit, such as 30 minutes or an hour, and challenge yourself to complete as much work as possible within that time frame. The sense of urgency and competition against the clock can enhance focus and productivity.

+ **The Power of Visualization:** Spend a few minutes visualizing yourself successfully completing the tasks at hand. Visualizing positive outcomes can increase motivation and help overcome procrastination.

Remember that not all techniques work universally. Experiment with different techniques and find the ones that resonate with you and align with your personal preferences and working style.

Conclusion

Effective time management is a critical aspect of maintaining mental health and achieving success in various areas of life. By prioritizing tasks, setting SMART goals, utilizing time blocking techniques, leveraging technology tools, delegating effectively, and implementing strategies to combat procrastination, you can optimize your productivity, reduce stress, and create a healthier work-life balance.

Remember, time management is a skill that requires practice and continuous improvement. Reflect on your experiences, identify areas for growth, and adapt your strategies accordingly. With dedication and consistent effort, you can develop strong time management skills and enhance your overall well-being.

Overcoming Procrastination and Boosting Motivation

Procrastination is a common struggle for many people when it comes to completing tasks or reaching their goals. It is a tendency to delay or postpone tasks, which often leads to increased stress and decreased productivity. In this section, we will explore strategies to overcome procrastination and boost motivation to help you achieve your mental health goals.

Understanding Procrastination

Procrastination can be influenced by various factors, including fear of failure, perfectionism, lack of motivation, and feeling overwhelmed by the task at hand. It not only affects our productivity but also impacts our mental well-being. To effectively overcome procrastination, it is important to understand its underlying causes.

One common reason for procrastination is the fear of failure. Setting high standards for ourselves can lead to a fear of not meeting expectations, which in turn causes us to delay starting or completing a task. Another factor is perfectionism, the belief that everything must be perfect before taking action. This mentality can paralyze us and prevent us from moving forward. Additionally, feeling overwhelmed by a task can lead to procrastination, as we may struggle to break it down into smaller, manageable steps.

Breaking the Procrastination Cycle

To break the cycle of procrastination, it is necessary to develop effective strategies that enhance motivation and minimize the impact of underlying factors. Here are some techniques you can implement:

1. **Set SMART goals:** Specific, Measurable, Achievable, Relevant, and Time-bound (SMART) goals provide a clear structure for your tasks, making them more manageable. Break down your larger goals into smaller, actionable steps, and assign realistic deadlines to each step.

2. **Prioritize tasks:** Create a to-do list and prioritize tasks based on urgency and importance. By focusing on high-priority tasks, you can avoid becoming overwhelmed and stay motivated to complete them.

3. **Use the Pomodoro Technique:** The Pomodoro Technique involves working in short bursts of intense focus, typically 25 minutes, followed by a short break. This technique helps maintain concentration and prevents burnout, increasing productivity and motivation.

4. **Practice self-compassion:** Be kind to yourself and acknowledge that everyone faces challenges and setbacks. Avoid self-criticism and negative self-talk that may contribute to feelings of inadequacy and lead to procrastination. Cultivate self-compassion by focusing on self-improvement rather than perfection.

5. **Break tasks into smaller steps:** Large tasks can be intimidating and overwhelming, leading to procrastination. Break them down into smaller, manageable steps to make them less daunting. Celebrate your progress as you

complete each step, which boosts motivation and provides a sense of accomplishment.

Boosting Motivation

Motivation plays a key role in overcoming procrastination and staying focused on your goals. Here are some strategies to boost your motivation:

1. **Find your "why":** Identify the reasons why achieving a particular goal is important to you. Connect with your deeper motivation, whether it is improving your mental well-being, reaching personal growth milestones, or making a positive impact on others. Keeping your motivation in mind can help you stay committed and focused.

2. **Visualize success:** Imagine yourself successfully completing the task or achieving your goal. Visualize the positive outcomes and the satisfaction you will experience. This mental imagery can enhance your motivation and provide a sense of purpose.

3. **Create a supportive environment:** Surround yourself with people who inspire and motivate you. Seek out individuals who share similar goals or have already achieved what you aspire to. Their support and encouragement can boost your motivation and hold you accountable.

4. **Use rewards and incentives:** Create a system of rewards for completing tasks or reaching milestones. Treat yourself to something enjoyable or engage in a pleasurable activity as a celebration of your progress. Rewards provide positive reinforcement and motivate you to continue working towards your goals.

5. **Practice positive self-talk:** Replace negative self-talk with positive affirmations. Remind yourself of your capabilities and past successes. Encourage and motivate yourself through positive self-talk, which can enhance your belief in your abilities and increase your motivation.

By implementing these strategies, you can overcome procrastination and boost your motivation to achieve your mental health goals. Remember, overcoming procrastination takes practice and dedication, but the rewards of increased productivity and improved well-being are well worth the effort.

Caveat: It is important to recognize that overcoming procrastination is an ongoing process. Everyone has their own unique challenges and what works for one person may not work for another. Experiment with different strategies and adjust them to fit your specific needs and circumstances. Be patient with yourself and persist in finding what works best for you.

Strategies for Increasing Productivity

In today's fast-paced world, productivity is a key factor in achieving success, both in personal and professional life. Being productive means managing your time effectively, staying focused on tasks, and achieving goals efficiently. In this section, we will explore some practical strategies that can help you increase your productivity and make the most out of your time.

Prioritizing and Setting Goals

One of the fundamental principles of productivity is prioritizing tasks and setting clear goals. By identifying and focusing on the most important tasks, you can ensure that you are making progress towards your objectives. Here are some strategies to help you prioritize effectively:

- **ABC Method:** Prioritize tasks using the ABC method, where A represents high-priority tasks, B represents medium-priority tasks, and C represents low-priority tasks. This method helps you stay organized and focus on tasks that have the most significant impact.

- **Eisenhower Matrix:** Use the Eisenhower Matrix, also known as the Urgent-Important Matrix, to categorize tasks based on their urgency and importance. This matrix helps you differentiate between what is essential and what is merely urgent, allowing you to allocate your time and energy wisely.

- **SMART Goals:** Set SMART (Specific, Measurable, Achievable, Relevant, Time-bound) goals to provide clarity and direction. SMART goals help you formulate clear objectives and create a roadmap to accomplish them.

Overcoming Procrastination and Boosting Motivation

Procrastination is a common barrier to productivity. It can lead to wasted time and increased stress. Overcoming procrastination requires understanding the underlying causes and developing strategies to boost motivation. Here are some techniques to help you combat procrastination and stay motivated:

- **Break Tasks into Smaller Steps:** Large tasks can be overwhelming and lead to procrastination. Break them down into smaller, more manageable steps. This approach makes the task feel less daunting and increases your motivation to get started.

- **Use the Pomodoro Technique:** The Pomodoro Technique involves working in short, focused bursts of 25 minutes, followed by a short break. This method helps you maintain concentration and overcome the tendency to procrastinate.

- **Create a Productive Environment:** Your environment can significantly impact your motivation. Create a dedicated and organized workspace that is free from distractions. Minimize interruptions such as phone notifications or social media to stay focused on the task at hand.

- **Utilize Positive Reinforcement:** Reward yourself for completing tasks or reaching milestones. Celebrating achievements reinforces positive behavior and motivates you to continue being productive.

- **Visualize Success:** Take a few moments to visualize the successful completion of your tasks or achieving your goals. This mental imagery can enhance motivation and increase your commitment to the task.

Strategies for Increasing Focus

Maintaining focus is crucial for productivity. Distractions can significantly hinder your ability to complete tasks efficiently. Here are some strategies to improve your focus:

- **Time Blocking:** Allocate specific blocks of time for different tasks or activities. By dedicating designated time slots for particular tasks, you can minimize interruptions and stay focused.

- **Single-Tasking:** Multitasking might seem efficient, but it often leads to reduced productivity and decreased quality of work. Instead, focus on one task at a time to ensure that you give it your full attention and produce better results.

- **Mindfulness Techniques:** Practice mindfulness techniques to enhance focus and concentration. Mindfulness involves being fully present and attentive to the task at hand, without judgment or distraction.

- **Manage Digital Distractions:** Digital devices, such as smartphones and social media platforms, can be significant sources of distraction. Minimize distractions by turning off notifications or using apps or browser extensions that block distracting websites during designated work periods.

⋄ **Take Regular Breaks:** Taking regular breaks can actually improve focus and productivity. Short breaks allow your brain to rest and recharge, reducing mental fatigue and increasing your ability to concentrate.

Optimizing Workflow and Efficiency

Streamlining your workflow and improving efficiency can have a significant impact on productivity. By optimizing your processes and eliminating unnecessary steps, you can save time and increase output. Consider the following strategies:

⋄ **Implement Time-Saving Tools:** Make use of productivity tools and technologies that can automate repetitive tasks or simplify complex processes. Task management apps, project management software, and automation tools can help you streamline your workflow.

⋄ **Delegate Tasks:** Learn to delegate tasks that can be done by others. Delegating frees up your time to focus on high-value tasks that require your expertise, ultimately increasing productivity.

⋄ **Eliminate Time Wasters:** Identify and eliminate activities that consume a significant amount of time but do not contribute much to your productivity or goals. Examples include excessive meetings, excessive email checking, or spending too much time on non-essential tasks.

⋄ **Continuous Learning and Skill Development:** Invest time in continuous learning and skill development. Acquiring new knowledge or improving existing skills can help you work more efficiently and stay updated with the latest advancements in your field.

⋄ **Regularly Evaluate and Adjust:** Reflect on your workflow regularly to identify areas for improvement. Analyze your productivity and make adjustments to your strategies as needed. This iterative process allows you to fine-tune your productivity over time.

Work-Life Integration

Maintaining a healthy work-life balance is crucial for overall well-being and sustained productivity. Here are some strategies to integrate work and personal life effectively:

+ **Set Boundaries:** Clearly define your working hours and personal time. Communicate these boundaries to colleagues, clients, and family members, and strive to maintain them as much as possible.

+ **Practice Self-Care:** Take care of your physical and mental health outside of work. Engage in activities that rejuvenate you, such as exercising, spending time with loved ones, pursuing hobbies, or practicing self-care techniques like meditation or deep breathing exercises.

+ **Schedule Personal Time:** Dedicate time for personal activities and interests. Schedule time for relaxation, hobbies, or other personal pursuits to ensure that you maintain a fulfilling personal life alongside your professional commitments.

+ **Build Supportive Relationships:** Cultivate relationships with supportive family members, friends, and colleagues who understand the importance of work-life integration. Surrounding yourself with a support system can help alleviate stress and enhance overall well-being.

+ **Set Realistic Expectations:** Avoid overcommitting yourself and learn to say no when necessary. Be realistic about what you can accomplish within a given timeframe, both professionally and personally.

Remember, increasing productivity is not about working longer hours but about working smarter and more efficiently. By implementing these strategies and finding a workflow that suits your individual needs, you can enhance your productivity and achieve a better work-life balance.

Case Study: Applying Productivity Strategies in Project Management

Let's consider a real-world example of applying productivity strategies in project management. Suppose you are managing a software development project with a tight deadline. To ensure productivity and meet the project's objectives, you can utilize various strategies:

1. **Prioritizing Tasks:** Identify critical project tasks and prioritize them according to their impact on project goals. This will help you focus on crucial activities and allocate resources effectively.

2. **Setting Clear Goals:** Establish specific, measurable goals for each project phase. Clearly define deliverables, timelines, and quality expectations to keep the team aligned and motivated.

3. **Breaking Down the Project:** Divide the project into smaller, manageable tasks or sprints. Breaking down complex tasks makes them less overwhelming and enables the team to work more efficiently.

4. **Using Task Management Tools:** Utilize project management tools that allow you to assign tasks, track progress, and collaborate effectively. This ensures transparency and streamlines communication within the team.

5. **Regularly Monitoring Progress:** Monitor the team's progress regularly to identify bottlenecks, address issues promptly, and make necessary adjustments. Keeping track of milestones and key performance indicators allows you to stay on top of the project's progress.

6. **Encouraging Open Communication:** Foster open and honest communication among team members. Encourage collaboration, share progress updates, and address concerns or conflicts promptly to maintain productivity and team morale.

7. **Optimizing Workflows:** Continuously evaluate and improve project workflows. Identify and eliminate unnecessary steps or bottlenecks to improve efficiency and ensure a smooth progression of the project.

8. **Emphasizing Work-Life Balance:** Consider team members' well-being and work-life balance. Encourage breaks, provide support when needed, and recognize individual contributions to maintain a healthy and productive work environment.

By implementing these strategies and adapting them to your project's specific needs, you can significantly enhance productivity, ensure timely project completion, and meet client expectations.

Exercises

1. Reflect on your current productivity levels. Identify any procrastination patterns or challenges that hinder your productivity. Develop an action plan to overcome these obstacles and improve your productivity. Consider using techniques discussed in this section, such as the Pomodoro Technique or task prioritization methods.

2. Choose a task or project you are currently working on. Apply the strategies discussed in this section to optimize your workflow and increase productivity. Track your progress and evaluate the impact these strategies have on your overall productivity and work quality.

3. Research and explore additional productivity tools or techniques that align with your preferences and work style. Experiment with different tools or approaches to find what works best for you. Keep a journal to record your experiences and reflect on the effectiveness of each technique.

4. Connect with a colleague or friend who has excellent time management and productivity skills. Interview them to learn about their strategies, habits, and mindset when it comes to productivity. Apply any key takeaways to your own routine and assess their impact on your productivity.

5. Create a work-life balance plan that outlines specific actions and strategies to integrate work and personal life effectively. Set realistic goals and commit to implementing these strategies consistently. Regularly evaluate your progress and make adjustments as needed.

Resources

+ Books:
    - "The 7 Habits of Highly Effective People" by Stephen R. Covey
    - "Deep Work: Rules for Focused Success in a Distracted World" by Cal Newport
    - "Getting Things Done: The Art of Stress-Free Productivity" by David Allen
    - "Atomic Habits: An Easy & Proven Way to Build Good Habits & Break Bad Ones" by James Clear

+ Websites:

– MindTools (www.mindtools.com): Provides a wide range of resources and tools for productivity, leadership, and personal development.

– Todoist (www.todoist.com): A popular task management app that helps organize and prioritize tasks efficiently.

– Toggl (www.toggl.com): A time-tracking tool that allows you to analyze how you spend your time and identify areas for improvement.

Key Takeaways

+ Prioritizing tasks and setting clear goals are crucial for effective time management and productivity.

+ Overcoming procrastination requires breaking tasks into smaller steps, using techniques like the Pomodoro Technique, and creating a productive and focused environment.

+ Strategies for increasing focus include time blocking, single-tasking, practicing mindfulness, managing digital distractions, and taking regular breaks.

+ Workflow optimization and efficiency can be improved through the use of productivity tools, delegation, eliminating time-wasting activities, continuous learning, and regular evaluation.

+ Integrating work and personal life involves setting boundaries, practicing self-care, scheduling personal time, building supportive relationships, and maintaining realistic expectations.

Creating Work-Life Balance

Work-life balance is a crucial aspect of maintaining good mental health. It refers to finding a healthy equilibrium between our personal and professional lives, allowing us to effectively manage our responsibilities and commitments while also prioritizing our well-being and personal fulfillment. In this section, we will explore various strategies and techniques that can help individuals create and maintain a healthy work-life balance.

Understanding the Importance of Work-Life Balance

Before diving into the strategies, let's first understand why work-life balance is essential for our mental health. In today's fast-paced world, we often find ourselves caught up in the demands of work, leaving little time for self-care and other important aspects of our lives. This imbalance can lead to chronic stress, burnout, and various mental health issues.

Achieving work-life balance allows us to:

- Reduce stress: Balancing work and personal life helps us manage stress effectively, preventing it from accumulating and causing harm to our mental health.

- Enhance well-being: By dedicating time to our personal lives, such as spending time with loved ones, engaging in hobbies, or pursuing interests, we promote our overall well-being and happiness.

- Improve productivity: Taking breaks and maintaining boundaries between work and personal life can actually boost productivity, as it allows us to rejuvenate and recharge.

- Prevent burnout: Prioritizing self-care and personal needs reduces the risk of burnout, which can negatively impact our mental health and overall satisfaction with life.

Assessing and Prioritizing Responsibilities

The first step in creating work-life balance is to assess our current responsibilities and commitments. This involves taking a comprehensive look at both our professional and personal obligations.

Exercise: Assessing Responsibilities   Take some time to make a list of all your current responsibilities, including work tasks, household chores, family obligations, social commitments, and personal goals. Once you have a clear picture, categorize these responsibilities based on their importance and urgency. This exercise will help you gain clarity and prioritize effectively.

Setting Boundaries and Establishing Routines

Once we have assessed our responsibilities, it's crucial to set boundaries and establish routines that ensure a healthy division between work and personal life. This helps us maintain focus, avoid overworking, and create dedicated time for self-care and personal activities.

Example: Establishing Work Time and Leisure Time   For those who work from home, it can be challenging to create a clear separation between work and personal life.   One effective strategy is to establish specific work hours and create a designated workspace. By doing so, we establish clear boundaries and signals to ourselves and others that work time is separate from leisure time. Once the work hours are over, make a conscious effort to disconnect from work-related tasks and engage in activities that promote relaxation and personal fulfillment.

Practicing Effective Time Management

Time management plays a vital role in achieving work-life balance. By effectively organizing and prioritizing our tasks, we can optimize productivity, reduce stress, and free up time for personal activities.

Technique: The Eisenhower Matrix   The Eisenhower Matrix, also known as the Urgent-Important Matrix, is a time management technique that helps prioritize tasks based on their urgency and importance.   It categorizes tasks into four quadrants:

+ **Urgent and Important** (Do First): Tasks that require immediate attention and have significant consequences if not addressed promptly.

+ **Important but Not Urgent** (Schedule): Tasks that are important but can be scheduled for later to maintain focus on high-priority tasks.

+ **Urgent but Not Important** (Delegate): Tasks that are time-sensitive but do not need your personal attention. Delegate them to others.

+ **Not Urgent and Not Important** (Eliminate): Tasks that are not urgent or important. Minimize or eliminate them to make room for higher-priority activities.

Using the Eisenhower Matrix can help you make informed decisions about task prioritization and ensure that your time allocation aligns with your goals and overall well-being.

Promoting Self-Care and Well-being

Self-care is a vital component of work-life balance. It involves actively taking care of our physical, emotional, and mental well-being to maintain optimal functioning and prevent burnout. Incorporating self-care practices into our daily routines is crucial for achieving work-life balance.

Exercise: Creating a Self-Care Routine   Reflect on activities or practices that bring you joy, relaxation, and rejuvenation. Make a list of self-care activities that you can easily incorporate into your daily or weekly routine. These activities can range from taking a walk in nature, practicing mindfulness or meditation, engaging in hobbies, or spending quality time with loved ones. Schedule specific self-care time slots in your calendar to ensure they are prioritized alongside other responsibilities.

Managing Technology and Digital Boundaries

In today's digital age, technology has become an integral part of our lives, blurring the lines between work and personal time. Effectively managing technology use and setting boundaries around its usage is crucial for work-life balance.

Tip: Digital Detox   Consider implementing regular digital detoxes to create dedicated time for unplugging from devices and online distractions. Set aside a specific period, such as a few hours or an entire day, where you disconnect from technology and focus solely on non-digital activities that promote relaxation and well-being.

Seeking Support and Communicating Needs

Lastly, seeking support and communicating our work-life balance needs is essential. Whether it's discussing workload concerns with a supervisor or seeking help from family members and friends, open communication can lead to understanding, collaboration, and finding solutions that support work-life balance.

Discussion: Communicating with Others   Initiate a conversation with your supervisor, colleagues, or loved ones to discuss your work-life balance needs. Clearly express your concerns, boundaries, and any adjustments that could help achieve a healthier work-life balance. By communicating openly, you can foster a supportive environment that respects and values your well-being.

Conclusion

Creating and maintaining a healthy work-life balance is crucial for our mental health and overall well-being. By prioritizing self-care, setting boundaries, practicing effective time management, and seeking support when needed, we can achieve a harmonious and fulfilling equilibrium between our personal and professional lives. Remember, work-life balance is a continuous process that requires regular evaluation and adjustments.

Stress Management Techniques

Understanding Stress and Its Impacts

Stress is an inherent part of life and can be defined as the body's response to any demand or pressure. It is a natural physiological and psychological reaction that prepares us to cope with challenges. However, when stress becomes overwhelming or chronic, it can have detrimental effects on our mental and physical well-being.

The Physiology of Stress

To understand the impacts of stress, it is crucial to comprehend the physiological processes involved. When faced with a stressful situation, the body activates the sympathetic nervous system, triggering the release of stress hormones such as cortisol and adrenaline. This initiates the "fight or flight" response, energizing the body to take action.

During this response, heart rate and blood pressure increase, breathing becomes rapid, and blood vessels constrict. These physiological changes divert blood flow away from non-essential functions, such as digestion, and towards critical areas like muscles and the brain. This heightened state of arousal allows us to respond quickly to stressors.

Acute vs. Chronic Stress

Acute stress refers to short-term stress triggered by a specific event or situation, such as public speaking or a tight deadline. In these instances, the body's stress response can be beneficial, helping us to focus and perform better. Once the stressor is resolved, the body returns to its normal state.

On the other hand, chronic stress occurs when stress persists over an extended period, often due to ongoing issues like work pressures, financial difficulties, or relationship problems. The constant activation of the stress response can have severe ramifications for both mental and physical health.

Manifestations of Stress

The impacts of stress on an individual's health can vary widely and may manifest in various ways. Some common physical effects of stress include headaches, elevated blood pressure, stomach problems, muscle tension, and weakened immune system. Furthermore, chronic stress has been linked to an increased risk of developing cardiovascular diseases, obesity, and diabetes.

Stress also exerts significant influence on mental health. It can contribute to the development or exacerbation of various mental health disorders, such as anxiety and depression. Chronic stress can negatively impact cognitive function, leading to difficulties with memory, concentration, and decision-making. Additionally, individuals experiencing high levels of stress may have trouble sleeping and often report feelings of irritability, mood swings, and decreased motivation.

Coping with Stress

Effective stress management is crucial for maintaining overall well-being. There are various strategies individuals can employ to cope with stress and minimize its impact on their lives. Some of these strategies include:

- 1. **Self-care:** Engaging in self-care activities such as exercise, adequate sleep, and relaxation techniques can help reduce stress levels.

- 2. **Social support:** Seeking support from friends, family, or support groups can provide emotional assistance and perspective during challenging times.

- 3. **Time management:** Prioritizing tasks, setting realistic goals, and organizing schedules can help individuals regain a sense of control and reduce stress levels.

- 4. **Stress reduction techniques:** Practices such as deep breathing, meditation, and mindfulness can activate the body's relaxation response, counteracting the physiological effects of stress.

- 5. **Problem-solving skills:** Developing effective problem-solving skills can help individuals address the sources of stress more efficiently, leading to a reduction in stress levels.

It is important to note that different strategies may work better for different individuals. It is essential to explore and find the techniques that resonate most with your unique needs and preferences.

Real-World Example: Workplace Stress

To illustrate the impacts of stress in a real-world context, let's consider workplace stress. Many individuals experience job-related stress due to factors such as high workloads, tight deadlines, conflicts with colleagues, or lack of job security.

Excessive and prolonged workplace stress can lead to burnout, a state of chronic physical and emotional exhaustion. Burnout not only affects an individual's mental health but can also hinder their productivity, job satisfaction, and overall well-being.

Organizations can play a crucial role in minimizing workplace stress by implementing policies and programs that promote work-life balance, provide opportunities for employee engagement and growth, and foster a supportive and healthy work environment. This can include initiatives like flexible work hours, stress management workshops, and regular check-ins with employees to address their concerns.

Key Takeaways

Understanding stress and its impacts is essential for cultivating effective stress management strategies. Stress can have both physical and mental health consequences, especially when experienced chronically. Engaging in self-care activities, seeking support from others, practicing stress reduction techniques, and developing problem-solving skills are key approaches to cope with stress effectively.

By addressing stress and implementing strategies to mitigate its negative effects, individuals can enhance their overall well-being and resilience in the face of challenges. Remember, managing stress is a lifelong endeavor and may require a combination of various techniques to find what works best for each individual.

Identifying Sources of Stress and Triggers

In order to effectively manage stress, it is important to first identify the sources of stress and triggers that impact our mental health. Stress can arise from various aspects of our lives, including work, relationships, finances, and health. By recognizing these stressors, we can develop strategies to cope with them and reduce their impact on our well-being.

Common Sources of Stress

The sources of stress can vary from person to person, but there are some common elements that tend to affect many individuals. Here are a few examples:

+ **Work-related stress:** This can include heavy workloads, tight deadlines, lack of control or autonomy, conflicts with colleagues or supervisors, job insecurity, and long working hours. It may also involve the pressure to consistently meet high expectations or perform at a certain level.

+ **Relationship stress:** Difficulties in personal relationships, such as conflicts with a partner, family members, or friends, can contribute to high levels of stress. This can arise from disagreements, misunderstandings, lack of communication, or unmet emotional needs.

+ **Financial stress:** Financial difficulties, such as debt, unemployment, or the inability to meet basic needs, can create significant stress. Concerns about financial stability, future planning, or the inability to afford necessary expenses can all contribute to a sense of anxiety and pressure.

+ **Health-related stress:** Health issues, whether physical or mental, can have a significant impact on our well-being. Chronic illnesses, pain, disabilities, and mental health disorders can all lead to increased stress levels. Additionally, concerns about our own health or the health of loved ones can be a significant source of stress.

Identifying Triggers

Triggers are specific events, situations, or circumstances that can exacerbate stress levels. These triggers may vary for each individual, but understanding and recognizing them is crucial for stress management. Here are some common triggers to be aware of:

+ **Environmental triggers:** Certain environments or settings can act as triggers for stress. This could be a crowded and noisy space, a cluttered or disorganized living area, or even excessive exposure to media or technology.

+ **Time-related triggers:** Time-related triggers can include deadlines, time pressures, or a lack of time management skills. Feeling rushed or constantly trying to catch up can greatly increase stress levels.

+ **Social triggers:** Interactions with specific individuals or situations involving social pressure can act as triggers. This may include uncomfortable social events, conflicts with friends or family members, or social comparisons and the fear of judgment or rejection.

- **Personal triggers:** Certain personal factors can act as stress triggers, such as perfectionism, self-criticism, negative self-talk, or excessive expectations. These internal factors can contribute to feelings of stress and anxiety.

- **Life transitions:** Significant life changes and transitions, such as moving to a new city, starting a new job, ending a relationship, or becoming a parent, can be major stress triggers. Even positive life changes can result in increased stress levels due to the adjustments they require.

Identifying Individualized Stressors

While the above examples cover many common stressors, it is important to remember that each person's experience of stress can be unique. It is crucial to take the time to reflect and identify the specific stressors that impact your mental health. Here are some strategies to help you identify individualized stressors:

- **Self-reflection and introspection:** Take some time to reflect on your life and activities. Consider what aspects of your daily routine or specific situations tend to cause stress. Keep a journal to track your emotions and stress levels in different situations.

- **Seek feedback from trusted individuals:** Reach out to friends, family members, or colleagues who may have a different perspective on your life and habits. They may be able to provide insights into stress triggers that you may not have considered.

- **Professional assistance:** If you find it challenging to identify your stressors or if they are significantly impacting your mental health, consider seeking support from a mental health professional. They can help you explore your stressors in a safe and supportive environment.

Managing and Coping with Stress Triggers

Once you have identified your sources of stress and triggers, it is important to develop effective strategies to manage and cope with them. Here are some strategies that can be helpful:

- **Stress management techniques:** Engage in stress management techniques such as deep breathing exercises, mindfulness meditation, or progressive muscle relaxation. These techniques can help you relax and reduce the impact of stress on your mind and body.

+ **Time management**: Prioritize your tasks and set realistic goals to manage your time effectively. Break down larger tasks into smaller, manageable steps, and delegate tasks when possible. This can help reduce the feeling of being overwhelmed.

+ **Assertive communication**: Develop effective communication skills to express your needs, set boundaries, and reduce conflicts. Learning to say "no" when necessary and asking for support can help reduce stress in relationships and work environments.

+ **Self-care practices**: Engage in activities that promote self-care and well-being, such as regular exercise, healthy eating, getting enough sleep, and engaging in hobbies or activities that bring you joy and relaxation.

+ **Seeking support**: Reach out to trusted individuals or seek professional help when needed. Talk to someone you trust about your feelings and experiences, and consider joining support groups or seeking therapy to address stress.

Remember, managing stress is an ongoing process, and what works for one person may not work for another. Experiment with different techniques and strategies to find what resonates with you and helps you effectively cope with your sources of stress and triggers.

Real-World Example: Let's consider the example of a college student who experiences stress related to academic pressures. The student may identify that tight deadlines, high expectations, and difficult coursework are significant stressors. They may develop strategies such as effective time management, breaking tasks into smaller steps, seeking academic support resources, and engaging in stress-reducing activities like exercise or meditation. By identifying and addressing the specific stressors associated with their academic workload, the student can approach their studies with reduced anxiety and better mental well-being.

Caveats and Considerations

It is important to note that identifying sources of stress and triggers is a personal process, and it may take time to gain insight into your individual stressors. Additionally, it is normal to experience stress in certain situations, and not all stress can or should be eliminated. Some stress can be motivating and drive us to perform at our best. The goal is to manage stress in a way that promotes well-being and prevents it from becoming overwhelming or chronic.

Moreover, it is crucial to seek professional help if stress becomes unmanageable or significantly impacts your daily functioning. Mental health professionals can provide guidance, support, and evidence-based interventions tailored to your specific needs.

Key Takeaways

+ Identifying sources of stress and triggers is essential for effective stress management.

+ Common sources of stress include work-related stress, relationship stress, financial stress, and health-related stress.

+ Triggers can be environmental, time-related, social, personal, or related to life transitions.

+ Individualized stressors vary from person to person and can be identified through self-reflection, seeking feedback from others, and professional assistance.

+ Effective strategies for managing stress triggers include stress management techniques, time management, assertive communication, self-care practices, and seeking support when needed.

Take a moment to reflect on your own sources of stress and triggers. Consider how you can apply the strategies mentioned to effectively manage and cope with them. Remember, self-care and seeking support are key components of maintaining good mental health.

Tools for Managing and Coping with Stress

Stress is an inevitable part of life, and learning to effectively manage and cope with it is crucial for maintaining good mental health. In this section, we will explore various tools and strategies that can help individuals better deal with stress. These tools encompass a wide range of techniques, from relaxation exercises to cognitive-behavioral strategies. By incorporating these tools into your daily routine, you can reduce the negative impact of stress on your well-being.

Relaxation Techniques

Relaxation techniques are invaluable for managing stress and promoting a sense of calm. These techniques help activate the body's relaxation response, counteracting the physiological changes that occur during times of stress. Here are a few commonly used relaxation techniques:

1. **Deep Breathing**: This technique involves taking slow, deep breaths, focusing on the sensation of the breath entering and leaving your body. Deep breathing triggers the body's relaxation response and helps reduce muscle tension and anxiety. To practice deep breathing, find a quiet and comfortable place, close your eyes, and take a deep breath in through your nose for a count of four, hold for a count of four, and then exhale slowly through your mouth for a count of four. Repeat this exercise several times until you feel more relaxed.

2. **Progressive Muscle Relaxation**: This technique involves systematically tensing and relaxing different muscle groups in the body, helping to release physical tension. To practice progressive muscle relaxation, start by tensing the muscles in your toes and feet for a few seconds, then relax them completely, noticing the difference in sensation. Move slowly up through each muscle group in your body, tensing and relaxing as you go. This exercise can be particularly helpful in relieving muscle tension caused by chronic stress.

3. **Guided Imagery**: This technique involves using your imagination to create a mental image or scenario that promotes feelings of relaxation and calm. Find a quiet place, close your eyes, and visualize yourself in a peaceful and serene environment. Focus on the sensory details of your imagined scene, such as the sights, sounds, and smells. Engaging your senses in this way can help shift your focus away from stress and induce a state of relaxation.

Cognitive-Behavioral Strategies

In addition to relaxation techniques, cognitive-behavioral strategies can be effective tools for managing and coping with stress. These strategies focus on identifying and challenging negative thought patterns and modifying harmful behaviors. Here are a few examples of cognitive-behavioral strategies:

1. **Cognitive Restructuring**: This technique involves identifying and challenging negative or irrational thoughts that contribute to stress and replacing them with more positive and realistic thoughts. Start by paying attention to your thoughts when you are feeling stressed. Are they rational and helpful, or are they overly negative and unproductive? Once you identify negative thoughts, challenge them by asking yourself for evidence to support or refute them. Replace these negative thoughts with more balanced and positive ones. For example, if you are feeling overwhelmed at work and thinking, "I can't handle this," challenge this thought by reminding yourself

of times when you have successfully managed challenging situations in the past.

2. **Problem-Solving**: This strategy involves breaking down a stressful situation into manageable components and developing a plan of action to address each component. Start by clearly defining the problem you are facing. Then brainstorm possible solutions and evaluate each one based on its feasibility and potential outcomes. Once you have selected a solution, create a step-by-step plan and take action. Taking proactive steps to address the problem can help reduce stress and increase feelings of control and empowerment.

3. **Behavioral Activation**: This strategy involves engaging in activities that bring joy and a sense of accomplishment, even when you are feeling stressed or down. During times of stress, it can be tempting to withdraw and avoid participating in activities that you usually enjoy. However, doing so can perpetuate negative emotions and make stress feel more overwhelming. Instead, make a conscious effort to engage in activities that boost your mood and provide a sense of fulfillment. This could be anything from going for a walk in nature, spending time with loved ones, or engaging in a hobby or creative pursuit.

Mindfulness and Meditation

Mindfulness and meditation practices have gained significant attention in recent years due to their effectiveness in reducing stress and promoting overall well-being. These practices involve bringing one's attention to the present moment, without judgment, and cultivating a state of heightened awareness and acceptance. Here are a few mindfulness and meditation techniques:

1. **Body Scan Meditation**: This technique involves systematically scanning your body from head to toe, paying attention to physical sensations, and bringing awareness to any areas of tension or discomfort. Start by finding a comfortable position and closing your eyes. Begin at the top of your head and slowly move your attention down through each part of your body, noting any sensations you experience. If you notice any areas of tension or discomfort, consciously relax those muscles and continue scanning. This practice can help you become more attuned to your body and recognize and release physical manifestations of stress.

2. **Breath Awareness Meditation:** This technique involves focusing your attention on the sensation of your breath as it enters and leaves your body. Find a quiet place, sit in a comfortable position, and close your eyes. Gently bring your attention to your breath, noticing the sensation of the breath as it moves in and out of your body. If your mind starts to wander, gently bring your focus back to your breath. Practice this meditation for a few minutes each day, gradually increasing the duration over time. This practice can help calm the mind, reduce stress, and cultivate a greater sense of presence and calm.

3. **Loving-Kindness Meditation:** This technique involves cultivating feelings of love, compassion, and kindness towards oneself and others. Find a quiet and comfortable place, close your eyes, and bring to mind someone you care about deeply. Repeat phrases such as "May you be happy, May you be healthy, May you be safe" silently to yourself. Then extend these wishes to other individuals, such as friends, family members, acquaintances, and even to yourself. This practice can help shift your focus away from stress and foster a sense of connection and well-being.

Additional Strategies

In addition to the techniques mentioned above, there are several other strategies that can help individuals better manage and cope with stress:

1. **Time Management:** Effective time management can help reduce stress by providing structure and organization. Prioritize your tasks, set realistic goals, and break large tasks into smaller, manageable steps. Use scheduling tools, such as calendars or to-do lists, to help you stay organized and on track.

2. **Social Support:** Building and maintaining strong social connections can provide a valuable source of support during times of stress. Reach out to friends, family members, or support groups to share your feelings and experiences. Having someone to listen and offer understanding can help alleviate stress and provide a fresh perspective.

3. **Healthy Lifestyle Choices:** Taking care of your physical health can have a positive impact on your mental well-being. Engage in regular exercise, eat a balanced diet, stay hydrated, and get enough sleep. These lifestyle choices can help regulate stress levels and promote overall resilience.

4. **Humor and Laughter:** Laughter has been shown to have numerous physical and mental health benefits, including reducing stress. Find opportunities to incorporate humor and laughter into your daily life, whether it's watching a funny movie, spending time with funny friends, or engaging in activities that make you laugh.

Remember, managing and coping with stress is a dynamic process that requires practice and self-awareness. Experiment with different strategies and find what works best for you. By incorporating these tools into your daily routine, you can develop resilience and enhance your ability to navigate life's challenges with greater ease.

Relaxation Techniques and Mind-Body Interventions

Relaxation techniques and mind-body interventions play a crucial role in promoting mental health and overall well-being. These techniques help individuals manage stress, reduce anxiety, enhance self-awareness, and cultivate a sense of inner calm. In this section, we will explore various relaxation techniques and mind-body interventions that can be incorporated into daily life to support mental health.

Understanding Stress and Its Impacts

Before delving into relaxation techniques, it is essential to understand the concept of stress and its impact on mental health. Stress is a natural response to demands or pressures that we encounter in our daily lives. While acute stress can be beneficial in challenging situations, chronic stress can have detrimental effects on our mental and physical well-being.

When we experience stress, our bodies release stress hormones like cortisol and adrenaline, which activate the "fight-or-flight" response. This response can lead to increased heart rate, elevated blood pressure, and heightened alertness. Prolonged activation of the stress response can contribute to anxiety, depression, and other mental health issues.

Relaxation Techniques for Stress Reduction

Relaxation techniques are effective tools for managing stress and promoting relaxation. These techniques help activate the body's relaxation response, which counteracts the physiological effects of stress. Here are some commonly used relaxation techniques:

1. **Deep Breathing**: Deep breathing exercises involve taking slow, deep breaths, expanding the abdomen, and exhaling slowly. This technique helps activate the body's relaxation response by slowing down the heart rate and promoting a sense of calm.

2. **Progressive Muscle Relaxation (PMR)**: PMR involves tensing and then releasing each muscle group in the body systematically. By alternating between tension and relaxation, this technique helps reduce muscle tension and promote a state of relaxation.

3. **Guided Imagery**: Guided imagery involves visualizing peaceful and calming scenes, such as a tranquil beach or a serene forest. By engaging the senses in a positive and soothing mental experience, guided imagery can help reduce stress and induce relaxation.

4. **Autogenic Training**: Autogenic training involves repeating specific phrases or visualizations to induce a state of relaxation. By focusing on sensations such as warmth or heaviness, this technique can help create a sense of deep relaxation and calm.

Mind-Body Interventions for Mental Well-being

In addition to relaxation techniques, various mind-body interventions can support mental well-being and promote a sense of balance and harmony between the mind and body. These interventions combine physical movements or activities with mindful awareness to enhance overall well-being. Here are some popular mind-body interventions:

1. **Yoga**: Yoga is a mind-body practice that combines physical postures, breathing exercises, and meditation. It promotes flexibility, strength, and balance while cultivating mindfulness and relaxation. Regular practice of yoga has been shown to reduce stress, anxiety, and depression.

2. **Tai Chi**: Tai Chi is a martial art that involves slow, deliberate movements, deep breathing, and focused attention. It emphasizes relaxation, balance, and flow of energy. Regular practice of Tai Chi has been associated with reduced stress, improved mental clarity, and enhanced overall well-being.

3. **Meditation**: Meditation involves training the mind to focus on a specific object, thought, or activity to achieve mental clarity and emotional calmness. Mindfulness meditation, in particular, has gained popularity for its ability to

reduce stress, increase self-awareness, and improve overall mental well-being.

4. **Art Therapy**: Art therapy utilizes creative processes such as drawing, painting, and sculpting to promote self-expression and emotional healing. Engaging in art therapy can help reduce stress, enhance self-esteem, and improve overall mental health.

5. **Biofeedback**: Biofeedback is a technique that allows individuals to gain awareness and control over their physiological processes, such as heart rate, blood pressure, and muscle tension. By using electronic devices that provide real-time feedback, individuals can learn to manage their physiological responses and promote relaxation.

Integration and Practical Tips

To derive maximum benefit from relaxation techniques and mind-body interventions, it is essential to integrate them into our daily lives. Here are some practical tips for incorporating these strategies:

+ **Consistency**: Set aside dedicated time each day for relaxation practices. Consistency is key to reap the long-term benefits of these techniques.

+ **Create a Relaxation Space**: Designate a quiet and comfortable space at home where you can engage in relaxation practices free from distractions.

+ **Practice Mindfulness**: Cultivate mindfulness by being fully present in the moment during relaxation practices. Pay attention to the sensations, thoughts, and emotions that arise without judgment.

+ **Start Small**: If you are new to relaxation techniques, start with shorter sessions and gradually increase the duration as you become more comfortable.

+ **Seek Guided Resources**: Utilize guided relaxation exercises through smartphone apps, online resources, or by working with a qualified professional to enhance your practice.

Remember that relaxation techniques and mind-body interventions are not a one-size-fits-all approach. Experiment with different techniques and find what works best for you. It is also important to note that while these strategies can be beneficial in promoting mental health, they are not a substitute for professional help. If you are struggling with severe stress or mental health issues, it is essential to seek support from a qualified mental health professional.

In conclusion, relaxation techniques and mind-body interventions are valuable tools for managing stress, promoting relaxation, and enhancing overall mental well-being. By integrating these practices into our lives, we can cultivate a greater sense of self-awareness, resilience, and inner peace.

Stress Reduction in Everyday Life

Stress is a common occurrence in our daily lives and can have a significant impact on our mental health. Fortunately, there are several effective strategies that can help reduce stress and promote overall well-being. In this section, we will explore practical techniques and lifestyle changes that can be incorporated into everyday life to minimize stress levels.

Identifying Sources of Stress

Before we delve into stress reduction techniques, it is essential to identify the sources of stress in our lives. These stressors can be categorized into different domains, such as work, relationships, financial concerns, and personal goals. Take a moment to reflect on your own life and pinpoint the specific factors that contribute to your stress levels. This self-awareness will allow you to target these stressors and implement appropriate strategies.

Managing Time Effectively

Time management plays a crucial role in stress reduction. Feeling overwhelmed and rushed can significantly contribute to stress levels. By implementing effective time management techniques, you can improve productivity, reduce the risk of burnout, and create a better work-life balance. Here are some strategies to consider:

- Prioritizing tasks: Identify the most important and urgent tasks, and allocate your time and energy accordingly.

- Setting realistic goals: Break down large tasks into smaller, manageable steps and set achievable deadlines.

- Creating a schedule: Use calendars or planner apps to plan your daily and weekly activities, allowing for designated time for work, leisure, and self-care.

+ Avoiding multitasking: Focus on one task at a time to improve efficiency and reduce stress.

+ Delegating responsibilities: If feasible, delegate tasks to others to lighten your workload.

Practicing Relaxation Techniques

Relaxation techniques are effective in reducing stress and promoting a sense of calm. Incorporating these techniques into your daily routine can help you manage stress and improve overall well-being. Here are some relaxation techniques to consider:

+ Deep breathing exercises: Take slow, deep breaths, focusing on your breath as it goes in and out. This can help activate your body's relaxation response and reduce stress.

+ Progressive muscle relaxation: Gradually tense and relax different muscle groups in your body, starting from your toes and working your way up to your head. This technique can help release physical tension and promote relaxation.

+ Guided imagery: Close your eyes and visualize a peaceful and calming place or situation. Engage your senses by imagining the sights, sounds, and smells associated with this place, allowing yourself to relax and let go of stress.

+ Mindfulness meditation: Practice being fully present in the moment, non-judgmentally observing your thoughts, emotions, and sensations. This practice can help you develop a calm and centered mindset, reducing stress and increasing self-awareness.

Engaging in Physical Activity

Regular physical activity is not only essential for physical health but also plays a significant role in managing stress. Engaging in exercise releases endorphins, the body's natural mood elevators, which can help reduce stress and improve overall well-being. Consider incorporating the following strategies into your routine:

+ Choose activities you enjoy: Find physical activities that you find enjoyable and engaging to enhance motivation and adherence.

+ Start with small steps: Begin with short bouts of exercise and gradually increase the duration and intensity to avoid overwhelming yourself.

+ Find an exercise buddy: Exercising with a friend or joining a group class can provide social support and make physical activity more enjoyable.

+ Incorporate mindfulness during exercise: Pay attention to your body and focus on the sensations and movements involved in the activity. This can enhance the mind-body connection and further reduce stress.

+ Engage in nature-based activities: Spending time in nature, such as going for a hike or practicing yoga outdoors, can have a calming effect on the mind and promote stress reduction.

Promoting Work-Life Balance

Achieving a healthy work-life balance is crucial for managing stress and maintaining overall well-being. Here are some strategies to help you find a balance between work and personal life:

+ Set boundaries: Clearly define your working hours and try to avoid work-related activities outside of these hours.

+ Take breaks: Incorporate regular breaks into your work schedule to rest and recharge. Use this time to engage in activities you enjoy or practice relaxation techniques.

+ Prioritize self-care: Make self-care activities, such as exercise, hobbies, and spending time with loved ones, a priority in your daily routine.

+ Learn to say no: Don't overcommit yourself. Learn to say no to tasks or responsibilities that can cause excessive stress and disrupt your work-life balance.

+ Disconnect from technology: Designate specific times where you disconnect from electronic devices to create mental and emotional space.

Seeking Support

Sometimes, despite our best efforts, stress can become overwhelming. It is important to reach out for support when needed. Here are some avenues for seeking support:

+ Friends and family: Share your feelings and concerns with trusted friends and family members who can provide emotional support and guidance.

* Support groups: Consider joining support groups or online forums where individuals with similar experiences can connect and offer mutual support.

* Professional help: If stress persists or becomes unmanageable, consider seeking professional help from mental health professionals who specialize in stress management and well-being.

* Employee assistance programs: Many workplaces offer employee assistance programs that provide confidential counseling and support services to employees.

Conclusion

Incorporating stress reduction strategies into everyday life is essential for maintaining optimal mental health and well-being. By identifying sources of stress, managing time effectively, practicing relaxation techniques, engaging in physical activity, promoting work-life balance, and seeking support when needed, you can minimize stress levels and foster a sense of calm and resilience in the face of life's challenges. Remember, stress reduction is a continuous process, and finding what works best for you may require some trial and error. Stay committed to prioritizing your mental health and well-being, and you will reap the benefits in all aspects of your life.

Mental Health Support Systems

Professional Help and Therapy

Types of Mental Health Professionals

When seeking mental health support, it is important to understand the various types of professionals who specialize in providing care and guidance. Here, we will explore the different roles and specialties of mental health professionals, each contributing their unique expertise to the field.

Psychiatrists

Psychiatrists are medical doctors who specialize in the diagnosis, treatment, and prevention of mental illnesses. They have extensive training in both general medicine and psychiatry, allowing them to consider the biological, psychological, and social factors that contribute to mental health conditions. Psychiatrists can prescribe medication, perform medical tests, and provide various forms of therapy, making them well-rounded professionals for comprehensive mental health care.

Psychologists

Psychologists are experts in the science of human behavior and the mind. They focus on understanding thoughts, feelings, and behaviors to help individuals develop healthier coping mechanisms and improve overall well-being. Psychologists may have doctoral-level training, such as a Ph.D. or Psy.D., and provide therapy through different modalities, including cognitive-behavioral therapy, psychodynamic therapy, or humanistic therapy. They work in diverse settings, such as private practice, research institutions, hospitals, and schools.

Counselors or Therapists

Counselors, also known as therapists, play a vital role in providing guidance and support to individuals experiencing emotional challenges or mental health disorders. They may have different specializations, including marriage and family therapy, substance abuse counseling, or career counseling. Counselors often use talk therapy to help clients explore their feelings, thoughts, and behaviors in a safe and non-judgmental environment. They focus on empowering individuals to develop coping strategies and make positive changes in their lives.

Clinical Social Workers

Clinical social workers are trained to address mental health problems within the context of social, environmental, and familial systems. They possess a master's degree in social work and are skilled in providing therapy, case management, and advocacy services. Clinical social workers work with individuals, families, and communities to improve overall mental and emotional well-being. They may also collaborate with other professionals to ensure comprehensive care and access to community resources.

Psychiatric Nurses

Psychiatric nurses specialize in providing care and support to individuals experiencing mental health challenges. They often work in collaboration with psychiatrists to administer medication, monitor treatment progress, and educate patients about their conditions. Additionally, psychiatric nurses may provide individual or group therapy sessions, create treatment plans, and offer education to individuals and their families. Their holistic approach to care encompasses both physical and emotional well-being.

Peer Support Specialists

Peer support specialists are individuals who have personal experience with mental health challenges and have received specialized training to offer support to others facing similar difficulties. These professionals provide empathetic listening, share their own recovery stories, and offer guidance based on their lived experiences. Peer support specialists serve as valuable resources and role models for individuals seeking help, as they offer unique insights and understanding.

Additional Mental Health Professionals

In addition to the professionals mentioned above, there are other individuals who play significant roles in the field of mental health. These may include addiction counselors, art therapists, music therapists, occupational therapists, and recreational therapists. Each brings a unique set of skills and interventions to facilitate healing and promote well-being.

It is important to note that while these professionals have specialized training, the choice of mental health provider depends on individual needs, preferences, and the specific services required. Collaborative care among different professionals can often be a beneficial approach, as it allows for a comprehensive and personalized treatment plan.

Remember, seeking help from mental health professionals is a sign of strength and a proactive step toward improving one's mental well-being. It is essential to find a provider who aligns with your values, offers a safe and supportive space, and empowers you on your journey to better mental health.

In the next subsection, we will delve deeper into the process of finding the right therapist and the different approaches to therapy.

Finding the Right Therapist

Finding the right therapist is a crucial step in the journey towards mental health and well-being. The therapeutic relationship plays a significant role in the effectiveness of therapy, as it lays the foundation for trust, open communication, and collaboration. In this section, we will explore the key considerations and steps involved in finding the right therapist for your needs.

Understanding Your Needs and Goals

Before starting your search for a therapist, it is important to have a clear understanding of your needs and goals. Take some time to reflect on what you hope to achieve through therapy and what specific challenges or issues you would like to address. Are you struggling with anxiety, depression, or trauma? Do you need help with relationship problems, grief, or self-esteem issues? Identifying your specific concerns will help you narrow down your search and find a therapist who specializes in the areas relevant to you.

Types of Mental Health Professionals

There are various types of mental health professionals who offer therapy services. Understanding the differences between them can help you make an informed decision. Here are some common types of mental health professionals:

- Psychologists: They have a doctoral degree in psychology and are trained to assess and treat a wide range of mental health issues. Psychologists often use evidence-based therapies such as cognitive-behavioral therapy (CBT), psychodynamic therapy, or interpersonal therapy.

- Psychiatrists: These medical doctors specialize in mental health. They can diagnose mental health disorders, prescribe medications, and provide therapy. Psychiatrists often work in collaboration with psychologists or other therapists.

- Licensed Professional Counselors (LPC): LPCs have a master's degree in counseling and are trained to provide therapy. They may specialize in various areas such as marriage and family therapy, addiction counseling, or career counseling.

- Social Workers: Licensed Clinical Social Workers (LCSW) have a master's degree in social work and are trained to provide therapy, case management, and advocacy. They may work in various settings such as hospitals, schools, or community mental health centers.

- Marriage and Family Therapists (MFT): These therapists specialize in working with couples and families to address relationship issues and improve communication and dynamics.

- Licensed Professional Clinical Counselors (LPCC): LPCCs hold a master's degree in counseling and are trained to provide therapy for individuals and groups. They often work in private practice, community agencies, or educational settings.

- Psychiatric Nurse Practitioners: These advanced practice nurses specialize in mental health and can prescribe medications, provide therapy, and manage mental health conditions.

- Other specialists: Depending on your specific needs, you may seek out therapists with specialized training or expertise, such as art therapists, music therapists, or trauma specialists.

Finding Therapists

Once you have a clear understanding of your needs and the type of therapist you are looking for, you can start the process of finding potential therapists. Here are some ways to find therapists:

- Personal Recommendations: Ask friends, family members, or healthcare professionals if they can recommend a therapist they have had a positive experience with. Personal recommendations can be valuable as they come from individuals who know you and your needs.

- Online Directories: Utilize online directories that provide listings of therapists in your area. Websites like Psychology Today, GoodTherapy, and TherapyDen allow you to search for therapists based on location, specialization, and insurance coverage.

- Professional Associations: Check the websites of professional associations relevant to the type of therapist you are seeking. These associations often have directories of members that you can search through.

- Insurance Provider: If you have health insurance, check if they have a list of therapists who are in-network. This can help minimize out-of-pocket expenses.

- Community Mental Health Centers: Local community mental health centers may offer affordable therapy services or be able to provide referrals to therapists in your area.

- Universities and Training Institutes: Contact local universities or training institutes that offer graduate programs in mental health. They often have clinics where graduate students provide therapy under the close supervision of licensed professionals.

Considerations in the Selection Process

Once you have a list of potential therapists, it is important to consider several factors before making a final decision. Here are some key considerations:

- Specialization and Expertise: Look for therapists who have experience and training in the specific issues you want to address. It is important to find someone who is knowledgeable about your concerns.

+ Therapeutic Approach: Different therapists may use different therapeutic approaches. Research the approaches they use and consider whether they align with your preferences and goals. Some common approaches include cognitive-behavioral therapy (CBT), psychodynamic therapy, mindfulness-based therapy, or solution-focused therapy.

+ Compatibility and Connection: During therapy, it is essential to feel comfortable and have a good rapport with your therapist. Consider whether the therapist's communication style, values, and personality resonate with you. A strong therapeutic alliance is key to successful therapy.

+ Logistics and Practicalities: Think about practical factors such as location, availability of appointment times, fees, and insurance coverage. It is important to find a therapist whose availability and logistics align with your needs.

+ Initial Consultation: Many therapists offer an initial consultation or phone call to discuss your needs and ensure a good fit. Take advantage of this opportunity to ask questions, discuss your concerns, and get a sense of the therapist's approach and style.

Finalizing the Decision

After considering all the relevant factors, you can make an informed decision and choose a therapist that feels like the best fit for you. It is important to remember that finding the right therapist may involve some trial and error. If, after a few sessions, you feel that the therapist is not meeting your needs or you do not have a strong connection, it is okay to explore other options and find someone else who is better suited to support you on your mental health journey.

Unconventional Tip: Mindful Decision-Making

When choosing a therapist, it can be helpful to engage in mindful decision-making. This involves approaching the decision with self-awareness, non-judgment, and intentionality. Take some time to sit quietly and reflect on what you value in a therapist. Notice any thoughts, emotions, or physical sensations that arise as you consider different options. By bringing mindful awareness to the decision-making process, you can tap into your intuition and make a choice that aligns with your needs and values.

Remember, finding the right therapist is a personal and individual process. Don't be discouraged if you don't find the perfect fit right away. Therapy is a collaborative journey, and with the right therapist, you can work towards improved mental health and well-being.

Different Approaches to Therapy

In the field of mental health, there are various approaches to therapy that can be utilized to address the specific needs of individuals. These approaches encompass a wide range of theoretical frameworks, techniques, and interventions aimed at promoting psychological well-being and facilitating positive change. In this section, we will explore some of the different approaches to therapy commonly used in mental health practice.

Psychodynamic Therapy

Psychodynamic therapy is an approach that originated from the theories of Sigmund Freud. It emphasizes the exploration of unconscious processes and childhood experiences to gain insight into current thoughts, emotions, and behaviors. The therapist and client work collaboratively to identify and understand the underlying causes of distress and to develop healthier ways of coping.

During psychodynamic therapy, the therapist may utilize techniques such as free association, dream analysis, and interpretation of transference and resistance. The goal is to bring unconscious conflicts and unresolved issues to conscious awareness, facilitating personal growth and healing.

Cognitive-Behavioral Therapy (CBT)

Cognitive-behavioral therapy (CBT) is a widely used approach that focuses on the relationship between thoughts, emotions, and behaviors. It is based on the idea that our thoughts and beliefs significantly influence our feelings and actions. CBT aims to identify and modify maladaptive thoughts and behaviors that contribute to psychological distress.

The therapist and client work together to identify negative thought patterns and cognitive distortions. Through various techniques, such as cognitive restructuring and behavioral experiments, individuals learn to challenge and replace unhelpful thoughts with more realistic and adaptive ones. CBT is often structured, goal-oriented, and time-limited, making it suitable for addressing specific problems or disorders.

Humanistic Therapy

Humanistic therapy is based on the belief that individuals possess the innate capacity for self-awareness, growth, and personal fulfillment. This approach emphasizes the importance of the individual's subjective experience and the therapeutic relationship as a catalyst for change.

One key humanistic therapy is person-centered therapy, developed by Carl Rogers. The therapist provides a supportive and non-judgmental environment where the client feels accepted and understood. The focus is on facilitating self-exploration, self-acceptance, and self-actualization. Therapeutic techniques in humanistic therapy may include active listening, empathy, and unconditional positive regard.

Existential Therapy

Existential therapy is rooted in the philosophical tradition of existentialism and explores the fundamental questions of human existence, such as the meaning of life, freedom, responsibility, and death. This approach emphasizes individual choice and the importance of taking responsibility for one's own life and choices.

Therapists utilizing existential therapy help clients explore and confront the anxieties and dilemmas inherent in the human condition. By examining their values, beliefs, and personal meaning systems, individuals can develop a greater sense of purpose, authenticity, and fulfillment.

Family Systems Therapy

Family systems therapy views individuals within the context of their family systems and emphasizes the interconnectedness and dynamics of family relationships. It recognizes that changes in one family member will affect the entire system and seeks to improve family functioning by addressing relational patterns and communication.

Therapists using family systems therapy work with families to identify and understand how their interactions and communication contribute to problems. Through techniques such as genograms, role play, and structural interventions, they help families develop healthier patterns of interaction and create a more supportive and nurturing family environment.

Group Therapy

Group therapy involves a therapeutic approach where multiple individuals with similar issues or goals come together under the guidance of a trained therapist. The group setting provides a supportive and interactive environment for participants to share experiences, gain insight, and develop coping skills.

Benefits of group therapy include universality (realizing you are not alone in your struggles), the opportunity for feedback and support from others, and the chance to practice new ways of relating and communicating. Group therapy can be used in conjunction with individual therapy or as a standalone treatment, depending on the needs of the individual.

Integration of Approaches

It is important to note that therapists often integrate different approaches and techniques, depending on the needs, preferences, and goals of the individual client. This integrative approach allows for flexibility and customization, ensuring that therapy is tailored to the unique circumstances of each person. Therapists may draw from various theoretical perspectives and interventions to create a comprehensive and individualized treatment plan.

Considerations and Challenges

When utilizing different approaches to therapy, it is essential to consider cultural, social, and contextual factors that may influence the effectiveness of the interventions. Therapists must be aware of their own biases and work towards cultural competence to provide appropriate and sensitive care to diverse populations.

Additionally, therapy is not a one-size-fits-all solution, and what works for one person may not work for another. Some individuals may require a combination of different approaches or a more specialized approach specific to their needs.

Conclusion

The field of mental health offers a multitude of therapeutic approaches to address the diverse range of psychological issues individuals may face. Psychodynamic therapy, cognitive-behavioral therapy, humanistic therapy, existential therapy, family systems therapy, and group therapy are just a few examples of the approaches available.

By understanding the principles and techniques underlying each approach, mental health professionals can tailor their interventions to best suit the needs of their clients. The integration of different approaches allows for a comprehensive and individualized approach to therapy, fostering positive change and promoting psychological well-being.

Benefits and Limitations of Therapy

Therapy, also known as psychotherapy or counseling, is a widely recognized and essential component of mental health treatment. It involves a therapeutic relationship between a trained professional and an individual seeking support and guidance. Therapy offers a safe and confidential space for individuals to explore their thoughts, emotions, and behaviors, with the goal of promoting personal growth, improving mental well-being, and enhancing overall quality of life. In this section, we will discuss the benefits and limitations of therapy, providing a comprehensive understanding of its role in mental health care.

Benefits of Therapy

Therapy offers numerous benefits that can significantly impact an individual's mental health and overall well-being. Some of the key benefits include:

1. **Emotional Support:** One of the primary advantages of therapy is the emotional support it provides. The therapist creates a non-judgmental and empathetic environment where individuals feel safe to express their thoughts and feelings without fear of criticism or rejection. This support can be particularly beneficial for individuals going through challenging life experiences, such as trauma, grief, or relationship difficulties.

2. **Insight and Self-Reflection:** Therapy facilitates self-reflection and introspection, helping individuals gain deeper insight into their thoughts, emotions, and behaviors. Through discussions and therapeutic techniques, individuals can develop a greater understanding of themselves, their values, and their motivations. This newfound insight can lead to personal growth and enable individuals to make more informed decisions that align with their goals and values.

3. **Skill Development:** Therapy equips individuals with valuable coping skills and strategies to manage stress, regulate emotions, and navigate life's challenges. Therapists may teach techniques such as relaxation exercises,

mindfulness practices, and effective communication skills, empowering individuals to develop healthy coping mechanisms and adapt to difficult situations more effectively.

4. **Behavioral Change**: Therapy can facilitate behavior change by helping individuals identify and modify negative patterns and habits. It provides a supportive framework for individuals to explore the underlying causes of their behaviors, gain awareness of triggers, and develop alternative, healthier ways of responding. This can be particularly advantageous for individuals struggling with issues such as addiction, compulsive behaviors, or unhealthy relationship patterns.

5. **Improved Relationships**: Therapy can enhance the quality of individuals' relationships by addressing interpersonal challenges and improving communication skills. Through therapy, individuals can gain a better understanding of their own needs and boundaries, as well as develop empathy and active listening techniques. This can lead to healthier and more fulfilling relationships with family, friends, and romantic partners.

These benefits highlight the significant impact therapy can have on individuals' lives by promoting self-awareness, personal growth, and emotional well-being.

Limitations of Therapy

While therapy can be highly effective, it is essential to acknowledge its limitations. Understanding these limitations can help individuals set realistic expectations and determine if therapy is the right fit for their specific needs. Some of the limitations of therapy include:

1. **Time Commitment**: Therapy is a time-intensive process that requires consistent attendance and active engagement. Depending on the individual, therapy can last for several weeks, months, or even years. This time commitment may not be feasible for everyone, especially those with demanding work or family responsibilities. It is essential to consider this factor when evaluating the suitability of therapy.

2. **Financial Considerations**: Therapeutic services can be costly, especially for individuals without access to insurance coverage or adequate financial resources. The cost of therapy can limit an individual's ability to seek regular or long-term treatment. It is crucial to explore different options for

affordable therapy, such as community mental health centers, sliding-scale fees, or free counseling services, if financial constraints are a concern.

3. **Treatment Effectiveness**: The effectiveness of therapy can vary depending on multiple factors, including the therapist's experience and expertise, the specific therapeutic approach used, and the individual's willingness to engage in the process. Finding the right therapist and therapeutic approach that aligns with an individual's unique needs and preferences can significantly impact the effectiveness of treatment. It may require some trial and error to find the right fit.

4. **Inherent Subjectivity**: Therapy relies on the subjective experiences and perspectives of both the individual and the therapist. The interpretation of these experiences can be influenced by personal biases, cultural differences, and other factors. While skilled therapists strive to maintain objectivity, there is an inherent element of subjectivity in the therapeutic process that can impact the outcomes of treatment.

5. **Scope of Practice**: Therapy has its limitations in dealing with certain mental health conditions or situations. For example, individuals experiencing severe psychiatric symptoms, such as acute psychosis or suicidal intent, may require more intensive interventions, such as psychiatric hospitalization. Therapists are trained to recognize such situations and collaborate with other mental health professionals to ensure individuals receive the appropriate level of care.

Understanding the limitations and potential challenges of therapy can help individuals make informed decisions about seeking treatment and manage their expectations throughout the therapeutic process.

In summary, therapy offers significant benefits in promoting emotional support, self-reflection, skill development, behavioral change, and improved relationships. However, it is crucial to consider the time commitment, financial considerations, treatment effectiveness, inherent subjectivity, and the scope of practice when seeking therapy. By understanding both the benefits and limitations of therapy, individuals can make more informed decisions and fully leverage its potential to enhance their mental health and overall well-being.

Remember, therapy is not a one-size-fits-all solution, and it may take time and effort to find the right therapist and approach that best suits each individual's needs and goals.

Considering Medication and Psychopharmacology

In the journey towards promoting mental health, it is important to consider the role of medication and psychopharmacology. Medication can be a valuable tool in the treatment of mental health disorders, particularly when used in combination with other therapeutic interventions. However, it is crucial to approach medication with caution and to carefully weigh the benefits and risks.

Understanding Medication and Psychopharmacology

Medication, in the context of mental health, refers to the use of drugs to alleviate symptoms and improve overall well-being. Psychopharmacology is the study of how drugs affect the mind and behavior. It involves understanding the mechanisms of action, side effects, and efficacy of various medications used in the treatment of mental health disorders.

Psychiatric medications work by influencing the balance of chemicals in the brain, such as neurotransmitters. By targeting specific neurotransmitter systems, these medications can help regulate mood, reduce anxiety, improve cognition, and manage other symptoms associated with mental health disorders.

Benefits of Medication in Mental Health Treatment

Medication can bring about significant benefits in the treatment of mental health disorders. Some of the key advantages include:

1. Symptom reduction: Medication can alleviate distressing symptoms associated with mental health disorders, such as depression, anxiety, hallucinations, and delusions. This can lead to improved functioning and a better quality of life.

2. Support for therapy: Medication can provide symptomatic relief, making it easier for individuals to engage in therapy and other interventions. It can enhance the effectiveness of therapy by reducing the intensity of symptoms.

3. Prevention of relapse: For some mental health disorders, such as bipolar disorder and schizophrenia, medication plays a crucial role in preventing relapse and maintaining stability. It helps individuals maintain a balance in mood and reduces the risk of recurrence of acute episodes.

4. Improved overall well-being: By addressing the underlying chemical imbalances in the brain, medication can improve overall well-being, promote emotional stability, and enhance daily functioning.

It is important to note that not all individuals with mental health disorders require medication as part of their treatment plan. The decision to use medication should be made in collaboration between the individual, their healthcare provider, and other members of the treatment team.

Considerations and Caveats

While medication can be beneficial, it is essential to consider several factors before starting or adjusting a medication regimen. Some considerations include:

1. Individualized approach: Each person's response to medication can vary, and there is no one-size-fits-all solution. Healthcare providers need to consider an individual's unique symptoms, medical history, genetics, and lifestyle factors when prescribing medication.

2. Potential side effects: Like any medication, psychiatric drugs can have side effects. It is important for individuals to be aware of the potential side effects and discuss them with their healthcare provider. Common side effects may include drowsiness, weight gain, sexual dysfunction, and changes in blood pressure.

3. Monitoring and follow-up: Regular monitoring is essential when taking psychiatric medication. Healthcare providers may need to adjust the dosage or switch medications based on the individual's response and any observed side effects. Open communication between the individual and their healthcare provider is crucial during this process.

4. Medication interactions: Psychiatric medications can interact with other medications, supplements, or substances, potentially leading to adverse effects or reduced effectiveness. It is important to inform healthcare providers about all medications and substances being used to ensure safe and effective treatment.

5. Education and informed consent: Individuals should be provided with comprehensive information about the medication, including its intended benefits, potential side effects, and alternatives. Informed consent is crucial, and individuals should feel empowered to ask questions and make decisions about their treatment.

Integrating Medication with Other Strategies

Medication is often most effective when used in conjunction with other strategies for mental health maintenance. It is important to adopt a holistic approach that includes psychotherapy, lifestyle modifications, and self-care practices. The goal is to create a comprehensive treatment plan that addresses both the biological and psychosocial aspects of mental health.

Therapy can help individuals develop coping skills, enhance self-awareness, and explore underlying issues contributing to their mental health symptoms. In combination with medication, therapy can provide a holistic approach to recovery and well-being.

Additionally, lifestyle modifications such as regular exercise, healthy eating, stress management techniques, and adequate sleep can all contribute to improved mental health. These lifestyle factors can complement the benefits of medication and enhance overall well-being.

Thinking Outside the Box

In the field of mental health, unconventional approaches can sometimes offer complementary support to medication and traditional treatment methods. Some individuals may find relief through alternative therapies such as acupuncture, herbal supplements, or biofeedback. While scientific evidence for these approaches varies, it is important to approach them with an open mind and involve healthcare professionals in decision-making.

Engaging in creative practices such as music therapy, art therapy, or dance therapy can also support mental health and serve as an outlet for self-expression. These forms of therapy can be used in combination with medication to enhance overall well-being and facilitate personal growth.

Conclusion

Considering medication and psychopharmacology is an important component of mental health treatment. While medication can provide significant benefits, it should be approached with caution and individualized to meet the unique needs of each person. It is essential to consider potential side effects, monitor and adjust dosage as needed, and integrate medication with other strategies for mental health maintenance. By taking a holistic approach that considers all aspects of an individual's well-being, we can empower them on their journey towards mental health and overall wellness.

Peer Support and Group Therapy

Importance of Peer Support

Peer support plays a crucial role in promoting mental health and well-being. It is a form of support where individuals with similar experiences, challenges, or conditions come together to provide mutual assistance, encouragement, and understanding. This section will explore the importance of peer support, its benefits, and its application in mental health.

Benefits of Peer Support

Peer support offers several unique benefits that distinguish it from other forms of support. These benefits include:

1. **Shared Experience:** Peer support allows individuals to connect with others who have faced similar challenges, providing a sense of validation and understanding. This shared experience can help reduce feelings of isolation and loneliness.

2. **Empowerment:** Peer support enables individuals to take an active role in their own recovery. By sharing their experiences and strategies for coping, peers can empower one another and foster a sense of self-efficacy.

3. **Role Modeling:** Peers who have successfully navigated their own mental health journeys can serve as role models for others. Witnessing someone who has overcome similar challenges can instill hope and inspire individuals to believe in their own ability to recover.

4. **Non-judgmental Environment:** Peer support groups provide a safe and accepting space for individuals to discuss their mental health concerns. Peers offer empathy and understanding without judgment, creating an atmosphere of trust and openness.

5. **Practical Support:** Peers can offer practical strategies and resources for managing mental health issues. This may include sharing information about treatment options, suggesting coping techniques, or providing recommendations for supportive services.

Application of Peer Support in Mental Health

Peer support is applicable in various mental health contexts and can complement professional treatment. Some key applications of peer support include:

1. **Support Groups:** Peer-led support groups provide spaces for individuals to share their experiences, challenges, and triumphs. These groups can focus on specific mental health conditions or broader well-being and recovery.

2. **Online Communities:** The advent of the internet has given rise to online peer support communities, where individuals can connect with others globally, irrespective of geographical limitations. These communities offer a convenient and accessible platform for seeking and providing support.

3. **Peer Mentoring:** Peer mentoring programs pair individuals who have successfully managed their mental health with those who are currently experiencing challenges. Mentors provide guidance, encouragement, and practical advice based on their own experiences.

4. **Advocacy and Activism:** Peers can play an active role in advocating for improved mental health policies, promoting awareness, and reducing stigma. They can use their collective voice to create meaningful change in their communities.

5. **Recovery-Oriented Services:** Peer support is increasingly integrated into formal mental health services, such as outpatient clinics and community-based programs. Peers may work alongside mental health professionals, offering support and guidance to individuals in their recovery journeys.

Challenges and Considerations

While peer support brings numerous benefits, there are also challenges and considerations to address. These include:

+ **Training and Supervision:** Peers should receive adequate training and ongoing supervision to ensure they have the necessary knowledge and skills to support others effectively. This helps maintain the quality and safety of peer support services.

+ **Confidentiality and Boundaries:** Peers must understand and adhere to ethical guidelines regarding confidentiality and appropriate boundaries in supporting others. Clear communication about the limitations of peer support is crucial.

+ **Potential Triggers:** Peer support may unintentionally trigger difficult emotions or memories for individuals participating in the group. Facilitators should create a supportive environment and establish guidelines for handling potential triggers.

✦ **Inclusivity and Diversity:** Peer support should be inclusive and account for diversity in terms of culture, race, gender, sexual orientation, and other aspects of identity. Ensuring an inclusive environment fosters a sense of belonging for all participants.

✦ **Ongoing Evaluation and Feedback:** Continuous evaluation of peer support programs and soliciting feedback from participants is crucial for maintaining their effectiveness. This allows for adjustments and improvements to meet evolving needs.

Real-World Example

To illustrate the importance of peer support, let's consider a real-world example. Sarah, a teenager struggling with anxiety, joins a peer support group specifically for adolescents with anxiety disorders. In this group, Sarah meets peers who have faced similar challenges and have found effective coping strategies. Through sharing experiences and learning from one another, Sarah gains a sense of support, empathy, and empowerment. The group provides a safe space for her to express her concerns without fear of judgment. Over time, Sarah's participation in the group contributes to her increased confidence, improved coping skills, and enhanced overall well-being.

Further Resources

For individuals interested in exploring peer support further, the following resources may be helpful:

✦ Mental Health America: `www.mhanational.org`

✦ National Alliance on Mental Illness: `www.nami.org`

✦ International Association of Peer Supporters: `www.inaops.org`

✦ Mental Health Commission of Canada: `www.mentalhealthcommission.ca`

Conclusion

Peer support offers a valuable and unique form of support for individuals dealing with mental health challenges. It provides a safe and empathetic environment, promotes empowerment and self-efficacy, and offers practical strategies for managing mental health issues. Incorporating peer support into mental health treatment and support systems can enhance overall well-being and contribute to individuals' recovery journeys.

Different Types of Support Groups

Support groups can be a valuable resource for individuals facing various mental health challenges. These groups provide a safe and supportive environment where individuals can connect with others who have similar experiences, share their thoughts and feelings, and gain insights and coping strategies. There are various types of support groups available, each catering to specific needs and circumstances. In this section, we will explore some of the different types of support groups that individuals may find helpful on their mental health journey.

1. Peer-Led Support Groups: Peer-led support groups are facilitated by individuals who have personal experience with a particular mental health condition. These groups are typically run by trained peers who have successfully navigated their own mental health challenges. Peer-led support groups provide a sense of validation and understanding, as members can relate to each other's struggles and offer guidance based on their own experiences. Examples of peer-led support groups include Alcoholics Anonymous (AA) and Narcotics Anonymous (NA) for individuals recovering from addiction.

2. Therapist-Led Support Groups: Therapist-led support groups are facilitated by mental health professionals such as psychologists, counselors, or social workers. These groups are structured and guided by the expertise and training of the facilitator. Therapist-led support groups provide a structured and therapeutic environment where participants can learn coping skills, receive guidance, and explore their emotions in a safe space. These groups are particularly beneficial for individuals who require professional guidance and assistance in managing their mental health. Examples of therapist-led support groups include Cognitive-Behavioral Therapy (CBT) groups for individuals with anxiety disorders or depression.

3. Online Support Groups: With the rise of technology and the internet, online support groups have emerged as a convenient and accessible option for individuals seeking support. Online support groups allow individuals to connect with others from the comfort of their own homes, making them particularly beneficial for those facing barriers such as distance or social anxiety. These groups can take various forms, including chat rooms, forums, or video conference platforms. Online support groups offer the opportunity for individuals to share

their experiences, ask questions, and receive support and advice from a supportive virtual community.

4. Condition-Specific Support Groups: Condition-specific support groups focus on a particular mental health condition or a related group of conditions. These groups bring together individuals who share a common diagnosis, enabling participants to discuss specific challenges, treatment options, and coping strategies related to their mental health condition. Condition-specific support groups can provide a wealth of knowledge and insights into managing symptoms and navigating the healthcare system. Examples of condition-specific support groups include groups for individuals with bipolar disorder, schizophrenia, or post-traumatic stress disorder (PTSD).

5. Caregiver Support Groups: Caregiver support groups cater to the unique needs of individuals who provide care and support for individuals with mental health conditions. These groups allow caregivers to connect with others facing similar challenges, share their experiences, and gain emotional support and practical advice. Caregiver support groups are beneficial in reducing feelings of isolation, burnout, and stress associated with caregiving. These groups provide a space for caregivers to discuss their concerns, learn self-care strategies, and access resources to better support their loved ones. Examples of caregiver support groups include groups for parents of children with ADHD or support groups for spouses of individuals with Alzheimer's disease.

It is important to note that support groups may vary in their structure, format, and focus. Some groups may be open-ended, offering continuous support, while others may follow a specific curriculum or program. Additionally, support groups can be offered in various settings, including community centers, hospitals, churches, or online platforms.

Joining a support group can be a valuable addition to an individual's mental health journey. It is essential to find a support group that aligns with one's needs, preferences, and comfort level. Individuals may need to try different groups or attend a few sessions before finding the right fit. Support groups should provide a safe and inclusive environment where individuals feel respected, supported, and empowered.

Example Scenario: Alicia has been struggling with depression and has recently started therapy. Her therapist suggests that she consider joining a support group to supplement her individual therapy sessions. Alicia decides to explore different types of support groups in her area and online. She discovers a therapist-led support group at a local mental health center that focuses on depression and anxiety. Intrigued by the structured approach and guidance from a professional, she attends a few sessions and feels a sense of relief and connection with others who share similar experiences.

Alicia also joins an online support group specifically for individuals with depression, allowing her to connect with a wider community and seek support from the comfort of her home.

   Exercise: Think about a mental health condition that you are interested in or have personal experience with. Research and find a support group related to that condition. Write a brief summary of the support group's focus, format, and potential benefits it may offer to individuals with that specific mental health condition.

Peer Support Models and Programs

Peer support programs play a crucial role in promoting mental health and well-being. These programs involve individuals with lived experience of mental health challenges providing support and guidance to their peers. Peer support models and programs offer unique benefits, as peers can relate to and understand each other's experiences in a way that professionals may not. In this section, we will explore different peer support models and programs, their effectiveness, and some examples of successful initiatives.

Types of Peer Support Models

There are various types of peer support models used in mental health settings. Let's take a closer look at some of the most common ones:

1. **Peer Support Groups:** Peer support groups are safe spaces where individuals with similar experiences come together to share their thoughts, feelings, and coping strategies. These groups can be facilitated by a peer support worker or can be self-led. They provide a sense of belonging and understanding, reducing feelings of isolation and stigma.

2. **Peer Specialists:** Peer specialists are individuals who have received specialized training and certification to provide support services. They may work in various settings such as hospitals, community centers, or educational institutions. Peer specialists use their own experiences to help others navigate their mental health journeys, providing guidance, resources, and emotional support.

3. **Peer-Run Crisis Services:** Peer-run crisis services offer immediate support to individuals in crisis. Peers who work in these services undergo rigorous training to develop skills in crisis intervention and de-escalation. These programs can include helplines, crisis text lines, or drop-in centers where individuals can seek support and guidance when they need it the most.

4. **Peer Navigation Programs:**   Peer navigation programs aim to guide individuals through the complex mental health system, providing information and advocacy. Peers who work as navigators help individuals access appropriate resources, understand treatment options, and navigate the challenges they may face during their recovery journey.

5. **Peer Coaching and Mentoring:**   Peer coaching and mentoring involve one-on-one support relationships between a peer coach/mentor and an individual seeking support.   Peer coaches/mentors provide guidance, encouragement, and accountability. They help individuals set goals, develop coping strategies, and build resilience.

Effectiveness of Peer Support Programs

Research has shown that peer support programs can have a positive impact on individual well-being and mental health outcomes. Here are some key findings:

- Peer support programs reduce feelings of isolation and loneliness by creating a sense of community and belonging.

- Peers, having experienced similar challenges, can provide empathy, validation, and understanding, leading to increased self-esteem and self-efficacy.

- Peer support programs empower individuals to take an active role in their own recovery, promoting autonomy and self-advocacy.

- Peers can share practical coping strategies and resources that have been helpful in their own journeys, providing practical support.

- Peer support can complement traditional mental health services, enhancing engagement and outcomes for individuals receiving professional treatment.

It is important to note that while peer support programs have significant benefits, they are not a substitute for professional mental health care. They work best as part of a comprehensive support system that includes both peers and professionals.

Examples of Successful Peer Support Initiatives

Peer support programs have gained recognition worldwide, and many successful initiatives have been implemented. Here are a few examples:

1. **Mental Health First Aid (MHFA):** MHFA is a training program that teaches individuals how to identify and respond to signs of mental health challenges. The program incorporates peer support principles, equipping participants with the skills to provide initial support to someone in crisis.

2. **Wellness Recovery Action Plan (WRAP):** WRAP is a peer-led program that helps individuals develop personalized plans for managing their mental health. The program focuses on self-advocacy, self-care, and crisis prevention.

3. **NAMI Peer-to-Peer:** The National Alliance on Mental Illness (NAMI) offers a peer-led educational program called Peer-to-Peer. It provides a supportive environment for individuals living with mental health challenges to learn about mental health, cope with symptoms, and develop recovery strategies.

4. **Hearing Voices Network (HVN):** HVN is an international network of support groups for individuals who experience auditory hallucinations or other unusual sensory experiences. The network encourages peer support, acceptance, and understanding of these experiences.

5. **Online Peer Support Communities:** With the advent of technology, online peer support communities have emerged as a valuable resource. Platforms like 7 Cups and Mental Health America's support community offer virtual spaces where individuals can connect with peers, share their stories, and receive support.

These examples demonstrate the diversity and effectiveness of peer support programs across different populations and settings.

Promoting and Navigating Peer Support Programs

If you are interested in accessing or participating in peer support programs, here are some steps to get started:

1. **Research Available Programs:** Look for peer support programs or organizations in your community or online. Conduct research to determine which programs align with your needs and preferences.

2. **Reach Out for Information:** Contact the program coordinators or facilitators to gather more information about the program structure, requirements, and any associated costs. They can also provide guidance on how to get involved or access services.

3. **Consider Training and Certification:** If you are interested in becoming a peer support worker, explore training and certification programs available in your region. These programs can provide you with the necessary skills and knowledge to effectively support others.

4. **Connect with Peer-Led Organizations:** Reach out to local or national peer-led organizations for additional resources and support. These organizations often have established networks and can connect you with peer support groups or other opportunities.

5. **Ensure Privacy and Confidentiality:** When participating in peer support programs, ensure that your privacy and confidentiality are respected. Understand the guidelines and protocols in place to safeguard your personal information.

Peer support programs can greatly enhance your mental health journey by providing understanding, guidance, and support. Remember, you are not alone, and there are people who have been through similar experiences and are willing to help.

Case Study: The Impact of Peer-led Support Groups

To illustrate the effectiveness of peer-led support groups, let's explore the case of Sarah, a young adult living with anxiety disorder. Sarah struggled with feelings of isolation and found it challenging to discuss her experiences with friends and family. She decided to join a local peer-led support group for individuals with anxiety disorders.

In the support group, Sarah connected with peers who understood her struggles firsthand. She received validation for her experiences and gained a sense of belonging. Within the supportive environment, peers shared coping strategies and resources that had helped them manage their anxiety.

Over time, Sarah noticed significant improvements in her mental well-being. She developed a stronger support network and gained confidence in managing her anxiety. Sarah eventually became a peer support worker herself, keen to support others who were going through similar challenges.

Sarah's story exemplifies the power of peer support programs in fostering understanding, empowerment, and recovery.

Conclusion

Peer support models and programs are valuable resources for individuals seeking mental health support. Whether through support groups, peer specialists, crisis services, navigation programs, or coaching and mentoring, peers offer unique perspectives and understanding. Such programs not only reduce feelings of isolation but also empower individuals to take control of their mental health journeys. By promoting the inclusion of peer support in mental health systems, we can create more holistic and effective approaches to supporting individuals on their path to recovery.

Remember, seeking support is a sign of strength, and connecting with peers who can relate to your experiences can make a significant difference in your mental health and overall well-being.

Online and Virtual Peer Support Communities

In today's digital age, technology has revolutionized the way we connect and communicate with others. As a result, online and virtual peer support communities have emerged as valuable resources for individuals seeking mental health support. These communities provide a safe and accessible platform for individuals to connect with others who share similar experiences, challenges, and goals. In this section, we will explore the benefits, challenges, and best practices of online and virtual peer support communities.

Benefits of Online and Virtual Peer Support Communities

Online and virtual peer support communities offer several advantages over traditional in-person support groups. Here are some of the key benefits:

- **Accessibility:** One of the primary advantages of online communities is their accessibility. Individuals can access support from the comfort of their own homes, eliminating geographical barriers. This is especially beneficial for individuals who live in remote areas, have limited mobility, or face transportation challenges.

- **Anonymity and Privacy:** Online platforms provide a level of anonymity that can be comforting for individuals who prefer to keep their struggles private. It allows participants to share their experiences openly without the fear of judgment or stigma that may be present in face-to-face interactions.

+ **24/7 Availability:** Unlike traditional support groups that meet at specific times, online communities are available 24/7. This ensures that individuals can access support whenever they need it, making it particularly helpful during times of crisis or when immediate support is required.

+ **Diverse Perspectives:** Online communities attract individuals from various backgrounds, cultures, and experiences. This diversity brings together a wealth of knowledge and perspectives, allowing for a richer learning and support environment. Participants can learn from each other's experiences and gain insights that they may not have encountered otherwise.

+ **Flexibility and Customization:** Online communities offer flexibility in terms of participation. Individuals have the option to engage as much or as little as they feel comfortable, and they can customize their level of involvement based on their needs and preferences. This flexibility can be empowering for individuals who may have limited time or energy to commit to traditional support groups.

+ **Continuity of Support:** Online communities provide a continuous source of support. Participants can establish ongoing connections and relationships, which can foster a sense of belonging and reduce feelings of isolation. This consistent support can contribute to long-term well-being and recovery.

Challenges and Considerations

While online and virtual peer support communities offer many benefits, it is important to be aware of the challenges and considerations associated with them. Here are some key factors to keep in mind:

+ **Quality and Credibility:** Not all online communities are created equal. It is essential to verify the credibility and quality of the platform and its members. Look for communities that are moderated or overseen by professionals or reputable organizations. This helps ensure that the information shared is accurate and that members adhere to respectful and supportive interactions.

+ **Safety and Security:** Online communities can be vulnerable to trolls, scams, or individuals with ill intentions. Users should take precautions to protect their personal information and be cautious when engaging with others. Familiarize yourself with the platform's privacy settings and reporting mechanisms to address any concerns promptly.

+ **Lack of In-Person Interaction:** While online communities can provide valuable support, they cannot replace the benefits of in-person interactions. Some individuals may find that face-to-face support groups offer a deeper sense of connection and understanding. It is important to find the right balance that meets your specific needs.

+ **Technology and Digital Literacy:** Accessing online communities requires basic technological proficiency and access to the internet. Not everyone has equal access to technology or the necessary digital literacy skills. Efforts should be made to ensure equitable access and provide support to individuals who may face barriers in participating.

+ **Potential for Misinformation:** Online communities are susceptible to misinformation. Participants should critically evaluate and verify the information they receive. Relying on evidence-based sources and seeking professional guidance when needed can help mitigate the risk of misinformation.

+ **Emotional Triggers:** Online communities may expose individuals to emotionally triggering content. It is crucial to practice self-care and set personal boundaries when engaging in these communities. Take breaks when needed and seek professional support if certain topics or conversations become overwhelming.

Best Practices for Online and Virtual Peer Support Communities

To ensure a positive and supportive experience in online and virtual peer support communities, it is helpful to follow some best practices. Here are some guidelines to consider:

+ **Respect and Empathy:** Treat others with respect, empathy, and kindness. Remember that individuals in the community may be going through challenging times, and the platform should be a safe space for everyone to share and seek support.

+ **Maintain Confidentiality:** Respect the privacy and confidentiality of others. Avoid sharing personal information or stories outside the community without explicit consent. Upholding confidentiality promotes trust and a sense of safety within the community.

+ **Verify Information:** Fact-check information before accepting it as accurate. This helps prevent the spread of misinformation and ensures that participants receive reliable and evidence-based support.

+ **Seek Professional Support:** Online communities can provide valuable peer support, but they should not replace professional help. If you or someone you know is in crisis or requires immediate assistance, reach out to a mental health professional or a helpline in your country.

+ **Engage Mindfully:** Be mindful of your own well-being when participating in online communities. Set boundaries, take breaks when needed, and seek professional help or support from loved ones if you are feeling overwhelmed.

+ **Report Concerns:** If you come across inappropriate behavior, harmful content, or feel unsafe within a community, report your concerns to the platform administrators or moderators. Reporting helps maintain a healthy and supportive environment for all participants.

+ **Contribute Positively:** Actively contribute to the community by offering support, sharing resources, and providing encouragement. Your contributions can make a significant difference in someone's mental health journey.

Real-World Example: Calming Anxiety Online Community

To illustrate the potential of online and virtual peer support communities, let's consider the "Calming Anxiety" online community. This community is specifically designed for individuals struggling with anxiety disorders. Members have the opportunity to connect with others, share coping strategies, and find support during difficult times. The following are some key features and activities within the community:

+ **Discussion Forums:** Members can engage in discussions on a variety of anxiety-related topics, such as managing panic attacks, challenging anxious thoughts, or coping with social anxiety. These forums facilitate peer-to-peer support and the exchange of personal experiences and strategies.

+ **Virtual Support Groups:** The community hosts virtual support group sessions facilitated by mental health professionals. These sessions provide a safe and structured space for members to share their struggles, ask questions, and receive guidance from both peers and professionals.

- **Guided Meditations and Relaxation Techniques:** The community offers a library of guided meditations, relaxation exercises, and breathing techniques specifically tailored to anxiety management. Members can access these resources at any time and practice them in the comfort of their own homes.

- **Expert Q&A Sessions:** Periodically, the community invites mental health experts to conduct live Q&A sessions. These sessions allow members to ask questions and receive evidence-based information from professionals who specialize in anxiety disorders.

- **Success Stories and Motivational Posts:** Members are encouraged to share their success stories and motivational posts to inspire others and foster hope. These stories highlight individual achievements, breakthroughs, and moments of strength in the face of anxiety.

- **Resource Library:** The community maintains a comprehensive resource library that includes articles, videos, and books related to anxiety disorders. Members can explore these resources at their own pace and delve deeper into understanding and managing their anxiety.

The "Calming Anxiety" online community exemplifies the power of online and virtual peer support communities in providing a holistic and accessible approach to managing mental health challenges.

In conclusion, online and virtual peer support communities play a crucial role in modern mental health strategies. They offer accessibility, anonymity, diverse perspectives, and 24/7 availability. However, it is necessary to consider factors such as quality and credibility, safety and security, and the potential for misinformation. By following best practices and engaging with mindfulness, individuals can harness the benefits of these communities while staying well-informed, supported, and connected in their mental health journey.

Navigating and Engaging with Support Groups

Support groups can be a valuable resource for individuals facing mental health challenges. They provide a safe and understanding environment where people with similar experiences can come together to share their stories, seek support, and learn from one another. Navigating and engaging with support groups effectively requires certain strategies and skills. In this section, we will explore some key principles and practical tips for making the most of support groups.

Benefits of Support Groups

Before diving into the strategies, let's first discuss the benefits of joining a support group. Support groups offer a range of advantages, including:

- **Validation and understanding**: Being part of a support group can help you feel validated in your experiences and emotions. It provides an opportunity to connect with others who truly understand what you're going through.

- **Learn from others**: Support groups offer a platform for sharing experiences, insights, and coping strategies. By listening to others' stories, you can gain new perspectives and learn effective ways to manage your own mental health challenges.

- **Sense of community**: Support groups provide a sense of community and belonging. Connecting with others who are going through similar struggles can help combat feelings of isolation and loneliness.

- **Emotional support**: In a support group, you can find emotional support and encouragement. Knowing that there are people who care and are rooting for your well-being can boost your resilience and motivation.

- **Practical advice and resources**: Support groups often provide access to valuable resources, such as information about mental health services, therapy options, and self-help materials. Additionally, fellow group members can offer practical advice based on their own experiences.

Finding the Right Support Group

To navigate and engage with support groups effectively, it's crucial to find the right fit. Here are some steps to help you find a suitable support group:

1. **Identify your needs**: Determine what specific mental health challenges or concerns you are facing. This will help you find a support group that aligns with your needs and goals.

2. **Seek professional recommendations**: Consult with mental health professionals, such as therapists or counselors, who can suggest support groups that may be beneficial for you. They can provide valuable insights and guide you towards groups that focus on your specific mental health condition.

3. **Online research:** Conduct online research to explore available support groups. There are numerous websites and online platforms dedicated to connecting people with various support groups. Look for groups that have a good reputation and positive reviews.

4. **Ask for recommendations:** Reach out to friends, family, or other individuals who have experience with support groups. They might be able to recommend groups they have found helpful or provide insights into support groups that cater to your specific needs.

5. **Attend meetings:** Once you have identified a potential support group, attend a few meetings to get a feel for the group dynamics, members, and overall atmosphere. This will help you assess whether the group is a good fit for you.

Remember, finding the right support group may take time and exploration. Don't be discouraged if you don't find the perfect fit immediately. Keep seeking and trying different groups until you find the one that best suits your needs.

Engaging in Support Groups

Once you have identified a support group that feels right for you, the following strategies can help you engage effectively:

+ **Active listening:** Listen attentively to others in the group. Give them your full attention and demonstrate empathy and understanding. Active listening allows you to learn from others' experiences and shows that you value their contributions.

+ **Share your experiences:** Open up and share your own experiences, thoughts, and feelings within the group. Sharing can be cathartic and may encourage others to do the same. It helps foster connection and mutual understanding.

+ **Respect boundaries:** Respect the boundaries and confidentiality of the group. Only share what you are comfortable sharing, and refrain from pressuring others to disclose personal information or experiences.

+ **Be non-judgmental:** Support groups are non-judgmental spaces where diverse perspectives and experiences are welcomed. Stay open-minded and avoid criticism or judgment. Remember that everyone's journey is unique, and what works for one person may not work for another.

- **Offer support:** Provide support and encouragement to fellow group members. Offering a kind word, expressing empathy, or sharing resources can make a big difference to someone who is struggling. Small acts of kindness can foster a supportive and nurturing environment.

- **Participate actively:** Take an active role in group discussions and activities. Contribute to conversations, ask questions, and offer insights. Active participation enhances the group's dynamics and fosters a collaborative and engaging atmosphere.

- **Respect diverse opinions:** Support groups often consist of individuals with diverse backgrounds and perspectives. It is important to respect and validate these differences. Engage in constructive dialogue, and be open to learning from the varied experiences within the group.

- **Follow group guidelines:** Every support group may have specific guidelines or rules to ensure a safe and respectful environment. Familiarize yourself with these guidelines and adhere to them. This helps maintain a positive group dynamic for everyone involved.

Extending Support Beyond Group Meetings

Support groups provide a valuable network of individuals who can help you on your mental health journey. To make the most of this network, consider the following suggestions:

- **Exchange contact information:** If group members are comfortable, exchange contact information with those you feel a connection with. This allows for continued support and connection outside of group meetings.

- **Stay connected online:** Many support groups have online platforms or social media groups where members can stay connected between meetings. Join these platforms to access additional resources, share insights, and continue discussions.

- **Reach out when needed:** Don't hesitate to reach out to fellow group members when you need support. They understand your struggles and can offer comfort and guidance. Be willing to reciprocate and support others when they reach out to you as well.

- **Attend social events:** Support groups often organize social events or gatherings. Attend these events to foster deeper connections and build relationships with group members in a more casual setting.

Support groups can provide ongoing support and a sense of community. By actively engaging with the group, staying connected with members, and extending support beyond meetings, you can maximize the benefits of being part of a support group.

Conclusion

Support groups can be a powerful tool for individuals facing mental health challenges. They offer validation, a sense of community, and practical advice. Navigating and engaging with support groups effectively involves finding the right fit, actively participating, and extending support beyond group meetings. By utilizing the strategies and principles outlined in this section, you can make the most of your support group experience and enhance your mental well-being. Remember, you are not alone on your journey to better mental health, and a supportive community can make a significant difference.

Family and Social Support

Impact of Social Relationships on Mental Health

Social relationships play a crucial role in shaping our mental health and overall well-being. The quality and quantity of social connections we have can significantly impact our emotional state, cognitive functioning, and even physical health. In this section, we will explore the various ways in which social relationships influence our mental health and its implications for fostering a supportive and nurturing social network.

The Importance of Social Connections

Humans are inherently social beings, and our need for social connections is deeply rooted in our biology. From an evolutionary perspective, belonging to a community or social group was fundamental for our survival. Our ancestors relied on social bonds to find food, provide protection, and reproduce. This need for social connections has persisted throughout the course of human history and remains essential for our psychological well-being.

Research consistently shows that individuals with strong social relationships experience better mental health outcomes. Having a network of supportive friends, family members, and peers acts as a protective factor against the development of mental health disorders. It contributes to higher levels of life satisfaction, self-esteem, and overall happiness. On the other hand, a lack of social connections is associated with feelings of loneliness, isolation, and an increased risk of mental health problems.

Emotional Support and Validation

One of the primary ways social relationships influence mental health is through the provision of emotional support and validation. When we are faced with challenging situations or stressful events, having someone we can turn to for emotional support plays a crucial role in helping us navigate those difficulties. Emotional support entails the provision of empathy, understanding, and reassurance, which can help us cope with stress, regulate our emotions, and feel more secure.

Validation is another important aspect of social relationships that impacts our mental health. When we feel understood and accepted by others, it boosts our self-esteem and promotes a sense of belonging. Validation assures us that our thoughts, feelings, and experiences are legitimate and worthy of recognition. Conversely, a lack of validation can contribute to feelings of self-doubt, invalidation, and is detrimental to our mental well-being.

Social Influence and Modeling Behavior

Our social interactions shape our thoughts, beliefs, attitudes, and behaviors through a process known as social influence. We are profoundly influenced by the people around us, and this influence extends to various aspects of our lives, including our mental health. Positive social influence can lead to the adoption of healthy coping mechanisms, positive self-perception, and optimism. Conversely, negative social influences can reinforce maladaptive behaviors, foster negative self-perception, and perpetuate mental health issues.

Modeling behavior is an important aspect of social influence. When we observe others who exhibit healthy attitudes and behaviors towards mental health, it can inspire and motivate us to make positive changes in our own lives. Conversely, witnessing negative attitudes or stigma towards mental health can perpetuate barriers to seeking help and hinder our well-being. Therefore, fostering social relationships that promote positive mental health attitudes and behaviors is crucial for creating a supportive environment.

Social Support and Stress Reduction

Social support, both tangible and intangible, is a powerful buffer against stress and its adverse effects on mental health. Tangible support refers to the provision of concrete assistance, such as financial help, transportation, or tangible resources. Intangible support, on the other hand, involves emotional support, advice, and guidance. Both forms of social support play a vital role in mitigating the negative impact of stress on mental well-being.

When we have a strong support system, we are more likely to perceive stressors as manageable and experience less distress in challenging situations. Social support offers a sense of security and reassurance, knowing that we can rely on others during difficult times. Furthermore, the act of seeking support from others and sharing our burdens can improve our mood, provide new perspectives, and promote problem-solving skills.

Social Isolation and Loneliness

In contrast to the positive impact of social relationships, social isolation and loneliness are associated with numerous mental health problems. Social isolation refers to a lack of social connections and minimal contact with others, while loneliness refers to the subjective experience of feeling disconnected or lacking companionship, even when surrounded by others. Both social isolation and loneliness can have severe consequences for mental health.

Prolonged social isolation and loneliness increase the risk of developing mental health disorders such as depression, anxiety, and substance abuse. They contribute to a heightened sense of vulnerability, lower self-esteem, and decreased life satisfaction. It is essential to recognize the impact of social isolation and loneliness on mental health and take proactive steps to foster social connections and reduce feelings of loneliness among individuals.

Strategies to Cultivate Supportive Social Relationships

Building and maintaining supportive social relationships is crucial for promoting mental health and well-being. Here are some strategies that can help cultivate positive and nurturing social connections:

+ **Quality over quantity:** Focus on building deep and meaningful relationships rather than having a large number of superficial connections.

+ **Open communication:** Engage in open and honest communication with others, expressing your thoughts, feelings, and needs while actively listening to others.

+ **Boundaries:** Establish and maintain healthy boundaries in relationships to ensure mutual respect and well-being.

+ **Shared activities:** Participate in activities and hobbies that align with your interests and values, as they provide opportunities to meet like-minded individuals.

+ **Support groups:** Consider joining support groups or seeking peer support from individuals facing similar challenges or experiences.

+ **Community involvement:** Engage in community activities, volunteering, or joining clubs or organizations to expand your social network.

Remember, nurturing social relationships requires time, effort, and reciprocity. It is a continuous process that involves both giving and receiving support. By actively investing in social connections, you can cultivate a strong support system that promotes positive mental health and enriches your overall well-being.

Conclusion

Social relationships have a profound impact on our mental health and well-being. They provide emotional support, validation, and act as a buffer against stress. Positive social connections foster positive attitudes and behaviors related to mental health, while a lack of social connections can contribute to feelings of loneliness and isolation. Recognizing the importance of social relationships and actively cultivating supportive connections is vital for maintaining good mental health. By fostering a nurturing social network, we can enhance our mental resilience, find solace during challenging times, and experience a greater sense of belonging and fulfillment.

Building a Supportive Social Network

Building a supportive social network is essential for maintaining good mental health. Humans are social beings, and our connections with others play a crucial role in our overall well-being. In this section, we will explore strategies to build and nurture a strong support system that can provide comfort, encouragement, and understanding during challenging times.

Understanding the Importance of Social Support

Social support refers to the network of relationships that individuals have with family, friends, peers, and other community members. It provides emotional, practical, and informational assistance, creating a sense of belonging and connectedness. Having a strong support system has been linked to numerous mental health benefits, including:

- Reduced stress levels: Social support can buffer the effects of stress by providing a sense of safety and protection. Having someone to confide in and share burdens with can help individuals cope with challenging situations.

- Increased self-esteem: Supportive relationships foster a positive self-image, boosting self-esteem. When surrounded by people who love and appreciate them, individuals feel valued and worthy, which enhances their mental well-being.

- Improved coping mechanisms: Supportive networks offer guidance, reassurance, and feedback, helping individuals develop effective coping strategies. When facing difficulties, they can turn to their support system for advice and perspective.

- Enhanced resilience: Resilience is the ability to bounce back from adversity and adapt to change. Social support provides resources, encouragement, and motivation, promoting resilience in individuals.

- Alleviated feelings of loneliness and isolation: Loneliness and social isolation are significant risk factors for mental health problems. Maintaining social connections helps combat these feelings and fosters a sense of belonging.

Building a Supportive Social Network

Building a supportive social network requires intentional effort and investment in nurturing relationships. Here are some strategies to help you establish and maintain a strong support system:

1. Identify individuals who support and uplift you. Start by identifying people in your life who genuinely care about your well-being and provide you with support. These may include family members, close friends, colleagues, or mentors. Focus on quality rather than quantity, as even a few meaningful connections can have a significant impact.

2. Seek out communities with shared interests.   Explore communities, clubs, or organizations that align with your interests and values. By engaging in activities you enjoy, you increase the chances of meeting like-minded individuals and potential sources of support.

3. Be open and authentic in your relationships.   To build deep and meaningful connections, it's important to be open and authentic. Share your thoughts, feelings, and experiences with trusted individuals, allowing them to understand and support you better. Vulnerability fosters empathy and strengthens relationships.

4. Communicate and express your needs.   Clearly articulate your needs and expectations to individuals within your support system. Let them know what kind of support you desire and how they can best provide it.   Open and honest communication helps build stronger connections and ensures your needs are met.

5. Be a supportive friend in return.   Building a support system is a two-way street. Offer support and be there for others in their time of need. Actively listen, provide validation and encouragement, and participate in their lives. By being a supportive friend, you strengthen your relationships and create a reciprocal system of support.

6. Use technology to your advantage.   In today's digital age, technology provides various avenues to connect with others.   Engage with online communities, participate in support groups or forums focused on mental health, and use social media mindfully to foster connections.

7. Seek professional support when needed.   While friends and family are essential sources of support, there may be times when professional help is necessary.   Mental health professionals can provide specialized support and guidance tailored to your needs. Don't hesitate to reach out if you require extra assistance.

Promoting an Inclusive and Supportive Network

Creating an inclusive and supportive social network involves embracing diversity and ensuring that everyone feels valued. Here are some tips to promote inclusivity within your support system:

1. **Embrace diversity.** Cultivate relationships with individuals from diverse backgrounds, cultures, and perspectives. Learn about their experiences, beliefs, and challenges. Embracing diversity enriches your support system and promotes understanding and empathy.

2. **Be mindful of biases and prejudices.** Examine your own biases and prejudices, and work towards overcoming them. Treat others with respect and fairness, valuing their unique qualities and contributions. Creating a non-judgmental environment fosters trust and openness.

3. **Foster a sense of belonging.** Actively work to ensure that everyone in your support system feels welcome and included. Encourage participation, listen attentively, and validate the experiences of others. Celebrate diversity and create an environment where everyone's voices are heard and valued.

4. **Address conflicts and disagreements respectfully.** Conflicts and disagreements are a natural part of any relationship. However, it's important to address them respectfully and constructively. Practice active listening, be open to different perspectives, and work towards finding common ground.

5. **Seek opportunities for education and understanding.** Educate yourself about various cultures, identities, and experiences to better understand and support others. Attend workshops or webinars, read diverse literature, or engage in conversations that promote learning and growth. Broadening your horizons fosters inclusivity within your support network.

Examples and Case Studies

To better illustrate the importance of building a supportive social network, let's consider a few examples:

Example 1: Sarah's Journey to Recovery Sarah has been struggling with anxiety and depression for several years. She decides to reach out to her close friends, explaining her situation and seeking support. Her friends listen empathetically, reassure her, and encourage her to seek professional help. They also offer to accompany her to therapy sessions and provide emotional support throughout her recovery journey. With the support of her friends, Sarah successfully manages her mental health and feels grateful for the strong support system she has built.

Example 2: The Power of Peer Support Groups   John recently lost his job, which significantly impacted his mental well-being. He joins a local peer support group for individuals facing unemployment. In this group, he finds people who understand his struggles and can offer guidance and encouragement. They share job search strategies, provide emotional support, and celebrate each other's successes. Through this peer support group, John regains confidence, finds new job opportunities, and forms lasting friendships that extend beyond employment support.

Exercises

1. Reflect on your current support system. Identify individuals who play a significant role in supporting your mental health and write down ways they have supported you in the past.

2. Consider joining a community or group with shared interests. Research local organizations or online communities that align with your hobbies or passions. Outline steps you can take to become involved and connect with like-minded individuals.

3. Engage in active listening with a friend or family member. Practice being fully present and attentive when someone shares their thoughts or experiences with you. Afterward, reflect on the effectiveness of your listening skills and areas for improvement.

4. Conduct a self-reflection exercise focusing on your biases and prejudices. Identify any unconscious biases you may hold and think about ways to overcome them. Consider how embracing diversity can enrich your support system.

5. Research and attend a webinar or workshop on a topic related to cultural competence or building inclusive communities. Take notes on key insights and ideas that can be applied to your own support network.

Additional Resources

1. *Support Networks and Mental Health*, Mental Health Foundation, available at: https://www.mentalhealth.org.uk/a-to-z/s/support-networks-and-mental-health

2. *Building Healthy Supportive Relationships*, ReachOut, available at: https://au.reachout.com/everyday-issues/family-friends-and-relationships/building-healthy-supportive-relationships

3. *The Importance of Social Support*, Psychology Today, available at: `https://www.psychologytoday.com/intl/basics/social-support`

Communicating with Family and Loved Ones

Effective communication with family and loved ones is crucial for maintaining good mental health. Building strong relationships and establishing open lines of communication can provide a supportive network during challenging times. In this section, we will explore strategies and techniques for effective communication that can contribute to positive mental well-being.

Active Listening

One of the fundamental principles of effective communication is active listening. Active listening involves fully engaging with the person speaking, showing genuine interest, and focusing on the message being conveyed. By practicing active listening, you can create a safe space for open and honest dialogue.

To practice active listening, it is essential to:

1. Pay attention: Give your full attention to the person speaking. Minimize distractions and maintain eye contact to demonstrate your focus and interest.

2. Show empathy: Try to understand the speaker's perspective by putting yourself in their shoes. Validate their feelings and emotions to create a sense of understanding and support.

3. Avoid interrupting: Allow the person to express themselves fully without interrupting. Interrupting can hinder their flow of thoughts and emotions and may discourage them from sharing openly.

4. Reflect and summarize: Periodically reflect on what the person is saying to ensure understanding. Summarize their thoughts and feelings to indicate that you are actively listening and comprehending their message.

By practicing active listening, you can foster effective communication by creating an environment of trust and understanding.

Expressing Emotions

Openly expressing emotions is a crucial aspect of effective communication with family and loved ones. When you express your feelings honestly and respectfully, it can strengthen your relationships and promote emotional connection. Here are some strategies for expressing emotions effectively:

1. Use "I" statements: Start your sentences with "I" to convey your own emotions and experiences rather than attributing them to others. For example, say "I feel upset when..." instead of "You always make me upset when..."

2. Be specific: Clearly articulate your emotions and the reasons behind them. Use specific examples to help the other person understand your perspective better.

3. Use non-verbal cues: Non-verbal cues such as facial expressions and body language can enhance the understanding of your emotions. Maintain eye contact, use appropriate gestures, and establish a comfortable physical distance to convey your emotions effectively.

4. Avoid blaming: Instead of blaming and criticizing, focus on expressing how you feel and the impact certain situations or behaviors have on you. This helps to prevent defensiveness and encourages a more constructive conversation.

5. Practice active assertiveness: Assertiveness allows you to express your emotions while respecting the feelings and perspectives of others. State your emotions clearly, set boundaries, and make requests in a confident and respectful manner.

By expressing emotions effectively, you can foster deeper connections and understanding within your family and loved ones.

Conflict Resolution

Conflict is a natural part of any relationship. When disagreements arise, it is important to have effective conflict resolution skills to maintain healthy relationships. Here are some strategies for resolving conflicts in a respectful and constructive manner:

1. Practice active listening: Give each person involved in the conflict an opportunity to express their thoughts and feelings. Encourage active listening by rephrasing and reflecting on what each person has said.

2. Identify common goals: Find common ground and shared goals to create a cooperative mindset. Focus on finding solutions that benefit all parties involved rather than trying to "win" the argument.

3. Use "I" statements: When discussing the conflict, use "I" statements to express your feelings and needs without blaming the other person. This reduces defensiveness and encourages open communication.

4. Seek compromise: Look for mutually beneficial compromises that address the needs and concerns of both parties. Be willing to give and take and find a middle ground that satisfies both sides.

5. Take a break if needed: If emotions are running high, it can be helpful to take a break from the conflict and allow everyone involved some time to cool down. This can prevent escalating the situation further and allow for more productive discussions later.

6. Seek professional help if necessary: In some cases, conflicts may be complex or deeply rooted. If you find it challenging to resolve conflicts within your family, seeking the assistance of a trained therapist or counselor can provide valuable support and guidance.

By utilizing these conflict resolution strategies, you can maintain healthier relationships and reduce the negative impact of conflicts on your mental well-being.

Cultivating Empathy and Understanding

Empathy and understanding are essential components of effective communication in family and loved ones. When you cultivate empathy, you can better comprehend the emotions and experiences of others. Here are some techniques for fostering empathy and understanding:

1. Practice active empathy: Put yourself in the other person's shoes and try to understand their perspective and emotions. This helps to develop a deep sense of understanding and allows for more empathetic communication.

2. Ask open-ended questions: Open-ended questions encourage the other person to share more information and provide insights into their thoughts and emotions. This can help you gain a deeper understanding of their experiences.

3. Validate feelings: Acknowledge and validate the emotions expressed by your family and loved ones. This creates a safe space for open dialogue and cultivates trust and understanding.

4. Avoid judgment and assumptions: It is important to suspend judgment and avoid making assumptions about the thoughts and emotions of others. Approach conversations with an open mind and a genuine willingness to understand.

5. Practice perspective-taking: Take the time to imagine yourself in the other person's situation. Consider their background, values, and experiences to gain a more comprehensive understanding of their thoughts and emotions.

6. Show appreciation and gratitude: Express appreciation for the other person's willingness to communicate openly. Gratitude can foster connection and encourage continued honest communication within your relationships.

By cultivating empathy and understanding, you can strengthen the bond with your family and loved ones and promote a healthier and more supportive environment for communication.

Conclusion

Effective communication with family and loved ones plays a vital role in maintaining good mental health. By practicing active listening, expressing emotions effectively, resolving conflicts constructively, and cultivating empathy and understanding, you can create stronger bonds and supportive relationships. Remember, open and honest communication is a two-way process; it requires effort, patience, and active participation from all parties involved.

Caregiver Roles and Mental Health Support

Caregivers play a crucial role in supporting the mental health of individuals who are in need of assistance due to physical or mental health challenges. The demands and responsibilities of being a caregiver can have a significant impact on their own mental well-being. This section will explore the various caregiver roles and provide strategies for maintaining good mental health while fulfilling these roles.

Understanding Caregiving

Caregiving refers to the provision of support and assistance to individuals who are unable to fully care for themselves due to illness, disability, or age-related conditions. This support can range from assisting with daily activities such as bathing, dressing, and meal preparation, to managing medication schedules and coordinating medical appointments.

The Impact of Caregiving on Mental Health

Caregiving is a demanding and often challenging role that can have significant consequences for the mental health of individuals taking on this responsibility. Caregivers may experience high levels of stress, anxiety, and depression as a result of their caregiving duties. They may also neglect their own physical and emotional needs while prioritizing the well-being of the individuals they care for.

Self-Care for Caregivers

It is essential for caregivers to prioritize their own mental health and well-being in order to provide optimal care to others. Here are some strategies for self-care:

1. Seek support: Reach out to friends, family, and support groups to share your experiences and concerns. It can be therapeutic to connect with others who are going through similar challenges.

2. Set boundaries: Establish clear boundaries and communicate your needs to others. It is important to know your limitations and not overextend yourself.

3. Take breaks: Schedule regular breaks and time for self-care. Engage in activities you enjoy, such as hobbies, exercise, or relaxation techniques.

4. Practice self-compassion: Be kind to yourself and acknowledge that you are doing the best you can. Offer yourself the same level of understanding and compassion that you extend to others.

5. Seek professional help: If you are experiencing persistent feelings of stress, anxiety, or depression, consider seeking support from a mental health professional. They can help you develop coping strategies and provide additional resources.

Building a Support Network

Caregivers often carry the weight of their responsibilities alone, but it is important to build a support network to share the burden and seek assistance when needed. Here are some ways to build a support network:

1. Engage family and friends: Reach out to family and friends who can provide emotional support and practical help. Communicate your needs and delegate tasks when possible.

2. Join support groups: Seek out local or online support groups specifically for caregivers. These groups provide a safe space to share experiences, gain insights, and receive support from others who understand the challenges of caregiving.

3. Utilize community resources: Research and utilize community resources that offer services and support for caregivers, such as respite care, meal delivery, or support hotlines.

Taking Care of Your Mental Health

Caregivers must prioritize their mental health to avoid burnout and provide the best care possible. Here are some strategies for taking care of your mental well-being:

1. Practice stress management techniques: Engage in stress-reducing activities such as deep breathing exercises, meditation, or yoga. These techniques can help manage feelings of overwhelm and promote relaxation.

2. Stay physically active: Regular physical activity has been shown to improve mood and reduce symptoms of stress and depression. Find activities that you enjoy and can easily incorporate into your daily routine.

3. Maintain a healthy lifestyle: Ensure you are getting enough sleep, eating a balanced diet, and staying hydrated. A healthy lifestyle can positively impact your mental well-being.

4. Take time for yourself: Schedule regular periods of time to focus on your own needs and interests. Engaging in self-care activities can help rejuvenate and restore your energy.

5. Monitor your own mental health: Pay attention to your own emotional well-being and seek help if needed. Do not dismiss signs of depression, anxiety, or other mental health concerns.

Case Study: Emily's Journey

Emily has taken on the role of caregiving for her aging mother who has recently been diagnosed with dementia. At first, Emily dedicated all her time and energy to caring for her mother, neglecting her own well-being. As a result, Emily experienced increased stress, exhaustion, and feelings of isolation. However, after reaching out for support, she joined a local caregiver support group and started practicing self-care techniques. Emily learned to set boundaries with her mother's care and prioritized activities that brought her joy. Over time, Emily's mental health improved, allowing her to provide better care for her mother while also taking care of herself.

Conclusion

Caregivers play a vital role in supporting the mental health of individuals in need, but it is crucial for them to prioritize their own mental well-being. By practicing self-care, building a support network, and implementing strategies to safeguard their mental health, caregivers can continue to provide compassionate care while maintaining their own well-being. Remember, taking care of yourself is not selfish, but a necessary step in providing the best care possible.

Addressing Stigma and Promoting Understanding

Addressing stigma surrounding mental health is crucial for promoting understanding and providing support to individuals who may be experiencing mental health challenges. Stigma often arises from a lack of knowledge and misconceptions about mental health disorders, leading to discrimination, prejudice, and marginalization. This section will explore strategies to combat stigma and promote a more empathetic and inclusive society.

The Impact of Stigma on Mental Health

Stigma surrounding mental health can have detrimental effects on individuals, further exacerbating their mental health struggles. It can lead to feelings of shame, isolation, and self-stigmatization. This, in turn, can discourage individuals from seeking help and support, worsening their condition and delaying their recovery process. Stigma can also affect the quality of care received by individuals, as healthcare professionals may hold biased attitudes or provide suboptimal treatment due to misunderstandings or stereotypes.

Educating the Public

One of the most effective ways to address the stigma surrounding mental health is through education. By providing accurate information about mental health disorders, their prevalence, and their impact, we can increase awareness and understanding in the general public. This can be done through various channels, such as schools, workplaces, and community organizations.

Educational campaigns can debunk common myths and misconceptions, such as the belief that mental health disorders are a sign of weakness or that they cannot be treated effectively. By promoting evidence-based information, we can empower individuals with knowledge and equip them with the tools to challenge stigmatizing beliefs they may encounter.

Promoting Open Dialogue

Creating safe and non-judgmental spaces for open dialogue is crucial for reducing stigma and promoting understanding. This can be accomplished through community events, support groups, or online forums where individuals can share their experiences and engage in meaningful conversations about mental health.

Encouraging individuals with lived experiences to share their stories can be particularly impactful. Personal narratives humanize the experiences of those living with mental health disorders, dispelling stereotypes and fostering empathy. Additionally, providing opportunities for individuals to ask questions, express concerns, and seek clarification can help dispel misconceptions and encourage informed discussions.

Challenging Language and Stereotypes

Language plays a significant role in perpetuating stigma surrounding mental health. The use of derogatory or demeaning terms can further marginalize and stigmatize individuals with mental health disorders. It is essential to promote the use of respectful and person-centered language when discussing mental health.

By challenging stereotypes and avoiding labels, we can shift the narrative and promote a more accurate and compassionate understanding of mental health disorders. Highlighting the individual's strengths, resilience, and unique experiences can help counteract negative assumptions and foster a more inclusive and accepting environment.

Collaboration with Media and Influencers

The media and social influencers play a powerful role in shaping societal attitudes and perceptions. Collaborating with media outlets, journalists, and influencers to promote accurate and sensitive portrayals of mental health is crucial. By avoiding sensationalism, stereotyping, and stigmatizing language, media can contribute to reducing stigma and fostering empathy.

Promoting positive stories of individuals overcoming mental health challenges, discussing the importance of seeking help, and showcasing the impact of supportive communities can help inspire others and challenge stigmatizing beliefs.

Media campaigns can also provide information about available resources and support services, encouraging individuals to seek help when needed.

Legislative Actions and Policy Changes

Legislative actions and policy changes can play a vital role in addressing stigma and promoting understanding of mental health. Developing and implementing anti-discrimination laws that protect individuals with mental health disorders can help reduce stigma and prevent unjust treatment in various settings, such as employment, education, and healthcare.

Moreover, advocating for increased access to mental health services and resources can help normalize seeking help and reduce barriers to treatment. By prioritizing mental health in policy and allocating adequate funding, governments can demonstrate their commitment to promoting mental well-being and combating stigma.

Addressing Intersectional Stigma

It is important to recognize that stigma surrounding mental health is often intersectional, meaning it intersects with other forms of discrimination based on factors such as race, ethnicity, gender, sexuality, or socioeconomic status. Individuals who belong to marginalized or oppressed communities may face compounded stigma and may encounter unique barriers to accessing mental health support.

Addressing intersectional stigma requires an intersectional approach. This involves acknowledging the complex interplay of various identities and systems of oppression and tailoring strategies to meet the specific needs of diverse populations. It is crucial to actively challenge discrimination, promote cultural humility, and support culturally sensitive mental health services and programs.

Resources and Support

To further promote understanding and combat stigma surrounding mental health, it is essential to provide easily accessible resources and support. This can include helplines, online platforms, and community-based organizations that offer information, guidance, and a safe space for individuals to seek help or support.

Additionally, training programs for mental health professionals, educators, and community leaders can enhance their knowledge and skills in addressing stigma and promoting understanding. These programs can focus on cultural competency, empathetic communication, and the use of evidence-based practices to provide optimal support to individuals with mental health disorders.

Conclusion

Addressing stigma and promoting understanding is crucial for creating a supportive and inclusive society for individuals experiencing mental health challenges.   Through education, open dialogue, challenging stereotypes, collaboration with media, legislative actions, addressing intersectional stigma, and providing resources and support, we can work towards reducing stigma and fostering a more empathetic and inclusive understanding of mental health.   By doing so, we can help individuals feel empowered to seek help and support, promoting their well-being and overall mental health.

Mental Health Strategies for Specific Populations

Children and Adolescents

Developmental Factors in Mental Health

Understanding the developmental factors that contribute to mental health is essential in promoting well-being and preventing mental health issues among children and adolescents. Various factors during this crucial stage of life can influence mental health outcomes and shape an individual's overall psychological well-being. In this section, we will explore these developmental factors and their implications for mental health.

Biological Factors

Biological factors play a significant role in shaping mental health during development. The changes that occur in the brain and body can have a profound impact on emotional regulation, cognitive function, and the overall mental well-being of children and adolescents. It is important to consider the following biological factors:

- **Hormonal Changes:** During puberty, there is a surge in hormone production, which can lead to emotional instability and mood fluctuations. For instance, increased levels of estrogen and testosterone can contribute to heightened emotional reactivity and impulsive behaviors.

- **Neurodevelopment:** The brain undergoes significant changes during adolescence, particularly in the prefrontal cortex, which is responsible for executive functions such as decision-making and impulse control. The development of these areas can impact various aspects of mental health, including risk-taking behaviors and self-regulation.

+ **Genetic Factors:** Certain genetic predispositions can make individuals more susceptible to mental health disorders. Understanding the interplay between genetics and the environment can help identify those at higher risk and implement appropriate preventive measures.

+ **Physical Health:** Physical well-being is closely intertwined with mental health. Chronic health conditions, disabilities, and nutritional deficiencies can impact cognitive functioning, mood, and overall mental well-being in children and adolescents.

Environmental Factors

Environmental factors play a critical role in shaping mental health outcomes during development. The experiences and influences children and adolescents encounter in their environment can contribute to the development of mental health disorders. Consider the following environmental factors:

+ **Family Environment:** The quality of the familial relationships, parenting styles, and family dynamics significantly impact mental health outcomes. A nurturing and supportive family environment can foster resilience and protect against mental health issues, while adverse experiences, such as abuse or neglect, can increase vulnerability.

+ **School Environment:** Schools play a crucial role in shaping the mental well-being of children and adolescents. Factors such as academic pressure, bullying, social isolation, and inadequate support systems can contribute to the development of mental health disorders.

+ **Peer Relationships:** During this stage of life, peers become increasingly influential. Positive peer relationships can provide support, while peer rejection, social exclusion, or involvement in negative peer groups can have detrimental effects on mental health.

+ **Socioeconomic Status:** Socioeconomic factors, including access to resources, educational opportunities, and social support networks, can influence mental health outcomes. Children and adolescents from disadvantaged backgrounds may face additional stressors and barriers to mental health support.

+ **Cultural Influences:** Cultural beliefs, values, and norms can shape the perception and experience of mental health. Understanding and respecting cultural differences is crucial in providing appropriate support and intervention for children and adolescents from diverse backgrounds.

Psychological Factors

Psychological factors, including cognitive, emotional, and behavioral aspects, are also important considerations when examining developmental factors in mental health. Understanding these factors can help identify risk factors and implement effective interventions. Some psychological factors to consider include:

+ **Cognitive Development:** Cognitive processes, such as problem-solving skills, emotional regulation, and self-esteem, undergo significant development during childhood and adolescence. Difficulties in these areas can contribute to the development of mental health disorders.

+ **Emotional Well-being:** Emotional resilience, the ability to cope with stress, and emotional regulation are essential aspects of mental health. Children and adolescents who struggle with identifying and managing their emotions are at higher risk for developing mental health disorders.

+ **Identity Formation:** The process of identity formation, including the exploration of personal values, beliefs, and sexual orientation, can significantly impact mental health outcomes. Self-acceptance, self-identity, and self-esteem are vital for positive mental well-being during this developmental stage.

+ **Social Skills:** Developing and maintaining healthy social relationships is crucial for mental health. Difficulties in social interactions, communication, or peer relationships can contribute to the development of mental health disorders.

+ **Trauma and Adverse Childhood Experiences (ACEs):** Exposure to traumatic events and adverse childhood experiences, such as abuse, neglect, or witnessing violence, can have long-lasting effects on mental health. Understanding and addressing these experiences through trauma-informed care is essential for supporting children and adolescents.

It is important to note that these developmental factors interact and influence each other. For instance, biological changes during puberty can impact cognitive and emotional development, which can, in turn, influence an individual's social interactions and relationships. Understanding the complexities of these interactions can help professionals develop effective strategies for promoting mental health and preventing mental health disorders among children and adolescents.

Summary

In this section, we explored the various developmental factors that contribute to mental health outcomes in children and adolescents. We discussed the biological, environmental, and psychological factors that shape mental well-being during this crucial stage of life. By understanding these factors, professionals can implement targeted interventions and support systems to promote positive mental health and prevent the onset of mental health disorders. It is crucial to adopt a holistic approach that considers the unique challenges and needs of individuals in different developmental stages, cultural contexts, and social environments. Together, we can foster a supportive and nurturing environment for the healthy development of young minds.

Early Intervention and Prevention Strategies

Early intervention and prevention strategies play a crucial role in promoting mental health and well-being among children and adolescents. By identifying potential risk factors and providing appropriate support, we can address mental health challenges before they become more severe. This section will explore various strategies that can be implemented in schools, families, and communities to ensure early intervention and prevention.

Identifying Risk Factors

Identifying risk factors is the first step in early intervention. Here are some common risk factors that may contribute to mental health issues in children and adolescents:

- **Family history of mental health issues:** Children with a family history of mental health disorders are more susceptible to developing similar conditions.

- **Adverse childhood experiences (ACEs):** ACEs, such as abuse, neglect, or household dysfunction, can have long-lasting impacts on mental health.

- **Socioeconomic status:** Children from low-income backgrounds may face additional stressors and limited access to resources, impacting their mental health.

- **Bullying and peer victimization:** Both physical and cyberbullying can lead to emotional distress and mental health problems.

- **Academic pressure:** High academic expectations and excessive workload can contribute to stress and anxiety in students.

- **Traumatic events:** Exposure to traumatic events, such as natural disasters or violence, can have a profound impact on mental health.

Promoting Protective Factors

While risk factors are important to consider, it is equally vital to focus on protective factors that can mitigate the impact of these risks. Protective factors are conditions or attributes that contribute to positive mental health outcomes. Here are some key protective factors for children and adolescents:

- **Strong family relationships:** Supportive and nurturing relationships with family members help build resilience and buffer against mental health issues.

- **Positive peer relationships:** Healthy friendships and social connections can enhance well-being and provide a support network during challenging times.

- **Strong social-emotional skills:** Developing emotional intelligence, empathy, and problem-solving abilities enables young individuals to navigate stressors effectively.

- **Effective parenting practices:** Parental involvement, consistent discipline, and open communication contribute to positive mental health outcomes.

- **Access to quality education:** Educational opportunities and supportive environments contribute to overall well-being and future success.

- **Community support:** Community resources, such as mental health services and recreational activities, provide additional support to children and adolescents.

School-Based Intervention Programs

Schools play a critical role in early intervention and prevention efforts. Implementing evidence-based intervention programs can effectively support students' mental health. Here are some examples of school-based intervention strategies:

- **Social-emotional learning (SEL) programs:** SEL programs promote the development of social and emotional skills, including self-awareness, self-management, and responsible decision-making.

- **Mental health education:** Schools can provide comprehensive mental health education to increase awareness, reduce stigma, and provide students with the knowledge and skills to take care of their mental well-being.

- **Crisis intervention teams:** Trained staff members can form crisis intervention teams to provide immediate support to students experiencing mental health crises or emotional distress.

- **Peer mentoring programs:** Peer mentoring programs pair older students with younger ones to provide guidance, support, and positive role modeling.

- **Screening and assessment:** Implementing mental health screening and assessment tools can help identify students who may be at risk and provide appropriate interventions.

Family and Community Involvement

Collaboration between families, schools, and communities is crucial for effective early intervention and prevention. Here are some strategies to involve families and communities:

- **Parent education programs:** Providing parents with information on child development, behavior management techniques, and available resources can empower them to support their child's mental health.

- **Community mental health partnerships:** Collaborating with mental health professionals and community organizations can ensure access to appropriate services and resources.

- **Outreach and awareness campaigns:** Raising awareness about mental health issues and available support services can reduce stigma and encourage help-seeking behaviors.

+ **School-family partnerships**: Regular communication between schools and families can promote a supportive environment for students and facilitate early identification and intervention.

+ **Community activities and programs**: Providing opportunities for children and adolescents to engage in positive, structured activities within the community enhances their mental well-being.

Case Study: Early Intervention in Schools

To illustrate the importance of early intervention and prevention strategies, let's consider a case study of a middle school implementing a comprehensive mental health program.

Background: The middle school has observed a growing number of students experiencing anxiety and depression symptoms, leading to academic and social challenges.

Intervention Strategies:

+ The school implements a social-emotional learning (SEL) curriculum that includes weekly lessons on emotional regulation, stress management, and interpersonal skills.

+ Teachers receive training on identifying signs of mental health distress and referring students to appropriate support services.

+ The school hosts regular mental health awareness events, inviting guest speakers from the community and providing resources for parents and students.

+ Partnership with a local mental health clinic enables on-campus counseling services and access to professionals for students in need.

+ The school establishes a peer mentoring program, where older students are trained to support and guide younger students with mental health challenges.

Outcome: As a result of these intervention strategies, the school observes a reduction in disciplinary issues, improved academic performance, and increased student well-being. Students report feeling more supported and empowered to seek help when needed.

Conclusion

Early intervention and prevention strategies are essential for promoting mental health and well-being in children and adolescents. By identifying risk factors, promoting protective factors, implementing school-based intervention programs, and involving families and communities, we can create supportive environments that foster positive mental health outcomes. Through these efforts, we can equip young individuals with the necessary tools and support for a mentally healthy future.

Creating a Supportive Environment for Children and Teens

Creating a supportive environment for children and teens is crucial for promoting their mental health and overall well-being. In this section, we will explore various strategies and approaches that can be employed to foster a nurturing and positive atmosphere for young individuals. By implementing these strategies, parents, educators, and community members can contribute to the development of resilient and emotionally healthy children and teens.

Understanding the Needs of Children and Teens

Before we delve into specific strategies, it is essential to recognize the unique needs of children and teens. During this phase of their lives, young individuals undergo rapid physical, cognitive, and emotional changes. They are navigating their identity formation, developing social skills, and facing increasing academic pressures. Additionally, they may encounter various stressors, such as peer pressure, bullying, and family conflicts.

To create a supportive environment, it is crucial to consider age-appropriate developmental milestones, individual differences, and the diverse backgrounds of children and teens. Recognizing their needs and challenges will enable us to tailor our approaches to meet their specific requirements.

Promoting Emotional Well-being

Emotional well-being is fundamental to the overall mental health of children and teens. Here are some strategies to promote emotional well-being in young individuals:

1. **Emotionally responsive communication:** Encourage open and honest conversations with children and teens. Provide a safe space for them to

express their feelings, thoughts, and concerns. Validate their emotions and actively listen to their experiences. This fosters trust and helps them develop healthy coping mechanisms.

2. **Emotion regulation skills:** Teach children and teens techniques to manage their emotions effectively. This can include deep breathing exercises, progressive muscle relaxation, and guided imagery. Additionally, encourage them to engage in activities they enjoy, such as art, music, or physical exercise, as these can serve as outlets for emotional expression.

3. **Building resilience:** Help children and teens develop resilience by teaching them problem-solving skills, promoting optimism, and encouraging a growth mindset. Teach them that setbacks and failures are opportunities for growth and learning. Provide support and guidance while also allowing them to experience natural consequences.

4. **Promoting self-care:** Educate children and teens about the importance of self-care and self-compassion. Encourage them to prioritize activities that promote well-being, such as engaging in hobbies, spending time with loved ones, getting adequate sleep, and maintaining a balanced lifestyle.

Creating a Safe and Inclusive Environment

A safe and inclusive environment is conducive to the mental health and well-being of children and teens. Here are some strategies to create such an environment:

1. **Addressing bullying and discrimination:** Establish a zero-tolerance policy for bullying and discrimination in schools, communities, and online spaces. Implement comprehensive anti-bullying programs that educate students about empathy, respect, and the negative impact of bullying. Encourage bystander intervention and provide resources for reporting incidents of bullying.

2. **Promoting diversity and inclusion:** Celebrate diversity and foster an inclusive atmosphere where differences are valued and respected. Incorporate culturally diverse books, media, and activities into educational settings. Educate children and teens about different cultures, religions, and lifestyles to promote empathy, understanding, and tolerance.

3. **Creating safe spaces:** Designate safe spaces in schools and community centers where children and teens can seek refuge and support. These spaces should

be free from judgment and provide resources for emotional support, such as counseling services or peer support groups.

4. **Encouraging positive peer relationships:** Foster positive peer relationships by promoting social skills, teamwork, and cooperation. Encourage activities and projects that require collaboration and emphasize the importance of empathy, respect, and kindness.

Involving Parents and Guardians

Parents and guardians play a vital role in creating a supportive environment for their children. Here are some strategies to involve parents and guardians in promoting mental health:

1. **Parent education programs:** Provide workshops and training programs for parents and guardians to enhance their knowledge and skills in promoting their child's mental health. These programs can cover topics such as effective communication, positive discipline, and recognizing signs of mental health issues.

2. **Parent support groups:** Establish support groups where parents and guardians can connect, share experiences, and seek guidance from one another. These groups can provide emotional support and practical strategies for addressing common challenges.

3. **Collaboration with schools and communities:** Encourage collaboration between schools, parents, and community organizations to create a holistic support system for children and teens. Foster regular communication and collaboration to address the unique needs of each child.

Addressing Trauma and Adversity

Children and teens who have experienced trauma or adversity require special attention and support. Here are some strategies for addressing trauma and adversity:

1. **Trauma-informed care:** Train educators, caregivers, and community members in trauma-informed care approaches. This involves understanding the impact of trauma on children's behavior and emotional well-being and responding with empathy and appropriate support.

2. **Access to mental health services:** Ensure that children and teens have access to mental health services, including counseling and therapy, particularly in communities affected by high levels of trauma or adversity. Advocate for increased funding and resources for mental health support in schools and community settings.

3. **Creating a nurturing environment:** Establish a nurturing and predictable environment for children and teens who have experienced trauma or adversity. Provide consistent routines, clear expectations, and opportunities for emotional expression and coping skills development.

Unconventional Approach: Animal-Assisted Therapy

One unconventional approach to creating a supportive environment for children and teens is through animal-assisted therapy. Animal-assisted therapy involves interactions between trained animals and individuals with the goal of improving their physical, emotional, and cognitive well-being. Studies have shown that animal-assisted therapy can reduce anxiety, increase self-esteem, and improve social skills in children and teens.

In animal-assisted therapy, trained animals, such as dogs or horses, are involved in therapeutic interventions, supervised by mental health professionals. The presence of animals can create a comforting and non-judgmental environment, promoting trust and emotional connection. It can particularly benefit children and teens who have difficulty expressing themselves verbally or who are resistant to traditional therapy approaches.

Conclusion

Creating a supportive environment for children and teens is a collaborative effort that involves parents, educators, communities, and mental health professionals. By understanding their needs, promoting emotional well-being, ensuring safety and inclusivity, involving parents and guardians, addressing trauma and adversity, and considering unconventional approaches, we can foster a nurturing environment that contributes to the overall mental health of young individuals. Taking these steps lays the foundation for a brighter and more resilient future for our children and teens.

Addressing Bullying and Peer Pressure

Bullying and peer pressure are common issues that children and adolescents face in their lives. These experiences can have a significant impact on their mental health and overall well-being. In this section, we will explore strategies for addressing bullying and peer pressure, empowering young individuals to navigate these challenges and promote resilience.

Understanding Bullying

Bullying refers to repetitive aggressive behavior that is intentional and involves an imbalance of power between the bully and the victim. It can occur in various forms, including physical, verbal, relational, and cyberbullying. Victims of bullying often experience fear, anxiety, depression, and low self-esteem. It is crucial for parents, educators, and communities to understand the dynamics of bullying to effectively address and prevent it.

To address bullying, it is important to recognize the signs and symptoms, such as unexplained injuries, changes in behavior or mood, and social withdrawal. Creating a safe and supportive environment where individuals feel comfortable reporting incidents of bullying is essential. Encouraging open communication and developing a zero-tolerance policy for bullying can help deter such behavior.

Prevention Strategies

Prevention plays a key role in addressing bullying and peer pressure. It is essential to promote an inclusive and respectful school and community environment. Education and awareness programs should be implemented to increase students' understanding of bullying, its consequences, and empathy towards others.

One effective prevention strategy is promoting social-emotional learning (SEL). SEL programs focus on developing emotional intelligence, empathy, communication skills, and conflict resolution techniques. By teaching children and adolescents how to navigate relationships and handle conflicts non-violently, they are better equipped to respond to bullying situations.

In addition to SEL, fostering positive relationships within schools and communities is crucial. Encouraging peer support and establishing mentoring programs can create a sense of belonging and provide opportunities for individuals to seek support from trusted peers and adults.

Empowering the Bystanders

Bystanders play a significant role in addressing bullying. Empowering bystanders to take action and support victims can help reduce the prevalence and impact of bullying. By providing education and awareness about the importance of bystander intervention, children and adolescents can learn to identify instances of bullying and make safe choices to address them.

One effective strategy is teaching bystanders the three Rs: Recognize, Report, and Respond. Bystanders should be encouraged to recognize bullying when it occurs, report the incidents to a trusted adult, and respond appropriately by supporting the victim or attempting to diffuse the situation.

Empowering bystanders also involves creating a supportive culture where individuals are encouraged to stand up against bullying. This can be achieved through anti-bullying campaigns, peer-led initiatives, and promoting empathy and inclusivity.

Peer Pressure and Resisting Negative Influences

Peer pressure is another significant challenge that children and adolescents face. It refers to the influence exerted by peers to conform to certain behaviors, beliefs, or attitudes. Negative peer pressure can lead to risky behaviors, increased stress, and compromised mental health.

To address peer pressure, it is important to foster self-esteem and assertiveness skills. Individuals should be encouraged to develop a strong sense of self-identity and confidence in their values and beliefs. Building resilience and teaching effective decision-making skills can strengthen their ability to resist negative peer influences.

Open and honest communication between parents, educators, and young individuals is essential in addressing peer pressure. Providing guidance on setting boundaries, making informed choices, and seeking support when needed can empower children and adolescents to navigate peer pressure in healthy ways.

Creating Safe Spaces and Support Systems

Creating safe spaces where young individuals feel comfortable expressing themselves and seeking support is crucial in addressing bullying and peer pressure. Schools, community centers, and online platforms should prioritize creating an inclusive and supportive environment.

Implementing regular check-ins and mental health support services can ensure that students have access to resources and guidance. Encouraging the formation of support groups or clubs centered around shared interests and experiences can foster a sense of belonging and connection.

Adults, including parents and educators, need to be vigilant in identifying and addressing instances of bullying and peer pressure. They should be available to listen, offer guidance, and facilitate dialogue about these issues.

Cultivating Empathy and Promoting Understanding

Cultivating empathy is a crucial aspect of addressing bullying and peer pressure. Empathy allows individuals to understand and share the feelings of others, promoting respectful and compassionate behavior. By teaching empathy from an early age, young individuals can develop a sense of social responsibility and treat others with kindness and understanding.

In order to promote understanding, it is important for educators and parents to foster open conversations about diversity, inclusion, and acceptance. Teaching children and adolescents about different cultures, identities, and perspectives can dispel stereotypes and reduce instances of bullying and peer pressure.

Furthermore, utilizing restorative practices can be an effective approach in addressing bullying. Restorative practices focus on repairing harm and restoring relationships through dialogue, accountability, and understanding. This approach encourages both the victim and the perpetrator to actively participate in finding resolutions, promoting empathy and personal growth.

Conclusion

Addressing bullying and peer pressure requires a multifaceted approach that involves education, prevention, empowerment, and support. By creating safe and inclusive environments, teaching empathy and assertiveness, and fostering resilience, young individuals can navigate these challenges and promote positive mental health. The strategies outlined in this section provide a foundation for promoting healthy relationships and helping children and adolescents develop the skills necessary to respond to difficult social situations.

Strategies for Promoting Resilience and Well-being

Resilience can be defined as the ability to bounce back from difficult experiences and adapt positively to adversity. It is an essential component of mental health and plays a significant role in promoting overall well-being. In this section, we will explore various strategies for promoting resilience and well-being in individuals, especially children and adolescents.

Building a Supportive Environment

Creating a supportive environment is crucial for promoting resilience and well-being in children and adolescents. Here are some strategies that can help:

+ **Foster positive relationships:** Encourage healthy and positive relationships with family members, friends, and peers. These relationships provide emotional support and act as a protective factor against adversity.

+ **Encourage open communication:** Create a safe space for children and adolescents to express their thoughts and feelings openly. Encourage them to seek support and communicate their needs effectively.

+ **Promote a sense of belonging:** Help children and adolescents feel accepted and valued within their communities. Foster an inclusive environment that respects diversity and promotes a sense of belonging for everyone.

+ **Provide consistent support:** Be available and provide consistent support to children and adolescents. Consistency in providing emotional support, guidance, and encouragement helps them build resilience and cope with challenges effectively.

+ **Encourage problem-solving skills:** Teach children and adolescents problem-solving skills to help them navigate through difficult situations. Encourage them to develop a positive outlook and find constructive solutions to their problems.

Developing Coping Skills

Coping skills are essential for managing stress, building resilience, and maintaining well-being. Here are some strategies for developing effective coping skills:

+ **Emotional regulation:** Teach children and adolescents to recognize and manage their emotions in healthy ways. Help them develop strategies like deep breathing, mindfulness techniques, and positive self-talk to regulate their emotions during challenging times.

+ **Stress management:** Teach children and adolescents stress management techniques such as relaxation exercises, time management skills, and prioritization. Encourage them to engage in activities that promote relaxation and reduce stress levels.

+ **Problem-solving:** Teach children and adolescents problem-solving skills to help them approach challenging situations effectively. Teach them to break down problems into manageable steps, brainstorm possible solutions, and evaluate the outcomes.

+ **Positive thinking:** Encourage children and adolescents to develop a positive outlook on life. Teach them to challenge negative thoughts and replace them with positive and realistic ones. Foster optimism and resilience by highlighting strengths and achievements.

+ **Seeking support:** Teach children and adolescents the importance of seeking support from trusted individuals when faced with challenges. Encourage them to reach out to family, friends, teachers, or mental health professionals when they need assistance.

Promoting Self-Care

Self-care is crucial for promoting resilience and well-being. Teaching children and adolescents the importance of self-care empowers them to prioritize their mental health. Here are some self-care strategies:

+ **Healthy lifestyle:** Encourage children and adolescents to adopt a healthy lifestyle, including regular exercise, nutritious diet, and sufficient sleep. Physical well-being significantly impacts mental health and resilience.

+ **Hobbies and interests:** Encourage children and adolescents to engage in activities they enjoy and are passionate about. Hobbies and interests provide a sense of fulfillment, reduce stress, and promote well-being.

+ **Time for relaxation:** Teach children and adolescents the importance of relaxation and downtime. Encourage them to engage in activities like reading, listening to music, or practicing mindfulness to relax their minds and bodies.

+ **Limit technology use:** Help children and adolescents set boundaries on technology use to ensure they have sufficient time for other activities and face-to-face interactions. Excessive screen time can negatively impact mental health.

+ **Encourage self-reflection:** Teach children and adolescents the importance of self-reflection and introspection. Help them develop self-awareness and emotional intelligence by encouraging journaling or creative expression.

Promoting Resilience through Education

Education plays a crucial role in promoting resilience and well-being. Here are some strategies for promoting resilience through education:

+ **Integrate social-emotional learning (SEL):** Incorporate social-emotional learning programs into the curriculum to help children and adolescents develop skills such as self-awareness, self-management, social awareness, relationship skills, and responsible decision-making.

+ **Promote growth mindset:** Teach children and adolescents about the concept of a growth mindset, which emphasizes the belief that abilities can be developed through dedication and hard work. Encourage them to view challenges as opportunities for growth and learning.

+ **Teach problem-solving skills:** Integrate problem-solving skills training into the curriculum to help children and adolescents develop critical thinking and creative problem-solving abilities. Provide opportunities for them to practice these skills in real-life scenarios.

+ **Provide mental health education:** Include mental health education as part of the curriculum to reduce stigma and increase awareness about mental health issues. Teach children and adolescents about common mental health disorders, coping strategies, and available support systems.

+ **Promote a positive and inclusive school culture:** Foster a positive and inclusive school culture that encourages empathy, respect, and acceptance. Implement anti-bullying programs, peer support initiatives, and regular community-building activities.

Encouraging Resilience in a Challenging World

In today's fast-paced and challenging world, it is crucial to equip children and adolescents with resilience skills to navigate through life successfully. Here are some additional strategies to encourage resilience:

+ **Encourage goal-setting:** Teach children and adolescents the importance of setting goals and working towards them. Help them break down long-term goals into smaller, achievable steps, and celebrate their progress.

- **Foster problem-solving skills:** Encourage children and adolescents to approach problems with a proactive mindset. Teach them to identify obstacles, brainstorm solutions, and evaluate the outcomes.

- **Promote adaptive thinking:** Encourage flexible thinking and the ability to adapt to new situations. Teach children and adolescents to embrace change, learn from failures, and adjust their strategies accordingly.

- **Provide opportunities for independence:** Allow children and adolescents to take on age-appropriate responsibilities and make decisions. Encourage autonomy and independence, which help foster resilience and self-confidence.

- **Celebrate strengths and achievements:** Recognize and celebrate the strengths and achievements of children and adolescents. Acknowledge their efforts and provide positive reinforcement, which boosts self-esteem and resilience.

Overall, promoting resilience and well-being in children and adolescents is a multifaceted process that requires a supportive environment, coping skills development, self-care practices, education, and encouragement. By implementing these strategies, we can help young individuals thrive in the face of challenges and build a solid foundation for their mental health and well-being.

Older Adults and Aging

Mental Health Challenges in Aging

As individuals age, they often face unique mental health challenges that can impact their overall well-being and quality of life. Aging is a natural process that brings about changes in physical, cognitive, and emotional abilities, which can increase the risk of mental health disorders and struggles. In this section, we will explore some of the common mental health challenges that older adults encounter and discuss strategies to promote healthy aging and well-being.

Depression and Anxiety

Depression and anxiety are two of the most prevalent mental health disorders among older adults. These conditions can have a significant impact on an individual's daily functioning, relationships, and overall mental well-being. While it is normal to experience occasional sadness or worry, persistent feelings of sadness, hopelessness, or excessive worrying may indicate a more severe mental health issue.

Several factors contribute to the higher risk of depression and anxiety in aging individuals. These factors include social isolation, loss of loved ones, chronic health conditions, and limited mobility. Additionally, changes in brain chemistry and hormonal imbalances associated with aging can also contribute to the development of these disorders.

To address depression and anxiety in older adults, it is crucial to identify symptoms early and provide appropriate interventions. Treatment options may include therapy, medication, and lifestyle adjustments. Cognitive-behavioral therapy (CBT) has been proven effective in treating depression and anxiety in older adults by helping them identify and change negative thought patterns.

Cognitive Decline and Dementia

Cognitive decline is another significant mental health challenge faced by older adults. While mild cognitive decline is a normal part of aging, severe cognitive impairment can lead to dementia, a progressive and irreversible decline in cognitive function. Dementia impairs an individual's memory, thinking, behavior, and ability to perform daily activities.

The most common form of dementia is Alzheimer's disease, accounting for approximately 60-70% of all dementia cases. Other types of dementia include vascular dementia, Lewy body dementia, and frontotemporal dementia. These conditions not only affect the individuals themselves but also place a significant burden on their caregivers and families.

Understanding the risk factors and adopting lifestyle choices that promote brain health can help mitigate the risk of cognitive decline. Engaging in mentally stimulating activities, such as puzzles and reading, staying socially active, maintaining a healthy diet, and engaging in regular physical exercise can all contribute to brain health and overall well-being.

In the case of dementia, although there is no cure, early detection and intervention can help manage symptoms and slow down the progression of the disease. Supportive services, memory-enhancing medications, and therapy focused on improving the individual's cognitive abilities and quality of life can all play a crucial role in dementia care.

Loneliness and Social Isolation

Loneliness and social isolation are prevalent issues among older adults and can have a significant impact on their mental health. With age, individuals may experience the loss of a spouse, friends, and relatives, resulting in a smaller social network. Physical limitations, such as decreased mobility or hearing impairment, can further exacerbate feelings of loneliness and isolation.

Loneliness and social isolation have been linked to increased rates of depression, anxiety, cognitive decline, and even mortality in older adults. It is essential to address these issues by promoting social engagement and creating supportive environments for older adults.

Community-based programs and support groups can provide opportunities for older adults to connect with others who share similar interests and experiences. Technology, such as video calls and social media, can also help bridge the gap and facilitate social connections for those who are physically isolated.

Encouraging older adults to participate in volunteer work, hobbies, and intergenerational activities can provide a sense of purpose and belonging. Furthermore, fostering relationships and maintaining open lines of communication with family and friends can help combat loneliness and isolation in older adults.

Substance Abuse and Medication Misuse

Substance abuse and medication misuse are often overlooked mental health challenges among older adults. Older adults may turn to substances such as alcohol or prescription drugs as a coping mechanism for physical pain, loss, or emotional distress.

With age, changes in metabolism and the body's ability to process substances can amplify the effects of alcohol and drugs, increasing the risk of addiction and other health complications. Polypharmacy, the use of multiple medications, can also contribute to medication misuse, leading to adverse drug reactions and interactions.

To address substance abuse and medication misuse in older adults, healthcare providers should screen for these issues during routine medical visits. Comprehensive assessments, including medication reviews, can help identify potential problems and facilitate appropriate interventions.

Treatment options may include therapy, support groups, medical detoxification, and medication management. Education on the risks and proper use of medications is also essential to prevent medication misuse in this population.

Promoting Healthy Aging and Well-being

Promoting healthy aging and well-being involves a holistic approach that encompasses physical, cognitive, and emotional aspects of an individual's life. Here are some key strategies to support mental health in older adults:

- **Physical Health:** Encourage regular physical activity, a balanced diet, and sufficient sleep to promote overall well-being. Regular exercise has been shown to improve mood, cognitive function, and physical health in older adults.

- **Mental Stimulation:** Engage in mentally stimulating activities such as puzzles, reading, and learning new skills to keep the brain active and maintain cognitive function.

- **Social Engagement:** Foster social connections by participating in community activities, joining clubs or support groups, and maintaining relationships with family and friends. Social connections provide a sense of belonging, support, and purpose.

- **Emotional Support:** Encourage open communication and emotional expression. Older adults should feel comfortable seeking help and support from their loved ones and healthcare providers when needed.

- **Regular Health Check-ups:** Encourage regular health check-ups and screenings to monitor and manage any underlying physical and mental health conditions.

- **Adaptive Strategies:** Assist older adults in adapting to age-related changes and limitations. Encourage the use of assistive devices, modifications to the living environment, and accessing appropriate support services.

- **Caregiver Support:** Provide support and resources for caregivers who play a crucial role in the mental health and well-being of older adults. Educate caregivers on self-care strategies and stress management techniques.

By implementing these strategies and addressing the mental health challenges specific to aging, we can improve the well-being and overall quality of life for older adults. It is essential to recognize the importance of mental health in the aging population and promote a society that values and supports the mental well-being of all individuals, regardless of age.

Note: The section on Mental Health Challenges in Aging should be complemented by appropriate citations and references to support the information provided. Additionally, real-life case studies and examples can be included to illustrate the challenges and potential solutions discussed.

Cognitive Decline and Dementia

Cognitive decline and dementia are significant mental health challenges faced by older adults. Dementia refers to a broad category of brain disorders that cause a gradual decline in cognitive function, affecting memory, thinking, behavior, and the ability to perform daily activities. Cognitive decline, on the other hand, refers to the normal age-related changes in cognitive abilities that may not necessarily lead to dementia.

Understanding Cognitive Decline

As individuals age, it is common for them to experience some changes in cognitive functioning. These changes can include a decline in processing speed, attention, and working memory. However, these changes are considered within the normal range and do not significantly impair daily functioning.

The exact causes of cognitive decline are not fully understood, but factors such as genetics, lifestyle, and chronic health conditions are believed to play a role. Some older adults may experience a more pronounced decline in cognitive abilities due to factors such as age-related neurodegeneration or the presence of underlying diseases.

While cognitive decline is a normal part of aging, it is important to identify when these changes go beyond what is expected and may be indicative of the onset of dementia.

Understanding Dementia

Dementia is a syndrome characterized by a progressive decline in cognitive abilities that is severe enough to interfere with daily functioning. The most common type of dementia is Alzheimer's disease, accounting for approximately 60-80% of cases. Other types of dementia include vascular dementia, Lewy body dementia, and frontotemporal dementia.

The exact cause of dementia depends on its type. Alzheimer's disease, for example, is associated with the accumulation of abnormal proteins in the brain, leading to the formation of plaques and tangles that disrupt neuronal communication. Vascular dementia, on the other hand, is caused by reduced blood flow to the brain due to a series of small strokes.

Dementia affects various aspects of cognitive function, including memory, attention, language, problem-solving, and orientation. As the condition progresses, individuals may experience personality changes, mood fluctuations, and difficulties with motor skills.

Diagnosis and Assessment

Diagnosing cognitive decline and dementia requires a comprehensive evaluation that includes a thorough medical history, cognitive testing, and assessment of functional abilities.   A healthcare professional, such as a neuropsychologist, geriatrician, or neurologist, may conduct these evaluations.

During the assessment, the healthcare professional may use various standardized tests and questionnaires to examine different aspects of cognitive functioning, such as memory, attention, language, and executive function. They may also assess daily functioning to determine the impact of cognitive decline on an individual's ability to independently carry out activities of daily living.

Diagnostic criteria for dementia often require the presence of cognitive impairment in multiple domains, such as memory and language, and evidence that the decline significantly interferes with daily functioning.   Additionally, the diagnosis involves ruling out other possible causes of cognitive impairment, such as medication side effects, vitamin deficiencies, or depression.

Treatment and Support

While there is currently no cure for dementia, early diagnosis and interventions can help manage the symptoms, improve quality of life, and slow down disease progression.   Treatment plans for dementia typically involve a combination of pharmacological and non-pharmacological interventions.

Pharmacological treatment may include medications that target symptoms such as memory loss, sleep disturbances, agitation, and depression. It is important to note that these medications may not halt or reverse the underlying disease process but may provide temporary relief from certain symptoms.

Non-pharmacological interventions focus on maximizing cognitive and functional abilities, as well as providing support to individuals and their caregivers. These interventions may include cognitive rehabilitation, cognitive stimulation programs, and lifestyle modifications such as regular physical exercise, a healthy diet, and social engagement.

Additionally, support services such as counseling, support groups, and respite care can help individuals and their caregivers cope with the challenges associated with dementia. It is essential to involve a multidisciplinary team, including healthcare professionals, social workers, and occupational therapists, to provide comprehensive care and support.

Cognitive Stimulation and Brain Health

Promoting brain health and cognitive stimulation is crucial for individuals experiencing cognitive decline or at risk of developing dementia. Engaging in activities that challenge the brain and promote cognitive function can help maintain cognitive abilities and potentially delay the onset of dementia.

Cognitive stimulation activities may include puzzles, reading, playing musical instruments, learning a new language, or participating in mentally stimulating games. It is important to choose activities that are enjoyable and suited to an individual's interests and abilities.

Lifestyle factors also play a significant role in brain health. Regular physical exercise, a balanced diet, adequate sleep, and managing chronic conditions such as hypertension and diabetes are all important for maintaining cognitive function.

In addition to these conventional strategies, emerging research has shown promising evidence for unconventional approaches to cognitive stimulation, such as virtual reality (VR) and brain-computer interfaces. VR can create simulated environments that provide cognitive challenges and promote brain health, while brain-computer interfaces allow individuals to control devices using their brain activity, which can help enhance cognitive functioning.

Conclusion

Cognitive decline and dementia are complex mental health issues that pose significant challenges for individuals, families, and healthcare systems. Understanding the differences between normal age-related cognitive changes and dementia is crucial for appropriate diagnosis and intervention.

Early detection, comprehensive assessment, and a combination of pharmacological and non-pharmacological interventions can help manage symptoms, slow down disease progression, and improve the overall quality of life for individuals with dementia. Additionally, promoting brain health and engaging in cognitive stimulation activities are vital for maintaining cognitive abilities and potentially delaying the onset of dementia.

By implementing these strategies and providing comprehensive support, we can strive to improve the lives of individuals affected by cognitive decline and dementia, while continuing to advance our knowledge and approaches to treatment and care.

Strategies for Healthy Aging and Brain Health

As individuals age, it is important to proactively take steps to maintain brain health and promote overall well-being. Aging is accompanied by changes in cognition, memory, and concentration, but there are various strategies that can help mitigate these changes and support healthy aging. This section will discuss key strategies for healthy aging and brain health, including physical exercise, cognitive stimulation, social engagement, nutrition, and stress management.

Physical Exercise

Physical exercise plays a crucial role in promoting brain health and healthy aging. Regular exercise has been shown to improve cognitive function, enhance memory, and reduce the risk of age-related cognitive decline and neurodegenerative diseases, such as Alzheimer's disease.

Aerobic exercises, such as walking, swimming, and cycling, increase blood flow to the brain, which enhances the delivery of oxygen and nutrients. This process promotes the growth of new neurons and strengthens neural connections, improving overall cognitive function. Aim for at least 150 minutes of moderate-intensity aerobic exercise or 75 minutes of vigorous-intensity aerobic exercise per week.

In addition to aerobic exercise, strength training exercises are also beneficial for brain health. Strength training promotes the growth of new neurons and increases the levels of brain-derived neurotrophic factor (BDNF), a protein that supports the survival and growth of neurons. Incorporate resistance exercises, such as lifting weights or using resistance bands, at least two days per week.

Cognitive Stimulation

Engaging in activities that stimulate the brain is essential for maintaining cognitive function and promoting healthy aging. Regular mental stimulation helps preserve existing neural connections and promotes the formation of new connections.

Activities such as puzzles, crosswords, reading, learning a new language, or playing a musical instrument can help keep the mind active and enhance cognitive function. These activities challenge the brain's ability to think, reason, and remember, which strengthens neural networks and promotes neuroplasticity.

Additionally, brain-training programs and online cognitive exercises can be useful tools for cognitive stimulation. These programs provide specific exercises that target various cognitive domains, such as memory, attention, problem-solving, and executive function. Incorporate these activities into your daily routine to keep your brain sharp and flexible.

Social Engagement

Maintaining social connections and engaging in social activities is crucial for healthy aging and brain health. Social interaction stimulates the brain, improves cognitive function, and reduces the risk of cognitive decline.

Participating in social activities, such as joining clubs, volunteering, or attending social gatherings, provides opportunities for intellectual engagement, emotional support, and mental stimulation. Interacting with others promotes positive emotions, reduces stress, and enhances overall well-being.

Additionally, staying socially connected helps build resilience and protects against the negative impact of loneliness and isolation on brain health. Make an effort to maintain relationships with family, friends, and community members, and seek out opportunities for social engagement.

Nutrition

Proper nutrition is essential for healthy aging and brain health. A well-balanced diet rich in nutrients can support cognitive function, protect against neurodegenerative diseases, and promote overall brain health.

Include a variety of fruits, vegetables, whole grains, lean proteins, and healthy fats in your diet. Antioxidant-rich foods, such as berries, leafy greens, and nuts, help reduce oxidative stress and inflammation in the brain, which are associated with cognitive decline.

Omega-3 fatty acids, found in fatty fish (e.g., salmon, sardines) and walnuts, are particularly beneficial for brain health. These fatty acids help maintain the integrity of brain cell membranes and support the communication between brain cells.

It is important to limit the consumption of saturated and trans fats, as they can increase the risk of cognitive decline. Also, stay hydrated by drinking an adequate amount of water, as even mild dehydration can impair cognitive function.

Stress Management

Chronic stress can negatively impact brain health and accelerate cognitive decline. Therefore, effective stress management techniques are essential for healthy aging.

Engaging in stress reduction activities, such as deep breathing exercises, meditation, or yoga, can help activate the body's relaxation response and counteract the detrimental effects of stress on the brain.

Additionally, getting enough restful sleep is crucial for brain health. Poor sleep quality or insufficient sleep can impair cognitive function and increase the risk of developing neurodegenerative diseases. Establish a consistent sleep routine and create a sleep-friendly environment to ensure adequate and high-quality sleep.

Incorporate stress management techniques into your daily routine, such as mindfulness practices or engaging in hobbies or activities that you enjoy, to reduce stress levels and promote optimal brain health.

Conclusion

Maintaining brain health and promoting healthy aging requires a holistic approach that includes physical exercise, cognitive stimulation, social engagement, proper nutrition, and stress management. By incorporating these strategies into daily life, individuals can support cognitive function, enhance memory, and reduce the risk of age-related cognitive decline and neurodegenerative diseases. It is never too early or too late to start implementing these strategies for healthy aging and brain health. So, let's embrace them and embark on the journey towards a healthier and sharper mind.

Addressing Loneliness and Social Isolation

Loneliness and social isolation are significant issues that can have a detrimental impact on mental health. It is essential to address these challenges and provide strategies to support individuals in overcoming feelings of loneliness and isolation. This section will explore the causes and consequences of loneliness and social isolation, as well as practical methods to promote social connection and build a supportive community.

Understanding Loneliness and Social Isolation

Loneliness refers to the subjective perception of being alone or lacking meaningful social connections, while social isolation is the objective absence of social contact and engagement. Both can occur concurrently or independently, and they can affect people of all ages and backgrounds.

There are several factors that contribute to loneliness and social isolation:

- ✦ Geographic location: Living in rural areas or isolated communities can limit access to social interactions and support networks.

- ✦ Life transitions: Events such as moving to a new city, starting a new job, or retirement can disrupt social connections and lead to feelings of isolation.

- Loss or bereavement: The death of a loved one or the end of a significant relationship can cause profound loneliness.

- Physical and mental health: Chronic illnesses, disabilities, or mental health disorders can impact one's ability to engage in social activities and build relationships.

- Technology use: While technology can facilitate connections, excessive reliance on social media can lead to feelings of loneliness and isolation.

The consequences of loneliness and social isolation on mental health are significant. Research shows that prolonged periods of isolation can increase the risk of depression, anxiety, cognitive decline, and even mortality. It is crucial to address these issues proactively and develop strategies that promote social connectedness.

Building Social Connections

Addressing loneliness and social isolation requires a multi-faceted approach that focuses on building social connections and enhancing community support. Here are some strategies that can help:

1. Foster a sense of belonging: Encourage participation in social activities and groups that align with individuals' interests and values. This can include joining clubs, volunteering, or taking part in community events. Creating a supportive and inclusive environment is essential in promoting a sense of belonging.

2. Strengthen existing relationships: Encourage individuals to reach out to friends, family, and acquaintances. Scheduling regular phone calls, video chats, or in-person meetings can help maintain and strengthen social connections. In some cases, mediation or conflict resolution techniques may be necessary to address relationship challenges.

3. Develop new relationships: Provide guidance on how to meet new people and make friends. This can involve enrolling in classes or workshops, participating in hobby groups, or attending social events. Encouraging individuals to step out of their comfort zone and initiate conversations can lead to meaningful connections.

4. Utilize technology mindfully: While technology can contribute to feelings of isolation, it can also facilitate social connections. Encourage the use of online communities, support groups, and social media platforms that promote positive interactions and shared interests. However, it is important to set healthy boundaries and avoid excessive screen time.

5. Reach out to support services: Inform individuals about available support services, such as helplines, counseling, or therapy programs. These resources can provide a safe space for individuals to express their feelings and receive professional guidance on managing loneliness and isolation.

6. Promote intergenerational connections: Encourage interactions between different age groups to foster mutual understanding and support. Programs that facilitate intergenerational activities, such as mentoring or volunteering, can create opportunities for meaningful connections and combat social isolation.

7. Create inclusive communities: Advocate for inclusive policies and initiatives that promote social cohesion and combat loneliness. This can involve working with local governments, community organizations, and businesses to create accessible and inclusive spaces that foster social connections among diverse populations.

Case Study: The Silver Connections Program

The Silver Connections program is an innovative initiative designed to address loneliness and social isolation among older adults. The program brings together older adults in a supportive community setting to engage in a variety of activities and social interactions.

The core components of the Silver Connections program include:

- Weekly social gatherings: Participants meet regularly to participate in group activities such as group exercises, art classes, or game nights. This provides opportunities for social interaction and helps build a sense of belonging.

- Intergenerational partnerships: The program collaborates with local schools and universities to facilitate partnerships between older adults and younger generations. This allows for mentorship opportunities and breaks down age-related stereotypes.

* Volunteer opportunities: Participants are encouraged to engage in volunteer work within their community. This not only provides a sense of purpose and fulfillment but also creates opportunities for social interaction with like-minded individuals.

* Technology training: The program offers technology training sessions to help older adults become more comfortable with digital platforms and social media. This empowers them to connect with others online and overcome technological barriers to social engagement.

* Supportive counseling services: The program provides access to counseling services where participants can discuss their emotions, concerns, and experiences related to loneliness and social isolation. This ensures that individuals receive both emotional support and practical guidance.

The Silver Connections program has demonstrated positive outcomes, including reduced feelings of loneliness and increased social connections among participants. It serves as a model for community-based initiatives that effectively address loneliness and social isolation.

Conclusion

Addressing loneliness and social isolation requires a multi-dimensional approach that focuses on building social connections, fostering a sense of belonging, and creating supportive communities. By implementing strategies such as fostering intergenerational connections, promoting inclusive environments, and utilizing technology mindfully, we can combat the detrimental effects of loneliness and social isolation on mental health.

Remember, loneliness and social isolation can impact anyone, and it is our collective responsibility to create an environment that promotes social connectedness and supports individuals in overcoming these challenges.

Supportive Services for Older Adults

As individuals age, they may face unique challenges to their mental health and well-being. It is essential to provide supportive services that address these specific needs and promote positive mental health outcomes for older adults. This section will explore various supportive services available for older adults, focusing on interventions and strategies that can enhance their overall well-being.

Geriatric Mental Health Assessment

Before implementing any supportive services, it is crucial to conduct a comprehensive geriatric mental health assessment for older adults. This assessment should encompass a range of factors, including physical health, cognitive functioning, emotional well-being, social support, and any existing mental health conditions or concerns.

The assessment should involve both self-report measures and direct observations. Evaluation tools such as the Geriatric Depression Scale (GDS) and Mini-Mental State Examination (MMSE) can be useful in identifying symptoms of depression, cognitive impairments, and potential mental health issues.

An accurate and thorough assessment will serve as a foundation for developing individualized supportive services and intervention plans tailored to the specific needs of each older adult.

Counseling and Psychotherapy

Counseling and psychotherapy are valuable supportive services for older adults experiencing mental health challenges. Talk therapy can provide a safe and supportive environment for older adults to express their feelings, cope with life changes, and address emotional concerns related to aging.

Various therapeutic approaches can be effective for older adults, including cognitive-behavioral therapy (CBT), interpersonal therapy (IPT), and reminiscence therapy. These approaches can help older adults develop coping skills, identify negative thought patterns, improve problem-solving abilities, and enhance their overall psychological well-being.

It is essential for mental health professionals working with older adults to possess knowledge of the aging process, empathy, and good communication skills. They should also be aware of any unique considerations related to working with this population, such as cognitive impairments or sensory changes.

Social Support Programs

Social support is crucial for the mental health and well-being of older adults. Social isolation and loneliness can have detrimental effects on their overall functioning and can contribute to the development or worsening of mental health issues. Implementing social support programs can help combat these challenges and promote positive mental health outcomes.

One example of a social support program is senior centers, which provide opportunities for older adults to engage in social activities, build new connections, and participate in recreational programs. These centers often offer a range of programs such as exercise classes, hobby groups, educational workshops, and community outings.

Another type of social support program is the senior companion program, where trained volunteers provide regular companionship and assistance to older adults who may be socially isolated or in need of extra support. These programs not only promote social interaction but also help older adults maintain a sense of purpose and fulfillment.

Intergenerational programs, where older adults interact with younger generations, can also be beneficial. These programs foster relationships and mutual learning between different age groups, which can be a source of social support and stimulation for older adults.

Health Promotion and Education

Health promotion and educational programs designed specifically for older adults can play a significant role in supporting their mental health. These programs aim to empower older adults to take an active role in managing their physical and mental well-being.

Health promotion programs often provide education on topics such as nutrition, physical activity, medication management, stress reduction techniques, and sleep hygiene. By increasing their knowledge and awareness, older adults can make informed decisions related to their health and engage in behaviors that promote mental well-being.

Furthermore, educational programs can help older adults recognize the signs and symptoms of common mental health disorders such as depression or anxiety. Increased awareness enables them to seek timely intervention and access appropriate mental health services.

Caregiver Support Services

Caregivers play a crucial role in the lives of older adults, especially those with chronic illnesses, disabilities, or cognitive impairments. Supporting caregivers is essential as their well-being directly impacts the mental health of the older adults they care for.

Caregiver support services are designed to provide assistance, education, and respite to individuals caring for older adults. These services may include support groups, counseling, educational workshops, and respite care programs that offer temporary relief to caregivers.

Support groups allow caregivers to connect with others facing similar challenges, providing them with a safe space to share experiences, seek advice, and receive emotional support. Counseling services can help caregivers manage stress, improve coping skills, and enhance their overall well-being.

Respite care programs offer short-term breaks to caregivers by providing temporary care for older adults. These breaks are essential for the caregiver's mental health as they allow time for self-care, rest, and rejuvenation.

Technology-Based Interventions

Advancements in technology have made it possible to deliver supportive services to older adults through innovative means. Technology-based interventions can improve access to mental health services, particularly for those who may have limited mobility or live in rural areas.

Telehealth and teletherapy enable older adults to receive mental health support remotely, eliminating barriers such as transportation or geographical distance. Through videoconferencing or telephone sessions, older adults can access counseling services, participate in mental health assessments, and receive support from mental health professionals.

Mobile applications and online platforms can also provide older adults with self-help resources, psychoeducation, and tools for managing symptoms of mental health disorders. These technological interventions offer convenience, flexibility, and privacy, making mental health support more accessible for older adults.

Conclusion

Supportive services for older adults play a vital role in promoting their mental health and overall well-being. By conducting comprehensive assessments, offering counseling and psychotherapy, implementing social support programs, providing health promotion and education, supporting caregivers, and utilizing technology-based interventions, we can enhance the mental health outcomes of older adults.

It is essential to consider the unique needs and challenges faced by older adults when developing and implementing these supportive services. By addressing their mental health concerns and promoting positive aging, we can ensure that older adults maintain an optimal level of mental well-being and enjoy a fulfilling and meaningful life.

LGBTQ+ Community

Mental Health Disparities and Challenges

Mental health disparities refer to the unequal distribution of mental health resources, access to care, and outcomes among different populations. These disparities can be influenced by various factors, including socioeconomic status, race and ethnicity, gender, sexual orientation, and geographical location. Addressing these disparities is crucial for promoting mental well-being and ensuring equitable mental health care for all individuals.

Socioeconomic Factors

Socioeconomic status (SES) plays a significant role in mental health disparities. Individuals from lower SES backgrounds often face greater challenges in accessing mental health services, resulting in limited treatment options and poorer mental health outcomes. Limited financial resources can prevent individuals from seeking proper care, leading to delayed or inadequate treatment.

Moreover, individuals from lower SES backgrounds may experience higher levels of stress due to factors such as unemployment, poverty, and inadequate housing. Chronic stress can contribute to the development of mental health disorders and exacerbate existing conditions. Additionally, limited access to educational and employment opportunities can further perpetuate mental health disparities.

Addressing socioeconomic factors requires a comprehensive approach that focuses on reducing poverty, improving access to education and employment opportunities, and providing affordable and accessible mental health services to underserved communities.

Racial and Ethnic Disparities

Racial and ethnic disparities in mental health care are evident in the unequal prevalence, diagnosis, treatment, and outcomes of mental health disorders among different racial and ethnic groups. African Americans, Hispanic Americans, Native Americans, and Asian Americans often face barriers in accessing culturally competent and linguistically appropriate mental health care.

Factors contributing to these disparities include cultural stigma, lack of diversity among mental health professionals, language barriers, and distrust in the healthcare system. Additionally, racial and ethnic minority groups may experience higher levels of discrimination, marginalization, and socioeconomic disadvantages, which can negatively impact their mental health.

To address these disparities, it is essential to promote cultural competency training for mental health providers, increase the representation of diverse professionals in the field, and implement policies that ensure equitable access to mental health resources for all racial and ethnic groups.

Gender Disparities

Gender disparities in mental health are evident in the differential prevalence, symptoms, and treatment-seeking behaviors between men and women. Women are generally more likely to experience common mental health disorders such as depression and anxiety, while men are more likely to experience alcohol and substance use disorders.

Societal expectations and gender norms can influence the expression and recognition of mental health symptoms, with women often being encouraged to seek help and men being discouraged from displaying vulnerability. Moreover, gender-based violence, including domestic violence and sexual assault, can significantly impact the mental health of individuals, primarily women.

Efforts to address gender disparities in mental health should focus on promoting gender-inclusive mental health services, challenging harmful gender norms, and addressing the specific mental health needs of marginalized gender communities.

Sexual Orientation and Gender Identity Disparities

Lesbian, gay, bisexual, transgender, and queer/questioning (LGBTQ+) individuals often experience unique mental health disparities. They are at a higher risk of experiencing mental health disorders, including depression, anxiety, substance abuse, and suicide ideation, compared to their heterosexual and cisgender counterparts.

Discrimination, social stigma, and internalized homophobia/transphobia can contribute to heightened stress levels and a sense of isolation among LGBTQ+ individuals. Moreover, limited access to affirming healthcare services and competent mental health providers can further exacerbate mental health disparities.

Addressing mental health disparities among LGBTQ+ individuals requires creating safe and inclusive spaces, promoting LGBTQ+ affirmative mental health care, and advocating for policies that protect their rights and well-being.

Geographical Disparities

Geographical location can significantly impact access to mental health resources and services. Rural communities often face unique challenges, including limited availability of mental health providers, transportation barriers, and a lack of specialized services. As a result, individuals living in rural areas may experience higher rates of mental health disorders and limited treatment opportunities.

Telehealth and telepsychiatry can play a crucial role in bridging the geographical gap in mental health care. These technologies enable individuals in remote areas to access mental health services through virtual platforms, reducing the barriers associated with distance and transportation.

Addressing geographical disparities requires expanding mental health services in underserved areas, utilizing telehealth technologies, and promoting collaborations between urban and rural mental health providers.

Challenges in Mental Health Disparities Research

Research on mental health disparities faces several challenges that need to be addressed to develop effective strategies. These challenges include limited funding for disparities research, inconsistent data collection methods, and a lack of standardized measures for assessing mental health outcomes across diverse populations.

To overcome these challenges, there is a need for increased investment in disparities research, the development of culturally appropriate measurement tools, and the inclusion of diverse populations in research studies. Additionally, community-based participatory research approaches can enhance the relevance and impact of mental health disparities research by involving affected communities in study design and implementation.

Real-World Example

A real-world example of mental health disparities can be seen in the context of access to mental health care in low-income neighborhoods. Individuals living in economically disadvantaged areas often have limited resources and face barriers such as lack of insurance coverage, shortage of mental health providers, and stigma associated with seeking help. As a result, these populations experience higher rates of untreated mental health disorders and poorer outcomes.

To address this disparity, community organizations, healthcare providers, and policymakers can collaborate to establish community mental health clinics, increase funding for mental health services in low-income areas, and implement outreach programs to raise awareness about mental health and available resources. Additionally, addressing systemic issues such as poverty and inequalities in education and employment can also contribute to reducing mental health disparities.

In conclusion, mental health disparities exist among different populations due to various factors such as socioeconomic status, race and ethnicity, gender, sexual orientation, and geographical location. Addressing these disparities requires a multi-faceted approach that focuses on improving access to resources, reducing stigma, promoting cultural competency, and advocating for policy changes. By addressing mental health disparities, we can work towards a more equitable and inclusive mental health system that provides quality care for all individuals, regardless of their background or circumstances.

Intersectionality and Minority Stress

Intersectionality refers to the interconnected nature of social identities such as race, gender, sexuality, and class, and how they interact to create unique experiences and challenges for individuals. It recognizes that people's experiences of discrimination and oppression are influenced by multiple aspects of their identity, and that these intersections can compound and intensify these experiences.

In the context of mental health, intersectionality plays a crucial role in understanding the concept of minority stress. Minority stress refers to the unique stressors experienced by individuals who belong to marginalized groups due to their intersecting identities. These stressors can include prejudice, discrimination, and social marginalization, all of which contribute to increased mental health disparities and negative well-being outcomes.

One example of intersectionality and minority stress is the experience of a transgender person of color. They may face discrimination not only based on their gender identity but also due to their racial background. This combination of identities can lead to higher levels of stress, increased risk of mental health disorders such as depression and anxiety, and reduced access to mental health support services.

Understanding intersectionality and minority stress is crucial for mental health professionals, as it allows them to provide more effective and inclusive care. By recognizing the unique challenges faced by individuals with intersecting marginalized identities, mental health professionals can tailor treatment approaches to address these specific stressors.

There are several strategies that mental health professionals can employ to support individuals experiencing intersectionality and minority stress:

1. Provide Culturally Competent Care: Mental health professionals should be knowledgeable about the cultural and social contexts in which their clients exist. This includes understanding the impact of intersecting identities and how they influence mental health experiences. A culturally competent approach ensures that mental health professionals take into account the unique challenges faced by their clients and provide appropriate support.

2. Create Safe Spaces: It is crucial to create safe and inclusive spaces where individuals can openly discuss their experiences without fear of judgment or discrimination. This can be achieved by promoting an environment that respects and values all intersecting identities, such as through the use of inclusive language and policies.

3. Advocate for Social Change: Mental health professionals should use their platform to advocate for social change. This involves addressing systemic inequalities and working towards creating a more equitable society. By challenging oppressive systems and advocating for policies that aim to reduce discrimination and marginalization, mental health professionals can contribute to the overall well-being of individuals with intersecting identities.

4. Collaborate with Community Organizations: Building partnerships with community organizations that specialize in advocating for the rights and well-being of marginalized groups can enhance the support available to individuals experiencing intersectionality and minority stress. These organizations often have specific knowledge and expertise in addressing the unique challenges faced by individuals with intersecting identities.

To illustrate these concepts, let's consider the case of Maria, a Latina lesbian who is experiencing significant distress due to the intersectionality of her identities. As a mental health professional, it is important to acknowledge and understand the challenges Maria faces as a result of being a member of both the LGBTQ+ community and a racial minority group. By employing a culturally competent approach, the mental health professional can work collaboratively with Maria to develop strategies that address her specific stressors and promote her mental well-being.

In conclusion, intersectionality and minority stress are crucial considerations in mental health care. By recognizing and addressing the unique challenges faced by individuals with intersecting marginalized identities, mental health professionals can create more inclusive and effective support systems. Advocating for social change and collaborating with community organizations are important steps in reducing disparities and promoting the well-being of individuals experiencing intersectionality and minority stress.

Culturally Sensitive Mental Health Care

Culturally sensitive mental health care is an essential aspect of providing effective and inclusive support to individuals from diverse cultural backgrounds. It recognizes the influence of culture on mental health and understands that cultural factors impact one's perception, expression, and experience of mental health issues. In this section, we will explore the principles and practices of culturally sensitive mental health care, highlighting the importance of cultural competence, the challenges faced by mental health professionals, and strategies for delivering culturally appropriate care.

Understanding Cultural Competence

Cultural competence refers to the ability to interact effectively with individuals from various cultural backgrounds. It involves developing knowledge, awareness, and skills to understand and respect cultural differences. In the context of mental health care, cultural competence enables mental health professionals to recognize the influence of culture on an individual's beliefs, values, and behaviors related to mental health.

To provide culturally sensitive care, mental health professionals need to engage in ongoing self-reflection and self-awareness. This involves examining their own cultural biases, assumptions, and prejudices that might affect their interactions with clients from different cultures. By being mindful and open-minded, mental health professionals can create a safe and supportive environment for individuals to express their concerns and seek appropriate care.

Challenges in Culturally Sensitive Mental Health Care

Culturally sensitive mental health care is faced with various challenges that can hinder the delivery of effective support. Some of the common challenges include:

1. Language and Communication: Language barriers can impede effective communication between mental health professionals and individuals from different cultural backgrounds. It is important to provide interpreters or ensure access to culturally appropriate mental health resources in the individual's native language.

2. Stigma and Cultural Beliefs: Cultural beliefs and stigmatization surrounding mental health can create additional challenges. Some cultures may perceive mental health issues as taboo, making it difficult for individuals to seek help. Mental health professionals must be sensitive to

these cultural beliefs and work collaboratively with individuals, families, and communities to reduce stigma and promote understanding.

3. Mistrust and Power Dynamics: Historical and systemic factors, such as colonization, racism, and discrimination, can contribute to mistrust and power dynamics in mental health care. Mental health professionals must actively address these issues and work toward building trust and empowering individuals to actively participate in their treatment.

4. Cultural Competence Training: Many mental health professionals receive limited training in cultural competence, which can result in gaps in knowledge and understanding of diverse cultural practices. It is essential for professionals to continuously engage in education and training to enhance their cultural competence skills.

Strategies for Culturally Sensitive Mental Health Care

To overcome the challenges and provide culturally sensitive mental health care, mental health professionals can employ several strategies:

1. Cultural Assessment: Conducting a thorough cultural assessment is crucial in understanding an individual's cultural background, beliefs, and values. This assessment can inform the development of a personalized treatment plan that is aligned with the individual's cultural preferences.

2. Collaborative Decision-Making: Mental health professionals should adopt a collaborative approach to decision-making, respecting the individual's autonomy and involving them in setting treatment goals and strategies. This approach acknowledges the individual as an expert in their own cultural context and supports their active participation in their treatment process.

3. Culturally Tailored Interventions: It is important to develop culturally tailored interventions that consider the specific needs and preferences of individuals from different cultural backgrounds. This may involve incorporating traditional healing practices, religious or spiritual beliefs, and community resources into the treatment plan.

4. Building Trust and Rapport: Establishing a trusting and empathetic relationship is essential in culturally sensitive care. Mental health professionals should actively listen, validate, and respond to the concerns of individuals with cultural humility and respect.

5. Collaboration with Cultural Consultants: Mental health professionals can collaborate with cultural consultants who possess expertise in specific cultural practices and beliefs. These consultants can provide valuable insights and guidance, ensuring the provision of culturally appropriate care.

Case Study

To illustrate the importance of culturally sensitive mental health care, let's consider the case of Amira, a young woman from a Middle Eastern cultural background who seeks therapy for anxiety. Amira's cultural beliefs value collectivism and place great importance on family ties. In Amira's culture, discussing personal problems with a stranger, such as a therapist, is considered taboo.

In this case, a culturally sensitive mental health professional would acknowledge and respect Amira's cultural beliefs while working collaboratively with her. The therapist may focus on involving Amira's family in the therapy process, ensuring that they understand the benefits of therapy and the positive impact it can have on Amira's well-being. The therapist would also explore alternative modes of therapy, such as group therapy or peer support, which align with Amira's cultural preference for a collective approach to problem-solving.

Through these culturally sensitive strategies, the mental health professional can create a safe and supportive environment for Amira, addressing her anxiety while respecting her cultural traditions and values.

Resources for Culturally Sensitive Mental Health Care

To enhance cultural competence and provide effective mental health care, mental health professionals can access various resources. Some valuable resources include:

+ Books and Articles: There are numerous books and articles available that explore the intersection of culture and mental health care. These resources provide insights into diverse cultural practices and help mental health professionals develop a broader understanding of cultural influences.

+ Cultural Competence Training: Mental health professionals can seek out training programs or workshops focused on cultural competence and diversity. These training opportunities can provide practical skills and strategies for delivering culturally sensitive care.

+ Cultural Consultants and Community Leaders: Collaborating with cultural consultants and community leaders can offer valuable guidance and knowledge about cultural practices and beliefs. These individuals can provide insights into cultural nuances and help shape culturally appropriate interventions.

* Professional Organizations and Networks: Joining professional organizations and networks that focus on cultural diversity and mental health can facilitate ongoing learning and provide a platform for connecting with other professionals in the field.

Conclusion

Culturally sensitive mental health care recognizes the impact of culture on mental health and emphasizes the importance of delivering personalized, culturally appropriate support. By developing cultural competence, addressing the challenges faced, and employing strategies for culturally sensitive care, mental health professionals can enhance the quality of care and promote positive outcomes for individuals from diverse cultural backgrounds. By working collaboratively and respecting cultural values, mental health professionals can create a safe space where individuals feel seen, heard, and supported on their mental health journey.

Let's remember: mental health care should be inclusive, affirming, and sensitive to the diversity of the human experience.

LGBTQ+ Rights and Advocacy

The rights and advocacy of the LGBTQ+ community are crucial aspects of promoting mental health and well-being among individuals who identify as lesbian, gay, bisexual, transgender, queer, and other diverse gender and sexual identities. This section explores the importance of LGBTQ+ rights, the challenges faced by this community, and strategies for promoting equality and inclusivity.

Understanding LGBTQ+ Rights

LGBTQ+ rights are fundamental human rights that aim to ensure equality, protection, and non-discrimination for individuals regardless of their sexual orientation, gender identity, or expression. These rights include the right to life, liberty, and security of person, the right to privacy, the right to equal protection under the law, and the right to be free from torture, cruel, inhuman or degrading treatment or punishment.

It is important to understand that LGBTQ+ rights are not universal and vary across different countries and jurisdictions. While some countries have made significant progress in recognizing and protecting these rights, others still have laws and social norms that discriminate against LGBTQ+ individuals. Advocacy for LGBTQ+ rights aims to promote equality and create a more inclusive society for all.

Challenges Faced by the LGBTQ+ Community

The LGBTQ+ community continues to face unique challenges that can have a detrimental impact on mental health and well-being. These challenges include:

1. Discrimination and Prejudice: Many LGBTQ+ individuals experience stigma, discrimination, and prejudice in various areas of their lives, such as employment, housing, healthcare, and education. This can lead to feelings of shame, low self-esteem, and social isolation.

2. Bullying and Harassment: LGBTQ+ individuals, particularly youth, are more likely to experience bullying and harassment in schools, workplaces, and online spaces. This can have a significant negative impact on mental health, leading to anxiety, depression, and suicidal ideation.

3. Minority Stress: LGBTQ+ individuals often face unique stressors related to their sexual orientation or gender identity, including internalized stigma, family rejection, and fear of coming out. These stressors can contribute to mental health disorders and substance abuse.

4. Lack of Supportive Resources: Many LGBTQ+ individuals struggle to find supportive resources, such as mental health services, that are inclusive and understanding of their specific needs. This can make it difficult to access appropriate care and support.

Strategies for Advocacy

Advocacy for LGBTQ+ rights is essential for promoting positive mental health outcomes and creating a more inclusive society. Here are some strategies and approaches to advocate for LGBTQ+ rights:

1. Education and Awareness: Increasing awareness and understanding of LGBTQ+ identities, experiences, and issues is crucial. This can be achieved through educational initiatives in schools, workplaces, and communities. Efforts should encompass curricula, training programs, and awareness campaigns to challenge stereotypes and promote acceptance.

2. Legal Reform: Advocacy efforts should aim to change discriminatory laws and policies to ensure equality and protection for LGBTQ+ individuals. Lobbying for comprehensive anti-discrimination laws, legal recognition of same-sex

relationships, and gender-affirming healthcare are examples of legal reform strategies.

3. Community Support: Building and strengthening LGBTQ+ support networks and organizations is essential for promoting mental health and well-being. These communities offer safe spaces, peer support, and resources for individuals to connect and advocate collectively.

4. Collaboration and Allies: Working in collaboration with other social justice movements and coalitions can amplify the voices and impact of LGBTQ+ advocacy. Building alliances with feminist organizations, racial justice movements, and disability rights advocates can create a more inclusive and intersectional approach to advocacy.

5. Policy and Health System Changes: Advocating for LGBTQ+ inclusive policies within healthcare systems and mental health services is critical. This includes promoting LGBTQ+ cultural competence training for healthcare providers, ensuring access to gender-affirming care, and addressing mental health disparities within the community.

6. Empowering LGBTQ+ Youth: Supporting LGBTQ+ youth is of utmost importance as they often face unique challenges. This can be achieved through initiatives such as LGBTQ+ student clubs, mentorship programs, and providing safe spaces and resources.

It is crucial to approach LGBTQ+ advocacy with cultural humility, meaning a willingness to learn from and respect the diverse experiences and voices within the community. Advocacy efforts should be guided by the principles of equity, justice, and inclusivity.

Example: Advocacy Campaign

To illustrate the practical application of LGBTQ+ rights advocacy, let's consider an example of an advocacy campaign focused on promoting transgender rights in a particular jurisdiction. Here are the key components of the campaign:

1. Research and Data: Conducting research to gather data on the experiences and challenges faced by transgender individuals within the jurisdiction. This data will help identify the specific areas that require advocacy.

2. Community Engagement: Engaging with the transgender community to understand their needs, concerns, and aspirations. This can be achieved through focus groups, interviews, and surveys.

3. Policy Analysis: Reviewing existing laws and policies to assess their impact on transgender individuals. Identifying areas of improvement, such as legal

recognition of gender identity, access to gender-affirming healthcare, and protection from discrimination.

4. Awareness and Education: Developing educational materials, workshops, and training programs to raise awareness about transgender issues among the general public, healthcare professionals, educators, and policymakers.

5. Media and Social Media Campaign: Utilizing traditional and social media platforms to share stories, amplify voices, and challenge misconceptions about transgender individuals. This can help create a more accepting and supportive environment.

6. Lobbying and Advocacy: Engaging with policymakers, legislators, and stakeholders to advocate for policy changes that promote transgender rights. This may involve meetings, public hearings, and grassroots initiatives.

7. Collaboration and Support: Building alliances with other LGBTQ+ organizations, human rights groups, and supportive individuals to gain collective strength and increase the impact of the advocacy campaign.

By adopting a multifaceted approach that combines research, community engagement, policy advocacy, and educational initiatives, this campaign can make significant strides in promoting transgender rights and inclusivity within the jurisdiction.

Resources for LGBTQ+ Rights and Advocacy

Here are some resources that can provide further information and support for LGBTQ+ rights and advocacy:

1. Human Rights Campaign: A prominent LGBTQ+ civil rights organization that advocates for equality and provides resources for advocacy initiatives. Website: `https://www.hrc.org/`

2. GLAAD: A media advocacy organization that works to amplify LGBTQ+ voices and representation in the media. Website: `https://www.glaad.org/`

3. National Center for Transgender Equality: An organization dedicated to advancing the equality of transgender people through advocacy and education. Website: `https://transequality.org/`

4. The Trevor Project: A leading organization providing crisis intervention and suicide prevention services to LGBTQ+ youth. Website: `https://www.thetrevorproject.org/`

5. International Lesbian, Gay, Bisexual, Trans and Intersex Association (ILGA): A global federation advocating for LGBTQ+ rights at an international level. Website: `https://ilga.org/`

Remember, advocacy is an ongoing process, and it's vital to continuously learn, adapt, and collaborate to create a more inclusive and equitable society for all LGBTQ+ individuals.

Building Affirming and Inclusive Communities

Building affirming and inclusive communities is crucial for promoting mental health and well-being among individuals belonging to the LGBTQ+ community. LGBTQ+ individuals often face unique challenges and mental health disparities due to societal stigma, discrimination, and prejudice. In this section, we will explore strategies to create safe and inclusive spaces that support the mental health needs of LGBTQ+ individuals.

Understanding LGBTQ+ Mental Health Disparities and Challenges

Research has consistently shown that LGBTQ+ individuals experience higher rates of mental health disorders compared to the general population. These disparities can be attributed to various factors, including minority stress, discrimination, lack of social support, and internalized homophobia or transphobia. It is important to acknowledge and understand these challenges to develop effective strategies for building affirming and inclusive communities.

Minority Stress: LGBTQ+ individuals often experience minority stress, which refers to the chronic stress resulting from stigmatization, prejudice, and discrimination. This chronic stress can lead to adverse mental health outcomes such as depression, anxiety, and substance abuse.

Discrimination and Lack of Social Support: Discrimination and lack of social support contribute significantly to the mental health disparities faced by LGBTQ+ individuals. Experiencing rejection or marginalization from family members, friends, and community can have detrimental effects on mental well-being.

Internalized Homophobia or Transphobia: Internalized homophobia or transphobia refers to the internalization of negative beliefs and attitudes towards one's own sexual orientation or gender identity. This self-stigmatization can lead to feelings of shame, low self-esteem, and psychological distress.

Creating Affirming and Inclusive Spaces

Creating affirming and inclusive spaces is key to support the mental health of LGBTQ+ individuals and cultivate a sense of belonging. Here are some strategies to consider:

Education and Awareness: Promote education and awareness about LGBTQ+ issues to foster understanding and empathy within the community. This can be done through workshops, training sessions, and inclusion of LGBTQ+ topics in educational curricula.

Language and Communication: Use inclusive language and avoid making assumptions about individuals' sexual orientation or gender identity. Respect individuals' chosen names and pronouns, and be open to learning and correcting mistakes.

Policy and Advocacy: Advocate for LGBTQ+ inclusive policies in schools, workplaces, and public spaces. Support organizations and initiatives that promote equality, anti-discrimination, and LGBTQ+ rights.

Supportive Networks: Establish LGBTQ+ support groups or networks where individuals can connect, share experiences, and find peer support. These groups can play a significant role in reducing isolation and increasing resilience.

Inclusive Healthcare: Ensure healthcare providers receive training on LGBTQ+ cultural competency to provide inclusive and affirming care. Provide resources and referrals to LGBTQ+ friendly healthcare providers and ensure confidentiality and privacy.

Culturally Sensitive Mental Health Care

LGBTQ+ individuals may face challenges accessing culturally sensitive mental health care. It is essential for mental health professionals to understand the unique needs and experiences of this community. Here are some guidelines for providing culturally sensitive care:

Creating Safe Spaces: Design therapy spaces that are safe, welcoming, and affirming for LGBTQ+ clients. Consider displaying LGBTQ+ inclusive symbols or resources to signal a supportive environment.

Engaging in Active Listening: Practice active listening to understand clients' experiences, concerns, and goals. Create an open and non-judgmental atmosphere where clients feel comfortable sharing their thoughts and emotions.

Addressing Minority Stress: Incorporate interventions that specifically address minority stress, like cognitive-behavioral therapy (CBT) or acceptance and commitment therapy (ACT). Help clients develop coping skills to navigate discrimination and build resilience.

Support Network Integration: Encourage clients to build and nurture supportive networks within the LGBTQ+ community.   Connect them with relevant community organizations, support groups, or social activities.

Culturally Competent Language: Use appropriate and inclusive language in therapy sessions. Familiarize yourself with LGBTQ+ terminology, and respect clients' preferred terms for their sexual orientation or gender identity.

LGBTQ+ Rights and Advocacy

Advocacy plays a crucial role in promoting equality and improving mental health outcomes for LGBTQ+ individuals. Here are ways to support LGBTQ+ rights and advocate for inclusive communities:

Supporting LGBTQ+ Organizations: Contribute time, resources, or donations to LGBTQ+ organizations that are working towards equality, social justice, and mental health support.

Participating in Pride Events: Attend Pride events to show support and solidarity with the LGBTQ+ community. These events provide opportunities to learn, celebrate diversity, and raise awareness about LGBTQ+ issues.

Using Social Media for Advocacy: Utilize social media platforms to share educational resources, LGBTQ+ stories, and promote inclusivity.   Amplify the voices of LGBTQ+ advocates and organizations to reach a wider audience.

Advocacy in Educational Settings: Collaborate with educational institutions to promote LGBTQ+ inclusive policies, curriculum, and support systems. Advocate for the inclusion of LGBTQ+ history and culture in educational materials.

Legislative Advocacy: Stay informed about local and national legislation that impacts LGBTQ+ rights and mental health. Communicate with policymakers and legislators to express support for LGBTQ+ inclusive policies.

In conclusion, building affirming and inclusive communities is instrumental in supporting the mental health and overall well-being of LGBTQ+ individuals. By promoting education, providing supportive spaces, delivering culturally sensitive mental health care, and advocating for LGBTQ+ rights, we can work towards creating a society where everyone feels valued, accepted, and supported.

Mental Health in the Workplace and Education

Workplace Mental Health

Understanding Workplace Stress and Burnout

Work can be a significant source of stress for many individuals. Workplace stress refers to the physical, emotional, and mental strain experienced by employees in their job environment. It arises when the demands of the job exceed an individual's ability to cope effectively. If left unmanaged, excessive workplace stress can lead to burnout, which is a state of chronic physical and emotional exhaustion.

Causes of Workplace Stress

There are several factors that contribute to workplace stress. Understanding these causes can help individuals and organizations develop strategies to mitigate their impact. Some common causes of workplace stress include:

1. **Workload:** Having an excessive or unrealistic workload can lead to stress. This may include having too many tasks to complete within a limited time frame or being expected to meet high productivity targets.

2. **Lack of Control:** When employees have limited control over their work environment, decision-making processes, or the tasks assigned to them, it can increase stress levels.

3. **Lack of Support:** A lack of support from colleagues, supervisors, or the organization as a whole can contribute to workplace stress. This may include a lack of communication, feedback, or resources necessary to complete tasks effectively.

297

4. **Unclear Expectations:** When expectations and goals are not clearly defined, employees may experience stress. Uncertainty about what is expected of them can increase pressure and anxiety.

5. **Work-life Balance:** Difficulties in balancing work responsibilities with personal life commitments can lead to stress. Long working hours, inflexible schedules, and limited time for rest and relaxation can take a toll on an individual's well-being.

6. **Job Insecurity:** Fear of job loss or concerns about job stability can create significant stress for employees. This is particularly true during times of economic uncertainty or organizational restructuring.

Effects of Workplace Stress

Workplace stress can have detrimental effects on both the individual and the organization. Some common effects of workplace stress include:

1. **Decreased Productivity:** When employees are stressed, their ability to concentrate, make decisions, and perform tasks efficiently may be compromised. This can result in decreased productivity and quality of work.

2. **Increased Absenteeism:** Chronic workplace stress can lead to increased absenteeism as employees may take time off to cope with physical and emotional symptoms associated with stress.

3. **Deteriorating Mental and Physical Health:** Prolonged exposure to workplace stress can negatively impact an individual's mental and physical health. It can lead to symptoms such as anxiety, depression, insomnia, headaches, and digestive issues.

4. **Strained Relationships:** Workplace stress can affect relationships with colleagues, supervisors, and loved ones outside of work. Irritability, mood swings, and decreased social interaction can strain personal and professional relationships.

5. **Decreased Job Satisfaction:** High levels of stress can diminish job satisfaction and overall happiness at work. It may lead to increased job dissatisfaction, reduced motivation, and a higher likelihood of seeking alternative employment.

Strategies for Managing Workplace Stress

To effectively manage workplace stress and prevent burnout, individuals and organizations can implement various strategies.   Here are some practical approaches:

1. **Identify and Address Stressors:** By identifying the specific factors causing stress, individuals can begin to develop strategies to address them. This may involve setting boundaries, seeking support, or initiating conversations with supervisors or HR departments.

2. **Implement Stress Management Techniques:** Engaging in stress-reducing activities such as physical exercise, mindfulness meditation, and deep breathing can help individuals manage workplace stress. These techniques can promote relaxation and improve overall well-being.

3. **Promote Work-life Balance:** Employers can support work-life balance by promoting flexible work arrangements, encouraging breaks throughout the day, and discouraging a culture of overwork. Employees can also prioritize self-care and set boundaries to ensure they have time for rest and relaxation.

4. **Build Supportive Relationships:** Nurturing supportive relationships with colleagues and supervisors can provide a support system to cope with workplace stress.   Open communication, collaboration, and a sense of community can help foster a healthier work environment.

5. **Develop Time Management Skills:** Effective time management can reduce stress by helping individuals prioritize tasks, set realistic goals, and manage deadlines.   Time management techniques, such as creating to-do lists and breaking tasks into smaller, manageable chunks, can enhance productivity and reduce stress levels.

6. **Seek Professional Support:** When workplace stress becomes overwhelming, individuals may benefit from seeking professional support. This may involve reaching out to a therapist, counselor, or mental health professional who can provide guidance and support.

Case Study: Managing Workplace Stress

Consider the case of Sarah, a project manager in a fast-paced technology company. She is frequently assigned demanding projects with tight deadlines and is responsible for managing a team of employees. Sarah has been experiencing increasing levels of workplace stress, which is impacting her overall well-being and job performance.

To address her workplace stress, Sarah decides to implement some strategies:

+ She starts practicing mindfulness meditation for a few minutes each day during her lunch break to help reduce stress and improve focus.

+ Sarah sets boundaries by clearly communicating her availability and avoiding excessive work hours. She delegates tasks to team members and seeks support from her supervisor when needed.

+ She reevaluates her workload and creates a realistic schedule by breaking down complex projects into manageable tasks. This helps Sarah prioritize and allocate her time effectively.

+ Sarah reaches out to her colleagues for support and initiates regular team meetings to foster open communication and collaboration. She also attends a stress management workshop organized by the company to learn additional coping strategies.

By implementing these strategies, Sarah successfully manages her workplace stress, improves her overall well-being, and enhances her job performance.

Conclusion

Understanding workplace stress and its potential consequences is crucial for both employees and organizations. By implementing effective strategies to manage workplace stress, individuals can protect their mental and physical health while organizations can create a healthier work environment. Prioritizing well-being and fostering supportive relationships and work-life balance can lead to increased job satisfaction, productivity, and overall success. It is important for individuals and organizations to work collaboratively to reduce workplace stress and promote a positive and thriving work culture.

Strategies for Promoting Mental Health at Work

Promoting mental health at work is crucial for creating a positive and supportive work environment. When employees feel mentally well, they are more engaged, productive, and satisfied with their jobs. In this section, we will explore various strategies that organizations can implement to foster mental health in the workplace.

Developing a Mental Health Policy

One of the first steps in promoting mental health at work is developing a comprehensive mental health policy. This policy should outline the organization's commitment to supporting employee mental well-being and provide guidelines for addressing mental health issues in the workplace. It should also promote a stigma-free environment where employees feel comfortable discussing mental health concerns.

Creating a Positive Organizational Culture

A positive organizational culture plays a vital role in promoting mental health at work. It is essential to foster a culture that values work-life balance, open communication, and employee well-being. This can be achieved by creating supportive policies, such as flexible work arrangements, opportunities for personal growth and development, and recognition of employee achievements.

Promoting Work-Life Balance

Achieving a healthy work-life balance is essential for maintaining good mental health. Employers can promote work-life balance by encouraging employees to take regular breaks, enforcing reasonable working hours, and offering employee assistance programs. It is also essential to discourage presenteeism (being physically present at work but not fully productive due to mental health issues) and support employees in prioritizing their well-being outside of work.

Building Resilience and Coping Skills

Resilience is the ability to bounce back from adversity, and building resilience is crucial for maintaining good mental health. Employers can provide resources and training programs focused on building resilience and developing coping skills. These programs may include workshops, seminars, or access to mental health professionals who can provide guidance and support.

Promoting a Supportive Workplace Environment

Creating a supportive workplace environment is key to promoting mental health. Employers can foster this environment by encouraging open communication, active listening, and empathy. Managers should be trained in recognizing signs of mental health issues and responding appropriately. Peer support programs and employee resource groups can also be implemented to provide a safe space for employees to connect and seek support.

Reducing Workplace Stressors

Workplace stress is a significant factor contributing to poor mental health. Employers should aim to identify and reduce workplace stressors to promote mental well-being. This can include ensuring reasonable workloads, clarifying roles and responsibilities, and providing employees with the necessary resources and support to perform their jobs effectively. Creating a positive work environment that encourages collaboration and teamwork can also help reduce stress.

Providing Mental Health Education and Training

Educating employees about mental health and building awareness is essential for promoting mental health at work. Organizations can provide mental health training programs to equip employees with the knowledge and skills necessary to address mental health issues. These programs can cover topics such as stress management, resilience-building, recognizing signs of mental health issues, and accessing available resources and support.

Offering Employee Assistance Programs

Employee Assistance Programs (EAPs) are employer-sponsored programs designed to support employees in managing personal challenges, including mental health issues. EAPs typically offer confidential counseling services, referrals to mental health professionals, and other resources to address a range of personal and work-related concerns. Implementing an EAP demonstrates the organization's commitment to employee well-being and provides a valuable support system for employees.

Evaluating and Monitoring Mental Health Initiatives

Regularly evaluating and monitoring the effectiveness of mental health initiatives is crucial for continuous improvement. Organizations should collect feedback from employees, track key metrics related to mental health, and make adjustments or enhancements to their programs as needed. By measuring the impact of their strategies, organizations can ensure that they are effectively promoting mental health in the workplace.

In conclusion, promoting mental health at work requires a multi-faceted approach that includes developing a mental health policy, creating a positive organizational culture, promoting work-life balance, building resilience, reducing workplace stressors, providing education and training, offering employee assistance programs, and evaluating and monitoring initiatives. By implementing these strategies, organizations can create a supportive work environment that prioritizes employee mental well-being. Remember, a mentally healthy workforce is a productive and successful one.

Addressing Workplace Harassment and Discrimination

In this section, we will explore strategies for addressing workplace harassment and discrimination, which are critical components of promoting a healthy and inclusive work environment. Harassment and discrimination can have profound negative effects on both individuals and organizations, including decreased job satisfaction, increased turnover, and diminished productivity. By implementing effective strategies, employers can create a safe and supportive workplace for all employees.

Understanding Workplace Harassment and Discrimination

Workplace harassment refers to any unwelcome conduct, behavior, or action that creates a hostile or intimidating work environment. It can take various forms, including verbal, physical, or written harassment, and can be based on characteristics such as race, gender, age, religion, disability, or sexual orientation. Discrimination, on the other hand, involves treating certain individuals or groups less favorably based on their protected characteristics.

It is important to understand that workplace harassment and discrimination are not only morally wrong but also illegal. They violate various laws and regulations, including Title VII of the Civil Rights Act, the Americans with Disabilities Act (ADA), and the Age Discrimination in Employment Act (ADEA), among others. Organizations have a legal obligation to prevent, address, and remedy instances of harassment and discrimination.

Creating a Culture of Respect and Inclusivity

The first step in addressing workplace harassment and discrimination is to create a culture of respect and inclusivity. This requires a commitment from both the organization and its leaders to foster an environment where individuals are valued, respected, and treated fairly. Here are some strategies to promote a positive work culture:

- Develop clear policies: Establish robust policies that prohibit harassment and discrimination in any form. These policies should clearly define the behaviors that are considered unacceptable and outline the consequences for violating them.

- Implement effective training programs: Provide comprehensive training programs to educate employees about their rights, the organization's policies, and how to identify and report instances of harassment and discrimination. Training should be regularly updated and mandatory for all employees.

- Lead by example: Leaders should set the tone for respectful behavior by modeling appropriate conduct and responding promptly to any concerns or complaints. They should also actively promote diversity and inclusion within the organization.

- Foster open communication: Encourage employees to speak up if they witness or experience any form of harassment or discrimination. Establish accessible channels, such as anonymous reporting mechanisms, to ensure employees feel safe and empowered to report incidents.

- Conduct regular assessments: Regularly assess the workplace culture through surveys or focus groups to identify potential issues and areas for improvement. Use the feedback to inform policies and practices.

- Establish a zero-tolerance policy: Emphasize that harassment and discrimination will not be tolerated in any circumstances. Take immediate and appropriate action when allegations are substantiated.

Implementing Effective Reporting and Investigation Procedures

In addition to creating a culture of respect, organizations must implement effective reporting and investigation procedures to address instances of workplace harassment and discrimination. This ensures that complaints are taken seriously, investigated thoroughly, and resolved promptly in a fair and impartial manner. Here are some essential steps for establishing and maintaining effective procedures:

- Establish multiple reporting channels: Provide various reporting options, such as a designated contact person, hotline, or online reporting system. This allows individuals to choose their preferred method and ensures confidentiality and privacy.

- Train designated investigators: Designate trained individuals who will handle complaints and conduct investigations. These investigators should have the necessary skills and knowledge to investigate allegations objectively and impartially.

- Conduct thorough investigations: Promptly initiate a thorough investigation when a complaint is received. Interviews should be conducted with all relevant parties and any supporting evidence should be gathered. The investigation process should be well-documented.

- Ensure confidentiality and protection against retaliation: Guarantee the confidentiality of all parties involved and protect individuals from retaliation. Whistleblower protections should be in place to encourage reporting without fear of negative consequences.

- Imposition of appropriate consequences: If the investigation substantiates the allegations, take appropriate action against the perpetrator, which may include disciplinary measures such as warnings, suspension, or termination. Communicate the outcome to the parties involved while respecting privacy concerns.

- Periodic review and evaluation: Regularly review the effectiveness of reporting and investigation procedures to identify any gaps or areas for improvement. Consider feedback from employees and incorporate best practices to enhance the process.

Training and Education for Employees

Education and training play a crucial role in preventing workplace harassment and discrimination. By providing employees with the knowledge and tools to recognize, prevent, and address these issues, organizations can empower their workforce to create a respectful and inclusive workplace. Here are some key components of training and education programs:

- Awareness training: Provide employees with the knowledge to recognize what constitutes harassment and discrimination. Train them on the different forms of harassment, its impact on individuals and the organization, and the legal implications.

- Bystander intervention training: Empower employees to intervene and support colleagues who experience harassment or discrimination. Bystander intervention training educates employees about the role they can play in preventing and addressing these issues.

+ Cultural sensitivity training: In today's diverse workforce, cultural sensitivity training is essential to foster inclusivity and respect. It helps employees understand and appreciate different cultures, beliefs, and perspectives, reducing the likelihood of discriminatory behavior.

+ Supervisory training: Provide specialized training to supervisors and managers on their role in preventing and addressing workplace harassment and discrimination. This training should emphasize their responsibility to create a respectful and inclusive work environment, as well as their role in handling complaints.

Monitoring and Evaluation of Progress

Continuous monitoring and evaluation of workplace practices are crucial to ensure the effectiveness of strategies in addressing workplace harassment and discrimination. Here are some ways organizations can evaluate their progress:

+ Regular data collection: Collect data on reported incidents, investigation outcomes, and employee feedback to identify trends and patterns. This can help determine the effectiveness of prevention strategies and guide targeted interventions.

+ Conduct climate surveys: Use surveys to gauge employee perceptions of the workplace climate, including their sense of safety, fairness, and job satisfaction. Analyze the results to identify areas that require improvement.

+ Benchmark against best practices and legal requirements: Regularly review best practices and legal requirements related to workplace harassment and discrimination. Compare organizational policies and practices to these benchmarks to ensure compliance and identify areas for enhancement.

+ Seek external input: Engage external experts or auditors to assess the effectiveness of workplace policies, training programs, and investigation procedures. Their objective assessment can provide valuable insights and recommendations.

By implementing comprehensive strategies to address workplace harassment and discrimination, organizations can create an environment where all employees feel valued, respected, and safe. These strategies not only comply with legal obligations but also contribute to a more productive and inclusive work culture. It is the collective responsibility of the organization, leaders, and employees to ensure that this commitment to a harassment-free workplace is upheld.

Now you have learned about strategies for addressing workplace harassment and discrimination. The next section will focus on creating a supportive organizational culture that promotes mental health and well-being.

Creating a Supportive Organizational Culture

Creating a supportive organizational culture is crucial for promoting mental health in the workplace. When employees feel valued, respected, and supported, it contributes to their overall well-being and fosters a positive work environment. In this section, we will explore strategies and practices that can help organizations create a culture that prioritizes mental health and well-being.

Leadership and Role Modeling

Leadership plays a vital role in shaping the organizational culture. When leaders prioritize mental health and well-being, it sends a clear message to employees that their mental health matters. Leaders should actively promote an open and inclusive environment that encourages dialogue about mental health and reduces stigma.

To create a supportive organizational culture, leaders can:

- Communicate openly about mental health: Leaders should openly discuss mental health, emphasize its importance, and encourage employees to seek support when needed. They can share their own experiences to foster a sense of empathy and understanding.

- Lead by example: Leaders should prioritize self-care and work-life balance, demonstrating to employees that mental well-being is not only valued but also essential for productivity and success. By setting boundaries, taking breaks, and engaging in stress-reducing activities, leaders can inspire employees to do the same.

- Provide resources and support: Leaders should ensure that employees have access to mental health resources and support services. This can include providing information about counseling services, mental health hotlines, and employee assistance programs. They can also encourage employees to take advantage of these resources without fear of judgment or repercussions.

Promoting Work-Life Balance

Work-life balance is essential for maintaining mental well-being. Organizations can take proactive steps to support their employees in achieving a healthy balance between work and personal life.

Some strategies for promoting work-life balance include:

+ Flexible work schedules: Offering flexible work hours or remote work options can give employees more control over their time, reducing stress and promoting work-life balance. This can be particularly beneficial for employees with caregiving responsibilities or personal commitments.

+ Encouraging breaks and holidays: Encouraging regular breaks throughout the workday and supporting employees' use of vacation time can prevent burnout and improve overall well-being. Organizations can create a culture that values rest and relaxation by discouraging excessive overtime and prioritizing employee downtime.

+ Providing wellness programs: Implementing wellness programs focused on physical activity, stress management, and mindfulness can contribute to employees' overall well-being. These programs can include gym memberships, yoga or meditation classes, and workshops on stress reduction techniques.

Communication and Support

Open and effective communication is essential for creating a supportive culture where individuals feel comfortable discussing their mental health concerns. Organizations should provide channels for employees to express their needs and concerns without fear of judgment or reprisal.

Some practices for promoting open communication and support include:

+ Mental health awareness training: Offering training programs that increase awareness and understanding of mental health issues can create a more empathetic and supportive workplace. These programs can educate employees on recognizing signs of mental health distress and how to provide appropriate support.

+ Establishing support networks: Organizations can create support networks or employee resource groups focused on mental health. These communities provide a safe space for individuals to connect, share experiences, and offer support to one another. Support networks can be particularly valuable for employees from marginalized or underrepresented groups who may face additional challenges related to mental health.

+ Employee feedback mechanisms: Establishing channels for employees to provide feedback on organizational policies, practices, and initiatives regarding mental health is essential. This can include regular surveys, focus groups, or anonymous suggestion boxes. Actively seeking and implementing employee feedback creates a sense of ownership and fosters a culture of continuous improvement.

Recognition and Rewards

Recognizing and rewarding employees' contributions and achievements can significantly impact their mental health and overall job satisfaction. Organizations should implement mechanisms to acknowledge employees' efforts and create a positive workplace culture.

Some strategies for recognition and rewards include:

+ Employee appreciation programs: Implementing employee appreciation programs can help foster a sense of belonging and boost morale. This can include simple gestures such as thank-you notes, public recognition during team meetings, or employee of the month awards. By celebrating achievements, organizations show their commitment to valuing and supporting their employees.

+ Professional development opportunities: Offering opportunities for professional growth and development demonstrates a commitment to employee well-being and career advancement. Organizations can provide access to training programs, conferences, or mentorship opportunities, empowering employees to enhance their skills and reach their full potential.

Evaluation and Continuous Improvement

Creating a supportive organizational culture is an ongoing process that requires evaluation and continuous improvement. Organizations should regularly assess the effectiveness of their strategies and make necessary adjustments to ensure the well-being of their employees.

Some practices for evaluation and continuous improvement include:

- Employee surveys: Conducting regular surveys to gather feedback on the organization's mental health initiatives and overall workplace climate provides valuable insights. Employee surveys can help identify areas of improvement and measure the effectiveness of existing programs and practices.

- Collaboration with mental health experts: Organizations can collaborate with mental health experts or consultants to assess their mental health support systems and develop evidence-based strategies. Mental health professionals can provide guidance on best practices and help tailor initiatives to the organization's specific needs.

- Creating a learning culture: Organizations should foster a culture of learning and growth, encouraging employees to continually develop their knowledge and skills related to mental health support. Providing opportunities for workshops, seminars, or webinars on mental health topics can empower employees and enhance their ability to support themselves and their colleagues.

By implementing these strategies, organizations can create a supportive and inclusive culture that prioritizes mental health and contributes to the overall well-being and success of their employees.

Return-to-Work and Accommodation Programs

Return-to-work programs and accommodation programs play a crucial role in supporting individuals with mental health challenges in the workplace. These programs aim to facilitate the successful reintegration of employees into the workforce after a mental health-related absence or to provide necessary workplace adjustments for those managing mental health conditions. In this section, we will explore the importance of return-to-work and accommodation programs, discuss their key components, and provide strategies for their effective implementation.

Understanding Return-to-Work Programs

Return-to-work programs are structured interventions designed to assist employees in transitioning back to work after a mental health-related leave of absence. They focus on creating a supportive and inclusive environment that facilitates a successful return to regular job duties. These programs recognize the unique needs and challenges faced by individuals with mental health conditions and aim to provide appropriate support during the reintegration process.

Components of Return-to-Work Programs

Return-to-work programs typically involve several key components that contribute to their effectiveness. These components include:

1. **Planning and coordination:** A structured return-to-work plan should be developed in collaboration with the employee, their healthcare provider, and relevant stakeholders. This plan outlines the gradual return to work process, any necessary workplace adjustments, and the allocation of resources and supports.

2. **Communication and education:** Open and transparent communication is essential during the return-to-work process. Employers should ensure that all employees are aware of the program and understand its purpose. Additionally, education and training sessions can help reduce stigma and provide employees with a better understanding of mental health conditions.

3. **Reasonable accommodations:** Employers should make reasonable accommodations to support the employee's successful return to work. These accommodations may include flexible work hours, modified duties, or changes to the physical work environment. By providing appropriate adjustments, employers demonstrate their commitment to creating an inclusive workplace.

4. **Monitoring and support:** Regular monitoring and support are critical to ensure a smooth transition back to work. This may involve regular check-ins, providing access to employee assistance programs (EAPs), or assigning a mentor or buddy to the returning employee for additional support.

5. **Evaluation and feedback:** Ongoing evaluation and feedback are essential to assess the effectiveness of the return-to-work program. Employers should gather feedback from both the employee and relevant stakeholders to identify potential areas for improvement and make necessary adjustments to the program.

Effective Implementation Strategies

To ensure the successful implementation of return-to-work programs, organizations should consider the following strategies:

1. **Leadership commitment:** The commitment of organizational leaders is crucial in fostering a culture that supports mental health and employee well-being. Leaders should actively promote the return-to-work program, allocate necessary resources, and lead by example in creating an inclusive and supportive work environment.

2. **Collaboration and cross-functional teams:** Collaboration between HR departments, managers, supervisors, and healthcare professionals is essential for the effective implementation of return-to-work programs. Cross-functional teams can collaborate to develop return-to-work policies, ensure adherence to legal requirements, and provide necessary support to returning employees.

3. **Training and education:** Providing comprehensive training and education to supervisors and managers equips them with the knowledge and skills needed to support employees throughout the return-to-work process. This includes training in mental health awareness, effective communication, and strategies for managing workplace accommodations.

4. **Regular program evaluation:** Continuous evaluation of the return-to-work program allows organizations to identify strengths and areas for improvement. Regular assessment of program outcomes, feedback from employees, and benchmarking against best practices can inform necessary adjustments to enhance the program's effectiveness.

5. **Promoting a culture of open communication:** Organizations should create a culture that encourages open communication and reduces the stigma associated with mental health. Implementing channels for employees to share their experiences, concerns, and feedback can foster a supportive workplace environment and strengthen the effectiveness of return-to-work programs.

Case Study: Successful Implementation of a Return-to-Work Program

To illustrate the effective implementation of a return-to-work program, let's consider the case of Company XYZ, a large multinational corporation. Company XYZ recently introduced a comprehensive return-to-work program to support employees with mental health challenges. Here are the key steps they took:

1. **Policy development:** Company XYZ developed a return-to-work policy in consultation with human resources, legal, and occupational health experts.

The policy outlined the eligibility criteria, the process for developing return-to-work plans, and the available accommodations and supports.

2. **Leadership support:** Senior leaders at Company XYZ actively promoted the return-to-work program and emphasized its importance in creating an inclusive and supportive workplace culture. They allocated resources to ensure the smooth implementation of the program and encouraged managers and supervisors to actively participate.

3. **Training and education:** Company XYZ provided comprehensive training and education to managers and supervisors on mental health awareness, stigma reduction, and effective communication strategies. This training equipped them with the necessary skills to support employees through the return-to-work process.

4. **Individualized return-to-work plans:** Employees participating in the program worked collaboratively with their healthcare providers, HR representatives, and supervisors to develop individualized return-to-work plans. These plans identified suitable accommodations, outlined a gradual return-to-work schedule, and addressed any necessary workplace adjustments.

5. **Ongoing monitoring and support:** Company XYZ implemented regular check-ins and provided access to an EAP for all employees participating in the return-to-work program. Supervisors and managers maintained open lines of communication, ensuring that employees felt supported throughout their transition back to work.

6. **Program evaluation:** To assess the effectiveness of their return-to-work program, Company XYZ conducted regular evaluations. They gathered feedback from employees, identified areas for improvement, and made adjustments to the program based on the feedback received. This continuous evaluation helped enhance the program's effectiveness over time.

By implementing these strategies, Company XYZ successfully integrated their return-to-work program into their organizational culture, resulting in improved employee well-being, increased productivity, and enhanced retention rates.

Conclusion

Return-to-work and accommodation programs are invaluable tools for helping individuals with mental health challenges integrate successfully back into the workplace. By implementing structured return-to-work plans, providing necessary workplace adjustments, and fostering a supportive organizational culture, employers can create an inclusive environment that prioritizes employee well-being. Through collaboration, education, and ongoing evaluation, organizations can ensure the effectiveness of their return-to-work programs and support the mental health of their workforce.

Mental Health in Education

Prevalence of Mental Health Issues in Schools

Mental health issues among school-aged children and adolescents have become a growing concern worldwide. The prevalence of these issues in schools has been increasing steadily over the years, with a significant impact on students' well-being and academic performance. It is essential to understand the scope of the problem and its implications to develop effective strategies for supporting the mental health needs of students.

Scope of the Problem

The prevalence of mental health issues in schools is staggering. According to the World Health Organization (WHO), approximately one in five children and adolescents worldwide have a mental health disorder. This means that in a typical classroom of 30 students, around six of them are likely to be experiencing mental health challenges.

Common mental health issues among school-aged children and adolescents include anxiety disorders, depression, attention-deficit/hyperactivity disorder (ADHD), and conduct disorders. These conditions can significantly impact students' emotional well-being, cognitive abilities, and social relationships.

Impact on Academic Performance

The impact of mental health issues on academic performance is substantial. Students experiencing mental health challenges often struggle with concentration, memory, and problem-solving skills, making it difficult for them to engage effectively in learning activities. They may experience a decline in academic achievement, leading to poor grades and a lack of motivation.

Furthermore, mental health issues can also affect students' attendance and school participation. Students may experience difficulties attending school regularly due to anxiety, depression, or other mental health-related symptoms. This absenteeism can lead to a significant loss of instructional time and exacerbate the academic challenges they face.

Factors Contributing to Mental Health Issues in Schools

Several factors contribute to the prevalence of mental health issues in schools. Understanding these factors is crucial for developing effective prevention and intervention strategies:

1. **Academic Pressure**: High academic expectations, stress from exams, and the pressure to perform well can contribute to mental health issues among students. The intense competition for grades and college admissions can lead to increased levels of anxiety and depression.

2. **Social Challenges**: Students face various social challenges in schools, such as bullying, peer pressure, and social exclusion. These experiences can significantly impact a student's mental health and well-being.

3. **Family Environment**: Family dynamics and relationships play a vital role in a student's mental health. Negative family environments, such as abuse, neglect, or parental mental health issues, can contribute to the development of mental health disorders.

4. **Socioeconomic Factors**: Socioeconomic factors, such as poverty, limited access to resources, and unstable living conditions, can increase the risk of mental health issues among students.

5. **Traumatic Events**: Exposure to traumatic events, such as natural disasters, violence, or loss of a loved one, can have a profound impact on a student's mental health.

Challenges in Identifying Mental Health Issues

Identifying mental health issues in schools can be challenging due to various reasons:

+ **Stigma**: Mental health stigma can prevent students, parents, and even educators from seeking help or talking about mental health openly. Stigma can perpetuate feelings of shame and silence, making it harder to identify and address mental health issues.

- ◆ **Lack of Awareness:** Many mental health issues in schools go unnoticed due to a lack of awareness or knowledge about the signs and symptoms. Educators and parents may not be equipped with the necessary skills to identify and address these challenges effectively.

- ◆ **Co-occurring Issues:** Mental health issues often co-occur with other problems, such as substance abuse, learning disabilities, or physical health conditions. This complexity can make it difficult to identify and address the underlying mental health concerns.

Strategies for Promoting Student Well-being

Promoting student well-being and addressing mental health issues in schools requires a comprehensive and multi-faceted approach. Here are some strategies that can be implemented:

1. **Mental Health Education:** Incorporate mental health education into the school curriculum to raise awareness, reduce stigma, and provide students with the knowledge and skills to take care of their mental health.

2. **Early Intervention:** Implement early intervention programs that identify and support students at risk of developing mental health issues. This can involve regular mental health screenings, counseling services, and access to appropriate interventions.

3. **Creating Supportive Environments:** Foster a positive and supportive school environment that promotes positive mental health. This can include implementing anti-bullying policies, promoting inclusivity and diversity, and providing mental health resources and support for students.

4. **Teacher Training:** Provide professional development and training for teachers and school staff on recognizing the signs of mental health issues and providing appropriate support. This can include workshops on mental health literacy, active listening skills, and strategies for promoting well-being in the classroom.

5. **Collaboration with Mental Health Professionals:** Establish partnerships with mental health professionals and community organizations to provide comprehensive support and resources for students. This collaboration can involve referrals, counseling services, and access to specialized interventions.

Case Study

To illustrate the prevalence of mental health issues in schools, let's consider the case of Alex, a 13-year-old student struggling with anxiety. Alex often feels overwhelmed by academic pressure and is afraid of social interactions due to past bullying experiences. As a result, Alex's grades have been declining, and absenteeism is becoming more frequent.

In this case, it is crucial for the school to identify and address Alex's mental health challenges. Through early intervention and support, the school can provide counseling services, implement a personalized academic plan, and collaborate with parents to create a supportive environment for Alex's well-being.

Additional Resources

To learn more about mental health issues in schools and effective strategies for support, the following resources are recommended:

+ American School Counselor Association: `www.schoolcounselor.org`

+ National Alliance on Mental Illness: `www.nami.org`

+ Centers for Disease Control and Prevention: `www.cdc.gov/childrensmentalhealth`

+ Mental Health America: `www.mhanational.org`

+ World Health Organization: `www.who.int/mental_health/policies/school/en`

In conclusion, the prevalence of mental health issues in schools is a significant concern affecting students' well-being and academic performance. By understanding the scope of the problem and implementing effective strategies, schools can create a supportive environment that promotes student well-being and addresses their mental health needs.

School-Based Mental Health Support Systems

In recent years, there has been a growing recognition of the importance of addressing mental health issues in schools. School-based mental health support systems play a vital role in promoting the well-being of students and creating a positive and nurturing educational environment. These systems encompass a range of strategies and interventions designed to identify, prevent, and address mental health concerns among students. In this section, we will explore various components of school-based mental health support systems and discuss their implementation and effectiveness.

Roles and Responsibilities

Implementing a comprehensive school-based mental health support system involves the collaboration of various stakeholders, including educators, counselors, school administrators, parents, and community organizations. Each individual plays a unique role in creating a supportive environment and addressing the mental health needs of students.

Educators have a crucial role in recognizing early signs of mental health problems in students. They can provide emotional support, facilitate a positive learning environment, and implement preventive measures. Counselors are essential in assessing and identifying mental health concerns, providing counseling services, and coordinating with other mental health professionals. School administrators also play a critical role in creating policies that support mental health, allocating resources, and promoting a safe and inclusive school culture.

Parents and families are important partners in school-based mental health support systems. They can actively engage with the school and collaborate with educators and counselors to address their child's mental health needs. Community organizations, such as mental health agencies and non-profit organizations, can provide additional resources, training, and services to enhance the effectiveness of school-based support systems.

Screening and Assessment

An integral part of a school-based mental health support system is the screening and assessment process. Screening involves the identification of students who may be at risk of mental health issues or require further evaluation. Screening tools may include questionnaires or checklists that focus on various domains, such as behavior, emotional well-being, and academic performance.

Assessment, on the other hand, involves a more comprehensive evaluation of a student's mental health needs. It may include interviews, observations, and standardized assessments conducted by trained professionals, such as school counselors or psychologists. Assessment tools should be culturally sensitive and consider the diverse backgrounds and experiences of students.

Screening and assessment allow for early identification of mental health concerns, enabling targeted interventions and support for students. It also helps in monitoring the progress of students receiving mental health services and making necessary adjustments to their support plan.

Prevention and Promotion

Prevention and promotion are fundamental components of school-based mental health support systems. These strategies focus on fostering positive mental health and well-being, reducing the risk of mental health problems, and promoting resilience among students.

Universal prevention programs aim to enhance the overall mental health of all students, regardless of their specific needs. These programs often involve the implementation of evidence-based practices, such as social-emotional learning (SEL) curricula, mindfulness programs, and anti-bullying initiatives. They promote skills development, resilience, and overall well-being.

Targeted prevention programs focus on specific groups of students who may be at higher risk of developing mental health issues. This may include students experiencing academic difficulties, social isolation, or adverse life events. Targeted interventions may involve individual counseling, group therapy, or skill-building workshops tailored to the specific needs of these students.

School-based mental health support systems should also address the needs of students with diagnosed mental health disorders. This includes providing appropriate accommodations, individualized support, and collaborating with external mental health service providers. Additionally, stigma reduction efforts should be integrated into the prevention and promotion strategies, fostering an inclusive and accepting school community.

Intervention and Treatment

For students with identified mental health needs, school-based mental health support systems should provide a range of intervention and treatment options. These may include individual counseling, group therapy, psychoeducation sessions, and referral to external mental health services.

Individual counseling sessions can be conducted by school counselors or mental health professionals and offer a safe and confidential space for students to express their feelings and concerns. Group therapy sessions provide an opportunity for students to connect with peers facing similar challenges, share experiences, and learn coping skills. Psychoeducation sessions aim to provide students with information about mental health topics, self-care strategies, and resources available to them.

Collaboration with external mental health service providers, such as psychologists or psychiatrists, is essential for more specialized assessments and treatment. School-based mental health support systems should establish strong partnerships with community mental health agencies to ensure a continuum of care for students requiring more intensive interventions.

Evaluation and Continuous Improvement

To ensure the effectiveness of school-based mental health support systems, ongoing evaluation and continuous improvement are crucial. Evaluation involves monitoring the implementation of strategies and interventions, assessing their impact on student outcomes, and gathering feedback from students, parents, and school staff.

Regular data collection through surveys, interviews, and academic performance indicators can provide insights into the strengths and weaknesses of the support systems. This information can be used to make informed decisions about resource allocation, training needs, and program adjustments.

Continuous improvement involves a commitment to evidence-based practices and staying up-to-date with the latest research in the field of mental health. School staff should engage in professional development opportunities to enhance their knowledge and skills in supporting student mental health. Collaboration with mental health experts, researchers, and other schools can facilitate knowledge exchange and promote innovative approaches to school-based mental health support.

Challenges and Considerations

Implementing and sustaining a comprehensive school-based mental health support system can present various challenges. Limited resources, including funding, staff, and time, may pose barriers to the implementation of a robust support system. The stigma associated with mental health may also hinder open discussions and access to services.

Considerations of cultural diversity and equity are crucial in developing inclusive support systems. Culturally sensitive practices and interventions must be incorporated to address the unique mental health needs of diverse student populations. Additionally, collaboration between mental health professionals and educators is necessary to ensure a shared understanding of roles, responsibilities, and effective communication.

It is important to note that school-based mental health support systems are not a substitute for professional mental health services. They serve as a crucial foundation for early identification, prevention, and intervention, but students with more severe or complex mental health needs may require additional support from external providers.

Conclusion

School-based mental health support systems play a vital role in promoting the mental health and well-being of students. By implementing comprehensive strategies that include screening, prevention, intervention, and collaboration with external providers, schools can create a positive and supportive environment for all students. However, ongoing evaluation, continuous improvement, and addressing challenges such as limited resources and stigma are necessary to ensure the effectiveness and sustainability of these support systems. By prioritizing student mental health, schools contribute to the overall development and success of their students.

Strategies for Promoting Student Well-being

In this section, we will explore various strategies for promoting student well-being. It is important to prioritize the mental health and overall well-being of students, as it directly impacts their academic performance, social interactions, and overall quality of life. By implementing these strategies, educators and schools can create a supportive environment that fosters emotional well-being and resilience in students.

Creating a Supportive School Climate

A supportive school climate plays a crucial role in promoting student well-being. It involves creating an environment where students feel safe, valued, and respected. Here are some strategies to cultivate a supportive school climate:

- **Positive Relationships:** Foster positive relationships between students, teachers, and staff members. Encourage open communication, empathy, and mutual respect.

- **Bullying Prevention:** Implement comprehensive anti-bullying policies and programs. Raise awareness about the harmful effects of bullying and provide resources for reporting and addressing bullying incidents.

- **Inclusive Practices:** Embrace diversity and promote inclusivity within the school community. Celebrate different cultures, backgrounds, and abilities, and ensure that all students feel included and valued.

+ **Safe Physical Environment**: Ensure a physically safe environment for students by addressing safety concerns, conducting regular safety checks, and providing appropriate measures to prevent accidents.

+ **Trained Staff**: Provide professional development and training for teachers and staff on mental health awareness, trauma-informed practices, and how to support students' well-being effectively.

Promoting Emotional Intelligence

Emotional intelligence refers to the ability to recognize, understand, and manage one's emotions and the emotions of others. Developing emotional intelligence equips students with essential skills for navigating challenges, building positive relationships, and enhancing overall well-being. Here are some strategies for promoting emotional intelligence:

+ **Emotion Recognition**: Teach students to identify and label their emotions accurately. This can be done through activities like emotion charts, guided discussions, or reflective writing exercises.

+ **Emotion Regulation**: Provide students with tools and techniques for regulating their emotions effectively. Teach deep breathing exercises, mindfulness techniques, and strategies for calming oneself during periods of stress or anxiety.

+ **Empathy Building**: Foster empathy in students by encouraging them to consider others' perspectives and experiences. Engage in activities like role-playing, group discussions, and community service projects that promote empathy and compassion.

+ **Conflict Resolution**: Teach students conflict resolution skills, such as active listening, compromise, and assertive communication. Provide opportunities for students to practice these skills through group activities or scenarios.

+ **Self-Reflection**: Encourage students to engage in self-reflection to better understand their thoughts, feelings, and behaviors. This can be facilitated through journaling prompts, guided reflections, or mindfulness activities.

Building Resilience

Resilience is the ability to bounce back from adversity and adapt positively to challenges. By fostering resilience in students, educators can empower them to overcome obstacles, persevere in the face of setbacks, and maintain a positive outlook on life. Here are some strategies for building resilience:

- **Growth Mindset:** Foster a growth mindset in students, emphasizing that intelligence and abilities can be developed through effort and practice. Encourage students to embrace challenges, learn from failures, and believe in their own potential.

- **Positive Self-Talk:** Teach students to replace negative self-talk with positive and encouraging thoughts. Help them recognize and challenge negative self-perceptions and reinforce positive affirmations.

- **Goal Setting:** Guide students in setting realistic and achievable goals. Teach them the importance of breaking down larger goals into smaller, manageable steps. This helps students build confidence and motivation as they experience success along the way.

- **Problem-Solving Skills:** Provide opportunities for students to develop problem-solving skills. Engage them in activities that require critical thinking, decision-making, and finding solutions to real-life problems.

- **Supportive Networks:** Encourage students to seek support from trusted adults, friends, or peer groups when facing challenges. Foster a sense of belonging and connectedness within the school community.

Promoting Physical Well-being

Physical well-being is closely linked to mental health. By promoting healthy habits and an active lifestyle, schools can contribute to the overall well-being of students. Here are some strategies for promoting physical well-being:

- **Physical Education:** Provide regular physical education classes that promote a variety of physical activities, including team sports, individual exercises, and recreational activities.

- **Healthy Eating Habits:** Educate students about the importance of a balanced diet and healthy eating habits. Offer nutritious food options in school cafeterias and provide resources for students to make informed food choices.

- **Physical Activity Breaks:** Incorporate physical activity breaks during classroom instruction to help students increase their movement and reduce sedentary behavior.

- **Sleep Education:** Teach students about the importance of adequate sleep for their physical and mental well-being. Provide information on healthy sleep habits and the potential consequences of sleep deprivation.

- **Health Promotion Campaigns:** Organize health promotion campaigns that raise awareness about the benefits of physical activity, healthy eating, and other wellness-related topics. Engage students in planning and implementing these campaigns to foster a sense of ownership and empowerment.

Collaboration with Mental Health Professionals

Collaborating with mental health professionals is essential for effectively promoting student well-being. These professionals can provide valuable expertise, resources, and support to students, educators, and families. Here are some strategies for collaboration:

- **School-Based Mental Health Services:** Partner with mental health professionals to offer on-site counseling services, support groups, and mental health screenings. This ensures early intervention and timely support for students who may need additional assistance.

- **Professional Development:** Conduct ongoing professional development sessions for educators to enhance their understanding of mental health issues, crisis intervention techniques, and best practices for supporting students' well-being.

- **Communication and Referral:** Establish effective communication channels between educators and mental health professionals to facilitate referrals and promote continuity of care. This includes sharing relevant information, progress reports, and collaborating on care plans.

- **Parent and Community Engagement:** Involve parents and the wider community in promoting student well-being. Organize workshops, support groups, or information sessions that address mental health topics and provide resources for families.

- **Multi-Disciplinary Teams:** Create multi-disciplinary teams comprising educators, mental health professionals, and other relevant stakeholders. These teams can collaboratively develop and implement comprehensive strategies to support student well-being.

By implementing these strategies, schools can create an environment that supports the mental health and well-being of students. It is important to remember that promoting student well-being is an ongoing and collaborative effort involving educators, mental health professionals, families, and the wider community. Through these collective efforts, we can support students in reaching their full potential and thriving academically, socially, and emotionally.

Teaching Mental Health Literacy

Mental health literacy refers to the knowledge and understanding of mental health conditions, including their causes, symptoms, and available treatments. It also involves the ability to recognize signs of mental distress in oneself and others, and to know when and where to seek help. In this section, we will explore various strategies for teaching mental health literacy to students, equipping them with the necessary knowledge and skills to navigate the complexities of mental health.

Importance of Mental Health Literacy

Mental health literacy is essential for promoting overall well-being and reducing the stigma surrounding mental health. By educating students about mental health, we can empower them to recognize and address their own mental health needs, as well as support their peers who may be struggling. Furthermore, teaching mental health literacy can help create a more inclusive and understanding school environment, where mental health is prioritized and addressed openly.

Incorporating Mental Health Education in the Curriculum

Integrating mental health education into the curriculum is an effective way to ensure that students receive comprehensive and ongoing instruction about mental health. Here are some practical strategies to incorporate mental health literacy into different subject areas:

- **Health Education:** Mental health should be included as a core component of health education curriculum. Topics such as stress management, emotional well-being, and coping strategies can be taught alongside physical health education.

+ **Science and Biology:** The biological basis of mental health can be explored in science and biology classes. Students can learn about the brain and its role in mental processes, the impact of neurotransmitters on mood and behavior, and the concept of neuroplasticity.

+ **English and Language Arts:** Literature can be used to discuss mental health themes and experiences. Reading and analyzing books, poems, and plays that explore mental health issues can help students develop empathy and a deeper understanding of mental health challenges.

+ **Social Studies and History:** Mental health education can be integrated into social studies and history lessons by examining the historical context of mental health treatment and the evolution of social attitudes towards mental illness. This can foster critical thinking and challenge stigmatizing beliefs.

+ **Mathematics and Statistics:** The prevalence and impact of mental health conditions can be explored using mathematical and statistical analysis. Students can examine data on mental health disorders, analyze trends, and interpret survey results related to mental well-being.

Developing Mental Health Literacy Programs

In addition to incorporating mental health education into existing curriculum, dedicated mental health literacy programs can be developed to provide more comprehensive instruction. These programs can be delivered through workshops, guest speakers, and interactive activities. Here are some key components that can be included in such programs:

+ **Promoting Awareness:** Programs should begin by raising awareness about the importance of mental health and challenging the stigma associated with mental illness. This can be done through presentations, videos, and personal stories shared by individuals with lived experiences.

+ **Building Knowledge:** Students should be provided with accurate and up-to-date information about mental health conditions. This includes teaching them about different types of disorders, their symptoms, and potential risk factors. It is also important to address common myths and misconceptions to dispel any misunderstandings.

+ **Developing Coping Strategies:** Students should be equipped with practical coping strategies to manage their own mental health and support their peers. This can involve teaching relaxation techniques, stress management skills, and methods for promoting self-care and resilience.

+ **Effective Communication:** Programs should emphasize the importance of open and non-judgmental communication about mental health. Students should learn how to have supportive conversations, actively listen to others, and express their own thoughts and feelings in a constructive manner.

+ **Resources and Support:** Mental health literacy programs should provide information about available resources, both within the school and the wider community. Students should be aware of helpline numbers, counseling services, and other support networks that can provide assistance if needed.

Assessment and Outcomes

Assessing the effectiveness of mental health literacy programs is crucial to ensure their impact on students' knowledge and attitudes. Here are some ways to evaluate the outcomes of such programs:

+ **Pre- and Post-tests:** Administering pre- and post-tests can measure the change in students' knowledge and understanding of mental health topics. This can include multiple-choice questions, short answers, or even role-playing scenarios to assess their ability to apply the knowledge in practical situations.

+ **Student Feedback:** Gathering feedback from students about their experiences in the program can provide valuable insights. Surveys or focus group discussions can be conducted to understand their perceptions, suggest improvements, and determine the program's impact on their attitudes towards mental health.

+ **Observations:** Observing changes in classroom dynamics, such as increased empathy, supportive behaviors, or a more open dialogue about mental health, can indicate the program's success in creating a positive and inclusive environment.

+ **Long-term Monitoring:** Following up with students after the completion of the program can help determine the long-term impact of mental health literacy education. Tracking changes in mental health knowledge, attitudes, and behavior over time can provide insights into the program's effectiveness in promoting lasting change.

Examples of Mental Health Literacy Activities

To make mental health literacy education engaging and interactive for students, here are a few examples of activities that can be included:

- **Personal Stories:** Inviting individuals with lived experiences to share their stories can help students develop empathy and reduce stigma. Students can also be encouraged to share their own experiences and reflections in a safe and supportive environment.

- **Role-playing Scenarios:** Presenting students with role-playing scenarios related to mental health can help them practice empathetic communication, problem-solving, and decision-making skills. This can build their confidence in supporting friends or peers who may be experiencing mental health challenges.

- **Media Analysis:** Analyzing portrayals of mental health in movies, TV shows, or news articles can facilitate critical thinking and media literacy. Students can identify stereotypes, highlight misconceptions, and discuss the potential impact of media on public perceptions of mental health.

- **Crisis Response Planning:** Guiding students through the process of creating crisis response plans can empower them to take action in times of mental health emergencies. This can involve teaching them how to recognize warning signs, identify supportive individuals, and develop strategies to ensure their safety or that of others.

- **Community Outreach:** Engaging students in mental health advocacy projects such as organizing awareness campaigns, fundraisers, or peer support groups can foster a sense of social responsibility while promoting mental health literacy in the wider community.

Additional Resources

Here are some additional resources for teaching mental health literacy:

- Mental Health America (MHA) - https://www.mhanational.org/

- National Alliance on Mental Illness (NAMI) - `https://www.nami.org/Home`

- Substance Abuse and Mental Health Services Administration (SAMHSA) - `https://www.samhsa.gov/`

- World Health Organization (WHO) - `https://www.who.int/mental_health/en/`

- Active Minds - `https://www.activeminds.org/`

By incorporating mental health education into the curriculum, implementing dedicated mental health literacy programs, and evaluating their outcomes, educators can create a supportive and inclusive learning environment that nurtures the mental well-being of students. Teaching mental health literacy equips students with lifelong skills to navigate challenges, promote resilience, and seek help when needed.

Supporting Educators' Mental Health

In our rapidly changing educational landscape, educators play a critical role in shaping the future of our society. However, the demanding nature of their work can take a toll on their mental health and well-being. It is essential to provide support systems and strategies to enhance the mental health of educators, allowing them to thrive personally and professionally. This section explores the various ways we can support educators' mental health and create a positive and inclusive work environment.

Understanding the Challenges

Educators face a unique set of challenges that can impact their mental health. Increased workload, high-stress environments, tight deadlines, and the pressure to meet performance expectations all contribute to the potential for burnout and emotional exhaustion. Additionally, the emotional labor involved in working with students who may come from diverse backgrounds or have specific needs can further add to the emotional strain experienced by educators.

Promoting Self-Care Practices

Encouraging educators to prioritize their own well-being and practice self-care is crucial for maintaining their mental health. Self-care practices help individuals recharge, reduce stress, and improve overall well-being. Some practical self-care strategies that can be promoted include:

+ Establishing work-life boundaries: Encouraging educators to set clear boundaries between work and personal life can help prevent burnout. This includes promoting the importance of taking breaks, disconnecting from work-related communication outside of working hours, and finding time for hobbies and leisure activities.

+ Providing resources for stress management: Educators can benefit from learning and utilizing various stress management techniques. This may include offering workshops or access to resources such as mindfulness exercises, relaxation techniques, and stress reduction strategies.

+ Prioritizing physical health: Encouraging regular physical exercise, maintaining a balanced diet, and getting adequate sleep are vital components of self-care. Providing resources and programs that support these practices can have a positive impact on educators' overall well-being.

Fostering a Supportive Work Environment

Creating a supportive work environment that promotes open communication, collaboration, and empathy can significantly contribute to educators' mental health. Key considerations include:

+ Building positive relationships: Encouraging collegiality and teamwork among educators fosters a supportive work culture. Creating opportunities for educators to connect, collaborate, and share experiences can strengthen relationships and provide a sense of community.

+ Encouraging mental health literacy: Providing training and resources to enhance educators' understanding of mental health issues can help reduce stigma and improve their ability to recognize signs of distress in themselves and their colleagues. This can facilitate early intervention and support.

+ Establishing support networks: Developing support networks within the educational setting, such as mentorship programs or peer support groups, can provide educators with spaces to discuss challenges, seek advice, and share resources. These networks can serve as a source of emotional support and professional development.

+ Addressing work-related stressors: Identifying and addressing work-related stressors, such as excessive workload or challenging classroom dynamics, is crucial for promoting educators' mental health. Implementing strategies such as workload management, providing professional development opportunities, and promoting effective classroom management techniques can help alleviate stressors and improve job satisfaction.

Access to Mental Health Resources

Ensuring educators have access to mental health resources and support services is vital in promoting their well-being. Educators should know where and how to access these resources when needed. Key considerations include:

+ Employee assistance programs: Providing educators with access to employee assistance programs can be valuable. These programs offer confidential counseling and support for a range of personal and professional issues.

+ Professional development on mental health: Incorporating mental health awareness and self-care into professional development programs can enhance educators' knowledge and skills in managing their mental health. This can involve workshops, seminars, or online resources.

+ Collaboration with mental health professionals: Establishing relationships with mental health professionals in the community can create pathways for educators to seek assistance when needed. Collaborative partnerships can facilitate timely access to appropriate support.

+ Policies and procedures: Implementing clear policies and procedures related to mental health can support educators in seeking help without fear of negative consequences. This includes ensuring confidentiality, non-discrimination, and reasonable accommodations for those with mental health conditions.

Taking Care of the Caregivers

It is crucial to recognize that educators may also act as caregivers outside of their professional roles. Balancing caregiving responsibilities, such as taking care of children or elderly family members, with their work responsibilities can further strain educators' mental health. Providing support and resources to address the unique challenges faced by caregiving educators is essential.

Unconventional Approach: Mindful Moments in the Classroom

One unconventional approach that can positively impact educators' mental health is integrating mindful moments into the classroom routine. Mindful moments are short, intentional pauses that allow educators and students to pause, breathe, and refocus. These moments can help reduce stress, improve focus, and create a calm and supportive environment. Educators can incorporate mindful moments at the beginning or end of each class, during transitions, or at any time they feel it may benefit their students' well-being. This practice not only promotes students' mental health but also supports educators' well-being by creating a more peaceful and harmonious classroom environment.

Conclusion

Supporting educators' mental health is crucial for creating a positive and inclusive educational environment. By recognizing the unique challenges they face, promoting self-care practices, fostering a supportive work environment, providing access to mental health resources, and addressing the needs of caregiving educators, we can empower educators to thrive both personally and professionally. Implementing innovative approaches, such as integrating mindful moments in the classroom, can further enhance their well-being and contribute to overall student success. Remember, taking care of the caregivers is not only essential but also beneficial to the entire educational community.

Crisis Intervention and Suicide Prevention

Recognizing Mental Health Crises

Warning Signs and Risk Factors

Recognizing warning signs and understanding the risk factors associated with mental health crises is crucial for early intervention and prevention. By being knowledgeable about these signs and factors, individuals can identify when someone might be in distress and provide appropriate support. In this section, we will explore the common warning signs and risk factors for mental health crises.

Common Warning Signs

1. **Changes in behavior:** Watch out for sudden or significant changes in a person's behavior, such as increased aggression, withdrawal from social activities, or noticeable changes in energy levels.

2. **Emotional instability:** Pay attention to frequent or intense mood swings, prolonged sadness or irritability, or feelings of hopelessness.

3. **Social withdrawal:** Notice if a person starts to isolate themselves from family, friends, or activities they used to enjoy without a clear reason.

4. **Changes in appetite or sleep patterns:** Keep an eye out for significant changes in eating or sleeping habits, such as increased or decreased appetite, insomnia, or oversleeping.

5. **Decline in personal hygiene:** Be aware of a noticeable decline in personal care and grooming, which may indicate a lack of motivation or emotional distress.

6. **Expressing suicidal thoughts or behaviors:** Take any mention or indication of suicide seriously and seek immediate help.

7. **Loss of interest:** Notice if a person loses interest in activities they previously enjoyed, including hobbies, socializing, or work/school-related activities.

8. **Intense anxiety or panic attacks:** Look out for symptoms such as rapid heartbeat, shortness of breath, trembling, or a sense of impending doom.

9. **Difficulty concentrating or making decisions:** Be aware if a person experiences persistent difficulty in focusing, remembering, or making even simple decisions.

10. **Unexplained physical symptoms:** Pay attention to unexplained physical complaints, such as headaches, stomachaches, or body aches, which may be psychosomatic manifestations of psychological distress.

It is important to note that these warning signs are not definitive proof of a mental health crisis but serve as indicators that someone may be struggling and in need of support.

Risk Factors

While warning signs provide observable cues, understanding the risk factors associated with mental health crises helps in identifying individuals who may be more vulnerable to developing mental health issues. Some common risk factors include:

1. **Family history:** Having a family history of mental health disorders can increase an individual's susceptibility to developing similar conditions.

2. **Previous history of mental health disorders:** Individuals with a previous history of mental health disorders are at a higher risk of experiencing a recurrence or developing new mental health challenges.

3. **Chronic medical conditions:** Certain chronic medical conditions, such as diabetes, cancer, or cardiovascular diseases, can contribute to increased stress levels and negatively impact mental well-being.

4. **Traumatic life events:** Exposure to traumatic experiences, such as physical or sexual abuse, natural disasters, or loss of a loved one, can have long-lasting effects on mental health.

5. **Substance abuse:** Substance abuse, including alcohol and drug addiction, can significantly impact mental health and increase the risk of developing mental health disorders.

6. **Social isolation:** Lack of social connections and support networks can contribute to feelings of loneliness and increase the risk of mental health issues.

7. **High levels of stress:** Chronic or excessive stress, whether related to work, relationships, or financial concerns, can significantly impact mental well-being.

8. **Environmental factors:** Living in an environment with high levels of violence, poverty, or discrimination can increase the risk of mental health problems.

It is important to understand that risk factors are not deterministic but rather increase the likelihood of developing mental health issues. Additionally, the presence of risk factors does not guarantee mental health challenges, as resilience, protective factors, and effective coping strategies can mitigate their impact.

Case Study: Identifying Warning Signs and Risk Factors

Let's consider a case study to apply our knowledge of warning signs and risk factors.

Julia, a 17-year-old high school student, has recently experienced the loss of her parent. Her friends have noticed significant changes in her behavior over the past few weeks. Julia has become socially withdrawn, no longer participates in extracurricular activities she once enjoyed, and her grades have started to decline. She often expresses feelings of sadness, hopelessness, and guilt. In addition, Julia has experienced a visible change in her physical appearance, neglecting personal hygiene and losing weight due to a decreased appetite.

In this case, the warning signs observed include changes in behavior, social withdrawal, decline in personal care, and the expression of intense negative emotions. The risk factors present include the recent loss of a parent and the potential for traumatic grief, as well as the age group's vulnerability to mental health challenges.

To support Julia, her friends and teachers should reach out to her, expressing concern and offering emotional support. They can encourage her to seek professional help from a school counselor or mental health provider, who can provide appropriate interventions to address her grieving process and support her mental well-being.

Resources and Support

Recognizing warning signs and risk factors is the first step towards helping someone in a mental health crisis. If you or someone you know is in immediate danger or experiencing a mental health emergency, please call emergency services or a local crisis hotline in your country.

Several resources and support options are available to assist individuals in crisis or seeking further information:

- National Suicide Prevention Lifeline: 1-800-273-TALK (1-800-273-8255) - Crisis Text Line: Text "HELLO" to 741741 (available 24/7) - National Alliance on Mental Illness (NAMI) Helpline: 1-800-950-NAMI (1-800-950-6264) -

MentalHealth.gov: A comprehensive online resource for mental health information and support in the United States.

Remember, your actions can make a difference in someone's life. Stay informed, be compassionate, and be willing to reach out and provide support when needed.

Assessing and De-escalating Crisis Situations

Assessing and de-escalating crisis situations is a critical skill for mental health professionals, as it helps ensure the safety and well-being of individuals in distress. Crisis situations can arise due to various factors, such as acute mental health symptoms, traumatic events, emotional crises, or interpersonal conflicts. Effectively assessing the situation and implementing appropriate strategies is essential to minimize potential harm and promote a sense of calm and stability. In this section, we will explore the key steps and techniques involved in assessing and de-escalating crisis situations.

Key Principles in Crisis Assessment

When faced with a crisis situation, mental health professionals should abide by certain key principles to ensure a comprehensive assessment. These principles include:

1. Safety first: The safety of the individual in crisis, as well as the safety of those around them, should be the primary concern. It is crucial to promptly assess any immediate threats and take appropriate measures to ensure physical safety.

2. Non-judgmental attitude: Maintaining a non-judgmental and empathetic approach is essential to build trust and rapport with the individual in crisis. Avoiding blame or making assumptions creates a safe environment for open communication.

3. Active listening: Actively listening and allowing the individual to express their emotions and thoughts without interruption is crucial. This helps the mental health professional gain a comprehensive understanding of the crisis situation and the individual's needs.

4. Collaborative approach: In crisis situations, working collaboratively with the individual empowers them and promotes their involvement in decision-making. It is essential to respect the individual's autonomy while providing necessary support and guidance.

5. Cultural sensitivity: Recognizing and respecting cultural differences is vital in crisis assessment. Mental health professionals should be aware of cultural norms, values, and beliefs that may influence the individual's perception of the crisis and their help-seeking behaviors.

Steps in Crisis Assessment

1. Establish rapport: Begin by introducing yourself and creating a safe and non-threatening environment. Use active listening skills to show empathy, validate the individual's feelings, and establish rapport.

2. Gather information: Ask open-ended questions to elicit information about the crisis situation. Encourage the individual to share their thoughts, feelings, and the events leading up to the crisis. Use paraphrasing and summarizing techniques to ensure accurate understanding.

3. Conduct a risk assessment: Assess the level of risk involved in the crisis situation. Identify any immediate danger to the individual or others and take appropriate actions to ensure safety. Factors to consider include the presence of self-harm ideation, access to lethal means, history of violence, or safety concerns in the immediate environment.

4. Evaluate coping strategies: Determine the individual's current coping strategies and their effectiveness in managing the crisis. This assessment helps identify potential strengths that can be utilized and any maladaptive coping mechanisms that may worsen the situation.

5. Explore support systems: Inquire about the individual's support systems, such as family, friends, or community resources. Assess the availability and adequacy of these resources in providing support during the crisis.

6. Assess immediate needs: Determine the immediate needs of the individual, such as medical attention, shelter, or emotional support. This assessment guides the development of a crisis intervention plan that addresses these needs effectively.

7. Formulate a crisis intervention plan: Based on the gathered information and assessment, collaboratively develop a crisis intervention plan with the individual. The plan should be tailored to the individual's specific needs, strengths, and available resources. It may involve referrals to other professionals, setting short-term goals, and identifying appropriate interventions.

De-escalation Techniques

De-escalation techniques aim to reduce the intensity of the crisis and maintain the safety of the individual and others involved. The following strategies can be employed during crisis situations:

1. Establishing safety: Ensure a safe environment by removing any potential hazards or triggers that may escalate the crisis. Maintain physical distance, allowing personal space for the individual.

2. Active listening and validation: Continue to actively listen and validate the individual's emotions and experiences. Use non-judgmental and empathetic responses to convey understanding and support.

3. Calming techniques: Teach and encourage relaxation techniques such as deep breathing exercises, grounding exercises, or guided imagery. These techniques can help the individual manage their anxiety and regain a sense of control.

4. Distraction and redirection: Divert the individual's attention away from the crisis by engaging them in activities or discussions unrelated to the immediate situation. This technique can help shift their focus and reduce emotional intensity.

5. Crisis communication: Use clear, concise, and straightforward language to communicate with the individual. Avoid complex or ambiguous statements that may exacerbate confusion or frustration.

6. Collaborative problem-solving: Engage the individual in problem-solving by exploring alternatives and potential solutions to mitigate the crisis. This approach empowers the individual and promotes autonomy.

7. Reframing and perspective-taking: Help the individual reframe their perspective by challenging negative thought patterns or cognitive distortions. Encourage them to consider alternative viewpoints and explore positive aspects of the situation.

8. Use of physical space and body language: Pay attention to your own body language, maintaining a calm and non-threatening demeanor. Allow for personal space and avoid actions or gestures that may escalate tension.

Remember, de-escalation techniques may vary based on the individual's unique needs and the specific crisis situation. It is important to continuously assess and adapt interventions as necessary.

Case Example

To illustrate the assessment and de-escalation process, let's consider a case example:

John, a 25-year-old university student, visits the campus counseling center in a distraught state. He has been experiencing intense anxiety and panic attacks due to academic stress and relationship difficulties. Upon assessment, the counselor determines that John is in a crisis situation and needs immediate support.

The counselor takes the following steps:

1. Establishes rapport: The counselor introduces themselves, creates a safe space, and demonstrates empathy and understanding.

2. Gathers information: The counselor asks open-ended questions to understand John's distress, triggers, and previous coping strategies.

3. Conducts a risk assessment: The counselor assesses the level of risk to determine if John is a danger to himself or others. They identify that John has been experiencing suicidal thoughts but has no immediate plan or access to means.

4. Evaluates coping strategies: The counselor explores John's current coping strategies, which include isolating himself and avoiding social interactions. They acknowledge these strategies and discuss their effectiveness.

5. Explores support systems: The counselor inquires about John's support systems and identifies that he has a close friend and supportive family.

6. Assesses immediate needs: The counselor recognizes that John needs emotional support, practical guidance with academic stress, and connection to resources for relationship issues.

7. Formulates a crisis intervention plan: Collaboratively, the counselor and John develop a plan that involves regular counseling sessions, referral to an academic advisor, and recommendations for self-care practices.

During the session, the counselor uses active listening, validation, relaxation techniques, and reframing to de-escalate John's distress. They address his immediate safety concerns and work towards building resilience and coping skills.

Conclusion

Effectively assessing and de-escalating crisis situations requires mental health professionals to apply a systematic approach that prioritizes safety, active listening, collaboration, and cultural sensitivity. By following the key principles of crisis assessment and employing de-escalation techniques, professionals can provide the necessary support to individuals in distress, promoting their well-being and facilitating their journey towards recovery. Remember, crisis situations can be emotionally charged, and ongoing professional development and supervision are crucial to enhance skills in crisis intervention.

Role of Mental Health Professionals in Crisis Intervention

Crisis intervention is a critical aspect of mental health care, as it involves providing immediate support and assistance to individuals experiencing a mental health crisis. Mental health professionals play a vital role in crisis intervention, using their expertise and training to help individuals navigate through challenging situations and provide the necessary support for stabilization and recovery. In this section, we will explore the various roles that mental health professionals play in crisis intervention.

Assessment and Triage

One of the primary roles of mental health professionals in crisis intervention is conducting assessments to gather information about the individual's current state and determine the level of risk and urgency. They utilize a variety of assessment tools and techniques to evaluate the individual's mental health status, including interviews, observations, and standardized assessments. This assessment process involves gathering information about the individual's symptoms, thoughts, feelings, and behaviors, as well as any potential risk factors.

Based on the assessment, mental health professionals then triage the individual to determine the appropriate level of care and intervention needed. This may involve determining whether the individual requires immediate hospitalization, referral to specialized services, or can be managed through outpatient care. The triage process helps ensure that individuals in crisis receive the appropriate level of support and intervention.

Crisis Intervention Planning

Once the assessment and triage process is complete, mental health professionals are responsible for developing a crisis intervention plan. This plan outlines the goals, strategies, and interventions that will be employed to address the individual's immediate needs and ensure safety and stabilization. The plan is individualized, taking into account the unique circumstances and needs of the individual.

The crisis intervention plan may involve various strategies, such as safety planning, coping skills development, and connectiing the individual with appropriate resources and services. Mental health professionals work collaboratively with the individual to establish achievable goals and identify steps to mitigate the crisis. The plan also considers the individual's support system, involving family, friends, and other relevant stakeholders to provide a holistic approach to crisis intervention.

Emotional Support and Active Listening

During crisis intervention, mental health professionals provide emotional support and engage in active listening to help individuals express their thoughts and emotions. They create a safe and non-judgmental space where individuals can freely share their experiences, concerns, and fears. Mental health professionals use active listening techniques, such as reflective listening and empathy, to understand the individual's perspective and validate their feelings.

By providing emotional support, mental health professionals establish a therapeutic alliance with the individual, which is essential for promoting trust, openness, and collaboration. This support helps individuals feel heard, validated, and understood, enhancing their overall well-being and promoting a sense of hope and resilience.

Crisis De-escalation and Safety Planning

Mental health professionals are trained in crisis de-escalation techniques to manage and reduce the intensity of the crisis situation. They employ various strategies for de-escalating heightened emotions and managing potential risks, such as self-harm or harm to others. The goal is to ensure the immediate safety of the individual and those around them.

Additionally, mental health professionals assist individuals in developing safety plans. Safety planning involves identifying potential triggers, warning signs, and coping strategies that can help the individual manage future crises effectively. Mental health professionals work collaboratively with the individual to develop personalized safety plans that address their specific needs and circumstances.

Collaboration and Referral

Mental health professionals play a crucial role in collaborating with other professionals and organizations to ensure comprehensive care and support for individuals in crisis. They work closely with medical professionals, emergency services, and community organizations to coordinate resources, referral services, and follow-up care.

In some cases, mental health professionals may need to facilitate immediate hospitalization or transfer to a higher level of care to ensure the safety and well-being of the individual. They communicate relevant information about the individual's crisis situation, assessment findings, and intervention plan to ensure a smooth transition and continuity of care.

Follow-up and Post-Crisis Support

After the crisis has been managed, mental health professionals provide follow-up and post-crisis support to promote continued recovery and resilience. They assess the individual's progress, monitor for any potential relapse or new challenges, and provide ongoing support and intervention as needed.

Follow-up care may involve individual therapy, group support, medication management, or referral to other specialized services based on the individual's needs. Mental health professionals also collaborate with the individual's support system, including family members and caregivers, to ensure a comprehensive and holistic approach to post-crisis support.

It is important to note that crisis intervention is a specialized area of mental health care, and mental health professionals involved in crisis intervention should receive specialized training and ongoing professional development to effectively support individuals in crisis.

Summary

The role of mental health professionals in crisis intervention is multifaceted and crucial in providing immediate support and assistance to individuals in crisis. They assess and triage individuals, develop personalized crisis intervention plans, provide emotional support and active listening, de-escalate crises, coordinate referrals and collaborate with other professionals, and offer follow-up and post-crisis support. Mental health professionals in crisis intervention play a significant role in helping individuals navigate through challenging situations and promoting their overall well-being and recovery.

Collaborative Crisis Response and Emergency Services

In times of crisis, collaborative response and emergency services play a crucial role in providing immediate support and assistance to individuals experiencing a mental health crisis. This section will explore the various components of collaborative crisis response and emergency services, including the roles of different professionals, crisis assessment and intervention techniques, and strategies for post-crisis support and recovery.

Roles of Different Professionals

Collaborative crisis response involves the coordinated effort of multiple professionals from different disciplines. These professionals work together to ensure a comprehensive and effective response to the crisis. Here are some key roles and responsibilities in a collaborative crisis response team:

+ **Mental Health Professionals:** Mental health professionals, such as psychiatrists, psychologists, and social workers, bring their expertise in assessing and managing mental health crises. They can provide immediate psychological support, conduct risk assessments, and develop safety plans for individuals in crisis.

- **Emergency Medical Services (EMS) Personnel:** EMS personnel, including paramedics and emergency medical technicians (EMTs), play a critical role in responding to crisis situations. They provide medical assistance, ensure the physical safety of individuals, and, if necessary, transport them to hospitals or specialized mental health facilities.

- **Law Enforcement Officers:** In some cases, law enforcement officers are involved in crisis response, particularly when there is a risk of harm to oneself or others. Their role is primarily focused on ensuring public safety, de-escalating potentially dangerous situations, and facilitating access to appropriate mental health services.

- **Crisis Workers:** Crisis workers, often employed by crisis hotlines or mobile crisis teams, are trained to respond to mental health crises over the phone or in person. They provide immediate support, conduct risk assessments, and connect individuals in crisis with appropriate resources and services.

- **Medical Professionals:** Medical professionals, such as emergency room physicians and nurses, contribute to crisis response by providing medical evaluations, assessing for physical health complications, and administering necessary treatments.

- **Community Support Workers:** Community support workers, including peer support specialists and case managers, offer ongoing support and advocacy to individuals following a crisis. They help connect individuals with community resources, coordinate follow-up care, and assist in navigating the mental health system.

Effective collaboration among these professionals ensures a multidimensional approach to crisis response, addressing both the immediate needs of individuals and the underlying factors contributing to the crisis.

Crisis Assessment and Intervention Techniques

Crisis assessment is an essential component of collaborative crisis response. It involves gathering information, evaluating the individual's current mental state, and determining the level of risk. The following assessment techniques are commonly used in crisis situations:

- **Risk Assessment:** A thorough risk assessment helps determine the level of immediate danger to the individual and others. It involves assessing factors such as the presence of suicidal thoughts, violent ideation, access to lethal means, and history of self-harm or harm to others.

+ **Safety Planning:** Creating a safety plan is an important intervention in crisis situations. A safety plan involves developing strategies and actions that the individual can take to keep themselves safe and manage their crisis triggers. It often includes identifying supportive people, coping strategies, and emergency contact information.

+ **De-escalation Techniques:** De-escalation techniques are used to calm individuals in crisis and reduce the risk of harm. It involves active listening, empathetic communication, and employing non-confrontational strategies to engage the individual in a supportive dialogue.

+ **Crisis Intervention:** Crisis intervention aims to stabilize the individual in crisis and provide immediate support. This can include crisis counseling, crisis hotlines, crisis respite services, and mobile crisis teams that offer on-site assessments and interventions.

+ **Safety Measures:** In situations where an individual poses an immediate risk to themselves or others, safety measures may be implemented. These measures can include hospitalization, involuntary commitment, or involving law enforcement to ensure the safety of all parties involved.

+ **Referral and Follow-up:** After the crisis is stabilized, individuals are typically referred to appropriate mental health services for ongoing support. This may involve referrals to outpatient therapy, support groups, psychiatric evaluations, or other relevant services.

Collaborating on these assessment and intervention techniques helps ensure a comprehensive approach to crisis response, addressing immediate safety concerns while also considering long-term support and recovery needs.

Strategies for Post-Crisis Support and Recovery

After a crisis has been managed, individuals require ongoing support to aid in their recovery and prevent future crises. Collaborative post-crisis support involves a range of strategies aimed at promoting resilience, well-being, and long-term stability. Here are some key strategies:

- **Crisis Follow-up:** Ensuring follow-up with mental health professionals is crucial to assess progress, adjust treatment plans if necessary, and provide ongoing support. This may include regular therapy sessions, medication management, and monitoring of symptoms.

- **Peers Support Networks:** Peer support networks, facilitated by trained individuals with lived experience of mental health challenges, offer valuable support and understanding to individuals following a crisis. These networks provide a sense of belonging, hope, and empowerment.

- **Supportive Services:** Connecting individuals with community resources and support services can help address any underlying issues and prevent future crises. This may include assistance with housing, employment, financial resources, and access to healthcare.

- **Education and Awareness:** Education and raising awareness about mental health can reduce stigma, increase understanding, and promote early intervention. Providing information about coping strategies, self-care techniques, and available resources empowers individuals to take an active role in their mental health journey.

- **Family Involvement:** Engaging family members or loved ones in the recovery process can significantly impact an individual's long-term well-being. Family therapy, education on mental health, and open communication can foster a supportive and understanding environment.

- **Self-Care and Wellness:** Encouraging individuals to prioritize self-care and wellness is vital in preventing future crises. This may involve developing healthy coping mechanisms, engaging in hobbies and interests, and promoting a balanced lifestyle that includes adequate sleep, proper nutrition, and regular physical activity.

Collaborative post-crisis support focuses on comprehensive care, addressing the physical, emotional, and social aspects of an individual's well-being. It aims to promote recovery, build resilience, and establish a strong support network for long-term mental health.

An Unconventional Approach: Crisis Text Line

One unconventional yet highly effective approach in collaborative crisis response is the Crisis Text Line. The Crisis Text Line is a 24/7 helpline that individuals in crisis can reach out to via text message. It provides immediate crisis counseling and support to individuals who may be more comfortable expressing their distress through written communication.

The Crisis Text Line uses an innovative platform and a network of trained volunteers to respond to text messages from individuals in crisis. Through empathetic and non-judgmental conversations, the volunteers assess the level of risk and provide crisis intervention strategies. If necessary, they can facilitate appropriate emergency services or referrals for ongoing support.

This unconventional approach effectively reaches out to individuals who may be hesitant or unable to access traditional crisis services. It offers an accessible and anonymous platform for people to seek support, helping to prevent crises and provide immediate assistance when needed.

Conclusion

Collaborative crisis response and emergency services are essential in providing timely and comprehensive support to individuals experiencing a mental health crisis. By involving professionals from various disciplines, employing effective assessment and intervention techniques, and implementing strategies for post-crisis support and recovery, collaborative crisis response seeks to stabilize the immediate crisis, address underlying issues, and promote long-term well-being.

The Crisis Text Line serves as an example of an unconventional but effective approach to crisis intervention, expanding the accessibility and reach of crisis support services. Incorporating such innovative initiatives alongside traditional crisis response systems can help ensure a more inclusive and responsive mental health support system.

Remember, collaborative crisis response is a shared responsibility. By working together, we can make a significant difference in the lives of those experiencing mental health crises and contribute to building a stronger and more compassionate society.

Post-Crisis Support and Recovery

After a mental health crisis, it is essential to provide individuals with the necessary support and resources for their recovery. Post-crisis support and recovery aim to help individuals regain stability, improve their well-being, and prevent future crises. This section will discuss the important components and strategies involved in post-crisis support and recovery.

Comprehensive Assessment and Evaluation

The first step in post-crisis support is to conduct a comprehensive assessment and evaluation of the individual's mental health needs. This involves gathering information about the crisis, understanding the underlying factors that contributed to it, and identifying any co-occurring mental health disorders.

A thorough evaluation can help mental health professionals develop an individualized treatment plan for the person in crisis. The assessment may involve interviews, standardized questionnaires, psychological testing, and collaboration with other healthcare providers involved in the individual's care. By understanding the unique needs and challenges faced by the individual, professionals can tailor their support and interventions accordingly.

Developing a Safety Plan

A critical component of post-crisis support is the development of a safety plan. A safety plan is a personalized, written document that outlines strategies and resources for managing future crises and preventing self-harm or suicide. The plan is collaboratively developed with the individual in crisis, their support network, and mental health professionals.

The safety plan typically includes warning signs and triggers of an impending crisis, coping strategies to address these triggers, and a list of emergency contacts. It may also involve identifying safe and supportive environments or activities that can help the individual during times of distress. Regular review and update of the safety plan are essential to ensure its ongoing relevance and effectiveness.

Therapeutic Interventions

Therapeutic interventions play a crucial role in post-crisis support and recovery. Different modalities may be utilized, depending on the individual's needs and preferences. Some common therapeutic approaches include:

- **Cognitive-Behavioral Therapy (CBT):** CBT is a widely used evidence-based therapy that focuses on identifying and modifying negative thought patterns and behaviors. It helps individuals develop healthy coping skills, improve problem-solving abilities, and build resilience.

- **Dialectical Behavior Therapy (DBT):** DBT is particularly effective for individuals who struggle with emotional regulation and self-destructive behaviors. It combines elements of CBT with techniques to enhance mindfulness, distress tolerance, interpersonal effectiveness, and emotional regulation.

+ **Supportive Psychotherapy:** Supportive psychotherapy provides a safe and non-judgmental space for individuals to express their thoughts and emotions. It primarily focuses on empathy, validation, and the development of healthy coping strategies.

+ **Group Therapy:** Group therapy allows individuals to connect with others who have experienced similar challenges. It provides a support system, reduces feelings of isolation, and encourages the development of interpersonal skills.

+ **Medication Management:** In some cases, medication may be necessary to manage underlying mental health conditions. Psychiatric evaluation and ongoing medication management can be essential aspects of the recovery process.

It is important to note that therapeutic interventions should be tailored to each individual's unique needs and preferences. Flexibility and collaboration between the individual, mental health professionals, and support systems are crucial for effective recovery.

Psychoeducation and Skills Training

Psychoeducation and skills training are integral components of post-crisis support. Education about mental health conditions, coping strategies, and techniques for self-management can empower individuals to take an active role in their recovery.

Psychoeducation involves providing individuals with information about their specific mental health condition, its symptoms, potential triggers, and available treatment options. It aims to increase their understanding, reduce stigma, and enhance their ability to make informed decisions about their care.

Skills training equips individuals with practical tools and techniques to manage their mental health. These may include stress management techniques, problem-solving skills, assertiveness training, and communication skills. By learning these skills, individuals can better navigate challenges and maintain their well-being.

Ongoing Support and Follow-up Care

Post-crisis support should extend beyond immediate interventions and incorporate ongoing support and follow-up care. This involves regular check-ins, monitoring of progress, and making any necessary adjustments to the treatment plan.

Mental health professionals, support groups, and other members of the individual's care team can provide ongoing support and encouragement. This support may include therapy sessions, case management services, access to community resources, and crisis helpline information.

Follow-up care is essential for preventing relapse and promoting long-term recovery. It provides an opportunity to address any emerging challenges, reinforce coping strategies, and ensure the individual is receiving appropriate care and support.

Reintegration and Social Support

Reintegration into daily life and the social support network is a critical aspect of post-crisis recovery. The individual may face challenges in rebuilding relationships, pursuing education or employment opportunities, and finding a sense of purpose. Social support from family, friends, and peers can play a vital role in this process.

Supportive social networks provide understanding, validation, and a sense of belonging. They can offer practical help, such as assistance with accessing resources or managing daily responsibilities. Social support also promotes social connectedness, reduces feelings of isolation, and contributes to overall well-being.

Reintegration and social support may involve joining support groups, engaging in community activities, participating in hobbies, and seeking out positive social interactions. It is essential to create an environment that fosters inclusivity and reduces stigma, allowing individuals to feel safe and supported as they rebuild their lives.

Encouraging Self-Advocacy and Empowerment

Post-crisis support and recovery are not just about treating symptoms but also about building resilience and empowering individuals to take control of their mental health. Encouraging self-advocacy and empowerment is crucial in promoting long-term well-being.

Self-advocacy involves advocating for one's own mental health needs, rights, and preferences. It empowers individuals to actively participate in their treatment, make informed decisions, and express their concerns. Mental health professionals and support systems should work collaboratively with individuals, valuing their input and encouraging their autonomy.

Empowerment emphasizes individuals' strengths, resources, and abilities to manage their mental health. It involves helping individuals recognize their personal agency, build self-confidence, and set achievable goals. Empowered individuals are more likely to engage in self-care practices, seek appropriate support, and continue their recovery journey beyond the immediate post-crisis period.

Unconventional Approach: Nature-Based Therapies

In addition to conventional therapeutic approaches, nature-based therapies have gained recognition for their potential benefits in post-crisis support and recovery. These interventions involve connecting individuals with nature, such as engaging in ecotherapy, nature walks, horticultural therapy, or wilderness therapy.

Nature-based therapies offer unique opportunities for relaxation, stress reduction, and promoting overall well-being. They provide a sense of connection to the natural world, which can enhance self-awareness, foster emotional regulation, and improve mood. These interventions can be particularly valuable for individuals who find solace and inspiration in nature.

Conclusion

Post-crisis support and recovery play a crucial role in helping individuals navigate their mental health challenges, regain stability, and prevent future crises. By conducting comprehensive assessments, developing safety plans, providing therapeutic interventions, and offering ongoing support and follow-up care, individuals can be empowered to take an active role in their recovery. Emphasizing self-advocacy, promoting social support, and integrating nature-based therapies can further enhance the post-crisis recovery process. Remember, recovery is a journey, and with the right support and resources, individuals can thrive beyond their mental health crises.

Suicide Prevention and Intervention

Understanding Suicide and Its Causes

Suicide is a complex and multifaceted issue that requires a comprehensive understanding of its causes in order to effectively address and prevent it. In this section, we will explore the various factors that contribute to suicide, including psychological, social, and environmental determinants.

Psychological Factors

Psychological factors play a significant role in suicidal ideation and behavior. Individuals who experience mental health disorders, such as depression, anxiety, bipolar disorder, and schizophrenia, are at higher risk for suicide. These conditions can lead to feelings of hopelessness, worthlessness, and despair, which can contribute to suicidal thoughts and actions.

Additionally, individuals who have a history of trauma or abuse may be more prone to suicidal behavior. Traumatic experiences, such as physical or sexual abuse, can have profound impacts on a person's mental well-being, leading to increased vulnerability to suicidal thoughts.

Social Factors

Social factors also contribute to suicide risk. One important factor is social isolation and lack of social support. When individuals feel disconnected from others and lack a network of supportive relationships, they may be more susceptible to suicidal tendencies. This is particularly true for marginalized and stigmatized populations, such as LGBTQ+ individuals and those experiencing racial or ethnic discrimination.

Furthermore, interpersonal conflicts, such as relationship difficulties, bullying, or conflicts within the family, can contribute to the development of suicidal thoughts. These conflicts can create significant emotional distress and feelings of entrapment, leading individuals to consider suicide as a way to escape their pain.

Environmental Factors

Environmental factors, including access to lethal means, can greatly influence suicide rates. Easy access to weapons, medications, or other harmful substances increases the likelihood of completed suicides. This is especially concerning in regions with high gun ownership rates, where firearms are commonly used in suicide attempts.

Media coverage of suicide can also have a profound impact on suicide rates. Research has shown that sensationalized or detailed reporting of suicides can lead to copycat behavior, known as suicide contagion. Responsible reporting guidelines, which emphasize the importance of avoiding explicit details and promoting help-seeking resources, are crucial in mitigating this effect.

The Interplay of Factors

It is important to note that suicide is rarely caused by a single factor but rather results from the interplay of multiple factors. For example, an individual may have a genetic predisposition for mental illness and experience social isolation, which can further exacerbate their vulnerability to suicidal thoughts.

Understanding the complex interaction of these factors is crucial in developing effective prevention strategies. It is essential to take a holistic approach, addressing both individual risk factors and broader societal influences to create an environment that supports mental well-being and reduces the risk of suicide.

Suicide Risk Assessment

To effectively intervene and provide support to individuals at risk of suicide, it is essential to conduct a thorough suicide risk assessment. This assessment involves evaluating the presence and severity of suicidal ideation, as well as the presence of any risk factors or warning signs.

Some common risk factors to assess include a history of previous suicide attempts, family history of suicide, access to lethal means, and a lack of social support. Warning signs may include expressing feelings of hopelessness or being a burden, withdrawing from social activities, or making direct or indirect statements about suicide.

It is important to approach suicide risk assessment with empathy and sensitivity, creating a safe and nonjudgmental space for individuals to share their feelings and experiences. Additionally, proper training in suicide risk assessment is crucial for professionals who work with individuals at risk.

Prevention Strategies

Preventing suicide requires a comprehensive and multifaceted approach. Some key strategies include:

1. Mental Health Promotion: Promoting mental health and well-being through awareness campaigns, education, and access to mental health services. This includes reducing stigma around seeking help for mental health issues.

2. Early Intervention: Identifying and addressing mental health concerns at an early stage, with a focus on prevention and early intervention programs in schools, colleges, and workplaces.

3. Crisis Hotlines and Support Services: Establishing and promoting crisis hotlines and support services that provide immediate help and guidance to individuals in distress.

4. Restricting Access to Lethal Means: Implementing policies and interventions to limit access to lethal means, such as firearms and medications, particularly for individuals at risk.

5. Training and Education: Providing training to healthcare professionals, educators, and community members on suicide prevention, risk assessment, and intervention strategies.

6. Building Supportive Communities: Fostering social connectedness, reducing social isolation, and promoting supportive networks within communities.

7. Postvention Support: Providing support and resources to individuals who have been affected by suicide, including family members, friends, and communities.

8. Research and Surveillance: Conducting ongoing research and surveillance to better understand the underlying causes of suicide, identify high-risk populations, and evaluate the effectiveness of prevention strategies.

Remember, suicide is a preventable tragedy, and by implementing comprehensive prevention efforts, we can work towards reducing suicide rates and promoting mental well-being. It is crucial to destigmatize mental health issues, prioritize early intervention, and provide support to individuals at risk. Together, we can make a difference in saving lives and promoting mental health.

Risk Assessment and Safety Planning

Risk assessment and safety planning are crucial components of suicide prevention and intervention. It involves evaluating the individual's level of risk for suicidal behavior and developing strategies to ensure their safety and well-being. This section will discuss the key elements of risk assessment and safety planning, providing guidelines and tools to effectively address suicidal risks.

Understanding Suicidal Risk Factors

To conduct a comprehensive risk assessment, it is important to understand the various factors that contribute to suicidal behavior. These risk factors can be categorized into three main domains: individual factors, social factors, and environmental factors.

Individual Factors   Individual factors include mental health conditions, previous suicide attempts, family history of suicide, substance abuse, impulsivity, access to lethal means, and presence of chronic pain or physical illness. These factors can increase an individual's vulnerability to suicidal ideation and behaviors.

Social Factors   Social factors encompass interpersonal conflicts, relationship difficulties, lack of social support, exposure to suicidal behavior in others, history of childhood abuse or neglect, and stigma associated with mental health issues. These factors can contribute to feelings of isolation, hopelessness, and despair.

Environmental Factors   Environmental factors refer to socio-cultural influences, such as economic hardship, unemployment, limited access to mental health care, community violence, and media portrayals of suicide. These factors can shape an individual's attitudes, beliefs, and behaviors related to suicide.

Assessing Suicidal Risk

When conducting a risk assessment, it is important to adopt a holistic and empathetic approach, considering both objective and subjective indicators of suicidal risk. Here are some key steps involved in assessing suicidal risk:

Establishing Rapport   Building a trusting and supportive relationship is crucial when conducting a risk assessment. Create a safe and non-judgmental space where the individual feels comfortable discussing their thoughts and feelings.

Gathering Information   Collect relevant information about the individual's current mental health status, personal history, and social context. This may involve conducting interviews, reviewing medical records, and administering standardized assessment tools.

Screening for Suicide Ideation   Use validated screening tools to assess the presence and severity of suicidal ideation. These tools can help determine the urgency and intensity of the individual's distress.

Assessing Risk Factors   Evaluate the individual's risk factors, considering both immediate and long-term risks. Focus on identifying factors that contribute to the individual's vulnerability, as well as factors that may increase the likelihood of imminent harm.

Evaluating Protective Factors   Identify protective factors that can mitigate the individual's risk for suicide. Protective factors include positive social support, access to mental health care, effective coping skills, and a sense of belonging.

Determining Imminent Risk Assess the individual's level of imminent risk for suicide. Consider the presence of warning signs, such as a specific plan, means, recent loss, or escalating distress. Assess their intent and capability to carry out a suicidal act.

Formulating a Risk Level Based on the assessment findings, assign a risk level that reflects the individual's level of risk for suicide. Common risk levels include low, moderate, high, and imminent risk. This categorization helps guide subsequent safety planning interventions.

Safety Planning

Safety planning involves collaboratively developing a personalized set of strategies to enhance an individual's safety and reduce the risk of suicide. Safety plans are typically created in partnership with the individual, taking into account their unique strengths, needs, and support systems. Here are the key components of a comprehensive safety plan:

Identifying Warning Signs Work with the individual to identify their personal warning signs that indicate an escalation of distress or increased suicide risk. These signs can be emotional, cognitive, and behavioral in nature.

Coping Strategies Identify coping strategies that the individual can use to manage suicidal thoughts or urges. Encourage the use of healthy coping mechanisms, such as engaging in relaxation techniques, reaching out to support networks, and engaging in activities that promote well-being.

Social Support Identify and involve key individuals in the individual's support network who can offer help during times of crisis. This may include family members, friends, mental health professionals, and crisis hotlines. Ensure that the individual has access to contact information for these support resources.

Professional Support Facilitate the individual's access to mental health professionals and supportive services. Provide them with information about available resources, such as therapists, psychiatrists, or community mental health centers. Assist with scheduling appointments, if needed.

Means Restriction   Collaborate with the individual to develop strategies for reducing their access to lethal means, such as firearms, medications, or sharp objects. This may involve enlisting the help of family members or taking steps to secure and limit access to potentially dangerous items.

Emergency Contacts   Compile a list of emergency contacts that the individual can reach out to during a crisis. Include local crisis hotlines, helplines, and emergency services. Ensure that the individual knows when and how to contact these resources.

Developing a Crisis Response Plan   Create a step-by-step plan that outlines the individual's actions to take in the event of a crisis. This plan should include specific steps to follow, such as contacting a trusted person, going to a safe place, and seeking immediate professional help.

Special Considerations

When conducting risk assessments and safety planning, it is important to consider the unique needs and circumstances of different populations. Here are some special considerations to keep in mind:

Youth and Adolescents   When working with young individuals, pay attention to developmental factors, including impulsivity, peer influences, and family dynamics. Involve parents or guardians in the safety planning process and ensure that the plan addresses the school environment.

Elderly Population   Consider the increased risk factors associated with aging, such as physical health problems, social isolation, and bereavement. Assess the individual's ability to implement the safety plan independently and involve caregivers or support systems as necessary.

Cultural Sensitivity   Acknowledge and respect cultural factors that may influence an individual's understanding of and attitudes towards suicide. Ensure that risk assessments and safety planning approaches are culturally sensitive and appropriate.

High-Risk Professions   Certain professions, such as healthcare providers, first responders, and military personnel, may be associated with increased risk for suicide due to occupational stress and trauma exposure. Tailor risk assessments and safety planning to address the unique challenges faced by individuals in these professions.

Exercise: Creating a Safety Plan

In pairs or small groups, role-play a hypothetical situation involving an individual at risk of suicide. Take turns assuming the roles of the individual, mental health professional, and support person. Use the knowledge gained from this section to collaboratively develop a safety plan that addresses the specific needs and challenges presented in the scenario.

Additional Resources

Encourage the reader to explore additional resources, including crisis hotlines, suicide prevention websites, and mental health organizations that provide information on risk assessment and safety planning. Provide a list of reputable resources and contact information in an appendix.

Note: Risk assessment and safety planning are complex processes that require specialized training and expertise. If you are not a mental health professional, it is important to collaborate with qualified professionals when addressing suicide risk.

Providing Support to Individuals in Crisis

In times of crisis, individuals experiencing mental health difficulties require immediate support and intervention. This section focuses on the essential steps and strategies to provide effective support to individuals in crisis. It outlines practical tools and techniques that mental health professionals can utilize to address immediate needs, ensure safety, and facilitate the journey towards recovery.

Recognizing the Signs of Crisis

Before we delve into providing support, it is crucial to recognize the signs of a mental health crisis. Common signs include:

- Intense feelings of hopelessness, despair, or anxiety

- Suicidal ideation or threatening behavior

- Extreme changes in behavior or mood

- Social withdrawal or isolation

+ Disorganized thoughts or speech

+ Hallucinations or delusions

+ Marked changes in appetite, sleep patterns, or energy levels

+ Engaging in risky or self-destructive behaviors

It is essential to approach any indication of a mental health crisis with care and compassion. Never underestimate the severity of the situation, and take immediate action to provide support.

The Five Steps of Crisis Intervention

1. **Assessing the Situation:** The first step is to assess the individual's immediate safety and well-being. Ensure that you and the person in crisis are in a secure environment, free from any potential harm. Ask open-ended questions to understand their experiences, emotions, and thoughts. Active listening and empathy are crucial during this stage.

2. **Establishing Rapport:** Develop trust and establish a connection with the individual. Create a safe and non-judgmental space to encourage open communication. Show genuine concern and validate their feelings. Respect their autonomy and collaborative decision-making.

3. **Identifying Support Systems:** Explore and identify the individual's existing support systems, such as family, friends, or other professionals. Involve these support networks to provide additional assistance during the crisis. Collaborating with the person's trusted contacts can promote a sense of belonging and reinforce their support network.

4. **Developing a Safety Plan:** Collaborate with the individual to create a safety plan. This plan should include strategies to manage the crisis and prevent harm, such as identifying triggers, coping mechanisms, emergency contacts, and access to professional help. Ensure the plan is personalized, realistic, and addresses their specific needs.

5. **Follow-up and Referral:** After the crisis has stabilized, it is crucial to follow up with the individual to ensure their ongoing well-being. Connect them with appropriate resources and professionals, such as mental health services, crisis hotlines, or support groups. Regularly check in on their progress and offer ongoing support as needed.

Emergency Interventions

In certain situations, immediate intervention may be necessary to ensure the individual's safety. If the person is at risk of self-harm or harm to others, it is vital to know how to respond effectively.

+ **Dial Emergency Services:** If the crisis is acute and the individual's safety is in immediate danger, contact emergency services, such as 911. Provide all relevant details and remain on the line until help arrives.

+ **Stay with the Person:** If it is safe to do so, stay with the person until help arrives. Your presence can provide comfort and reassurance in an overwhelming situation.

+ **Remove Immediate Hazards:** Eliminate any immediate hazards or dangerous objects from the surroundings. This can help minimize the risk of self-harm or harm to others.

+ **Engage in Active Listening:** During the crisis, actively listen to the person's concerns and validate their emotions. Allow them to express themselves without judgment or interruption.

+ **Do Not Leave the Person Alone:** In most cases, it is essential to stay with the person until professional help arrives. Leaving them alone during a crisis may increase the risk of harm.

The Value of Connection and Empathy

When supporting individuals in crisis, compassion, connection, and empathy play a vital role in promoting their well-being. Here are some key strategies to foster these qualities:

+ **Active Listening:** Give your full attention to the individual and demonstrate genuine interest. Reflect their feelings and validate their experiences, showing that you understand and care.

+ **Non-Judgmental Attitude:** Free your mind from biases, assumptions, or stigmas, and refrain from passing judgment. Create a safe space for open dialogue and respectful expression of thoughts and emotions.

+ **Empathetic Language:** Use language that shows empathy and understanding. Acknowledge the person's suffering and struggles, while emphasizing hope and the potential for recovery.

- **Respect Personal Boundaries:** Be aware of personal space, physical contact, and cultural considerations. Respect the individual's boundaries, and ask for consent before offering physical comfort or support.

- **Inclusivity and Diversity:** Recognize and embrace the diverse backgrounds, identities, and experiences of individuals in crisis. Show respect for their unique perspectives, and adapt your approach accordingly.

Self-Care for Crisis Support Providers

Supporting individuals in crisis can be emotionally challenging and draining. Practicing self-care is crucial for maintaining your own well-being and effectiveness as a crisis support provider. Here are some self-care strategies:

- **Set Boundaries:** Establish clear boundaries between your personal and professional life. Allocate time for rest, relaxation, and activities that replenish your energy.

- **Seek Support:** Connect with peers or supervisors for supervision, debriefing, or peer support. Sharing your experiences with others who understand can help process emotions and reduce burnout.

- **Engage in Self-Reflection:** Regularly reflect on your emotions, thoughts, and reactions to the crises you encounter. Identify any triggers or signs of burnout and adjust your self-care strategies accordingly.

- **Practice Stress Management:** Engage in stress-reducing activities such as exercise, meditation, or hobbies. Prioritize self-care activities that promote relaxation and emotional well-being.

- **Continuous Learning:** Invest time in continuous professional development to enhance your crisis intervention skills and expand your knowledge base. Stay updated with the latest research, best practices, and resources in the field.

Conclusion

Providing support to individuals in crisis requires a compassionate and person-centered approach. Recognizing signs of crisis, following the five steps of crisis intervention, and utilizing emergency interventions when necessary are essential components of effective support. Connection, empathy, and self-care complete the foundation for assisting individuals through their crisis, towards recovery, and on the path to better mental health. Remember, by offering support, you are making a significant contribution to their journey of healing and resilience.

Suicide Prevention Strategies in Communities

Suicide prevention is a critical aspect of mental health care, and effective strategies in communities can make a significant difference in reducing suicide rates. In this section, we will explore various suicide prevention strategies that can be implemented at the community level. These strategies involve creating supportive environments, raising awareness, providing access to mental health services, and fostering a sense of connectedness within the community.

Supportive Community Environment

Creating a supportive community environment is essential in preventing suicide. Community members need to feel valued, included, and supported. Here are some strategies for establishing a supportive environment:

- **Promote Mental Health Literacy:** Educate community members about mental health, its importance, and the warning signs of suicide. Encourage open conversations about mental health to reduce stigma and increase awareness.

- **Training Programs:** Provide training programs on suicide prevention, such as Mental Health First Aid, to community members, educators, healthcare professionals, and other key individuals. These programs enable individuals to recognize the signs of distress and respond appropriately.

- **Collaboration with Community Organizations:** Collaborate with local organizations, such as schools, religious institutions, and non-profit organizations, to develop suicide prevention initiatives. By working together, communities can pool resources and expertise to address the issue effectively.

- **Support for High-Risk Groups:** Identify high-risk groups within the community, such as LGBTQ+ individuals, veterans, and individuals with a history of mental illness or substance abuse, and develop targeted support programs for them.

- **Fostering a Sense of Belonging:** Encourage community involvement and social connections by organizing community events, support groups, and volunteer opportunities. Helping individuals feel connected and engaged can enhance their mental well-being and decrease their risk of suicide.

Awareness Campaigns

Raising awareness about suicide is crucial to reduce stigma, promote early intervention, and ensure that individuals at risk receive the help they need. Here are some effective strategies for conducting awareness campaigns in communities:

+ **Media Campaigns:** Utilize various media platforms, such as television, radio, social media, and print media, to disseminate information about suicide prevention. These campaigns can provide education, share personal stories of recovery, and highlight available resources.

+ **Gatekeeper Training:** Train gatekeepers within the community, such as teachers, coaches, and community leaders, on how to identify and respond to individuals at risk of suicide. Empowering gatekeepers with knowledge and skills can help them bridge the gap between at-risk individuals and mental health services.

+ **School-Based Programs:** Implement suicide prevention programs in schools that focus on early identification, building resilience, and promoting access to support services. These programs can include classroom education, counseling services, and peer support initiatives.

+ **Partnerships with Local Businesses:** Collaborate with local businesses to raise awareness about suicide prevention. Display informational materials, distribute helpful resources, and promote mental health through workplace wellness programs. Encourage businesses to provide supportive environments for their employees.

+ **Community Events:** Organize events, such as walks, runs, or candlelight vigils, to honor those lost to suicide, raise awareness, and foster a sense of solidarity within the community. These events provide platforms for open discussions and encourage help-seeking behavior.

Access to Mental Health Services

Improving access to mental health services is vital in preventing suicide. Communities should strive to ensure that individuals at risk can easily access appropriate care and support. Here are some strategies to enhance access to mental health services:

- **Community-Based Mental Health Centers:** Establish or expand community mental health centers that offer a wide range of services, including counseling, therapy, crisis intervention, and support groups. These centers should be easily accessible, affordable, and tailored to the needs of the community.

- **Crisis Hotlines and Helplines:** Develop and promote local crisis hotlines and helplines that are available 24/7. These services provide immediate support, guidance, and resources for individuals in crisis.

- **Collaboration with Healthcare Providers:** Collaborate with healthcare providers, including primary care physicians, to ensure that mental health care is integrated into routine healthcare services. This approach increases the likelihood of early detection and intervention for individuals at risk.

- **Peer Support Services:** Establish peer support programs where individuals with lived experience of suicide attempts or mental health challenges can offer support and guidance to those currently struggling. Peer support can play a crucial role in reducing isolation and providing hope and understanding.

- **Transportation Services:** Address transportation barriers that may prevent individuals from accessing mental health services. Partner with local transportation providers or community organizations to offer free or discounted rides for mental health appointments.

Promoting Connectedness

Promoting social connections and a sense of belonging is a protective factor against suicide. Here are some strategies to foster connectedness at the community level:

- **Community Volunteer Programs:** Encourage community members to engage in volunteer work. Volunteering not only benefits the community but also provides individuals with a sense of purpose and connectedness.

- **Mentoring Programs:** Establish mentoring programs that pair individuals at risk with supportive mentors who can provide guidance, support, and encouragement. Mentoring relationships can create a sense of belonging and resilience.

- **Social Support Networks:** Encourage the formation of social support networks within the community. These networks can consist of friends, family, neighbors, or community groups that provide emotional support during challenging times.

+ **School and Workplace Initiatives:** Implement initiatives in schools and workplaces that promote positive social interactions, peer support, and a sense of community. Such initiatives can include team-building activities, mentoring programs, and wellness programs.

+ **Online Support Communities:** Develop and promote online support communities and forums for individuals at risk of suicide. These platforms can provide a safe space for sharing experiences, finding support, and connecting with others who have gone through similar struggles.

Additional Considerations

While implementing suicide prevention strategies in communities, it is crucial to consider the following:

+ **Evaluation and Continuous Improvement:** Regularly evaluate the effectiveness of suicide prevention programs and interventions within the community. Collect feedback from individuals involved and make necessary adjustments to ensure constant improvement.

+ **Cultural Sensitivity:** Develop suicide prevention strategies that take into account the cultural, social, and linguistic diversity of the community. Ensure that resources and interventions are culturally sensitive, inclusive, and accessible to all members of the community.

+ **Collaboration and Partnerships:** Engage in partnerships with relevant stakeholders, including mental health professionals, community organizations, schools, local government, and law enforcement agencies. Collaboration facilitates the coordination of efforts, sharing of resources, and the development of a comprehensive approach to suicide prevention.

+ **Addressing Root Causes:** Suicide prevention strategies should not only focus on addressing individual risk factors but also tackle the underlying social determinants of mental health, such as poverty, discrimination, and social inequality. Addressing these root causes can have a significant impact on reducing suicide rates in communities.

Remember, suicide prevention is a collective responsibility. By implementing community-based strategies, we can create supportive environments, raise awareness, enhance access to mental health services, and foster a sense of connectedness. Together, we can make a difference and save lives.

Advocacy for Mental Health and Suicide Prevention

Advocacy plays a vital role in promoting mental health and preventing suicide. By advocating for mental health awareness, resources, and support, individuals and communities can make a positive impact and reduce the stigma surrounding mental illness. This section will explore the importance of advocacy, strategies for effective advocacy, and how to support suicide prevention efforts.

Understanding the Importance of Advocacy

Advocacy involves speaking up, raising awareness, and engaging with policymakers and the public to promote positive change. In the context of mental health and suicide prevention, advocacy is crucial for several reasons:

1. **Reducing Stigma**: Advocacy helps challenge and dismantle the harmful stereotypes and misconceptions surrounding mental health. By fostering understanding and empathy, it creates a supportive culture that encourages individuals to seek help.

2. **Increasing Access to Resources**: Advocacy can help ensure adequate funding and resources for mental health services and programs. It aims to address the barriers that individuals face when trying to access mental health care, such as affordability, availability, and cultural sensitivity.

3. **Promoting Policies and Legislation**: Advocacy efforts can drive the development and implementation of policies and legislation that support mental health and suicide prevention. This includes initiatives to improve mental health education, increase funding for mental health research, and establish crisis helplines.

4. **Empowering Individuals**: Advocacy empowers individuals by giving them a voice and allowing them to share their experiences. It helps break the silence surrounding mental health and creates a sense of community, support, and validation for those who may feel isolated.

Strategies for Effective Advocacy

Effective advocacy requires careful planning and strategic actions. Here are some strategies to consider when advocating for mental health and suicide prevention:

1. **Raise Awareness:** Start by raising awareness about mental health and suicide prevention through various channels. Use social media platforms, community events, and personal conversations to share information, personal stories, and resources. Engage with local media to amplify your message.

2. **Form Partnerships:** Build relationships with organizations, community leaders, healthcare professionals, and mental health advocates. Collaborate on initiatives, coordinate efforts, and leverage combined resources to advocate for change.

3. **Educate Yourself:** Stay informed about mental health statistics, research, and best practices. Educate yourself on current policies and legislation related to mental health and suicide prevention. This knowledge will strengthen your advocacy efforts and make them more impactful.

4. **Engage with Legislators:** Reach out to local, state, and national policymakers to advocate for mental health reforms and initiatives. Prepare concise and compelling arguments that highlight the importance of mental health support and suicide prevention. Attend community meetings, participate in public forums, and share your perspective.

5. **Share Personal Stories:** Stories have the power to create empathy and inspire action. Share personal experiences related to mental health and suicide prevention to humanize the issue. This can be done through public speaking events, written articles, or testimonials.

6. **Support Mental Health Organizations:** Contribute to existing mental health organizations through volunteering, donations, or fundraising. By supporting these organizations, you can amplify their advocacy efforts and help them provide crucial resources and services.

7. **Promote Mental Health Education:** Advocate for comprehensive mental health education in schools, workplaces, and communities. Seek opportunities to address misconceptions, provide accurate information, and promote open conversations about mental health.

Supporting Suicide Prevention

Suicide prevention is a critical aspect of mental health advocacy. Here are some ways to support suicide prevention efforts:

1. **Raise Awareness:** Increase awareness about the warning signs of suicide and the available resources for support. Share information about helplines, crisis centers, and local mental health services.

2. **Promote Training Programs:** Encourage individuals and communities to participate in suicide prevention training programs such as Mental Health First Aid

or Applied Suicide Intervention Skills Training (ASIST). These programs equip participants with the skills to identify and respond to individuals at risk of suicide.

3. **Create Safe Spaces**: Foster environments that prioritize mental health and provide a safe space for individuals in crisis. This can be achieved through workplace policies, school initiatives, and community programs that promote mental health support and destigmatization.

4. **Support Survivors of Suicide Loss**: Advocate for the needs of individuals who have lost someone to suicide. Promote support groups, counseling services, and resources specifically tailored to survivors of suicide loss.

5. **Advocate for Research and Funding**: Support efforts to increase funding for suicide prevention research. Advocate for policies that prioritize research on effective prevention strategies, risk assessments, and mental health interventions.

6. **Engage the Media Responsibly**: Work with journalists and media outlets to ensure responsible reporting on suicide-related incidents. Advocate for the adherence to guidelines that emphasize sensitivity and avoid sensationalization. Promote media campaigns that provide hope, resilience, and information on available resources.

7. **Promote Peer Support**: Encourage the development of peer support networks and programs. Peer support has been shown to be effective in reducing suicide risk by providing understanding, empathy, and shared experiences.

Additional Resources

Advocating for mental health and suicide prevention requires ongoing education and engagement. Here are some additional resources to support your advocacy efforts:

- **National Alliance on Mental Illness (NAMI)**: NAMI offers numerous resources, including toolkits and guides, to support advocacy for mental health and suicide prevention. - **American Foundation for Suicide Prevention (AFSP)**: AFSP provides advocacy and policy resources to support suicide prevention efforts at the local, state, and national levels. - **World Health Organization (WHO) Mental Health Action Plan**: WHO's Mental Health Action Plan provides guidance and strategies for global mental health advocacy. - **Substance Abuse and Mental Health Services Administration (SAMHSA)**: SAMHSA offers tools, webinars, and resources to support mental health advocacy efforts in the United States.

Remember, advocacy is a powerful force for change. By taking action, raising awareness, and supporting suicide prevention efforts, you can contribute to a world where mental health is prioritized, stigma is reduced, and individuals are empowered to seek the help they need.

Cultural Competence and Global Mental Health

Cultural Influences on Mental Health

Intersection of Culture and Mental Health

The intersection of culture and mental health is a crucial area of study that highlights the influence of cultural factors on mental health experiences and outcomes. Culture encompasses a wide range of shared beliefs, values, customs, traditions, and behaviors that shape individuals' identity and worldviews. These cultural factors significantly impact how individuals perceive, understand, and seek support for mental health issues.

Cultural Influence on Mental Health Perceptions

Culture plays a significant role in shaping the perception of mental health and the expression of distress. Cultural norms, beliefs, and values influence how individuals interpret and label mental health symptoms, leading to variations in symptom recognition and interpretation across different cultural groups.

For example, some cultures may view mental health issues as a sign of personal weakness or moral failing, leading individuals to avoid seeking help due to the fear of stigma and discrimination. On the other hand, some cultures may attribute mental health symptoms to spiritual or supernatural causes, emphasizing the importance of religious or traditional healing practices.

The understanding of mental health also varies across cultures. Some cultures may have rich vocabularies and concepts to describe mental health experiences, while others may lack specific terminology. It is important to consider these cultural nuances when assessing and treating mental health concerns among individuals from diverse cultural backgrounds to ensure accurate diagnosis and appropriate interventions.

Cultural Factors in Help-Seeking Behaviors

Cultural factors significantly influence help-seeking behaviors and preferences for mental health support. Different cultures have distinct attitudes towards mental health services, which can influence individuals' decisions to seek professional help.

Stigma associated with mental health, particularly in collectivist cultures, may discourage individuals from seeking professional help and instead rely on informal support networks such as family, friends, or community members. Cultural values of self-reliance and privacy may also contribute to individuals' hesitation in seeking professional mental health services.

Moreover, cultural beliefs about the causes of mental illness may shape the preference for certain treatment modalities. For instance, cultures that prioritize holistic approaches to health may prefer interventions that incorporate mind, body, and spirit, such as traditional healing practices or alternative therapies, alongside conventional mental health treatments.

It is crucial for mental health professionals to be culturally sensitive and aware of the diverse help-seeking behaviors and preferences influenced by cultural factors. Engaging communities and respecting cultural beliefs and practices can facilitate a more inclusive and effective approach to mental health care.

Cultural Competence in Mental Health Services

Cultural competence is essential in providing effective mental health care to individuals from diverse backgrounds. It involves developing awareness, knowledge, and skills to understand and address cultural factors that influence mental health.

Cultural competence requires mental health professionals to be aware of their own cultural biases and assumptions that may impact their interactions with clients. It involves actively seeking cultural knowledge and understanding through ongoing education, training, and engagement with diverse communities.

Furthermore, cultural competence entails adapting treatment approaches to align with the cultural values, beliefs, and practices of the individuals being served. This includes taking into account cultural norms regarding language, communication styles, non-verbal cues, and trust-building.

Promoting cultural competence within mental health services can enhance the quality of care, increase accessibility, and reduce disparities among culturally diverse populations. It is a key step towards ensuring that mental health services are respectful, inclusive, and effective for individuals of all cultural backgrounds.

Challenges and Opportunities

The intersection of culture and mental health poses both challenges and opportunities. Cultural factors can act as barriers to accessing quality mental health care due to stigma, language barriers, limited cultural awareness among providers, and a lack of diversity in the mental health workforce.

However, embracing cultural diversity and promoting cultural competence can open doors to innovative and inclusive approaches in mental health care. Culturally tailored interventions that incorporate cultural values, beliefs, and practices have shown promising results in improving treatment engagement, adherence, and outcomes among diverse populations.

To address the challenges and seize the opportunities, it is essential to prioritize cultural competence training for mental health professionals and increase the representation of diverse cultures within the mental health workforce. Additionally, initiatives that reduce stigma, raise awareness about mental health, and promote culturally sensitive practices can enhance the accessibility and effectiveness of mental health services for all.

Conclusion

The intersection of culture and mental health highlights the profound influence of cultural factors on mental health experiences, help-seeking behaviors, and treatment outcomes. Understanding the dynamics between culture and mental health is crucial for providing culturally sensitive and effective mental health care.

Cultural competence, through the acknowledgment of cultural diversity, respectful engagement, and adaptation of interventions, plays a pivotal role in improving access, engagement, and outcomes in mental health services. Embracing cultural diversity and addressing cultural stigma are essential steps towards building a more inclusive and equitable mental health support system. By recognizing and honoring the intersection of culture and mental health, we can enhance the wellbeing of individuals from diverse backgrounds and foster a more compassionate and holistic approach to mental health care.

Cultural Competence in Mental Health Services

Cultural competence is an essential aspect of providing effective mental health services. It involves understanding and appreciating the influence of culture on an individual's mental health, as well as adapting interventions to meet the unique needs of diverse populations. In this section, we will explore the key principles and strategies for promoting cultural competence in mental health services.

Understanding Cultural Influence on Mental Health

Culture plays a significant role in shaping an individual's beliefs, values, behaviors, and perceptions of mental health. Different cultural groups may have distinct beliefs and practices regarding mental illness, help-seeking behaviors, and treatment preferences. For mental health professionals to provide culturally competent care, they need to understand the cultural context within which individuals experience and express their mental health concerns.

One important consideration is the concept of "cultural norms." Cultural norms refer to the shared expectations and rules within a particular cultural group. These norms influence how mental health symptoms are perceived and expressed, as well as the acceptability of seeking help. For example, in some cultures, mental health issues may be stigmatized or regarded as a spiritual issue rather than a medical one. Understanding these cultural norms is crucial to avoid misinterpretation or misdiagnosis.

Principles of Cultural Competence in Mental Health Services

Cultural competence in mental health services is built upon several key principles:

1. **Respect for diversity**: Mental health professionals must recognize and appreciate the diversity of cultural backgrounds and individual experiences. They should approach each individual with an open mind, without judgment or stereotypes.

2. **Self-reflection and awareness**: Mental health professionals should engage in ongoing self-reflection to identify their own cultural biases and assumptions. This self-awareness allows them to provide unbiased and non-discriminatory care.

3. **Culturally sensitive communication**: Effective communication is essential when working with individuals from diverse cultural backgrounds. Mental health professionals should use clear and simple language, avoid jargon or technical terms, and be mindful of non-verbal cues that may differ across cultures.

4. **Flexibility and adaptation:** Mental health interventions should be flexible and adaptable to meet the cultural needs and preferences of individuals. This may include incorporating culturally specific beliefs, practices, or traditional healing methods into treatment plans.

5. **Collaborative approach:** Cultural competence involves working collaboratively with individuals, their families, and communities. Mental health professionals should actively involve clients in treatment decision-making and seek their input regarding cultural considerations.

Strategies for Promoting Cultural Competence

To promote cultural competence in mental health services, mental health professionals can implement the following strategies:

1. **Cultural assessment:** Conducting a thorough cultural assessment is essential to understand an individual's cultural background, beliefs, and values. This assessment should go beyond asking about demographic information and include questions about cultural identity, language proficiency, religious or spiritual beliefs, and cultural practices regarding mental health.

2. **Cultural competence training:** Mental health professionals should engage in ongoing cultural competence training to enhance their knowledge and skills. This training may include workshops, seminars, or online courses that provide education on various cultural groups, cultural humility, and effective cross-cultural communication.

3. **Collaboration with community organizations:** Building partnerships with community organizations that serve specific cultural groups can enhance cultural competence in mental health services. These organizations can provide valuable insights into cultural practices, help navigate language barriers, and facilitate access to mental health care for underserved populations.

4. **Language services:** Offering language services, such as interpreters or translated materials, is crucial for effective communication with individuals who have limited English proficiency. Accessible and culturally sensitive materials can promote understanding and engagement in mental health treatment.

5. **Continuous evaluation and improvement**: Mental health professionals should regularly evaluate their practices to ensure they are aligned with the principles of cultural competence. Collecting client feedback, monitoring outcomes, and seeking input from diverse communities can help identify areas for improvement and promote ongoing learning.

Case Study: Culturally Competent Care for Latinx Population

To illustrate the importance of cultural competence in mental health services, let's consider a case study involving a Latinx individual seeking therapy for anxiety.

Juan, a first-generation immigrant from Mexico, expresses his anxiety symptoms differently than what is typically described in mainstream literature. His anxiety manifests as somatic complaints rather than typical cognitive symptoms. Without cultural competence, a mental health professional may overlook or misinterpret Juan's anxiety symptoms, leading to an inaccurate diagnosis and ineffective treatment.

By applying cultural competence principles, the mental health professional takes the time to learn about Juan's cultural background, beliefs, and experiences. This knowledge helps them recognize that somatic complaints may be a common way of expressing distress within the Latinx culture.

The mental health professional adapts their approach by incorporating somatic-focused interventions and exploring the cultural context of Juan's symptoms. They also collaborate with Juan to develop a treatment plan that integrates culturally relevant coping strategies, such as grounding techniques rooted in his cultural traditions.

Through this culturally competent approach, the mental health professional builds trust, engages Juan in therapy, and tailors the treatment to his specific needs. This leads to improved outcomes and a more positive therapeutic experience for Juan.

Conclusion

Cultural competence is critical in providing effective mental health services to diverse populations. By understanding the cultural influences on mental health, embracing key principles of cultural competence, and implementing specific strategies, mental health professionals can deliver care that is respectful, inclusive, and responsive to the unique needs of individuals from different cultural backgrounds. This approach not only improves therapeutic outcomes but also promotes equity and reduces disparities in mental health care.

Addressing Cultural Stigma and Barriers

Addressing cultural stigma and barriers is essential in promoting culturally sensitive and inclusive mental health services. Stigma associated with mental health is often rooted in cultural beliefs, misconceptions, and discriminatory practices that can prevent individuals from seeking help and accessing appropriate care. These barriers can vary across different cultures and ethnic groups, highlighting the importance of understanding and addressing them in a culturally competent manner.

Understanding Cultural Stigma

Cultural stigma refers to the negative attitudes, beliefs, and stereotypes associated with mental health that exist within a particular culture or community. It can lead to discrimination, social exclusion, and marginalization of individuals with mental health challenges. Cultural stigma often arises due to cultural norms around masculinity, femininity, family honor, and expectations of emotional resilience.

To address cultural stigma, it is crucial to raise awareness and challenge the stereotypes and misconceptions about mental health within specific cultural contexts. Education campaigns, community outreach programs, and engaging influential community leaders can play a significant role in changing attitudes and reducing stigma.

Cultural Barriers to Mental Health Care

Cultural barriers can act as significant obstacles to accessing mental health care. These barriers can include language barriers, lack of culturally appropriate services, differing help-seeking behaviors, and cultural mistrust of mental health professionals. It is essential to recognize and address these barriers to ensure that individuals from diverse cultural backgrounds can access the support they need.

Language barriers can hinder effective communication between mental health professionals and individuals seeking help. Providing interpretation services or employing bilingual professionals can help overcome this barrier and ensure effective communication.

Culturally appropriate services take into account the specific cultural beliefs, practices, and values of individuals and communities. By tailoring mental health interventions to align with the cultural context, it increases the likelihood of engaging individuals in treatment and enhances treatment outcomes.

Understanding help-seeking behaviors specific to different cultures is crucial in developing effective mental health support systems. Some cultures may rely more on informal support networks, community healers, or religious practices. Collaborating with these cultural resources can help bridge the gap between traditional healing practices and Western mental health care.

Cultural mistrust can arise from experiences of historical trauma, discrimination, or a lack of representation within the mental health system. Building trust through engagement, active listening, and nurturing culturally sensitive therapeutic relationships can help overcome this barrier and enable individuals to feel safe and supported in seeking mental health care.

Culturally Sensitive Assessment and Treatment

Addressing cultural stigma and barriers also involves adopting culturally sensitive approaches to assessment and treatment. Mental health professionals need to be aware of and respectful of cultural values, language, beliefs, and practices when conducting assessments and developing treatment plans.

Culturally sensitive assessment involves adapting assessment tools to be culturally appropriate and considering the impact of cultural factors on mental health symptoms. This includes acknowledging the influence of cultural beliefs, norms, and expectations on the expression and experience of mental health issues.

Culturally sensitive treatment plans recognize and integrate cultural values, beliefs, and strengths into interventions. This may involve incorporating traditional healing practices, involving family members, or seeking the guidance of community leaders or cultural mentors.

Collaborative partnerships with diverse communities can facilitate the development of culturally appropriate interventions and support services. Engaging community members in the design and implementation of mental health programs helps ensure that they are culturally responsive and relevant.

Ongoing cultural competency training for mental health professionals is essential in promoting understanding and reducing cultural stigma and barriers. It helps clinicians develop the necessary knowledge, skills, and attitudes to deliver culturally sensitive care and strengthens the overall mental health system's capacity to address the diverse needs of different cultural groups.

Case Study: Addressing Cultural Stigma in a Southeast Asian Community

In a Southeast Asian community, mental health stigma is prevalent due to cultural beliefs that mental illnesses are caused by supernatural forces or personal weaknesses. Access to mental health services is limited due to language barriers, a lack of culturally appropriate services, and cultural mistrust.

To address cultural stigma and barriers, a community-focused approach is implemented. Community leaders, religious leaders, and local cultural organizations are engaged in dialogue and education about mental health. This helps challenge misconceptions, reduce stigma, and increase awareness of available services.

Culturally appropriate mental health services are introduced, which include language interpretation services and the hiring of bilingual mental health professionals. These measures improve access to care and ensure effective communication between professionals and individuals seeking help.

Collaborative partnerships are established with traditional healers and community elders to integrate traditional healing practices into mental health interventions. This recognizes and respects the cultural beliefs and healing traditions of the community, enhancing engagement and treatment outcomes.

Ongoing cultural competency training is provided for mental health professionals to enhance their understanding of the community's cultural values, beliefs, and practices. This helps them tailor their assessments and treatment plans to be more culturally sensitive and responsive.

Through these efforts, cultural stigma is reduced, and individuals in the Southeast Asian community feel more comfortable seeking help for mental health issues. The integration of traditional healing practices and culturally appropriate interventions leads to improved mental health outcomes and stronger community support systems.

Key Takeaways

- Cultural stigma and barriers can prevent individuals from seeking help and accessing appropriate mental health care. - Understanding cultural stigma involves challenging stereotypes, raising awareness, and educating communities about mental health. - Cultural barriers, such as language barriers and lack of culturally appropriate services, need to be addressed to ensure equal access to care. - Culturally sensitive assessment and treatment involve adapting interventions to align with cultural beliefs, values, and practices. - Collaborative partnerships with communities and ongoing cultural competency training for mental health professionals are crucial in addressing cultural stigma and barriers.

Note: The case study and examples provided in this section are fictional and for illustrative purposes only.

Cultural Considerations in Assessment and Treatment

Cultural considerations play a crucial role in mental health assessment and treatment.   It is necessary to recognize and respect the diverse cultural backgrounds, beliefs, and values of individuals when assessing their mental health needs. Failing to do so can result in misdiagnosis, inadequate treatment, and a lack of trust between the client and therapist.

When conducting a cultural assessment, mental health professionals need to gather information about the client's cultural background, including their language, religion, ethnicity, and customs.   This information helps to understand how cultural factors may influence the client's perception of mental health, their help-seeking behaviors, and their preferences for treatment.

In conducting assessments, it is important to use culturally appropriate measures that are validated for use with diverse populations. Traditional diagnostic criteria and assessment tools developed in Western cultures may not fully capture the experiences and expressions of distress in other cultural contexts. Therefore, it is essential to consider the cultural validity and relevance of assessment measures.

One challenge in culturally sensitive assessment is dealing with language barriers. Mental health professionals should ensure the availability of interpreters or bilingual staff to facilitate effective communication with clients who are not fluent in the dominant language. It is crucial to avoid relying on family members or friends to interpret as this can compromise confidentiality and accuracy.

In addition to language barriers, cultural factors can significantly shape the expression and experience of mental health symptoms. Certain cultures may have distinct explanatory models for mental illness, such as attributing it to supernatural causes or imbalances in energy. Mental health professionals need to be aware of these cultural beliefs to better understand the client's perspective and develop appropriate treatment plans.

Treatment should be tailored to align with the client's cultural values and preferences. This may involve incorporating traditional healing practices, rituals, or ceremonies that are consistent with the client's cultural background. For example, in some Indigenous cultures, healing ceremonies involving smudging or sweat lodges may be important components of the therapeutic process.

Collaboration between the mental health professional and the client's community can also be beneficial. Community leaders, religious figures, or elders can provide invaluable insights into the cultural context and offer support in the healing process. Working together with the community can help overcome the stigma associated with mental illness, encourage help-seeking behaviors, and promote holistic well-being.

It is important to note that cultural considerations in assessment and treatment extend beyond ethnicity or nationality. Cultural factors can also be influenced by other aspects, such as gender, sexual orientation, socioeconomic status, and disability. Mental health professionals need to approach each client with an open mind and a willingness to learn about their unique cultural perspectives.

In conclusion, cultural considerations are essential in mental health assessment and treatment. Mental health professionals need to be aware of and respectful of the diverse cultural backgrounds and beliefs of their clients. By incorporating cultural sensitivity into assessment and treatment approaches, mental health professionals can provide more effective and appropriate care for individuals from diverse cultural backgrounds.

Global Mental Health Initiatives and Challenges

Mental health is a universal concern that affects individuals and communities across the globe. Global mental health initiatives aim to address the challenges and promote the well-being of individuals worldwide. However, mental health systems and services vary greatly across different countries and cultures, presenting unique challenges and opportunities. In this section, we will explore the initiatives and challenges in promoting global mental health.

The Global Burden of Mental Health Disorders

Mental health disorders contribute significantly to the global burden of disease, affecting people of all ages and backgrounds. According to the World Health Organization (WHO), approximately 1 in 4 individuals will experience a mental health disorder at some point in their lives. Mental health disorders, such as depression, anxiety, and substance use disorders, account for a substantial proportion of disability-adjusted life years (DALYs) globally.

However, the burden of mental health disorders is not evenly distributed. Low- and middle-income countries often face additional challenges due to limited resources, inadequate mental health policies, and stigma surrounding mental health. Furthermore, vulnerable populations, including refugees, immigrants, and individuals living in conflict zones or post-disaster settings, are particularly susceptible to mental health challenges.

Promoting Global Mental Health Initiatives

To address the global burden of mental health disorders, several initiatives and programs have been established. These initiatives aim to promote mental health, prevent mental health disorders, and ensure access to appropriate mental health services. Some key global mental health initiatives include:

1. **World Health Organization (WHO) Mental Health Action Plan:** The WHO has developed a comprehensive action plan that provides a framework for countries to strengthen their mental health systems. The plan focuses on promoting mental well-being, preventing mental health disorders, and providing quality mental health care.

2. **Grand Challenges in Global Mental Health:** This initiative, launched by the National Institute of Mental Health (NIMH) and the Global Alliance for Chronic Diseases, aims to identify innovative approaches to prevent and treat mental health disorders. It encourages research collaborations and supports the scaling-up of evidence-based interventions in low-resource settings.

3. **Mental Health Gap Action Programme (mhGAP):** Developed by the WHO, mhGAP aims to address the treatment gap for mental, neurological, and substance use disorders. It provides evidence-based guidelines for non-specialized health professionals in low-resource settings to identify and manage mental health disorders.

4. **Partnership for Global Mental Health:** This global alliance of organizations and individuals advocates for increased resources and improved policies for mental health. It collaborates with governments, academic institutions, and civil society to advance mental health initiatives worldwide.

These initiatives play a crucial role in raising awareness, promoting policy changes, and improving the availability and accessibility of mental health services globally.

Challenges in Global Mental Health

While the global mental health initiatives have made significant progress, several challenges persist. These challenges can hinder the effectiveness of mental health interventions and the achievement of mental health goals. Some key challenges in global mental health include:

1. **Stigma and Discrimination:** Stigma surrounding mental health remains a significant barrier in many cultures and societies. It can prevent individuals from seeking help and can lead to social exclusion and discrimination.

2. **Limited Resources and Funding:** Many low- and middle-income countries face resource constraints, including limited mental health professionals, infrastructure, and funding. This can impede the development and implementation of mental health programs and policies.

3. **Cultural and Contextual Factors:** Mental health disorders are influenced by cultural beliefs, values, and social norms. It is essential to consider cultural and contextual factors when designing and implementing mental health interventions to ensure their effectiveness and acceptability.

4. **Workforce Capacity and Training:** The shortage of trained mental health professionals is a common challenge across many countries. Addressing this issue requires investment in workforce capacity building, training, and retention strategies.

5. **Data and Research Gaps:** There is a lack of accurate and timely data on the prevalence and impact of mental health disorders in many countries. Additionally, there is a need for further research on culturally sensitive interventions and strategies to address mental health disparities.

Addressing these challenges requires collaboration between governments, international organizations, and local communities. It involves improving mental health policies, increasing funding for mental health services, reducing stigma, and building a skilled mental health workforce.

Unconventional Approach: Technology and Innovation

In an increasingly interconnected world, technology and innovation offer new opportunities to address global mental health challenges. Mobile mental health applications, telemedicine, and online platforms provide accessible and cost-effective ways to deliver mental health services, particularly in remote and underserved areas. Additionally, technology can support data collection, monitoring, and research efforts, enabling targeted interventions and evidence-based decision-making.

However, it is crucial to navigate the ethical, cultural, and privacy considerations associated with technology in mental health. Safeguarding data privacy, ensuring equity in access, and tailoring interventions to local contexts are essential aspects of utilizing technology effectively.

Resources and Collaborations

Promoting global mental health requires collaborative efforts and access to reliable resources. Here are some resources and organizations that can provide valuable insights and support:

- **World Health Organization (WHO)**: The WHO provides guidelines, reports, and toolkits on various mental health topics. Their website offers valuable resources for understanding global mental health challenges and initiatives.

- **Grand Challenges in Global Mental Health**: The Grand Challenges website provides information on research projects, funding opportunities, and resources related to global mental health.

- **Partnership for Global Mental Health**: The Partnership for Global Mental Health website offers resources, reports, and advocacy tools for promoting mental health globally.

- **Centers for Disease Control and Prevention (CDC)**: The CDC's website provides information on mental health initiatives, research, and resources, with a focus on public health approaches.

- **Mental Health Innovation Network (MHIN)**: MHIN is an online platform that shares innovative approaches and resources for mental health. It connects practitioners, researchers, and policymakers globally.

- **International Federation for Psychotherapy (IFP)**: IFP promotes the development and dissemination of psychotherapy globally. Their website offers resources and information on training programs and initiatives.

By utilizing these resources and fostering collaborations, individuals and organizations can contribute to the promotion of global mental health and the reduction of disparities in access to mental health care.

Conclusion

Global mental health initiatives play a pivotal role in addressing the challenges and promoting the well-being of individuals worldwide. By raising awareness, advocating for policy changes, and improving the availability and accessibility of mental health services, these initiatives contribute to reducing the burden of mental health disorders. However, significant challenges, such as stigma, limited resources, and cultural considerations, need to be addressed to ensure the effectiveness and sustainability of global mental health interventions. Through an interdisciplinary and collaborative approach, we can strive towards a world where mental health is a fundamental human right.

Indigenous Mental Health

Historical Trauma and Intergenerational Effects

Historical trauma refers to the cumulative emotional and psychological wounds experienced by a group of people who have endured a common history of profound suffering and oppression. It is the collective trauma that results from events such as colonization, slavery, mass violence, forced relocation, and cultural genocide. These traumatic experiences can have long-lasting effects on not only the individuals who directly experienced them but also on subsequent generations.

Intergenerational effects occur when the trauma experienced by one generation is passed down to the next through various mechanisms. This transmission of trauma can manifest in a variety of ways, including through family dynamics, cultural practices, and the transmission of beliefs and behaviors. The impact of historical trauma can be seen in the mental health and well-being of individuals and communities, as well as in their social, cultural, and political contexts.

Historical trauma can disrupt the development of cultural identity, leading to a loss of traditions, values, and language. This loss can contribute to a sense of disconnection and can affect individuals' self-esteem and sense of belonging. It can also result in unresolved grief and unresolved anger, which may be passed down through generations.

The intergenerational transmission of trauma can manifest in several ways. One mechanism is through family narratives and storytelling, where stories of trauma are passed down from one generation to another. These stories can shape the worldview of future generations and influence their perceptions of themselves and their place in the world.

Another mechanism is through epigenetic changes, which refer to modifications in gene expression that occur in response to environmental factors. Research has shown that trauma can lead to changes in gene expression that can be passed down to subsequent generations. These changes can potentially influence an individual's vulnerability to mental health disorders.

Furthermore, intergenerational trauma can be perpetuated through cultural practices and behaviors. For example, certain cultural norms and expectations may be influenced by the trauma experienced by previous generations. These expectations can create additional stress and pressure on individuals and contribute to the perpetuation of unhealthy coping mechanisms.

Addressing historical trauma and its intergenerational effects requires a comprehensive and culturally sensitive approach. This includes acknowledging and validating the experiences of individuals and communities impacted by historical trauma. It also involves fostering healing and resilience through the promotion of cultural identity, connection to community, and the restoration of cultural practices.

Therapeutic interventions that integrate traditional healing practices with evidence-based therapies can be effective in addressing intergenerational trauma. These interventions often emphasize the importance of storytelling, ceremony, and collective healing. Healing circles, support groups, and community-based initiatives can provide a safe space for individuals to share their experiences and find support from others who have had similar experiences.

In addition, addressing the root causes of historical trauma and working towards social and systemic change is essential. This may involve advocating for policies and practices that promote social justice, equality, and cultural autonomy. Collaborative partnerships between mental health professionals, community leaders, and policymakers are crucial for implementing effective strategies.

It is important to recognize that historical trauma and its intergenerational effects are complex and multifaceted. The experiences and impacts vary across different cultural groups and communities. Therefore, cultural humility and an understanding of the unique historical and cultural contexts are essential when working with individuals and communities affected by historical trauma.

By addressing historical trauma and its intergenerational effects, we can work towards healing, reconciliation, and the promotion of mental well-being for individuals and communities. It is through understanding and confronting the legacy of trauma that we can create a more compassionate and inclusive society.

Exercises

1. Reflect on your own cultural background and history. Are there any events or experiences that have had a lasting impact on your community? How have these events shaped your own identity and worldview? Share your thoughts in a journal or with a trusted friend or family member.

2. Research and explore the concept of epigenetics in the context of historical trauma. How does trauma influence gene expression and potentially impact mental health? Discuss your findings with a classmate or in an online forum.

3. Imagine you are a mental health professional working with individuals affected by historical trauma. Develop a culturally sensitive therapeutic intervention that combines traditional healing practices with evidence-based therapies. Describe the key elements of your intervention and discuss how it can address the intergenerational effects of trauma.

4. Create a support group or community initiative that provides a safe and inclusive space for individuals affected by historical trauma to share their experiences and find support. Develop a plan for organizing and implementing this initiative, including potential partnerships and resources needed.

5. Investigate current social justice and advocacy movements that aim to address the historical trauma experienced by specific cultural or ethnic groups. Choose one movement of interest and discuss its goals, strategies, and impact. How can you support these movements or get involved to contribute to positive change?

Additional Resources

1. Brave Heart, M. Y. (2003). The historical trauma response among natives and its relationship with substance abuse: A Lakota illustration. Journal of Psychoactive Drugs, 35(1), 7-13.

2. Duran, E., Duran, B., & Brave Heart, M. Y. (2008). Healing the American Indian Soul Wound. In J. R. Trimble & C. B. Fisher (Eds.), The Handbook of Ethical Research with Ethnocultural Populations and Communities. % New York, NY: American Psychological Association.

3. Walters, K. L., Mohammed, S. A., Evans-Campbell, T., Beltran, R. E., Chae, D. H., & Duran, B. (2011). Bodies don't just tell stories, they tell histories: Embodiment of historical trauma among American Indians and Alaska Natives. Du Bois Review: Social Science Research on Race, 8(01), 179-189.

4. Kirmayer, L. J., Gone, J. P., & Moses, J. (Eds.). (2014). Rethinking historical trauma: Narratives of resilience. Transcultural Psychiatry, 51(3), 299-319.

5. Brave Heart, M. Y. (1999). Gender differences in the historical trauma response among the Lakota. Journal of Health and Social Policy, 10(4), 1-21.

Conclusion

Historical trauma and its intergenerational effects represent a complex and significant aspect of mental health. Understanding the impact of collective trauma and the mechanisms through which it is transmitted is essential for providing effective support and healing to individuals and communities affected.

By fostering healing, resilience, and cultural revitalization, we can begin the journey towards breaking the cycle of intergenerational trauma. Through a combination of cultural sensitivity, therapeutic interventions, community initiatives, and social change, we can promote mental well-being and create a more inclusive and compassionate society for all.

Culturally Sensitive Approaches to Healing

In order to provide effective mental health services to indigenous communities, it is crucial to adopt culturally sensitive approaches to healing. These approaches recognize and respect the cultural values, beliefs, and practices of indigenous peoples, and aim to integrate traditional healing methods with modern therapeutic interventions. By incorporating cultural traditions, rituals, and community support, these approaches can enhance the effectiveness and acceptability of mental health interventions.

Understanding Cultural Healing Practices

Cultural healing practices within indigenous communities are diverse and rooted in long-standing traditions. These practices often emphasize the interconnectedness of the individual with their community, environment, and spiritual beliefs. For example, indigenous healing may involve ceremonies, storytelling, purification rituals, or the use of specific plants and herbs for medicinal purposes. These practices are often guided by traditional healers or elders who possess deep cultural knowledge and spiritual wisdom.

Holistic and Integrative Approaches

Culturally sensitive approaches to healing recognize the importance of a holistic understanding of health. They recognize that mental, emotional, physical, and spiritual well-being are interconnected and must be addressed collectively. This approach emphasizes the integration of traditional healing practices with evidence-based therapeutic interventions. By combining these approaches, individuals can benefit from culturally specific interventions while also accessing the benefits of modern mental health care.

Collaborative Partnerships and Knowledge Exchange

To ensure the effectiveness of culturally sensitive approaches to healing, it is essential to foster collaborative partnerships with indigenous communities. This involves engaging community members, elders, and traditional healers as equal partners in the development and delivery of mental health services. By actively involving the community in decision-making processes, service providers can gain valuable insights into cultural practices, beliefs, and community dynamics.

Knowledge exchange is another crucial aspect of culturally sensitive approaches to healing. This involves recognizing the expertise of traditional healers and integrating their knowledge with the expertise of mental health professionals. Through mutual learning and respect, a comprehensive understanding of mental health and effective treatment strategies can be achieved.

Addressing Historical Trauma and Intergenerational Effects

Culturally sensitive approaches to healing must also address the impact of historical trauma and intergenerational effects within indigenous communities. Historical trauma refers to the cumulative psychological and social impact of colonization, forced assimilation, and other forms of oppression experienced by indigenous peoples. These traumatic experiences can be passed down through generations, leading to unresolved trauma and mental health challenges.

To effectively address historical trauma, healing approaches must recognize and validate the experiences and feelings of individuals and communities. This may involve specific interventions designed to promote healing, resilience, and cultural revitalization. Examples include cultural ceremonies, land-based activities, and creative arts therapies that allow individuals to reconnect with their culture, strengthen their identity, and restore a sense of belonging.

Community-Based Mental Health Services

Culturally sensitive approaches to healing prioritize community-based mental health services. This involves establishing mental health programs within the community, delivered by individuals who have cultural knowledge and understanding. Community-based services provide a safe and familiar environment for individuals seeking support, reducing barriers to care and promoting a sense of trust and belonging.

In addition to individual therapy, community-based services may include group interventions, support networks, and community events focused on promoting mental wellness. These initiatives encourage social connectedness, foster peer support, and engage individuals in cultural activities that promote healing and well-being.

Training and Education

To implement culturally sensitive approaches to healing effectively, mental health professionals must receive adequate training and education. This training should encompass an understanding of indigenous history, culture, and practices, as well as the impact of historical trauma on mental health. Mental health professionals should develop skills in building rapport and trust with indigenous clients, demonstrating cultural humility, and adapting interventions to align with indigenous values and beliefs.

It is important to note that training should be an ongoing process that involves ongoing engagement with indigenous communities, cultural mentors, and elders. This allows mental health professionals to continuously learn and adapt their practices to meet the evolving needs of the community.

Conclusion

Culturally sensitive approaches to healing are essential for providing effective mental health services to indigenous communities. These approaches recognize the importance of incorporating traditional healing practices, respecting cultural values, and fostering collaborative partnerships. By integrating traditional knowledge with evidence-based interventions, mental health professionals can improve outcomes and promote healing, resilience, and well-being for indigenous individuals and communities.

Indigenous Rights and Mental Health Advocacy

In the context of mental health advocacy, it is essential to address the specific challenges and needs of indigenous communities. Indigenous peoples worldwide have faced historical trauma, cultural displacement, and ongoing marginalization, which have significantly impacted their mental well-being. Therefore, advocating for the recognition of indigenous rights and promoting culturally sensitive mental health services is crucial for ensuring equitable and effective care for these populations.

Historical Trauma and Intergenerational Effects

Historical trauma refers to the cumulative psychological and emotional harm experienced by indigenous communities due to colonization, forced assimilation, and other forms of historical oppression. These traumatic experiences have had long-lasting effects on the mental health of individuals and communities.

One significant impact of historical trauma is intergenerational trauma, where the consequences of trauma are passed down from one generation to another. The trauma experienced by ancestors can influence the mental health outcomes of subsequent generations through mechanisms such as epigenetic changes and the transmission of trauma narratives.

Understanding the historical trauma and intergenerational effects is crucial for mental health advocacy in indigenous communities. By acknowledging and addressing these issues, mental health professionals can provide more appropriate and culturally sensitive care.

Culturally Sensitive Approaches to Healing

To promote mental health and well-being in indigenous communities, it is vital to adopt culturally sensitive approaches to healing. These approaches acknowledge and respect the unique cultural beliefs, practices, and values of indigenous peoples.

Traditional healing practices, such as ceremony, storytelling, and connection to the land, play a crucial role in indigenous mental health. These practices provide a sense of belonging, cultural identity, and healing from historical trauma. Mental health advocacy should support and integrate traditional healing practices into mainstream mental health services.

Collaborative partnerships with indigenous communities and traditional healers are essential in developing culturally sensitive approaches to healing. By involving community members in the planning, implementation, and evaluation of mental health programs, services can be tailored to meet the specific needs and preferences of the indigenous population.

Indigenous Rights and Mental Health Advocacy

Advocacy for indigenous rights is a fundamental component of mental health advocacy in indigenous communities. The United Nations Declaration on the Rights of Indigenous Peoples (UNDRIP) provides a framework for promoting and protecting the rights of indigenous peoples worldwide. This declaration recognizes the right to health and the importance of indigenous peoples' own methods of health care, including their traditional medicines and practices.

Mental health advocacy should work towards ensuring that indigenous communities have equal access to quality mental health services. This includes advocating for the development of culturally appropriate assessment tools, treatment approaches, and research methods that respect and incorporate indigenous worldviews.

Indigenous rights and mental health advocacy should also address the social determinants of mental health in indigenous communities. This includes advocating for improved access to education, employment, housing, and other social and economic opportunities that contribute to overall well-being.

Advocacy efforts should involve collaboration with indigenous organizations, community leaders, and policymakers to address systemic barriers and promote policy changes that support indigenous rights and mental health.

Community-Based Mental Health Services

In indigenous communities, community-based mental health services play a vital role in providing accessible and culturally sensitive care. These services are often provided by community members who understand the unique needs and challenges faced by their community.

Community-based mental health services focus on prevention, early intervention, and recovery-oriented care. They prioritize holistic approaches that address the physical, mental, emotional, and spiritual aspects of well-being.

Mental health advocacy in indigenous communities should support the development and sustainability of community-based services. This includes providing resources, training, and funding opportunities for indigenous-led initiatives. It also involves advocating for policy changes that recognize and support the role of community-based mental health services.

Through community-based mental health services, indigenous communities can reclaim their cultural practices, promote resilience, and address the mental health disparities they face.

Collaborative Partnerships and Knowledge Exchange

Collaborative partnerships and knowledge exchange between mental health professionals, researchers, and indigenous communities are essential for effective mental health advocacy.

Partnerships should be built on principles of mutual respect, trust, and reciprocity. Mental health professionals should, first and foremost, acknowledge and value the knowledge and expertise of indigenous community members. The involvement of community elders, traditional healers, and cultural advisors can provide valuable insights into indigenous perspectives on mental health and healing.

Knowledge exchange should be a two-way process, where mental health professionals learn from the community's cultural teachings and practices while sharing evidence-based interventions that align with indigenous values and beliefs.

Through collaborative partnerships and knowledge exchange, mental health advocacy can promote positive change, empower indigenous communities, and contribute to the overall improvement of mental health outcomes in these populations.

Conclusion

Advocacy for indigenous rights and culturally sensitive mental health services is crucial in addressing the unique challenges faced by indigenous communities. By recognizing historical trauma, promoting culturally sensitive healing approaches, advocating for indigenous rights, supporting community-based services, and fostering collaborative partnerships, mental health advocacy can contribute to improved mental health outcomes and the overall well-being of indigenous peoples.

By addressing the intersection of cultural and mental health, we can embrace diversity, promote equity, and ensure that mental health strategies are inclusive and respectful of all individuals and communities.

Community-Based Mental Health Services

Community-based mental health services play a vital role in providing support and care to individuals with mental health issues within their local communities. These services aim to improve access to mental health care, reduce stigma, and promote a more integrated and holistic approach to mental health treatment.

Importance of Community-Based Mental Health Services

Mental health disorders can have a significant impact on individuals and their families, affecting their overall well-being, functioning, and quality of life. However, many people face barriers to accessing traditional mental health services, such as cost, distance, and stigma. This is where community-based mental health services step in, bringing care and support directly to individuals in their own communities.

These services provide a range of interventions and supports, including counseling, therapy, case management, psychiatric medication management, and peer support. They are usually provided by multidisciplinary teams of professionals, including psychologists, social workers, nurses, psychiatrists, and peer support workers.

Community-based mental health services not only address the immediate needs of individuals with mental health issues but also focus on empowering individuals, promoting their recovery, and enhancing their overall well-being. By providing services within the community, these programs help individuals maintain their connections with family, friends, and other support systems, which are crucial for their recovery journey.

Components of Community-Based Mental Health Services

Community-based mental health services are designed to be flexible, person-centered, and responsive to the unique needs of individuals and their communities. They often include the following components:

1. **Outreach and Education:** These services aim to raise awareness about mental health, reduce stigma, and promote early intervention. Outreach workers may organize community events, provide educational materials, or

conduct presentations to increase mental health literacy and encourage help-seeking behaviors.

2. **Screening and Assessment:** Community mental health centers often provide mental health screenings and assessments to identify individuals who may benefit from services. These assessments help determine the appropriate level of care and develop personalized treatment plans.

3. **Counseling and Therapy:** Community-based mental health services offer individual, group, and family therapy sessions. These sessions are facilitated by trained professionals who provide evidence-based interventions to address a range of mental health issues. Therapy may focus on developing coping skills, improving relationships, managing symptoms, and promoting overall well-being.

4. **Case Management:** Case managers support individuals in navigating the mental health system and accessing various resources and services. They assess needs, develop care plans, coordinate services, and provide ongoing support and advocacy. Case managers also help individuals with practical matters, such as housing, employment, and financial assistance.

5. **Psychiatric Medication Management:** Community-based mental health services often include access to psychiatrists or other prescribing professionals who can assess the need for medications, prescribe and monitor their use, and provide education about medication management. Medication management is typically integrated with other therapeutic interventions.

6. **Peer Support:** Peer support workers, who have lived experience with mental health challenges, play a crucial role in community-based mental health services. They provide understanding, empathy, and practical assistance to individuals by sharing their own recovery journeys. Peer support workers offer hope, encouragement, and guidance as individuals navigate their own paths to recovery.

7. **Collaboration and Referrals:** Community-based mental health services work closely with other community agencies, including primary care providers, schools, employment services, and housing agencies. They facilitate referrals and coordinate care to ensure individuals receive comprehensive support across various domains of their lives.

Examples of Community-Based Mental Health Services

Community-based mental health services can take various forms and operate in different settings. Here are a few examples:

1. **Community Mental Health Centers:** These centers are commonly found in urban and rural areas and provide a wide range of mental health services. They often offer counseling, therapy, medication management, case management, and other support services.

2. **Mobile Crisis Teams:** These teams respond to mental health crises in the community, providing immediate assessments, crisis intervention, and referrals to appropriate services. They can help de-escalate crises, offer support, and prevent unnecessary hospitalizations.

3. **Assertive Community Treatment (ACT) Programs:** ACT programs are designed to provide intensive, community-based support to individuals with severe and persistent mental illnesses, such as schizophrenia or bipolar disorder. ACT teams deliver a comprehensive range of services, including medication management, therapy, case management, and assistance with daily living skills.

4. **Clubhouse Programs:** Clubhouses are community centers that provide psychosocial support, skill-building activities, and vocational opportunities for individuals with mental health challenges. They aim to promote social connections, personal growth, and employment readiness.

5. **School-Based Mental Health Services:** These services bring mental health professionals into schools to provide assessments, counseling, and support for students. They aim to reduce barriers to accessing mental health care and promote early intervention for mental health concerns in young people.

Challenges and Considerations

While community-based mental health services offer many advantages, they also face challenges that need to be addressed. Some key considerations include:

+ **Funding and Resources:** Community-based mental health services often struggle with limited funding and resources, which can impact service availability and quality. Advocacy for increased funding and allocation of resources is crucial to ensure the sustainability and effectiveness of these services.

+ **Stigma and Discrimination:** Stigma surrounding mental health remains a significant barrier to accessing community-based services. Efforts to educate the public, challenge stereotypes, and promote understanding are essential to reduce stigma and discrimination.

+ **Workforce Development:** Building and maintaining a skilled workforce is critical for delivering high-quality community-based mental health services. Recruitment, training, and ongoing professional development of mental health professionals are necessary to ensure the availability of competent and compassionate care.

+ **Collaboration and Integration:** Collaboration between community-based services and other sectors, such as primary care, education, and social services, is vital for a comprehensive and integrated approach to mental health care. Improved coordination and information-sharing can enhance continuity of care and outcomes for individuals.

Conclusion

Community-based mental health services play a vital role in providing accessible, person-centered, and holistic care to individuals with mental health issues. By bringing services directly into local communities, these programs improve access, reduce stigma, and support individuals in their recovery journeys. However, continued advocacy, funding, and collaboration are needed to ensure the ongoing effectiveness and sustainability of these services. By investing in community-based mental health services, we can create stronger, healthier, and more resilient communities for everyone.

Collaborative Partnerships and Knowledge Exchange

Collaborative partnerships and knowledge exchange play a crucial role in promoting mental health within indigenous communities. These partnerships involve creating connections between mental health professionals, researchers, policymakers, and community members to facilitate the exchange of ideas, information, and resources. By working together, diverse stakeholders can develop culturally sensitive and effective mental health initiatives that honor the unique values, beliefs, and practices of indigenous cultures.

Understanding Collaborative Partnerships

Collaborative partnerships are built on the principles of mutual respect, trust, and shared decision-making. They aim to address mental health disparities and promote equitable access to culturally appropriate care. Such partnerships involve active engagement with indigenous communities, recognizing their inherent wisdom and expertise in their own mental health needs.

To establish effective partnerships, mental health professionals must engage in cultural humility, acknowledging and respecting the historical traumas experienced by indigenous communities. It is essential to approach collaborations with openness and a willingness to learn from community members. Indigenous knowledge holders, elders, and traditional healers should be actively involved in developing, implementing, and evaluating mental health programs.

Knowledge Exchange in Indigenous Mental Health

Knowledge exchange in indigenous mental health involves the reciprocal sharing of information, expertise, and experiences between different stakeholders. It acknowledges the value of both traditional indigenous knowledge and evidence-based practices in promoting mental well-being.

One aspect of knowledge exchange is the integration of indigenous healing practices and Western psychological approaches. For example, mental health professionals can work alongside traditional healers to incorporate traditional ceremonies, storytelling, and land-based healing practices into therapy sessions. This integration respects and honors indigenous cultural practices while addressing the psychological needs of individuals.

Additionally, knowledge exchange involves sharing research findings, best practices, and success stories related to indigenous mental health. This includes highlighting community-led initiatives, culturally appropriate interventions, and promising strategies for improving mental health outcomes. By sharing this knowledge, professionals can learn from each other and implement effective approaches in various indigenous settings.

Cultivating Collaborative Partnerships

Cultivating collaborative partnerships requires ongoing commitment and effort. Mental health professionals should actively seek opportunities to engage with indigenous communities, build trust, and establish meaningful relationships. Here are some strategies to promote successful collaboration:

+ **Community Engagement:** Mental health professionals should reach out to indigenous communities through community events, meetings, and cultural ceremonies. Building relationships based on trust and respect is essential for effective collaboration.

+ **Cultural Sensitivity:** Professionals should educate themselves about the history, culture, and values of the indigenous communities they work with. This helps promote understanding and ensures that interventions align with community needs and preferences.

+ **Participatory Approaches:** Including community members in the planning, implementation, and evaluation of mental health programs enhances their relevance and effectiveness. Indigenous voices should guide decision-making processes.

+ **Capacity Building:** Collaborative partnerships should focus on building the capacity of community members to deliver culturally appropriate mental health support. Training programs, workshops, and mentorship opportunities can empower indigenous individuals to take an active role in promoting mental well-being.

+ **Resource Sharing:** Collaborative partnerships should facilitate the sharing of resources, including funding opportunities, research findings, and culturally relevant mental health tools. This helps strengthen the collective knowledge and improves the overall capacity to address mental health challenges.

Case Study: Indigenous Mental Health Research Network

The Indigenous Mental Health Research Network (IMHRN) is an example of a collaborative partnership dedicated to indigenous mental health. The IMHRN brings together researchers, mental health professionals, community members, and policymakers to address the unique mental health needs of indigenous populations.

Through the IMHRN, stakeholders engage in knowledge exchange activities, such as conferences, workshops, and webinars. They share research findings, discuss best practices, and explore innovative approaches to indigenous mental health care. This network actively involves community members in research projects, ensuring that their voices and experiences shape the research process.

The IMHRN also advocates for policy changes that prioritize indigenous mental health and supports the development of culturally appropriate interventions. By fostering collaboration and knowledge exchange, the network aims to reduce mental health disparities and improve the overall well-being of indigenous communities.

Key Takeaways

Collaborative partnerships and knowledge exchange are critical for addressing mental health disparities among indigenous populations. When mental health professionals, researchers, and community members work together, they can develop effective, culturally sensitive interventions that honor indigenous cultural practices and promote mental well-being.

Successful collaboration requires mutual respect, trust, and shared decision-making. Mental health professionals should actively engage with indigenous communities, value traditional knowledge, and integrate indigenous healing practices into Western approaches. They should also prioritize capacity-building efforts, resource sharing, and inclusive research practices.

By cultivating collaborative partnerships and engaging in meaningful knowledge exchange, stakeholders can collectively work towards promoting mental health equity and supporting the mental well-being of indigenous communities.

Index

Milton Keynes UK
Ingram Content Group UK Ltd.
UKHW032033191024
449814UK00010B/560